The Whiz Kids and the 1950 Pennant

In the Series

Baseball in America

Edited by
Richard Westcott

The Whiz Kids
AND THE 1950 PENNANT

ROBIN ROBERTS
AND C. PAUL ROGERS III
FOREWORD BY PAT WILLIAMS
AND A SPECIAL TRIBUTE BY JAMES A. MICHENER

Best Regards
Robin Roberts
Enjoy the Whiz Kids!
Paul Rogers

TEMPLE UNIVERSITY PRESS
PHILADELPHIA

Temple University Press, Philadelphia 19122
Copyright © 1996 by Temple University
All rights reserved
Published 1996
Printed in the United States of America

⊗ The paper used in this publication meets the requirements of the American
National Standard for Information Sciences—Permanence of Paper for Printed
Library Materials, ANSI Z39.48–1984

Library of Congress Cataloging-in-Publication Data
Roberts, Robin, 1926–
The Whiz Kids and the 1950 pennant / Robin Roberts and
C. Paul Rogers III.
p. cm.—(Baseball in America)
Includes bibliographical references and index.
ISBN 1–56639–466–X (alk. paper)
1. Philadelphia Phillies (Baseball team)—History.
I. Rogers, C. Paul. II. Title. III. Series.
GV875.P45R63 1996
796.357′64′0974811—dc20   96–21349

For my Whiz Kids teammates
and for my wife, Mary

R.R.

For my mother Leigh Galloway Rogers,
who supported this project with great
enthusiasm, and my wife Lynn who endured
it with good cheer and understanding

C.P.R.

Contents

A Special Tribute

R obin Roberts! When I hear that name I shiver and chills run down my spine.

He is one of the finest professional athletes I have known, a powerful competitor, a gentleman by breeding and personal inclination, and altogether a splendid citizen. Why then the shivers and chills?

In 1974 the experts who vote baseball players in and out of the Baseball Hall of Fame in Cooperstown, New York, oldest and best of the halls of fame, passed over my cherished friend Robin Roberts, with his 286 big league pitching victories and his impeccable reputation as an almost ideal sportsman. Outraged at this miscarriage of justice, I launched a one-man campaign to get Roberts into the Hall of Fame in the 1975 balloting. I wrote newspaper columns singing Roberts's praises. I published comparable studies proving that other pitchers of much less worth had been voted in while he had not. And I made something of a bore of myself, but I know that I touched sensitive spots because several sports experts told me I had made a strong case for Robin.

However, several writers who made their living reporting on baseball let me know that they did not appreciate my sticking my nose into their business, and when the time came to elect the 1975 entrants into the Hall, the name of Robin Roberts was missing. This was a rebuke to me, not to Roberts, and I spent that year in silence. I had cost my friend election to the Hall of Fame and I was mortified that I had been the agent of his defeat.

But then strange things happened. A few sportswriters assured me that I had been more than right in my earlier attitude. It was ridiculous for them to have passed Roberts by because they were irritated with me, and in the following year's vote Robin Roberts leaped into the Hall of Fame. My miscalculation was forgotten. I could breathe easily again, and justice was done to one of our notable athletes.

I knew Roberts as one of the new breed of baseball players, a man with a college education, Michigan State, and a purist where the game was concerned. He was without guile. During an extended fishing trip with him to northern Alaska, he proved himself a likable gentleman who looked after the welfare of others. A fellow baseball player told me: "Robin has no curve ball, just a high hard ball with blinding speed. When he's in a tight spot, say the bottom of the eighth in a visiting ballpark, and he has only a 1–0 lead with two enemy runners on base, what he does is rear back, summon all his energy and throw his big fast one right down the middle of the plate. The batter knows it's coming, no slider, no tricky curve, so he digs in and takes a wild swipe at the ball. If he misses it's a strike out. If he connects, the ball is coming in so fast that it goes back the same way. It's a home run and Robin loses the game 2–1." When I agreed that I had seen this scenario unfold several times in tight ballgames, my informant added an explanation: "The important part of the story is that the batter can dig in at the plate, take the stance he prefers, and rest assured that Robin will not throw at his head to brush him back. We all know that Robin Roberts will not throw the brushback ball at our head, so we stand there and wait for the high fast one." Others told me that my hero Roberts was the gentleman ballplayer.

As I pointed out in my ill-fated articles calling for his election into the Hall of Fame, Roberts deserved credit beyond his mere won-loss record, which was an impressive 286–245, because he had played with one of the weakest hitting teams in the game, while more fortunate pitchers threw for the Yankees and their ilk with a murderer's row of heavy hitters on deck to drive in the runs. Roberts lost a number of superbly pitched ballgames by scores of 1–0 and 2–1, where even a scratch single might have won the game for him.

I tried to pattern my own professional life as a writer after Roberts. I would do my best. I would not resort to guile or self-promotion. I would play by the rules, and when a difficulty arose, I would throw that high, hard fastball right down the middle. If the reading public knocked it out of the park, so be it. If they accepted what I'd written, so much the better, but I would play by my rules and the great traditions of the writing profession. I adhered to this determination and was never regretful. I was a Robin Roberts kind of writer.

He left a splendid tradition in Philadelphia, the big husky stopper, the pitcher you used when you had to win the important game. In addition to his skills as a player, he contributed enormously to the spirit of his club and to the dignity of the game. He was a special athlete and I am proud to contribute a special statement to his story of the Whiz Kids.

James A. Michener

FOREWORD

I'll never forget that day in the spring of 1947. I had just turned seven years of age. My father, a high school teacher and coach, put me in the car and told me he was taking me to my first major league baseball game. We lived in Wilmington, Delaware, which was about an hour or so from Philadelphia. He took me up to see a doubleheader between the Philadelphia Athletics and the Cleveland Indians. Little did I know that that day was going to change my life.

The sights, sounds, and smells of that day have never left me even though it took place 48 years ago. I can still envision the towering light standards of Shibe Park as we approached the ballpark, looking down like giant cranes. I remember walking up the steps of that ancient ball-park as if it were yesterday. I can hear the sounds of the hawkers, partic-ularly the man at the lower front part of the stadium selling *Daily News* scorecard lineups. The smell of the hot dogs and the other smells com-ing from the concession area are vivid in my mind. But I think the thing that hit me hardest was coming up the steps and looking out over the panorama of a major league ballpark for the first time, then sitting in our seats upstairs along the third base line. The beauty of that field is still one of my most vital memories. I can see that little cart dragging the infield in figure eight fashion. The grounds crew with their giant hoses hosing down the infield. The fresh painted lines of the batter's box and the lines going down toward the foul poles. The beauty of the game, the excite-ment of the crowd. Listen, I'll never forget it.

In the years that followed I became a rabid A's and Phillies fan. I had a unique advantage because I grew up about two miles from the home of Bob Carpenter, the owner of the Phillies. His son Ruly and I were classmates from kindergarten until we graduated from high school. We played sports together and palled around. I guess the greatest advantage I had was that Ruly and his dad took me to Phillies games all through my youth and to spring training every year in Clearwater for a week to rub shoulders with the major league ballplayers.

Nineteen forty-eight, when I turned eight years of age, was another magical year because the Phillies had a farm club in Wilmington, the Wilmington Blue Rocks. There was a tremendous amount of excitement as the 1948 season started because the Phillies had spent a staggering sum of money, $25,000, to sign a young pitcher out of Michigan State named Robin Roberts. He made his professional debut in Wilmington. I can remember going out to see him pitch at the Wilmington ballpark on a number of occasions. Even as a young kid I could tell he was special and was going places. Well, he didn't last at Wilmington very long because halfway through the season he was called up to Philadelphia, which sparked even more interest.

As the Phillies began to put together a much improved product through 1948 and 1949, the anticipation of the 1950 season was absolutely magical. By then I was ten years of age and went to games through that season almost on a weekly basis. My mother was really the great baseball fan in our family. She was the one who drove me up there every weekend. I can remember vividly being at the ballpark to see a young right-handed pitcher named Bob Miller in his major league debut. I was there when Andy Seminick almost physically dismantled the entire New York Giants team in a violent brawl that erupted one Saturday afternoon at Shibe Park. I was there for game two of the World Series that year. My parents took me out of school and I got to see Robbie pitch against the Yankees. I'll never forget the sight of Joe DiMaggio hitting a towering home run into the left center field grandstands to beat the Phillies and the disappointment of driving home that night.

My memories of that season remain fresh and vivid. So you can imagine how excited I got when I learned that Robin Roberts was writing his memoirs of how the Whiz Kids were put together and how the 1950 season unfolded. In the years since then I really count it a privilege to have come to know Robbie as a friend, and a good one. I moved to Orlando nine years ago in my role as the general manager of the Orlando Magic, and I learned that Robin had established his home in nearby Tampa. Our paths have crossed many times and I always look forward to my meetings with Robin, primarily because he is one of the greatest storytellers in all of sports and his memory is absolutely flawless. He remembers every minute detail of every game and every event that ever took place in his life and has a wonderfully vivid way of sharing those stories.

As I have read this book, which recaptures all of those warm, precious memories of my youth, I can't begin to tell you how much I have enjoyed hearing Robin share every possible memory he has of that season, as well as the memories of his teammates who have reflected back on what easily is the most unique season in Phillies history. I have read this book with great joy and great passion, and I think the most important thing it has done for me is take me back 45 years in time, almost like in a time capsule, and allowed me to relive the 1950 season all over again with special insights that have absolutely revived my youth and given me one of the most pleasant reading experiences I can ever remember.

Imagine as a nine-, ten-, or eleven-year-old boy driving up with the owner of the team and his son, parking outside the ballpark, walking into the stadium and going right into the locker room, into the dugout, and out onto the field before games. The players all knew Ruly. I can still see Ruly walking over to the lockers and Puddinhead Jones, in his southern drawl, ragging on him. The memories of seeing the Granny Hamners and the Richie Ashburns and the Andy Seminicks, those are memories that will never leave, never, and I realize how absolutely fortunate I was.

Then I had one other marvelous experience. When I graduated from college at Wake Forest, I signed with the Phillies as a catcher. My roots are in baseball, and the first seven years of my sports career were in baseball. The Phillies signed me in 1960, and in 1962 they sent me to Miami, then one of their minor league affiliates in the Florida State League. In 1962 and 1963, the two years that I played in Miami, the manager was Andy Seminick. I was a catcher through school and college and into the Phillies' system and Andy was my boyhood idol. So it was another special treat to report that first day to play for Andy Seminick. Those two years I had the opportunity to talk to Andy about his days as a Phillie and the 1950 season and all the things that happened. So, it was really exciting to read in these pages about his part in that season.

Robin Roberts, as I said, is the greatest storyteller and has wonderful memories and insight into everything that happened. Inspired by Robin, I will relate one story that I will never forget. It is in regard to the 1949 game against Cincinnati when the Phillies hit five home runs in one inning. Andy hit two of them, and earlier in the game he had hit another. That game is mentioned in this book. Andy points out that it could have been seven home runs—Jones and Hamner apparently just missed them. Every year on that date in June, in the agate type of "Baseball To-day" that runs in every paper, that game is always mentioned. It also gets a highlight note each year in the baseball calendar, "This Day in Base-ball." So, a couple of years ago when that date came around, I called Andy, who lives in Melbourne, Florida, and said, "Andy, I just want to tell you that you are all over the papers again. Every paper in America is car-rying a note that this was the day of your greatest day in baseball." And I asked Andy a question. "Andy, 43 years later what is your most vivid memory of that night?"

You know what he said? "My most vivid memory is that the next day when I came to the ballpark and went to my locker there was a hand-written note from R. R. M. Carpenter, Sr., the owner of the Phillies, and in the handwritten note he simply said, 'Congratulations, I'm proud of you, you did a great job.' That's what I most remember." As I thought on that it really hit me. His vivid memory was not what the pitch was, or who he hit it off of, or what the count was, or what the score was. His most vivid memory was the words of encouragement that the owner of the team expressed to him with a handwritten note. That had some power to it.

It's been a privilege as I have gotten older to come to know some of these people, not just as boyhood idols running around on a baseball field, but as men that I have spent some time with and learned to really appreciate.

Pat Williams

The Whiz Kids and the 1950 Pennant

INTRODUCTION

When Paul Rogers approached me about writing a book on the Whiz Kids, I immediately thought it was a good idea and told Paul, "Let's do it." Even now, 45 years after our 1950 run to the National League pennant, I am identified more with the Whiz Kids than anything else in my big league career.

But more than that it seemed like an opportunity to tell about an organization, a manager and a system that was at once uncomplicated and successful. Bob Carpenter, our owner, had the resources to scout and sign top young talent, and Eddie Sawyer, who took over as manager in July 1948, was the perfect choice to develop and bring out the best in a young ballclub that had potential and considerable ability.

Eddie Sawyer and his coaches, simply put, let us play. The only pressure on us was to try to win each ballgame on the playing field. We had no other pressures, other than to perform to the best of our ability. Eddie kept it simple so we had very little to worry about except playing ball. Even our signs were simple. As a result, we played hard but we played relaxed. We were not concerned about being second-guessed, and thus we did not perform looking over our shoulder.

Perhaps a story involving my teammate Bubba Church is the best example of what this meant to us as a young ballclub. Shortly after Bubba was traded to Cincinnati in 1952 he gave up a home run on a 3–2 count in a tight ballgame. When Bubba returned to the bench at the end of the inning, Reds manager Luke Sewell came over and asked him, "How could you throw him that pitch?" Bubba was nonplussed to say the least. All he could think of to say was, "Well, I wanted him to hit a home run."

Bubba had never had anyone second-guess his pitch selection before. No one with the Phillies ever questioned a pitch, even a poor pitch. They knew that you were not intending to give up a home run. If you hung a curve, they knew you did not mean to hang it, that you were trying to get the batter out.

It makes it so much easier to pitch without the added pressure of worrying about someone questioning your pitches. It means as a pitcher you can relax and concentrate on executing and trying to get the hitters out. It also makes the catcher's job much easier if he knows his pitch calling is not going to be second-guessed by someone in the dugout.

Late in my career I pitched and also served as the pitching coach for the Chicago Cubs under Leo Durocher. The first game I pitched for the Cubs was against the Pirates in Forbes Field. Randy Hundley was a rookie and he was catching me that day. We were in the ninth inning with a one-run lead and Jerry Lynch, an excellent pinch hitter, was coming up.

Durocher, who was terrible about second-guessing pitches, came out and said, "Don't let this SOB beat you." Of course, I did not plan on letting Lynch beat me, but Leo wanted to get his two cents in and that was fine with me. As he turned around and started to walk away, I said, "Hey, Leo. What do you want me to throw him?"

Leo said, "Curve the SOB." So I curved him and Lynch hit a rope to right field for a base hit. The next batter was Manny Mota and I got him out and we won the game.

Afterwards we were flying back to Chicago and Hundley came up and asked to talk to me for a minute. I told him, "Sure, but I want you to know, you are as good a catcher as I ever pitched to. You can really catch."

After he thanked me he said, "I really like what you did with Mr. Durocher, asking him what pitch to throw. You know, he gets on me all the time about what pitches I'm calling."

I said, "That is really why I asked him what to throw Lynch. When the manager tells you what to throw, he can't second-guess you."

The next day I saw Leo and said to him, "You know, Leo, Randy Hundley is a fine catcher, but you've got him scared stiff worrying about what pitches to call. If you really want to tell him something, tell me and I'll tell him for you."

Leo said, "Oh, that kid, he doesn't even swear." Leo was right, Judas Priest was about the strongest thing Randy said. But the rest of the year

Randy Hundley was relaxed and played much better because he was not worried about being second-guessed all the time. I understood from having played with the Phillies how a young ballplayer needs to be free from those kind of concerns in order to play well.

The 1950 Phillies were fortunate to have Eddie Sawyer's quiet, strong leadership. Eddie never forced himself on us, but everyone knew who was boss. He did not flaunt his authority, but he was nonetheless in complete command of the ballclub.

We had very few meetings and Eddie had very few conversations with individual ballplayers. When he did talk to a player it was in private and it had a purpose, usually to correct a mistake or to give someone a quiet boost in confidence. It was a year after I joined the club in the middle of 1948 before Eddie had a conversation with me, and it was probably a year after that before I had another conversation with him.

Eddie Sawyer had been a Yankee farmhand and then a manager in the Yankee organization, and he was influenced by the great Yankee manager Joe McCarthy. Like McCarthy, he was not there to put on a show or impress the writers but simply to try to win ballgames.

In retrospect, it was uncanny how Eddie's leadership style got the best out of us. The Whiz Kids played hard all game, every game. Our effort to win games was remarkable. We were, for the most part, very young, and we appreciated the opportunity to play in the big leagues. Eddie seemed to understand that, and he created an atmosphere that allowed us just to concentrate on playing the game to the best of our abilities.

Eddie never panicked. He had the same low-key approach in the clubhouse and on the bench the entire year, from spring training to October 1, when we had to beat Brooklyn in Ebbets Field or face blowing the pennant. And Eddie kept the game simple.

The contrast with today's game is marked. When I was coaching baseball at the University of South Florida I had a young catcher named Scott Hemond who was a wonderful talent and became the number one draft choice of the Oakland A's. Scottie came over before the first game he was going to catch in college and asked me, "What signs do we use for you to call the pitches?"

I said, "Scottie, you've got to be kidding. I don't call the pitches. I watch the game. You're the catcher, you call the pitches."

Scottie was an outstanding prospect even then, but he had never called the pitches while catching. If that had happened during the Whiz Kids era, we would have laughed and said, "Hey, it's not that complicated," but now it is accepted practice in baseball for the pitching coach or the manager to call the pitch and relay it to the catcher so he can in turn relay it to the pitcher.

Cy Perkins, who was my mentor and a coach for the Phillies for many years, used to tell a story about when he was a young catcher just coming up with Connie Mack's Philadelphia Athletics. Mr. Mack told Cy, "One day you might have trouble deciding what pitch to call and if you do, look over to the bench and maybe I can help you." Cy was a cocky young ballplayer then and thought, "There's no way I'll ever need his help." But one day they were in a tough situation with men on base and a 2–2 count on the batter. Cy wasn't sure what to call, so he looked over to the bench at Mr. Mack. In response, the great Connie Mack just shrugged his shoulders. Mr. Mack had also always told Cy that there was an exception to every rule.

That story, to me, sums up the way baseball can be played and the way we played it in 1950. I mean, who knows what pitch to call? But whatever the pitch is, you have to execute. If you throw a low fastball, you better throw it. It better be a major league fastball with movement in a good location or a big league hitter is going to crush it. If you do execute and you do have major league ability, you will get the batter out more often than not even if he knows what pitch is coming.

The Whiz Kids were not just out there playing without any thought to the circumstances of the game. We had basic rules that Eddie Sawyer and our coaching staff emphasized. None of it was rocket science. Cy Perkins firmly believed that you throw the first pitch for a strike, throw strikes for two of the first three pitches, and never go deeper in the count than 2–2. Cy believed that and made me believe it, but you still have to have big league stuff to be successful.

We were taught the fundamentals of the game and focused on executing and using our ability. Under Eddie, we rarely had team meetings and never went over the hitters before the game, which, incidentally, was fairly common even back then.

Before the All-Star game in 1955, I remember Leo Durocher had a meeting to go over the hitters. I could not believe it. We were going over how to pitch to guys like Ted Williams, Yogi Berra, Al Kaline, and Mickey Mantle. To me, it was a total waste of time. The only way to get those guys out was to have big league stuff and put it where you wanted it, low and outside or in tight with good hooks and a moving fastball. But holding meetings, even before an All-Star game, was Durocher's style.

Later on in my career with the Phillies I played for a manager who, like Durocher, believed in meetings. One time in Cincinnati we had a pregame meeting to go over the Reds lineup, which was pretty formidable at that time, with guys like Ted Kluszewski, Frank Robinson, Gus Bell, Wally Post, and Ed Bailey. By the time the manager got through going over the Cincinnati batting order, he had not mentioned anybody making an out. So our starting pitcher that day stood up and said, "Skipper, these guys are too good for me, I can't pitch against them." Although our pitcher was kidding, unfortunately he was right. He got knocked out in the second inning.

Contrast that approach to my first start in the big leagues against the Pirates in June 1948. I arrived at the ballpark about 6:00. Ben Chapman, our manager then, told me I would be pitching, and by 8:05 I was on the mound. Nobody went over the Pittsburgh lineup with me, they just gave me the ball. Now the first guy in the Pirate lineup did seem like Jimmie Foxx to me (it was Stan Rojek) and I walked him on four pitches. But then I settled down and threw a good ballgame, although I lost 2–0.

I believe simply getting thrown into the fray was the best thing that could have happened to me. The Phillies just gave me the chance to compete and kept the game from becoming overly complicated.

The Phillies' approach was probably the exception to the rule even in 1950 and certainly does not exist today. I remember Tom Seaver once telling me that one of the teams he played for had a fake pitchout sign. I thought he was pulling my leg, but apparently it was true. Baseball, winning baseball, just does not have to be that complex.

As I have visited with my teammates on the Whiz Kids over the years, I have been amazed at how appreciative we all are at the way we were just allowed to play without any distractions or complications or constant meetings. And when we were traded to other organizations, we all had trouble adjusting, as Bubba's experience in Cincinnati suggests.

After the Phillies released him in 1960, Curt Simmons had a lot of success late in his career with the Cardinals. But he had been groomed under Eddie Sawyer and Cy Perkins and never could adapt to having pregame meetings to go over the hitters every time he pitched. Bob Gibson, who also hated pregame meetings, told me that Curt used to just hate to have to tell everyone how he was going to pitch each hitter. So Curt would go through the lineup saying "Low and away, high and tight and play them straight away" for every batter. Then he would say, "Play the big guys back and the little guys up," or if he got to a guy like Hank

Aaron, he would say, "Play him a little bit to pull, maybe three steps to pull."

Meanwhile, Gibson would be rolling on the floor, he would be laughing so hard. Curt would go through the entire meeting and manage to state only the obvious and never say anything about how he was really going to get anybody out. Gibson could not wait for Curt to pitch so that he could hear Curt go through his litany, "Play the big guys back and the little guys up."

Of course, as Connie Mack always said, there are exceptions to every rule. I witnessed this firsthand at the end of my career when I played with Joe Morgan and Jim Wynn on the Houston Astros. Curt would not have wanted to play those two in, even though each stood about 5'7".

Some of the veteran players on the Whiz Kids whom we had acquired from other teams were skeptical initially about the way Eddie ran the Phillies. They were amazed that not only did we not have meetings, but Eddie rarely even came into the clubhouse. But once they saw how it worked and how easy it was to play under that system, they became converts. It was pretty hard to second-guess Eddie's methods, because we were a winning club.

I pitched for 18 years in the big leagues and later coached college baseball for 8 years. It was always my experience that if you had good players who could perform and execute, your team would win. If you did not have good players you might need to have a lot of meetings and attempt to make the game more complicated because you were likely to lose anyway, and if you did at least it looked like you were trying.

I am reminded of something my wife Mary once said to me while I was coaching baseball at the University of South Florida. We had won a game with two outs in the bottom of the ninth inning when one of my kids got jammed on a pitch but managed to bloop a base hit just over third to drive in the winning run. As we were driving home from the game Mary suddenly said, "You know, it's all luck." Now I had been playing and coaching sports all of my life and Mary had sat through many of those contests. I had worked hard all of those years keeping in shape and trying to improve, and now my wife had decided that it was all luck.

While Mary is entitled to say anything she wants after all those years of going to ballgames, an athlete, especially after winning, certainly does not like to attribute success to luck. Although luck can make a difference, a winning team has to put itself in a position to succeed.

Our 1950 team had luck along the way, both good and bad, but it also had talent. Eddie Sawyer and his coaches developed that talent by just letting us play. We all knew our roles and performed them with confidence and without interference. We were probably not the best team in the National League in 1950. The Dodgers were a tremendous club that had won in 1947 and 1949 and would win four pennants in the next six years. But in 1950, under the unique leadership of Eddie Sawyer, we beat Brooklyn and everyone else and won the pennant.

If we had not won the last game of the season in Ebbets Field to take the pennant, perhaps no one would remember the Whiz Kids. But we did win, and it is how we won under Eddie Sawyer's direction that, to me, makes the Whiz Kids' story one worth telling.

Chapter 1
THE WHIZ KIDS WIN A PENNANT

Sunday, October 1, 1950, the day after my 24th birthday, is a day that I will never forget. On that day the Phillies won their first pennant in 35 years. We had come very close to blowing the pennant race and had to defeat the Brooklyn Dodgers in Ebbets Field in the last game of the regular season to avoid a tie and a best-of-three playoff with the Dodgers. We were dubbed the "Whiz Kids" by the press because of our youth, but if we had not beaten the Dodgers that day we would be remembered only for blowing the National League pennant.

Our success in 1950 was not totally unexpected, at least not to us. We had finished sixth in 1948 and third in 1949, and we all knew that we were coming into our own and could play with the better teams in the National League.

Our arrival as a top contender was an important milestone for the Phillies franchise and was of considerable significance to the city of Philadelphia, which had been plagued for years by bad baseball teams. Between 1917 and 1948 the Phils had reached the first division exactly one time, a fourth-place finish in 1932. Included in that span were 16 last-place and 9 seventh-place finishes. The American League Philadelphia Athletics, with whom we shared Shibe Park, had also been dismal since their great teams of the late 1920s and early 1930s. In fact, from 1936 to 1945 both Philadelphia teams finished last in six different years, including a clean sweep in 1940, 1941, and 1942.

Given that history, our 1950 ballclub had really captured the imagination of the city of Philadelphia. On September 20 we had a 7½-game lead over the Boston Braves and were 9 games up on the Dodgers. But we knew then that we were in for a dog fight. On September 10 we had lost southpaw starter Curt Simmons, who had 17 victories when his Pennsylvania National Guard Unit was called to active duty because of the escalating Korean conflict. Three days earlier, Bill "Swish" Nicholson, our veteran reserve outfielder who had twice led the National League in home runs during the War years, was diagnosed with diabetes and was out for the year. Bob Miller, a right-handed pitcher who had started the year with eight straight wins, had hurt his back slipping on some wet steps in a train station, and on September 15 Bubba Church, yet another starting pitcher, was frighteningly injured when struck in the face by a line drive off the bat of Cincinnati's Ted Kluszewski.

By the time we arrived in New York for the last long weekend of the season our lead was down to four games with six to play. But we managed to lose successive doubleheaders to the New York Giants in the Polo Grounds and then lost to the Dodgers 7–3 on Saturday, September 30, setting the stage for one of the most exciting games in baseball history.

Going into the final game, not only was our pitching depleted and exhausted, but we had gone into one of those inexplicable team batting slumps the last week of the season. That same week, our catcher, Andy Seminick, had injured his left ankle (it turned out to be broken) when knocked flying by the Giants' Monte Irvin in a play at the plate. After missing one game of one doubleheader, he kept playing, although with limited mobility and in considerable pain. The Dodgers, in contrast, were healthy and had played extremely well the last weeks of the season.

With our dissipated pitching staff, it was far from clear whom Manager Eddie Sawyer would name to start against the Dodgers. I had started games the previous Saturday, Wednesday, and Thursday. On Wednesday I had pitched five innings against the Giants (Sawyer took me out the inning after Hank Thompson hit a three-run homer to put us behind 5–2). Eddie then started me the following day in the second game of our doubleheader against the Giants. I pitched the complete game and got beat 3–1 when Whitey Lockman blooped a two-strike fastball over third base to drive in the winning run. The team and I were in one of those stretches where we could not believe how hard it was to win a ballgame.

So I honestly did not know who was pitching because Eddie had not told anyone. I did know that I had pitched a lot, but I had had two days rest so I thought I could pitch. The locker room was very tense and quiet before the game because we knew we had just about blown the pennant. About an hour before the game, Sawyer walked over to me by my locker, tapped me on the shoulder, handed me a new ball and wished me good luck. And that was the only time he ever did something like that before a ballgame.

Dodger ace Don Newcombe was starting for Brooklyn in our fifth head-to-head meeting of the year. To add a little more drama, both Newk and I were trying for our first 20-win seasons, although 20 wins never entered my mind until after the game was over. We were so focused on trying to win the pennant that everything else was secondary.

When I began to warm up I really did not feel particularly good, and I was not sure I could crank my arm up like I needed to. I was nervous and tense because so much was riding on the game. But for some reason I looked over at Newcombe warming up for the Dodgers and I thought, "Hell, he is just as scared as I am." I knew that Newk had pitched almost as much as I had and probably was just as tired, nervous, and anxious as I was. Once I realized that the opposing pitcher was in the same shape, I relaxed and never gave another thought to how tired or nervous I was supposed to be.

Ebbets Field was packed with a standing-room crowd of 35,073. Another 30,000 were turned away, but a fairly sizable minority contingent from Philadelphia managed to get into the park on that bright, mild afternoon.

Newcombe started strongly, retiring Eddie Waitkus, our leadoff hitter and first baseman, on a fly; Richie Ashburn, our center fielder, on a grounder; and Dick Sisler, our left fielder, on a strikeout. In the bottom half of the first, I uncharacteristically walked Cal Abrams, the Brooklyn leadoff man. Pee Wee Reese, the future Hall of Fame Dodger shortstop, then hit a long drive to center that Ashburn was able to corral. I retired Duke Snider and Jackie Robinson on routine outs to end the inning and proceeded to set the Dodgers down in order in the next two innings.

Reese led off the fourth with a double, the Dodgers' first hit. I got Snider when he hit little roller to the right of the plate and ran into it after he left the batter's box. Robinson then hit a comebacker to me and Carl Furillo flew out to end the inning. In the fifth, I again retired the Dodgers in order.

We were not able to get anything going against Newcombe early either, although we had four runners reach base on three singles and a walk in the first five innings. Nobody, however, got beyond first.

In the top of the sixth, Waitkus and Ashburn both grounded sharply to Dodger first baseman Gil Hodges, who tossed to Newk covering for the putouts. But with two outs Sisler stroked a hit between first and second that Hodges could not get. Del Ennis, our home-run leader and right fielder, followed with a Texas Leaguer to center that Snider, playing deep because of Del's power, could not reach. Our peerless third sacker, Willie "Puddinhead" Jones, then delivered a clutch single to Reese's left to bring in Sisler with the first run of the game. Shortstop Granny Hamner flied deep to the scoreboard in right, but Furillo was able to grab it and prevent any further damage.

Unfortunately, our lead was short lived. In the bottom half of the sixth with two outs, Reese, who was a thorn in my side all day, hit a line drive near the right field foul line, which was only 297 feet from home plate. The ball hit the screen and dropped down to a six-inch coping, where it stayed. Although the ball was in the field of play, it was unreachable and Reese, instead of a double, had a freak home run. For the rest of the game, the ball lay on that ledge, a constant reminder of why the score was tied.

Through eight and a half innings the score remained 1–1. We had managed a base runner against Newk in the seventh, eighth, and ninth innings but were unable to score. I had given up only three hits, including a single to Dodger catcher Roy Campanella in the eighth, while we had eight scattered hits against Newcombe.

When I trudged out to face Brooklyn in the bottom of the ninth, I knew that if the Dodgers scored we would very likely lose not only the ballgame but also the pennant. My wife Mary and I had planned on taking a vacation in Florida after the season with some of my World Series money, and I remember for a brief moment thinking, "If we don't win this ballgame, we're not going to get to Florida."

Cal Abrams led off the inning and I went to a 3–2 count on him. I thought the next pitch was a strike on the inside corner, but umpire Larry Goetz called it ball four. Now Goetz was an outstanding umpire, probably along with Al Barlick the finest in the league. In fact, Goetz was such an outstanding ball-and-strike umpire that National League President Warren Giles had called the umpiring crew and told them to put Goetz behind the plate again even though he had been the home plate umpire the day before. In any event the pitch, which was so important at the time, was very close, the kind that looks like a strike from the mound and looks like a ball at the plate.

Reese was next and tried to bunt Abrams over. I threw high and hard, which makes it tougher to bunt, particularly if your fastball has a hop on it, and Pee Wee fouled two off. With two strikes, I thought he might try to go to right field and I tried to throw in on him. I either did not get it far enough inside or Pee Wee guessed with me because he hit a rope to left field, his third hit of the game, putting runners on first and second with no one out.

I was now in real trouble. Sawyer had Jim Konstanty, our ace relief pitcher who would win the National League's Most Valuable Player Award, warming up, but Eddie left me in.

Duke Snider was the next batter. Although Duke was a very good hitter (his 1950 stats were a .321 batting average, 31 home runs, and 107 RBIs), I assumed that with the game on the line and no one out Duke would try to bunt the runners over. As a result, I popped the first pitch in there, thinking of nothing but breaking to cover the third base line to try to force Abrams at third when Snider bunted.

Well, Snider was not bunting. He ripped that first pitch right over my left shoulder on the second base side to center field. The ball was a low line drive, and as I turned to watch it I could see Abrams at second hesitate a moment to make sure Mike Goliat, our second baseman, could not get to it. Our center fielder, Richie Ashburn, was not known to have a strong throwing arm and the Dodgers often ran on him. Milt Stock, the Dodgers' third base coach, took a chance on Richie's arm and sent Abrams home to try to score the winning run. But Richie caught the ball on the first hop and threw a strike to Stan Lopata, our catcher, and Abrams was out at the plate by 15 feet.

Although Richie's throw was huge, we were still on the brink of disaster. Reese and Snider had each moved up with the play at the plate, meaning the Dodgers had runners on second and third with only one out. Eddie Sawyer came out to the mound to tell me to walk Jackie Robinson intentionally and pitch to Carl Furillo. So I walked Robinson to load the bases, bringing up Furillo, an excellent right-handed hitter who already had 106 RBIs to go with a .305 batting average.

When Eddie came out, he reminded me to be sure to keep the ball down on Furillo, who liked high fastballs. Well, my first pitch to Carl was about eye high, but it must have had something on it because he popped it up to Waitkus at first in foul territory. Although much in baseball is made about how precise pitching is, sometimes luck is involved. If I had thrown Furillo a low fastball, who knows, he might have slapped it up the middle.

Next was Gil Hodges, Brooklyn's first baseman and a dangerous clutch hitter who had already knocked in 113 runs that year. Gil took a strike and a ball and then hit a soft fly ball near the front of the scoreboard in right field, which was a short porch in Ebbets Field. Del Ennis in right field went back for the ball and had to battle the sun all the way. He stayed with it and caught the ball against his chest, getting us out of the inning unscathed.

I did not have much time to relax after the ninth because I was the leadoff hitter in the top of the tenth. Eddie told me to go ahead and hit, which was fine with me. He often let me hit in late innings in close games when I was pitching. I really did not feel tired, even though I had pitched a lot. I was young and charged up, and getting out of that last inning had not hurt any.

Normally, I lunged a lot at the plate because I had dreams of hitting the ball a long way, but in this type of situation I just tried to make contact. I took a ball from Newcombe, who was also still in the ballgame, and then swung at the next pitch and hit a bouncer up the middle for a base hit. I did not hit the ball very hard but it did get through the infield.

Eddie Waitkus, our leadoff batter, followed. On his way to the plate, he conferred with Sawyer about whether to try to bunt me over. He bunted the first pitch foul along the third base line and then squared away again and had to quickly dodge a high inside pitch from Newcombe. Sawyer then took the bunt off and Waitkus looped a Texas Leaguer in front of Snider in center. I easily made second since I could see that it was a base hit.

We now had runners at first and second with no outs and Ashburn coming to the plate. Richie bunted the first pitch along the third base line and I busted my tail to get to third, even sliding head-long into the base. But Newk made an excellent play on the ball and threw to Brooklyn third sacker Billy Cox to just nip me. If Newcombe had hesitated or bobbled the ball at all, I would have been safe and the bases would have been loaded with nobody out.

We still had runners on first and second with one out and Dick Sisler, a left-handed batter, coming up. Dick had had a good year at the plate with close to a .300 batting average, 12 homers, and 80 RBIs. He already had three hits against Newk, and we were hoping against hope that he could drive Waitkus in from second to give us the lead. Ashburn at first had great speed and had an excellent chance to score on an extra base hit.

Dick immediately got behind in the count two strikes, foul tipping the first pitch and fouling the second straight back. It was clear that Newcombe was really going after him, hoping to strike him out. After taking a ball high and outside, Dick hit another foul back into the press box behind home plate.

On the next pitch, Sisler made baseball history and made pennant winners of the Whiz Kids. He connected with a fastball out over the plate and hit a low trajectory blast to left field. Sitting in the dugout, I knew that the ball was hit hard but was not sure it was going out, because you do not normally expect a line drive hit to the opposite field to carry all the way out of the park. But Dick's blow did carry, landing in about the third row in left, 350 feet from home plate. We spontaneously erupted from the dugout to mob Dick at the plate.

We now had a 4–1 lead, which felt like a real cushion following the tension of the entire game and the suspense of the last of the ninth. Del Ennis struck out and Willie Jones bounced out to Reese at short to end the inning, and I went out to face the Dodgers, knowing that if I could get them out we had the pennant at long last.

There was no real conversation as I went out to pitch the bottom of the 10th. Sawyer put Jack Mayo into left field for defensive purposes, replacing Sisler. I felt good and probably had as good stuff as I had had all day.

Roy Campanella was the first batter and, with 31 home runs in 1950, was another powerful Dodger slugger. He took a fastball inside and then hit a foul pop-up over the Phillies dugout for strike one. On the next pitch Campy drove a line drive to left that Mayo quickly moved over to grab. Sisler probably would have made the play as well, but Jack had no trouble with the ball and, with his excellent speed, caught it easily for the first out.

Dodger manager Burt Shotton then sent Jim "Rip" Russell up to pinch hit for Billy Cox. Rip was a veteran switch-hitting outfielder with good power also; he had hit 10 home runs in a little more than 200 at bats. But with the pennant in sight, I was really pumped up and struck Russell out swinging on four pitches. It was only my second strikeout of the game and the first since the third inning.

Next Shotton inserted Tommy Brown to pinch hit for Newcombe. Tommy, who would become a teammate the following year when he was traded to the Phils, was a utility player who hit .291 and had seven pinch hits for the Dodgers in 1950. After a swinging foul back on the screen, Tommy hit a foul pop to Waitkus at first. Eddie grabbed the ball and the Whiz Kids had finally won the first pennant for the Phillies in 35 years.

When Eddie caught that last pop foul, I had a feeling that I never experienced again in athletics. It was a feeling of relief, complete satisfaction, and exhilaration all rolled together. In addition, I was simply grateful because we had almost blown the pennant and disappointed a lot of people, including ourselves. And my trip to Florida with Mary was safe.

Yet we knew we had overcome some tremendous obstacles in the last month of the season, with the loss of Curt Simmons to active duty, the injuries to our pitching staff, the loss of Bill Nicholson in early September, and the injury to Andy Seminick in the last week, and we had a sense of accomplishment in the face of real adversity. By winning that tension-filled final game against the Dodgers for the pennant, we had shown the baseball world that the Whiz Kids were indeed for real.

Chapter 2
A Dismal Team History

The Philadelphia Phillies' climb to the 1950 pennant really began when Robert R. M. Carpenter, Sr., of Wilmington, Delaware, bought the team in late 1943. Previously, the Phillies had been plagued for decades by what have been described as "five and dime" ownerships.

They started with William F. Baker, former police commissioner of New York City, who owned the franchise from 1913 until his death in 1930. In 1917, Baker began a practice that was to frustrate Phillies fans for 25 years—selling star players for cash. On December 17 of that year, in a move that appeared cold-blooded and calculating, Baker traded the incomparable Grover Cleveland Alexander and reliable catcher Bill Killefer to the Cubs for $60,000 and a young pitcher and catcher. The cash was the largest amount ever involved in a player transaction at that time. The press reported that Baker decided to unload Alexander after learning that his star pitcher had been drafted for military service in World War I and was waiting to be called to active duty.

Similarly, in June 1920 Baker dealt celebrated shortstop Dave Bancroft to John McGraw's Giants for $100,000 and two second-line players. In 1921 Baker traded Irish Meusel, who was batting .353 for the Phils after 89 games, to the Giants for three nondescript players and $30,000. Meusel immediately became a key figure in the Giants' 1921 pennant run.

Those transactions were the beginning of a vicious cycle for the Phillies. Faced with competing against Connie Mack's American League Athletics, who were either very good or as bad as the Phillies, the Phillies had trouble drawing fans to watch mediocre baseball. Until 1938, they played their home games in the increasingly dilapidated Baker Bowl, a nineteenth-century relic known as Philadelphia National Park before Baker bought the club in 1913. It was variously called the "Bandbox" because of its short right field porch and the "Hump" because it sat on an elevated plot over a railroad tunnel running under the outfield. Soot and grime from the Reading Railroad tracks across the street made the seats less than desirable, and during the 1920s and 1930s when a foul ball landed on the roof patrons covered their heads against showers of rust cascading down. Not only was Baker Bowl an unpleasant place to watch bad baseball, it had proven to be dangerous as well. In 1903, 12 people were killed and 232 injured in the right field bleachers when a rail collapsed as fans rushed to a balcony to watch a fire across the street. In May 1927, 10 rows of the same bleachers collapsed during a game, although fortunately without fatalities.

The Baker Bowl's seating capacity was allegedly 18,000 but was probably closer to 14,000. In any event it was the smallest park in the majors and its capacity was largely an academic issue since the Phillies drew so poorly, often less than 200,000 patrons a season. By selling star players for cash, Baker was actually able to make a little money with perpetually poor teams, miserable attendance, and an antiquated ballpark. (Baker even used sheep to keep the outfield grass trim, at least until a ram charged club president Billy Shettsline.)

Baker was also hampered by the strict Pennsylvania blue laws, which forbade Sunday baseball. The Pennsylvania Supreme Court upheld the blue laws as applied to professional baseball in 1927, ruling that baseball continued to fall under the "worldly employment" and "business" prohibitions. As a result, Philadelphia did not legalize Sunday baseball until 1934, the last major league city to lift the ban.

The salaries paid the players were, not surprisingly, meager. Lefty O'Doul got all of a $500 raise after his memorable 1929 season, in which he led the league in hitting with an imposing .398 batting average and 254 base hits, still a National League record. After O'Doul's second season with the Phils, in which he hit .383, he was traded to the Dodgers with Fresco Thompson, a quality second baseman who was also one of the games greatest wits, for three players and the inevitable check. (On one occasion after the trade Thompson was sent in to pinch run for a teammate who had reached first batting for a relief pitcher. Whereupon Thompson yelled into the Dodger dugout, "How do you like that? From captain of the Phillies to a pinch runner for a pinch hitter for a pinch pitcher!") The Phillies had finished last with those two and Baker probably figured he could not do any worse without them.

O'Doul was apparently eager to escape the tight-fisted Baker, a feeling shared by most of the high-caliber players who passed through. The story goes that Casey Stengel learned that he had been traded from the cellar-dwelling Phillies to the pennant-contending Giants in the clubhouse one rainy afternoon in 1921. The game had been postponed and the players were in their street clothes playing cards to pass the time. Stengel had been bothered by a bad back all season, but when he got word of the trade he put on his baseball uniform and, against the admonitions of the trainer, ran out onto the field in the pouring rain. He then proceeded to dash around the bases, sliding in the mud at each one. His last act as a Phillie was to gleefully leave his muddy uniform for Baker to have cleaned.

Baker was not above going to further lengths to curtail his payroll. In 1929, the Phillies had, for them, a banner year. They finished fifth and won 28 more games than their 43–109 eighth-place debacle of the year before. The main reason was a .309 team batting average and 153 team home runs. In addition to O'Doul and Don Hurst, a first baseman who hit 31 homers in only his second season, 1929 was the year that Chuck Klein emerged. In his first full year, Klein, the leading slugger in Phillies history until Del Ennis and then Mike Schmidt came along, hit .356, with 219 hits and 145 RBIs. He also hit 43 home runs to lead the league.

Klein was a left-handed dead pull hitter who took great advantage of the inviting right field wall in Baker Bowl. The wall, made of tin (and thus full of dents), stood about 35 feet high and was only 280 feet from home down the line. It had no curve but ran straight to the power alley, which was a mere 310 to 320 feet from the plate. Unbelievably, in mid-season Baker declared that "home runs have become too cheap" and tacked an additional 15 feet onto the existing right field screen. The new screen prevented Klein from reaching the 50-home-run mark and, according to the cynics, avoided a salary demand commensurate to the other 50-plus home run hitter in baseball, Babe Ruth.

Baker Bowl's tin right field wall produced much baseball lore. The legendary columnist Red Smith wrote, "It may be exaggerating to say the outfield wall cast a shadow across the infield, but if the right fielder had eaten onions at lunch the second baseman knew it." Pitchers felt like they could reach out and "thump" the wall. Brooklyn pitcher Walter Beck, who later pitched for the Phillies after they moved to Shibe Park, acquired the unhappy nickname "Boom-Boom" from trying to pitch in Baker Bowl: one boom off of the bat, the other off the tin wall.

On one typical afternoon, Beck was being tattooed by the Phils in Baker Bowl. Dodger manager Casey Stengel had made several trips to the mound and finally went out to remove Beck—whereupon Beck, in a fit of pique, hurled the ball against the tin in right field. Brooklyn right fielder Hack Wilson, who had been chasing line drives all afternoon, had leaned against the fence and dozed off in the brief interlude. Beck's heave clanged against the wall a few feet above Wilson's head, spurring Hack to action. He jumped, raced to the ball, and fired a strike to second base.

The Phillies' 1930 season was certainly one of the most peculiar in baseball history. After edging up to fifth place in 1929 under manager Burt Shotton (who would manage the Dodgers in 1950), there were expectations of a first division finish in 1930. And although the Phillies continued their prodigious slugging with a team batting average of .315 (second to the Giants' .319), they finished dead last with deplorable 52–102 record, 40 games behind the pennant-winning Cardinals.

In that year of the hitter, Klein hit .386 with 40 home runs and 250 hits. He set club records for doubles (59), RBIs (170), runs (158), total bases (445), and slugging percentage (.687). In Baker Bowl alone, Klein hit an astounding .439 with 26 home runs and 109 RBIs. Seven other Phils topped .300 for the season, led by O'Doul's .383. As a club they averaged six runs a game (944 total runs) and set any number of team batting marks.

One of the worst pitching staffs in history and a porous defense led the plunge to the cellar. The pitching staff had an outlandish earned run average (ERA) of 6.71, an all-time major league high, and the team made 239 errors. As a result the club gave up 1,199 runs, or 7.7 per game. The Phils gave up 10 or more runs in 45 games, 15 or more in 17 games, and 20 or more in 3 contests. In July they lost consecutive games by scores of 16–15 and 19–15. Right fielder Klein set a major league record with 44 outfield assists, as further testament to how much action he had that year playing in front of the tin wall.

Claude Willoughby typified the futility of the 1930 pitching staff. Aptly nicknamed "Weeping Willie," Willoughby compiled a 4–17 won-lost record and a 7.59 ERA, allowing 241 hits in 153 innings. Fresco Thompson, serving as team captain, once brought out the lineup card to the umpire in the pregame meeting at home plate with the pitcher's slot filled in as "Willoughby—and others."

William Baker died unexpectedly in December 1930 at the minor league meetings in Montreal, only a month after trading O'Doul and Thompson. Shortly before his death he had cast out long-time Phillies business manager Billy Shettsline and replaced him with Gerald P. Nugent, Sr. In a curious bequest, Baker willed his Phillies stock to his wife and Nugent's wife, Mrs. May Mallon Nugent, who was first his secretary and by then the club secretary. When Mrs. Baker died a few years later, she also willed her stock to Mrs. Nugent and her son Gerald, Jr. By 1933 Gerald Nugent, Sr., had become president of the club.

Nugent was a Philadelphia native and a long-time Phillies fan. Unfortunately, he was a man of little financial means, having previously worked as a shoe salesman. As a result, he was forced to run the franchise as Baker had, selling good ballplayers for cash to keep the team afloat.

As Nugent took over the Phillies were coming off a fourth-place finish, their first first-division finish in 15 years. The club had finished with a 78–76 record due largely to leading the league in hitting with a .292 average, 122 home runs, and 844 runs scored. Six regulars batted over .300 and Pinky Whitney hit .298. The Phillies had the league's top three RBI producers in Hurst (143), Klein (137), and Whitney (124), a feat never duplicated in either league.

The fans' hope for continued progress was quickly dissipated the following winter when Nugent traded one of his few dependable pitchers, Ray Benge, to the Dodgers for three marginal players and $15,000. Then, when the Phils started slowly in 1933, Nugent unloaded Whitney, one of the top third basemen in the league, and outfielder Hal Lee, who had hit .303 with 18 homers in 1932, to the Braves for two unhelpful players and much-needed cash.

The 1933 Phillies sank to seventh place and drew only 156,000 fans, despite a Triple Crown year by Klein and a banner performance by catcher Spud Davis, who batted .349. Klein and Davis finished first and second, respectively, in the batting race, and Klein and shortstop Dick Bartell started for John McGraw in the first All-Star game.

Nonetheless, the club seemed to have a black cloud hanging over it. In July of that year, second baseman Mickey Finn suddenly died while recovering from surgery for ulcers. Finn was the third Phillies player to die in five years. Dutch Ulrich, a pitcher, died just before the start of spring training in 1929 after a lengthy illness, and Walt Lerian, a young catcher, was killed that October when struck by a truck. In addition, shortstop Tommy Thevenow was seriously injured when he drove his car off the road during spring training in 1929, although he was able to recover and continue his career.

In November following the 1933 season, the inevitable finally occurred. Chuck Klein was sold to the Cubs for three inconsequential players and $65,000. The outcry was not as great this time and, for once, the timing may have been right. Klein, king of the so-called Baker Bowl hitters, became just an average player for the Cubs. By the 1935 World Series, he was the Cubs' fourth outfielder and was used as a pinch hitter in three games and in the outfield for two.

For the rest of the decade the Phillies failed to finish higher than seventh and landed in the cellar three more times. For much of the 1930s, a huge Lifebuoy Soap billboard adorned the tin wall in right field. Part of the sign proclaimed that "The Phillies Use Lifebuoy," underneath which some fan had scrawled late one night "And They Still Stink." That pretty much summed up local sentiment.

Although helped some when Pennsylvania legalized Sunday baseball in 1934, Nugent continued to keep the franchise afloat by selling ballplayers for cash. Bill Terry, manager of the Giants, was heard to comment, "Whenever I deal with Gerry Nugent I always have to give him a tip." But to his credit, Nugent was able to hang on to the franchise as long as he did because he was astute enough to pick up unheralded players who performed very well for the Phillies. They were typically sold after establishing their value so that Nugent could continue to pay the bills.

In June 1934, in a swap of first basemen with the Cubs, Nugent traded Don Hurst for a young Dolph Camilli. Hurst, another Baker Bowl hitter, turned out to be a colossal flop with the Cubs, batting just .199 in 51 games. At age 28 he was through as a major leaguer while Camilli became the Phillies' leading slugger for three years, twice batting over .300 with more than 100 RBIs. After the 1937 season Nugent traded him to the Dodgers for a player and $45,000 to provide some funds for 1938. Camilli later led Brooklyn to a pennant with an MVP season in 1941.

In 1939 Nugent traded Claude Passeau, a quality pitcher, to the Cubs for $50,000 and three players, one of whom was pitcher Kirby Higbe, a young fireballer. Higbe threw 283 innings and won 14 games for a terrible 1940 club, leading the league in strikeouts. In November, Nugent swapped Higbe to the Dodgers for three players and a whopping $100,000. Higbe proceeded to win 22 games for the pennant winners, but Nugent had turned a nifty profit on a throw-in from the sale of Passeau the year before.

Nugent also reacquired Chuck Klein early in the 1936 season. Although he gave up Curt Davis, a fine pitcher who won 19 and 16 games in 1934 and 1935, respectively, and Ethan Allen, a hard-hitting outfielder, Nugent also got a $50,000 check and another player in the deal. So in 1933 Nugent sold Klein for $65,000 and three years later secured another $50,000 to take him back.

Highlights in those years were few. Back home in Baker Bowl, Klein had a good year in 1936, although not up to his previous standards. On July 10 of that year though he did put on a memorable performance with four home runs in a 10-inning game against the Pirates. To add credibility to the feat, the game was played at Forbes Field in Pittsburgh. In 1935, the Phillies played in major league baseball's first night game, predictably losing 2–1 to the Reds at Crosley Field. A few days later they faced the Boston Braves in Baker Bowl in what would be the 40-year-old Babe Ruth's final game. The Babe went hitless.

The team finally left Baker Bowl to become tenants of the Athletics in Shibe Park in mid-season 1938. In the final game at Baker Bowl on June 30, only 1,500 diehards showed up. The Phillies closed the old park in typical fashion—they lost to the Giants 14–1.

The move to Shibe Park coincided with the beginning of the most woeful stretch in club history, a difficult achievement considering its previous 20 years. They finished dead last five straight years from 1938 to 1942. Their won-lost records were even worse than that statistic suggests—1938: 45–105; 1939: 45–106; 1940: 50–103; 1941: 43–111; 1942: 42–109. Their winning percentage was as low as .278 and never higher than .327. They finished 43, 50.5, 50, 57, and 62.5 games out of first. They finished 25.5, 18, 15.5, 19 and 18.5 games out of *seventh* place! In addition, the club was now a second-class citizen in its own home park. Before their move the Phils had a small but loyal following; afterwards Philadelphia baseball fans were much more likely to go to Shibe Park to watch the Athletics.

Prior to their move to Shibe Park, the Phillies had always had good hitting, even in their worst years. But in 1938 and thereafter their hitting went south. Klein hit only 8 home runs in 1938, to lead the team that collectively had only 40. The more normal dimensions of Shibe Park certainly contributed to the decline, but the Phils' bats were simply mediocre generally. In addition, the Phillies' pitching remained the worst in the league during that dismal period. In 1938 the team ERA was 4.93. The rest of the league had an ERA of almost a run and a half less. The Dodgers provided the next worst pitching with a team ERA of 4.07.

Suffering with the team during the late 1930s was workhorse right-handed pitcher Hugh Mulcahy. From 1937 through 1940 Mulcahy pitched well over 200 innings each year and rang up records of 8–18, 10–20, 9–16, and 13–22. Although considered a quality pitcher, he was saddled with the nickname "Losing Pitcher" Mulcahy because his name appeared so often in the box score as the losing pitcher.

Mulcahy's bad luck did not end there; in March 1941 he was the first major leaguer drafted into the U.S. Army. Thus, the Phils, who could ill afford it, were deprived of their best pitcher (and Nugent of one his most valuable assets) eight months before Pearl Harbor. Hugh missed four full seasons of baseball, and when he rejoined the club late in 1945 a South Pacific illness had weakened him considerably. He was unable to regain his pitching form.

The 1942 season was the last of the Nugent regime. Doc Prothro (father of NFL and college football coach Tommy Prothro) was replaced as manager after three hapless years by Hans Lobert, who had played third for the Phillies in the early teens. Lobert could only cajole the team to 42 victories, the lowest total in club history. He is perhaps best remembered for being so concerned about the opposition stealing his signs that he actually used a different set of signs for each player on the club. Bobby Bragan broke in with the Phillies in 1940 and played with them through 1942.

> **BRAGAN:** "Hans Lobert kept the players' pass list. He would sit by the clubhouse door several hours before game time with the list. To get the passes you would go over and give him the name of your guests who were supposed to be on the list. Bennie Warren, one of our catchers, had some friends named Scroggin, so he would say, 'Two for Scroggin.' Ike Pearson had someone named Chatfield, so he would say, 'Two for Chatfield' and so forth.
>
> "Hans would then use the names on that pass list for some of our signs. So a word sign like Chatfield could be my hit-and-run sign and Merrill May's bunt sign. Even today if I get a call from Ralph Branca, he'll say, 'How you doing, Chatfield?' Isn't that amazing?
>
> "Lobert also had different signs for each of us. He had amazing powers of recall. He did it to confuse the opposition, but sometimes he confused his own players."

Ike Pearson completed his fourth season with the Phillies' mound corps in 1942. Signed off the Ole Miss campus and rushed directly to the major leagues without minor league experience, "Mississippi Ike" had compiled records of 2–13, 3–14, 4–14, and 1–6 with the Phillies. He enlisted in the Marines after the 1942 season, commenting, "I want to be on a first place team."

Danny Litwhiler had a remarkable season in 1942, leading the Phillies with an unremarkable 9 home runs, 56 RBIs, and .271 batting average. However, he played every inning of every dreary game in left field that year without making an error, setting a record that he extended the next year to 187 games. Litwhiler's fielding prowess in 1942 was even more amazing considering that the previous year he had committed 15 errors, the worst in the league among outfielders.

In a late-season game in 1942 against the Cardinals, who were fighting the Dodgers for the pennant, Litwhiler nearly knocked himself unconscious scoring a run for the Phillies, who were about 60 games out of first place. He was ultimately rewarded for his hustle on June 1 of the next year when the Cards acquired him in a trade. As a result he played in both the 1943 and 1944 World Series for the pennant-winning Cardinals.

Danny later coached baseball at my alma mater, Michigan State, and I like to think I may have had something to do with him getting that job. In 1963, while I was pitching for the Baltimore Orioles, Michigan State hosted a banquet in Detroit to honor me. During the course of the evening Biggie Munn, the athletic director, said, "I guess you are wondering why we had this night for you?"

I said, "Well, yes, I was wondering."

He said, "I would like to talk to you about retiring and becoming our baseball coach."

I said, "I appreciate that, but I want to keep playing." But then I happened to ask, "Who have you interviewed?"

Biggie said, "Danny Litwhiler."

I said, "Well, you don't have to go any farther. Danny would be an excellent choice." Danny was hired and stayed on as baseball coach at MSU for 20 years.

The winter after the 1942 season was a tumultuous one for the franchise. Bill Veeck, later owner of the St. Louis Browns, Cleveland Indians, and Chicago White Sox (twice), was then owner of the Milwaukee Brewers of the Triple A American Association. He launched a plan to buy the Phillies from Nugent and immediately turn the team around by stocking it with the best players from the Negro Leagues. He had in mind Roy Campanella, Monte Irvin, Larry Doby (whom he, as owner of the Indians, later signed as the first black player in the American League), and Satchel Paige and Luke Easter (both of whom he also later signed), among others. Phillies Cigars had agreed to be one of the investors and Abe Saperstein, who ran the Harlem Globetrotters, was to help sign the top black players.

Nugent had apparently agreed in principal to the sale when Veeck, out of respect for Commissioner Kenesaw Mountain Landis, advised the commissioner of his plan to break baseball's unwritten color line. According to Veeck's autobiography, the next thing he knew the National League had taken control of the Phillies. Upon approaching National League President Ford Frick, Veeck was informed that the club had already been sold to lumber executive William D. Cox for (according to Veeck) about half of the amount he had offered Nugent.

While the sequence of events is somewhat unclear, it appears that the league, whose owners were weary of the Phillies' annual weak sister ballclubs and dispiritingly poor attendance, were negotiating to take over the team when Veeck entered the picture. Even with Nugent's ballplayers-for-cash philosophy, the franchise was increasingly covered in red ink, including substantial unmet financial obligations to the league. It seems likely that Veeck considerably speeded up the league's taking control of the Phillies as the baseball hierarchy strove to avoid integration for as long as possible.

Thus, by February 1943 Nugent no longer owned the team. In the decade of Nugent ownership the team had finished dead last six times, including five in succession, and had finished seventh four times.

> **BRAGAN:** "Gerry Nugent was a real fine owner with no money. He was a good person, a compassionate fellow. In 1942 my son was about to be born in Elizabeth, New Jersey, where my wife's folks lived. I asked permission to go for his birth and Hans Lobert said, 'Oh Bobby, babies are born every day.'
>
> "I said, 'Not mine,' but he wouldn't give me permission. We were playing in Boston, and when I went back to my room, Si Johnson, my roommate, who had been around a long time, said, 'Go ahead. All he'll do is fine you $25 or $50.'
>
> "So I got on the train and went down to Elizabeth. Monday was off, so I rejoined the club on Tuesday in Philadelphia. Hans said,

'We got your telegram and we're all proud you had a boy, but it will cost you $50 for leaving without permission.

"About a month after my son was born our two catchers, Ben Warren and Mickey Livingston, were hurt and we had an exhibition game in Allentown, Pennsylvania. I had caught in American Legion ball and in high school, so I told Lobert, 'If you need a catcher, I can catch.' So I caught the exhibition game. The next night we played Cincinnati and I caught my first game in the major leagues and threw Lonnie Frey, a real speedster, out twice. Nugent advertised it that Earl Naylor, an outfielder, would pitch and Bobby Bragan, shortstop, would catch. Sure enough, Naylor pitched five or six innings and we won the ballgame 4–2.

"After I caught that game Mr. Nugent sent me a check for $50 and said, 'I appreciate what you did, here is your $50 back.'"

President Frick's buyer, William D. Cox, was only 33 years old but had already achieved considerable wealth in the lumber business. He was a New Yorker who had played baseball at Yale and had had some ownership involvement in professional football. Cox proved to be a hard-working, hands-on owner who spent much of his waking hours trying to improve the team. His overzealousness also proved to be his undoing.

In his first move, Cox hired the highly regarded Bucky Harris as manager, replacing Lobert. Harris was the former "Boy Wonder" who as a 27-year-old manager–second baseman had won pennants with the Washington Senators in 1924 and 1925. In fact, Harris had managed continuously in the majors since 1924. He was available only because Clark Griffith had just let him go from his second term as the Washington skipper.

Cox quickly went about attempting to improve the team by actually purchasing players and making trades for players without requiring cash in return. Among the acquisitions was Schoolboy Rowe, former ace pitcher for the Detroit Tigers, who led the 1943 Phils with 14 wins. (Rowe also batted .300 in 82 games and was 15 for 49 as a pinch hitter.)

In late July the team was rocking along in sixth place with a greatly improved 40–53 record when the wheels began to come off the brief Cox regime. On July 28, with the team in St. Louis, Cox suddenly fired the popular Harris. Cox issued a press release announcing the firing and the appointment of Freddie Fitzsimmons (recommended to Cox by Dodger kingpin Branch Rickey) as the successor four hours before bothering to tell Harris. By that time Harris had learned of his dismissal from St. Louis sportswriters.

The Phillies were to play a night game against the Cardinals, with the proceeds of the game to benefit the Red Cross, a not uncommon occurrence during the war years. The players were so upset with Harris's firing and Cox's handling of it that they refused to leave the clubhouse and take the field, with Rowe reputedly the ringleader. Harris, although more than a little unhappy with the events of the day, had to step in to avert a strike. The Phillies played under Fitzsimmons and actually won the game, snapping an 11-game Cardinal win streak.

The dismissal was the result of a growing tension between Cox and Harris, who objected to Cox's hands-on ownership style. After the firing the acrimony escalated when Cox criticized Harris to the press and Harris responded in kind. In a meeting with Philadelphia sportswriters after his return to Philadelphia, Harris told them of Cox, "He's a fine guy to fire me—when he gambles on games his club plays."

The resulting bombshell immediately hit the papers and quickly got Commissioner Landis's attention. A hearing in the commissioner's Chicago office revealed that club secretaries had frequently obtained the odds and placed bets on Phillies games with bookies on Cox's instructions. Cox's only defense was his ignorance of baseball's anti-gambling rule.

On November 23, 1943, Landis declared Cox permanently banned from organized baseball. The Phillies thus became the only franchise in baseball to have two owners kicked out of the game: Horace Fogel had been ousted in 1912 for making unfounded claims about the integrity of umpires and rival managers and claiming that the pennant race was "crooked."

Surprisingly, the team continued to play improved baseball the rest of year, finishing in seventh place, their first time out of the basement since 1937. They won 22 games more than in 1942, and even defeated the powerful Cardinals nine times. The Cardinals dominated the league with a 105–49 record, winning the pennant by 18 games.

Seemingly insignificant amid the turmoil of the 1943 season was the September 12 purchase of catcher Andrew Wasil Seminick from Knoxville of the Southern Association. Seminick, who turned 23 that day, was one of ten children, the son of a Pennsylvania coal miner. In 22 games that year he batted .181 with 2 home runs and 2 doubles among his 13 base hits. With that inauspicious beginning, Seminick became the first Whiz Kid; he was to become the cornerstone of the 1950 pennant winners.

Chapter 3
THE CARPENTERS TAKE OVER

William D. Cox's ouster by Commissioner Kenesaw Mountain Landis meant that Cox had to sell his interest in the Phillies quickly. Cox had brought Nathan "Babe" Alexander to the organization, a bright young public relations director. Alexander contacted Robert R. M. Carpenter, Sr., of Wilmington, Delaware, who promptly purchased the team in late 1943 for a reported $400,000.

Cox's fire sale was a watershed in Phillies history. Bob Carpenter, Sr., a former vice president of DuPont Chemicals, was married to a Dupont, and, most importantly for the Phillies, was a man of great wealth. Carpenter really purchased the club for his son, Robert R. M. Carpenter, Jr., who had minimal interest in big industry but loved sports. Young Bob, at the age of 28, immediately became club president, with something of a blank check to build the ballclub.

Bob, Jr., had played baseball, football, and some basketball in prep school and attended Duke University, where he played on a Rose Bowl team under Wallace Wade. After departing college early to marry, he spent two years in DuPont's public relations department before leaving to involve himself in various sport ventures. He promoted prize fights around Wilmington, ran a professional basketball team called the Wilmington Blue Bombers, and helped to revitalize the football fortunes of the University of Delaware, which had fallen on hard times.

In the late 1930s, young Bob also served as president and eventually part-owner of the Wilmington Blue Rocks of the Class B Interstate

League, in partnership with the venerable Connie Mack. The Blue Rocks operated as a farm club for Mack's American League Athletics. Mack later played a role in the senior Carpenter's purchase of the Phillies from Cox, assuring Commissioner Landis that the Carpenters would breath some life into the moribund franchise.

Faced with a huge task, the Carpenters were not afraid to spend money to make money. The change in the operation of the Phillies was dramatic, even if the results were somewhat slow in coming. Carpenter hired marketing consultants to look for ways to increase ticket sales and revamped the team's financial systems. To bolster the club's image, he even ran a contest early in 1944 for a new team nickname, with the winner to receive a $100 war bond. From among 5,064 entries, the winner was "Blue Jays," submitted by the wife of the caretaker of Odd Fellows Grand Lodge in Philadelphia.

The strongest reaction to the proposed new name came from the student government at Johns Hopkins University in Baltimore, whose teams were also known as the Blue Jays. It passed a resolution, which it forwarded to Carpenter, calling the Phillies' adoption of the name Blue Jays "a reprehensible act which brought disgrace and dishonor to the good name of Johns Hopkins University."

Fan reaction to the new name was less than overwhelming. Although the Blue Jays name made the club stationery and the 1944 and 1945 teams wore Blue Jays patches on their uniforms, the name never really caught on. The local press continued to refer to the team alternatively as the Blue Jays until 1949, when the name was officially dropped.

More importantly, Phillies fans knew that under the Carpenter ownership their best players were no longer going to be sold to pay the bills. Further, the Carpenters soon made it abundantly clear that they were going to be a force to reckon with in the signing of new talent. At his first press conference Bob Carpenter, Jr., announced, "The first thing I want to do is build up the farm system. We're not going to beat anybody's brains out by trying to get a good club right off the bat. But we are going to start working for one systematically."

Young Bob was facing induction into the Army within months of becoming club president. In one of his first and most astute moves he appointed Herb Pennock, then minor league director of the Boston Red Sox, as general manager to carry out the rebuilding plan. Pennock, in fact, was the first real general manager the Phillies ever had. He was an old family friend of the Carpenters and was a highly regarded baseball man. He had pitched in the big leagues for 22 years, mostly for the Red Sox and the storied Yankee teams of the 1920s. He not only won 241 games in a Hall-of-Fame career, but was 5–0 in World Series games. The prototypical wily left-hander, Pennock was said to pitch more with his head than his arm.

The Phillies were certainly a severe test for Pennock's baseball acumen. When the Carpenters took over, the Phillies farm system consisted of a lone working agreement with Trenton in the Class B Interstate League. Bob, Jr., later recalled, "All we had to start with were 25 second-division ballplayers and one minor leaguer at Trenton, a fellow called Turkey Tyson." This was only a slight exaggeration; although players were in short supply during the war, the Phillies were so depleted that they could barely conduct spring training.

Pennock, like Carpenter, rejected a quick fix through the buying of established stars from other clubs. While with the Red Sox, Pennock had watched Tom Yawkey fruitlessly attempt to buy a pennant through the purchase of all-stars such as Lefty Grove, Jimmy Foxx, Wes Ferrell, Bill Werber, Ben Chapman, George Pipgras, and Pinky Higgins. Instead, Pennock went about signing the best new talent available and building a strong farm system.

Pennock began building the Phillies farm system by bringing over key personnel from the Yankee system, such as scout Johnny Nee and, in what appeared to be relatively insignificant at the time, Eddie Sawyer.

Sawyer had been a good-hitting outfielder in the Yankee chain whose playing career was cut short by a shoulder injury suffered while with Oakland in the Pacific Coast League. Sawyer subsequently began his managerial career in the Yankee chain as a player-manager in 1939 at the ripe old age of 28 and had managed at Binghamton in the Eastern League in 1942 and 1943.

SAWYER: "I got to be quite friendly with Herb Pennock in the early 1940s because he was farm director of the Red Sox and I was playing and managing in the Yankee organization. Every minor league that I managed in had a Red Sox farm club, so I got to see Herb quite often and we became good friends. Herb had talked to me about going to the Red Sox with him. It was sort of hard to work for [Yankee President] George Weiss because they didn't pile too many nickels on top of one another—and they didn't intend to, either. They weren't the easiest people to work for by a long shot.

"In the winter of '44, I had practically decided to join Herb in the Red Sox organization. I was with Binghamton in the Eastern League in '43 and we had had a good year. The winter meetings were in New York and Herb was going to meet me at the New Yorker Hotel to talk about different things. So I got on the sleeper out of Binghamton, got into New York City in the morning, picked up a paper at the station and read that Herb Pennock was the new general manager of the Phillies, which changed plans a little bit. When I saw Herb a little later, he told me, 'Don't worry, I've got a job for you no matter.'

"When I left New York all I knew was that I was going to be in a National League organization for the first time; I didn't know where I was going to go. And they didn't know. They didn't have a Triple A club because they didn't have enough players. The first club they bought was Utica in the Eastern League. I was already in that league, so that is where they put me and that was their top club.

"We had to get around and sign players as best we could. That first year in Utica we didn't even have good A players and that was the top farm club. The team didn't have a name, either, so I came up with the Blue Sox. There were the White Sox and the Red Sox in the league so we decided to call ourselves the Blue Sox."

The Phillies did not have a Triple A franchise until 1948, when they formed a working agreement with Toronto of the International League with Sawyer as manager.

Sawyer was a key ingredient in the new ownership's scheme to develop young players through a strong farm system. He had managed in the minors for the Yankees since 1939 and was known for his teaching ability and patience. In the off-season he was in fact a professor, teaching biology at his alma mater, Ithaca College, where he also served as assistant athletic director. Pennock thought so highly of Sawyer that he made it known to Eddie that he was to be groomed to take over the Phillies eventually.

Hiring Sawyer away from the Yankees proved to be one of the most important moves of the new regime. Sawyer had great success at Utica and later Toronto, developing Richie Ashburn, Granny Hamner, Jim Konstanty, Stan Lopata, and Putsy Caballero, among others. After becoming the Phillies' manager in July 1948, of course, he led our club to the 1950 pennant.

The Carpenter-Pennock plan eventually became known as "the five-year plan." Carpenter served in the Army from March 1944 until January 1946, so it was up to Pennock to implement the plan, backed by Carpenter money. Within a few years, the organization had working agreements with 11 minor league teams, up from part of one, and employed nine scouts and the franchise's first farm system director. To staff those clubs with the best new talent available, the Phillies doled out $1,250,000 in bonus money in four years, often outbidding wealthy teams like the Yankees, Cardinals, and Red Sox.

> **SAWYER:** "We did things pretty fast. Our scouts signed a lot of good young players. Of course, we rushed them to the major leagues pretty quickly, but we made sure they had a good foundation. The Carpenters knew what it took to build an organization and they relied on Herb Pennock. He knew how to start a farm system and develop it. Within a few years we had a bunch of teams in the minor leagues."

On an open date during the 1947 season, Carpenter went so far as to send the entire club to Egypt, Pennsylvania (near Allentown), to play a town team in an attempt to cement the signing of local phenom Curt Simmons (the game was ostensibly to dedicate a new community baseball diamond). Simmons pitched against the Phillies before a throng of 4,500 local partisans, striking out 11 future teammates. He had the lead when two of his outfielders collided trying to make the final putout in the ninth, enabling the Phillies to tie the score 4–4. The game was then called, and Carpenter treated the community to a chicken dinner at the local fire hall.

Carpenter may have hoped that the 17-year-old Simmons would get shelled, tempering the bidding war and lowering Curt's price. The ploy obviously did not work. Shortly thereafter Pennock personally signed Simmons to a $65,000 bonus, the largest paid by organized baseball at that time.

The Phillies continued to languish the first two years of the five-year plan, returning to the basement in 1944 and 1945 after rising to seventh in Cox's sole year of ownership. Experienced ballplayers were in very short supply during the war years, and the new capital was used for signing youngsters.

In 1944 and 1945, with Freddie Fitzsimmons continuing as manager, the Phils trained in Wilmington, Delaware, because of wartime travel restrictions.

> **ANDY SEMINICK:** "We had a lot of cold and snow in 1944, so most of our training was done indoors. We played a lot of basketball and ran up and down the steps trying to get in condition. Fitzsimmons played basketball with us and, man, was he tough. He just knocked everyone around. He also gave each player a broomstick about eight feet long and we used it for conditioning by swinging it around in different positions. It seemed to work very well."

In 1944 the Phils finished 61–92, 43¹/₂ games in arrears of the champion Cardinals. The club nearly matched the 64–90 record of the 1943 team, which ended up 41 games out, but a respectable last place was still last place. Philadelphia fans were understandably glum and skeptical of the new ownership.

The team ERA in 1944 was 3.64, the club's best pitching performance since the dead ball era. The staff was led by southpaw Ken Raffensberger who, although going 13–20, fashioned a solid 3.06 ERA. He was the winning pitcher in that year's All-Star game, still the sole Phillies hurler ever to win that game. Ron Northey came of age that year with 22 home runs, 104 RBIs, a .288 batting average, and a league-leading 24 outfield assists.

Twenty-three position players passed through the roster, with many appearing only briefly. Chuck Klein pinch hit a few times as a last vestige of the past while both Granny Hamner and Andy Seminick played in about 20 games with little distinction, giving bare hint of the future.

Seminick and Del Ennis, who was in the South Pacific in 1944 and 1945, are the only two Whiz Kids who were signed by the Phillies before Carpenter bought the team. Andy's road to the major leagues was arduous, particularly when contrasted with the Carpenter-era bonus babies. His baseball journey was so trying that he was the subject of a 1951 feature article in the *Saturday Evening Post* entitled "The Ballplayer Nobody Wanted."

At 17 Andy quit school and went to work in the mines in his hometown of Muse, Pennsylvania, even though Duquesne University recruited him to play football. Andy had begun playing baseball with his town team at age 15 and was able to get a job in the mines because the miners wanted him to keep playing for the Muse team. After three years in the mines shoveling coal all day and playing baseball two or three nights a week, he injured his back stepping on a lump of coal. While recuperating, he decided his best chance of escaping the mines was professional baseball.

After his release from the hospital in 1940, Andy headed for McKeesport, about 30 miles away, where a couple of Pirate farm teams were training. The Pirates head scout, Leo Mackey, and the legendary Pie Traynor thought enough of Andy to sign him to a Class D contract with London, Ontario, in the PONY League. Unfortunately, Andy's professional debut did not go well. After hitting only .156 in 19 games during which he committed 7 errors, he was given his outright release.

A subsequent tryout with Oneonta of the Canadian-American League was unsuccessful, so Andy headed to Detroit where his oldest sister resided. There he worked in a milk bottle cap factory, played some semipro ball, and got a chance to work out with the Tigers, where his boyhood hero Mickey Cochrane had played. After three weeks of morning workouts at Navin Field, Andy received a special-delivery letter from the Tigers on Labor Day telling him not to come out anymore.

A fourth opportunity that summer failed to materialize when Andy, delayed in traveling to Chicago for a tryout with the Giants, arrived as the team was packing to leave for their next city. Manager Bill Terry told him, "Sorry kid, you're too late." Still Andy persevered, saving money over the winter so that he could pay his way to spring training and try to hook on with a club.

> **SEMINICK:** "I decided to try the Knoxville Smokies camp in Tallahassee, Florida, because they had signed a couple of ballplayers from my home area. The Smokies were an independent club in the Southern Association. So I rode the bus down from Detroit and asked the Knoxville manager, Freddie Lindstrom, who was a Hall of Famer, for a tryout. I must have caught an hour and a half of batting practice before I even swung a bat. I was about wore out. I finally got up and hit. I think I had about a dozen swings and they signed me for $75 a month. I guess they saw something because they sent me to their Class D affiliate Elizabethton, Tennessee, in the Appalachian League."

The Elizabethton manager, Hobe Brummette, liked Andy's long-ball potential but was less than taken with him as a catcher. As a result, Andy played second base and the outfield more than he caught. But he stuck and had a solid season, hitting .263 with 16 home runs and 86 RBIs in 112 games. More importantly, Andy met and married a local girl, Gussie Irene Anderson, during that 1941 season.

He returned to Elizabethton in 1942, hitting a more impressive .325 and earning a contract with Knoxville for 1943. With the wartime shortage of players (he kept getting rejected by the Army because of a knee injured at Elizabethton in 1942) Andy found himself in demand.

> **SEMINICK:** "I went to work with a defense plant in Kingston, Tennessee, during the off-season, running a bulldozer and making good money. Knoxville sent me a contract for $150 a month, which was about what I was making a week at the plant. I sent them a weekly pay stub from my paycheck, which I think was for $175, and they right away sent me another contract for $350 a month. I was reluctant even then, but one of the guys I worked with urged me to give it a shot. I didn't want to give up baseball, but I was married and making good money and I wasn't sure if I should give that up."

At first Andy was a utility player with the Smokies, filling in at first base, second base, and the outfield. At midseason, when the Phillies bought Smokies catcher Bob Finley (later baseball coach at Southern Methodist University), manager Buddy Lewis, an old catcher himself, tried to step in. After a couple of games he made Andy the regular catcher, and Andy responded by hitting .303 with 16 homers and 83 RBIs.

> **SEMINICK:** "While I was catching at Knoxville, Phillies manager Bucky Harris came by at the All-Star break to scout a shortstop named Ray Hamrick. I had a pretty good day, hitting a home run to tie the game and hitting another home run in extra innings to win the ball game. Bucky Harris made a statement to the paper the next day that 'Looks like we bought the wrong catcher.'"

Late in the 1943 season, the Phillies tried to buy Andy when two of their catchers were hurt, only to be beaten to the punch by Bill Veeck, the boy-wonder president of the Triple A Milwaukee Brewers. Veeck paid $15,000 for Andy on September 12 and sold him the same day to the Phillies for $35,000 and pitcher Newt Kimball. By outmaneuvering Bill Cox for Seminick, Veeck made $20,000 in less than 24 hours and obtained Kimball, a major league pitcher.

> **SEMINICK:** "Shortly after the end of our season in Knoxville, I got a call from Bill Veeck telling me that he had bought my contract from Knoxville and sold me to Philadelphia the same

day. I told him I couldn't report because I had gotten called up to the service. Veeck told me he would give me $500 just to report and so I did, because $500 was a lot of money in those days. Sure enough when I got to Philadelphia there was a $500 check waiting for me. It turned out pretty well for me since the Army rejected me because of my bad knees."

Although Veeck certainly made a buck at the Phils' expense, the club had acquired a catcher who would pay long-term dividends as a cornerstone of our 1950 pennant winners. And the team avoided a major mistake in the Seminick transaction. The player Veeck really wanted from the Phillies was not Kimball, but Del Ennis, then a rookie outfielder with Trenton.

SEMINICK: "When I reported to the Phillies, I didn't have a decent pair of spikes, so I went by a local department store on my way to the ballpark. The only spikes they had in my size were a pair with yellow tongues and laces. They looked ridiculous and only made me more nervous. The first five times I went to bat, I struck out. I didn't even foul one off. Then I grounded out to short and grounded out to first. Finally, on my eighth at bat, I hit a home run off Harry Feldman of the Giants, for my first hit in the big leagues.

"A couple of days later I was catching and dove for a pop fly and broke a bone in my wrist. I didn't tell the manager about it and asked the trainer to keep it quiet. I managed to hit one more home run and after the season was over had it X-rayed. I ended up with it in a cast most of the winter."

During the wintry 1944 spring training in Wilmington, Delaware, Fitzsimmons tried Andy in left field, at third base, and at shortstop, where he almost made the team. After opening the season on the big league roster, however, the Phillies sent Andy to the Buffalo Bisons in the International League, where he played most of the year in left field. He was called up for another cup of coffee late that year and batted .222 in 63 at bats.

On September 9, 1944, the Phillies signed another future Whiz Kid, 16-year-old Ralph "Putsy" Caballero from New Orleans. Since the club was firmly in the cellar, it activated Caballero and played him in four ballgames, two at third base. As a result, Caballero became the youngest third baseman in major league history and the youngest Phillie ever, distinctions that still stand today.

CABALLERO: "I had finished high school at 16 because we only had seven grades in grammar school back then. I was going to LSU on a baseball and basketball scholarship but Mel Ott, who was from the New Orleans area, wanted me to sign with the Giants. But the Phillies wanted to sign me too. I called Mel Ott and he told me, 'I'm treating you like a father would. Whoever offers you the most money, sign with them.' The Phillies were offering $10,000 to sign me and my Dad, who was a druggist in New Orleans, said, 'Putsy, if you go to college it will take you years to save $10,000. So go ahead and sign and go back to college in the off-season.' So Dad and I went to Philadelphia to sign with Herb Pennock and Bob Carpenter."

Although perhaps never fulfilling his early promise, after some time in the minor leagues Caballero became the Phils' regular third baseman in 1948 at the age of 21 and was a valuable utility infielder for the team through 1952.

On September 14, 1944, just five days after signing Caballero, the Phillies signed another high schooler, 17-year-old Granville Wilbur Hamner of Richmond, Virginia. Granny Hamner, whose father drove an ice truck, was a streetwise, cocky kid who became one of the finest shortstops in the National League and a key to the success of our 1950 pennant winners. The signing of teenagers Caballero and Hamner were prime examples of Carpenter's aggressive plan to spend money to sign young talent.

Hamner was a three-sport star at Benedictine High School and had worked out with several professional teams over the 1944 summer. He had even traveled on his own nickel to Brooklyn to try out with the Dodgers. Branch Rickey reportedly thought that the kid was a little too brash, leaving Hamner with no way home until Coach Jake Pitler took pity on him and loaned him the train fare back to Richmond.

Granny had an older brother, Garvin, who was playing for the independent Richmond Colts in the Piedmont League. Garvin arranged for Granny to work out with the club, and he impressed Colts' manager Ben Chapman, who was shortly to succeed Fitzsimmons as the Phillies' manager. Chapman contacted several major league teams, including his old Yankee teammate Herb Pennock of the Phillies. After a tryout in Shibe Park, Pennock signed Granny for a bonus of $8,000.

HAMNER: "I had worked out with several other clubs. But the Phillies didn't have anybody. I thought I could get to the big leagues quicker if I signed with them, so that's what I did."

Granny was correct. The next day he joined the Phillies. He got into 21 games in 1944 and hit a respectable .247 in 77 at bats.

HAMNER: "We had a really poor club. The quality of play had really diminished, so coming to the big leagues at that age wasn't as bad as it sounds. There were a few good players still around. But they were all getting older. We didn't get big crowds to watch us. So it wasn't too hard to break in."

Contemporary accounts suggest that it was a little tougher to break in than Granny remembered almost 50 years later. Granny made nine errors in his short stint in 1944, including five in one game. (Hamner recalled, "I made seven one afternoon, but the scorers were generous. They only charged me with five.") The Philadelphia fans, sparse though they were, began to boo Granny unmercifully. One afternoon in particular the fans got to Granny. He came to the dugout with tears in his eyes and was consoled by manager Fitzsimmons, who then stepped out of the dugout and challenged any fan who had booed the kid to come down and fight. No one took him up on it.

When the season ended, Granny returned to Richmond to begin his senior year of high school.

In October 1944 the Phillies also signed Granny's older brother Garvin for a small bonus. The Richmond Colts had attempted to sell Garvin during the summer to the Giants but the sale was voided, leaving him a free agent. Garvin, also an infielder, played part of the 1945 season with the Phils, hitting .198 in 30 games.

A couple of years later the St. Louis Browns noticed the name G. Hamner on the list of minor leaguers available for the baseball draft. They quickly put in a claim, thinking that they were getting Granny. Instead the Browns ended up with Garvin, by then no longer considered a prospect. Garvin never made it back to the major leagues after his 1945 stint with the Phillies.

In 1945 the Phillies farmed Granny out to Utica to regain his confidence and play under the watchful eye of Eddie Sawyer. Upon Granny's arrival, Sawyer told him, "You're my shortstop this season even if you boot a dozen a game. And I am going to sock the first fan that rides you."

At the season opener, Granny booted the first ball hit in his direction and threw the next one over the first baseman's head. When the fans started to boo, Granny dropped his glove, walked over to the bleachers and challenged anyone to come down and discuss the issue in person. Again, no one took up the challenge and Granny went on to have a solid season, hitting .258 in 104 games.

> **ASHBURN:** "Granny was a tough kid, let me tell you. When we went to spring training with the Phillies, they had a bunch of veteran ballplayers. They didn't particularly like a young kid coming in there with his attitude. He had very little respect for those old players and he would tell them what he thought. Granny could play better than those veterans. They would try to run him out of the batting cage. Well, Granny was a street fighter. A lot of Granny's friends in Richmond, Virginia, are probably still in prison. He was a tough kid. He didn't want to put up with all that crap. We just practically grew up together, playing in the minor leagues."

The 1945 season for the parent Phils appeared to be a step backward. The team again finished in last place, this time with a miserable 46–108 record. Pennock (Carpenter was still in the army) canned Fitzsimmons on June 30 after the club had won only 17 out of its first 67 games. In his stead, Pennock chose Ben Chapman, his hard-bitten former Yankee teammate, who had been suspended for the season two years previously for slugging a minor league umpire.

The Phillies had acquired Chapman as a player in a trade for catcher Johnny Peacock a few weeks before Pennock named him manager. Brooklyn had purchased Ben from Richmond the previous year to pinch hit and shore up their war-depleted pitching staff. Although Chapman's long career with the Yankees, Senators, Red Sox, Indians, and White Sox had been as a fleet-footed outfielder, he had some success as a Dodger pitcher in 1944, winning 5 and losing 3 with 6 complete games and a 3.40 ERA. In 1945 he was 3–3 with the Dodgers.

Chapman's acerbic nature and sharp tongue were legendary. As a player, he had been traded or sold at least half a dozen times. Even Yankee manager Joe McCarthy, who was known for his ability to handle difficult personalities, eventually got rid of Ben.

Although fiercely competitive, Chapman could do little with the 1945 Phillies. He forbade card playing or drinking in the clubhouse and required that all conversation in the dugout had to be about baseball. Although improving slightly from their woeful start, the club still finished 52 games behind the pennant-winning Cubs and 15 games behind the seventh-place Reds. The team batting average of .246 was worst in the league, as was the team ERA of 4.64. Nineteen pitchers paraded through Shibe Park. Dick Barrett led (if you can call it leading) the starters with 7 wins 20 losses and a 5.43 ERA. The Phils led the league in errors and were last in home runs.

Chapman inherited a wartime team with five players under 21 years of age and nine over 35. The oldtimers included Jimmie Foxx, who hit the last seven homers of his illustrious career and even pitched 23 innings with a sparkling 1.57 ERA; old Giant catcher Gus Mancuso; and former Dodger ace Whitlow Wyatt, who turned in a forgettable 0–7 performance. With Ron Northey in the service, Vince DiMaggio (Joe's and Dom's brother), acquired from the Pirates for pitcher Al Gearheauser in March, supplied the team's only power. The oldest ballplaying DiMaggio hit 19 home runs, including a club record four grand slams. No one else hit more than seven round-trippers.

Solid performances were turned in by first sacker Jimmy Wasdell, who batted an even .300 in 134 games, and reliever Andy Karl, who was needed a league-leading 67 times and responded with a 2.98 ERA in 188 innings of work. The only future Whiz Kids to see any action were Andy Seminick, who got into 80 ballgames, and Granny Hamner, who had another late-season trial after hitting .258 at Utica.

It was, all things considered, a dreary showing. With Connie Mack's Athletics finishing in the cellar as well, Philadelphia fans were understandably discouraged. Through the 1945 season the Phillies had finished at the bottom of the National League heap, usually by large margins, seven out of eight years. And it did not appear that Carpenter's so-called five-year plan was paying any dividends at all.

But the team continued to lay some important groundwork. Of no little consequence down the road were the coaches Chapman brought to the Phillies upon his hiring as manager. Further cementing the Yankee connection, Chapman brought in Pennock's old Yankee battery mate Benny Bengough; Cy Perkins, another old catcher who had caught for the A's for many years and spent 1931 in the Yankees bullpen; and Chapman's good buddy Dusty Cooke, who had broken in with the Yankees the same time as Ben. Dusty was initially hired as the trainer, a skill he learned in the Navy during the war, but later became a coach. All three men were still with us in 1950, though Chapman, the man who hired them, was fired midway through the 1948 season.

After the dismal showing of 1945, Carpenter, just back from the service, and Pennock refused to stand pat. With literally hundreds of big leaguers returning from the war, quality players were available. While still sticking to their plan of aggressively signing young talent, Carpenter and Pennock saw that they could immediately fashion a more competitive postwar club by prudently buying returning veterans from other teams.

> **SAWYER:** "In 1946 the Phillies trained in Miami Beach. When I showed up I asked Ben, 'What do you want me to do?'
>
> "Ben said, 'Just hit fungoes to the second basemen.'
>
> "I thought there would be two or three of them. There were about 30 of them. Danny Murtaugh was one, Moon Mullen, Fred Daniels, Charlie Letchas, I could name a bunch. They were all coming back from the service."

As a result, the Phillies fielded an entirely new infield, and a quality one at that. They purchased first baseman Frank McCormick, the 1940 National League MVP, from the Reds, slick-fielding second baseman Emil Verban from the Cardinals, and the entire left side of the infield, veteran third sacker Jim Tabor and 35-year-old shortstop Skeeter Newsome, from the Red Sox. Several pitchers of merit returned to the Phillies from the service, including Schoolboy Rowe, Tommy Hughes, Frank Hoerst, and Hugh Mulcahy, back after missing five full seasons to the war. Hopes were high that the pitching would be much improved from the staff's woeful 1945 performance.

Unfortunately, the Phils started slowly and spent the first two months of the season in their accustomed basement position. But in late June they got hot and within a week moved from last to sixth. The club continued to play well for the rest of the season and finished in fifth place with a 69–85 record, their best showing since the 1932 fourth-place team.

More importantly, the Phils captured the imagination of their fans with their competitiveness. Chapman demanded a fighting, hustling ballclub, and the Phils responded. They won many games with eighth- and ninth-inning rallies and never seemed to give up. Dressed in sharp new uniforms with red and white trim, the team began to be known as the Fightin' Phillies. They beat the Cardinals, 1946 World Champions, 8 times and won 10 ballgames from the Cubs, the 1945 pennant winners and third-place finishers in 1946.

With the war finally over, 1946 was a great year for baseball. With the return of the troops and the relief that peace was at hand at last, fans flocked to ballparks all over the country. In Philadelphia, the Fightin' Phillies drew an astonishing total of 1,045,247 patrons to Shibe Park—astonishing because in 1945 the club could draw only 285,000. The team's previous attendance record was only 515,365, established in 1916 before the advent of night or Sunday baseball. (The 1916 team, following their 1915 pennant, had finished second under manager Pat Moran, losing the pennant to Brooklyn in the last two days of the season.) In 1946 the Phillies, long playing the neglected stepchild to Connie Mack's Athletics, outdrew their Philadelphia rivals by almost 425,000. Crowds of 25,000 to 30,000 became commonplace.

Andy Seminick continued to improve both behind and at the plate, finally becoming the regular catcher. He caught 118 games, appeared in 124, and hit a solid .264 with 12 round-trippers. Hamner and Caballero, however, had gone into the military.

Hughes, Hoerst, and Mulcahy were unable to regain their earlier form, but the veteran Schoolboy Rowe led the pitching with an 11–4 record and sparkling 2.12 ERA before being sidelined by injury. Canadian southpaw Oscar Judd finished 11–12 and another lefty, hardluck Ken Raffensberger, won 8 and lost 15 despite a 3.63 ERA in a team-leading 196 innings. Future Whiz Kid pitcher Sylvester "Blix" Donnelly was acquired from the Cardinals in midseason and finished 4–6 (3–4 in 12 games with the Phillies). The team ERA of 3.99 was still last in the league, but a great improvement over the previous year.

Late in 1946 the Phillies outbid the Yankees and the Cubs to sign a 20-year-old pitching prospect from Chicago named Lou Possehl.

> **POSSEHL:** "My hometown team, the Cubs, offered me about $10,000 less than the Phillies. The Yankees offered $15,000 and the Phillies offered $18,000. So we took the money. I bought my father a brand new Chevrolet for $600.
>
> "I signed in August and went right to the Phillies. I had just shut out a good semi-pro team in Chicago 1–0. Ben Chapman heard about it and said, 'I'm going to start the kid Sunday in Cincinnati.'
>
> "I joined the team in Chicago and then we went down to St. Louis. Chapman sent Blix Donnelly and I ahead of the team to Cincinnati to rest up and go watch Cincinnati play. Well, hell, I

didn't know what I was looking at. Blix Donnelly told me, 'Don't worry about it kid, these guys are lousy hitters.'

"We had a doubleheader on Sunday. Blix Donnelly pitched the first game and he got bombarded. Nothing but line shots all over the joint and we lost about 13–4. I was scared to death. He had told me they weren't good hitters. I started the second game and I only gave up four hits but I'm losing 1–0 after seven innings. But we got four runs and I get the win 4–1."

Lou was up and down with the Phillies for several years before an arm injury ended his career.

SAWYER: "It's a shame Lou didn't stick in the major leagues because he was a fine pitcher. He never had much breaking stuff but he could throw hard. Wonderful guy, he would pitch anytime. He played hard, too. He loved to pitch but he never could get beyond Triple A."

The new infield in 1946 solidified the team's defense and put up respectable numbers on offense. McCormick hit a solid .284 and made only one error all year. He played 131 straight games without an error and had a record .999 fielding percentage.

The Phillies had a new outfield in 1946 as well, with the return of Ron Northey from the military, the acquisition of Johnny Wyrostek from the Cardinals, and the emergence of Del Ennis. Northey slugged 16 home runs and Wyrostek showed real promise, hitting .281 in 145 games. But Del was the real story. Discharged from the Navy on April 5, he joined the Phillies about a week later. Chapman, impressed with the strength of Del's wrists, began working him into the lineup in left field.

ENNIS: "I didn't really expect to stay with the Phillies, but they had to give me a 30-day trial because I was on the national defense list. I never had spring training. I pinch hit in Pittsburgh in my first game, then I got into the starting lineup. In my second game in left field, I hit a bases-loaded double to beat the Pirates. A few days later against the Cubs in Chicago, I hit two homers in one game, one off Claude Passeau and one off Hi Bithorn."

Del became a fixture in the Phillies' lineup, hitting .313 (fourth in the league), leading the team with 17 home runs and making the All-Star team. For his impressive debut, Del was named the *Sporting News* National League Rookie of the Year.

Ennis was homegrown talent from the Olney section of Philadelphia, where the Phillies signed him back in 1943. Del was first noticed by the Phillies in 1942, when Nugent still owned the club. Jocko Collins, the Phillies only scout back in those lean years, took the streetcar (costing the Phillies 7½ cents) out to Olney to check out a hot tip on a southpaw pitcher for Olney High, one "Lefty" Gilbert. His attention was quickly diverted to a 16-year-old outfielder with a seemingly effortless swing.

> **ENNIS:** "I had a pretty good day that day. I hit two home runs with the bases loaded, doubled with the bases loaded, and then later hit another home run. I ended up with three home runs and 12 runs batted in for the day. Jocko was the first scout to see me play. Back then I was just an unrecognized kid with no intention of playing professional baseball. I didn't have any idea of playing in the major leagues. I just played ball because I was good at it. I was going to join the Navy after graduation."

Del was a shy teenager and initially resisted Collins's efforts to sign him to a professional contract because he did not believe he was ready for more advanced competition. He even resisted playing with Port Richmond, a fast semi-pro team managed by Collins, preferring to spend the summer playing in his local league. In August, Del finally signed Collins's proffered contract with Rome, New York, a Phillie farm team in the Canadian-American League. But the league suspended operations because of the war before Del could play, leaving all the players, Del included, as free agents.

Del was again reluctant to sign a professional contract, but guided by his father he signed in March 1943 with Trenton of the Class B Inter-State League, with whom the Phils had a working agreement.

> **ENNIS:** "I was always a home boy and I was going into the Navy in September, so I commuted from home back and forth every game, to Trenton, to Hagerstown, to Lancaster—even all the away games and everything. Dick Carter, one of our pitchers and later a scout and a coach for the Phillies, and I used to ride together all the time to every game.
>
> "In fact, in August I was hitting .409 and didn't even know it. I didn't know anything about averages or RBIs or anything. All I did was play ball every day and come home. Even in high school I had just played and never knew anything about statistics."

As green as Del was, he was a major league prospect from the outset. In 140 games with Trenton in 1943, he hit a lusty .346 with 37 doubles, 16 triples, 18 home runs, and 93 RBIs. In September the Phillies called up nine players from the Trenton roster to finish the season with the big club, Ennis included. But Del declined. He was going into the Navy the first of October and wanted to spend the next few weeks at home with his parents.

Although Del did not join the Phillies, Herb Pennock was sharp enough to sign Ennis to a major league contract for $50, since technically he was the property of Trenton. After Del entered the Navy, the Yankees offered him $25,000 to sign with them and the Cubs also offered a substantial bonus. But Del was the bargain basement property of the Phillies and had to turn down both offers.

Once in the Navy, Del was shipped to the Great Lakes Training Station near Chicago where he played baseball with established major leaguers like Joe Gordon, Bob Feller, and Billy Herman. Later he became a signalman for the Hawaii Sea Frontier, saw action in the Pacific, and made a Navy baseball team in which he was the only player without major league experience.

> **ENNIS:** "We had Vander Meer, Dickey, York, Rowe, and other guys who were all major leaguers. Those guys thought I could play so I made the team and we traveled all over the South Pacific, playing ball to entertain the troops. I went to something like 17 islands. At some places we would have to make the baseball field before we could play a game. But that is where I got my really good experience, playing ball in the Navy."

Word of Ennis's baseball exploits in the Pacific reached the states and a number of clubs attempted to persuade Pennock to throw Del in on proposed trades. The general manager held fast to his plan of keeping young talent, and the local product became one of the best bargains and greatest outfielders in Phillies history.

> **ENNIS:** "Ben Chapman did a good job with that 1946 club and worked hard with me. I had a lot to learn and it wasn't until about June that I began to think I had a chance to stay with the team all season. Chapman would give me one thing each week to practice on, like how I caught fly balls. He also worked with my batting. When I first came up I used to hit the ball a lot to right and right center field. So he got me way up on the plate and got me to use a heavier bat and choke it a little bit. That way I could shorten my swing and pull a lot of balls.

"Schoolboy Rowe was one of my neighbors and we used to go back and forth to the park together. When he wasn't pitching he would sit on the bench and tell me when the opposing pitcher was going to throw a curveball or a fastball. He could really read pitchers' motions. When I was at bat he would whistle when a curveball was coming and I knew to expect a curve. He really helped me a lot and taught me to study the pitchers."

With the emergence of Ennis and a fifth-place finish, 1946 was certainly a turning point for the Phillies. While not yet pennant contenders, the club was now respectable. The team was still a veteran one, but younger players were beginning to contribute and the Carpenter-Pennock five-year plan seemed to be back on track. Only three future Whiz Kids—Ennis, Seminick, and Donnelly—were with the team for the bulk of the year, but more were shortly to come.

Chapter 4
1947: Jackie Robinson, Treading Water, and Building for the Future

After the tremendous enthusiasm generated by the Phillies' fifth-place finish in 1946, Philadelphians' expectations for 1947 were greater than ever. Unfortunately, the club could not deliver, slipping into a seventh-place (i.e., last-place) tie with the Pirates. Nevertheless, the team remained competitive, winning 62 games, only 7 fewer than the year before. Their disappointing position in the standings did not seem to discourage the fans; a remarkable 907,332 of them made their way to Shibe Park in 1947.

The Phillies' season had a number of highlights, particularly for a tail-end ballclub. For example, 41,660 (40,952 paid) fans crammed into Shibe Park on May 11 to watch the Phillies beat the pennant-bound Dodgers 7–3 and 5–4 behind the pitching of veterans Dutch Leonard and School-boy Rowe. The crowd was the largest ever to that point in Philadelphia baseball history and was about eight thousand over the listed capacity for Shibe Park.

Of course, 1947 was the year Jackie Robinson broke the game's color barrier and the Phillies unhappily played a key role in that watershed event. Robinson was handpicked by Dodger president Branch Rickey to integrate baseball, and he chose well. Jackie was a very intelligent, college-educated athlete (he had lettered in four sports at UCLA) who had a remarkable inner spirit and drive. He had promised Rickey that he would not fight back initially at the expected racial taunts, and he did not. Jackie was able to keep his composure against bean balls, flying spikes, and repugnant verbal abuse while competing fiercely on the playing field and earning the respect of everyone in baseball, even those heaping abuse on him.

The first time I saw Jackie Robinson play was in 1946. I was playing in a summer college league in Vermont, and on a day off three of us decided to make the long drive up to Montreal to see Jackie perform. Rickey had signed Jackie to a professional contract on October 23, 1945, and assigned him to play for the top Dodger farm club in Montreal for the 1946 season, where there was likely to be less racial pressure. Jackie put on quite a show that day, going three for four with a home run and a steal of home while playing errorless ball at second base. It was easy to see that Jackie was a remarkable player. Of course, I did not have an inkling that we would later face each other so often in crucial situations in the major leagues.

Robinson faced tremendous resistance throughout the National League in 1947. During the Dodger spring training in Havana, Fred "Dixie" Walker, a native of Birmingham, Alabama, circulated a petition among a number of his teammates threatening a boycott if Robinson were promoted to the Dodgers. Branch Rickey and manager Leo Durocher quashed the threat, and they traded former Phillies hurler Kirby Higbe, also one of the instigators of the petition, to the Pirates shortly after the season began. Rickey kept Walker only for the 1947 season before banishing him to the Pirates in the deal that brought the Dodgers Billy Cox and Preacher Roe.

Walker later regretted his actions, calling the petition "the biggest mistake of my life." Ironically, Dixie, who played for Brooklyn from 1939 through 1947, was called "the People's Cherce" and was one of the most popular players in Dodger history. The older brother of my future teammate Harry Walker, he was a fine ballplayer, batting .306 in 18 big league seasons. Bobby Bragan, another Birmingham native on the '47 Dodgers who threatened to boycott, later became a close friend of Jackie's. Bragan went on to manage the Pirates, Braves, and Indians and was noted for his fair treatment of Latin-American and African-American ballplayers.

Early in 1947, the veteran players on the Cardinals, whose roster was full of southerners, allegedly attempted to organize a player strike throughout the National League. Some clubs, including the Phillies, actually took votes about whether to play against Robinson.

ANDY SEMINICK: "When Jackie Robinson first came into the league, each club was to vote about whether they were going to play or not. I remember Pittsburgh voted not to play and we voted we would play. We had a meeting and Skeeter Newsome, our shortstop at the time, got up and said, 'This is something real serious and you better be thinking real hard about not playing.' He wanted to play and he was trying to tell everyone not to vote not to play. We voted to play. There might have been a few guys who voted not to play, but most guys wanted to play."

Phillies manager Ben Chapman, also from Birmingham, and first-base coach Dusty Cooke of North Carolina were particularly rough on Jackie, as were some of the Phillies' other veteran ballplayers from the south. When the Phillies first visited Ebbets Field in mid-April, Chapman, Cooke, and others taunted Robinson with vicious racial insults for the entire three-game series. The invective was so severe that two of Jackie's teammates from Alabama, Eddie Stanky and Dixie Walker, leapt to his defense, Stanky calling Chapman a "coward" and telling him to "pick on somebody who can fight back." Fans protested to Commissioner Happy Chandler, the press took up Robinson's cause and Broadway columnist Walter Winchell even castigated Chapman on his national Sunday night radio broadcast.

LOU POSSEHL: "I was with the Phillies at the beginning of '47 when Jackie Robinson came up. They called him every name in the book. How he took it I'll never know. When he was in the on-deck circle he would just put his head down over the bat. We had a lot of guys from the South, like Jim Tabor, Skeeter Newsome, Dusty Cooke, and Ben Chapman. They just let him have it. Unbelievable. He went through hell. He had to be quite a man to do what he did.

"I grew up in a rough neighborhood in Chicago, so it wasn't anything I hadn't heard before. It didn't shock me but it surprised me that they would get after a guy so bad like they were after him. I mean enough is enough."

Commissioner Chandler and National League president Ford Frick both warned Bob Carpenter that the racial baiting of Robinson had to cease. Chapman was forced to agree but defended himself by saying, "There is not a man who has come to the big leagues since baseball has been played who has not been ridden. We will treat Robinson the same as we do Hank Greenberg of the Pirates, Clint Hartung of the Giants, Joe Garagiola of the Cardinals, Connie Ryan of the Braves or any other man who is likely to step to the plate and beat us." According to Ben, Robinson "did not want to be patronized" and had simply received the treatment afforded all rookies.

> **HARRY WALKER:** "Sure Chapman rode Robinson. He rode anybody. If you were Polish, Jewish, Italian, Irish, English, Indian, or whatever. If he could beat you by getting under your skin and make you forget what you were doing, he would do it. He didn't give anything to anybody. He fought hard and played hard all of his life. He gave a hard time to a lot of players. I remember he rode the hell out of Harry Danning when he was catching in New York, just to needle him because he was Jewish."

> **MAJE McDONNELL:** "Chapman said, 'Look, when I came up to the big leagues they called me every name in the book. Let's see what he's made of.' He told us, 'Get on him, get on him good.'"

The Dodgers arrived in Philadelphia on May 9 for their first series of the season at Shibe Park. Bob Carpenter pushed hard for a public reconciliation and Chapman, possibly fearing for his job, asked Robinson to shake hands with him for the photographers before the first game. Jackie, after considerable thought, agreed and the two met on neutral ground behind home plate. Newspapers all over the nation ran the photos. Afterwards Chapman continued to deny that he had treated Robinson unfairly and went so far as to say that he would "be glad to have a colored player" on his team.

Chapman and others continued to ride Robinson, but toned down or eliminated the racial epithets. Jackie had quickly earned their respect as a ballplayer, and the negative publicity from Chapman's initial confrontation with Robinson was sobering.

> **McDONNELL:** "I'll say this, when it got to be August Chapman said, 'Gentleman, no more. He showed me he can play.' So we gave him the silent treatment after that."

By June 1948, when I was called up to the Phillies, the taunting of Robinson was largely in the past. Chapman, however, had tried other tactics against Jackie, which, he recognized, had also failed.

> **PUTSY CABALLERO:** "Chapman had a rule in 1948 when Jackie moved over to second base [Robinson had played first base as a rookie in 1947] that if we went into him and didn't knock him

down, we were automatically fined. That was a team rule. We had to try to knock him down even after the play was over. The more we tried to hurt him, the good Lord would punish us. Somebody fractured an ankle, Andy [Seminick] hurt his shoulder one time, another guy got a bruised elbow. So we finally had a meeting and Chapman told us to play him like any other player. We were just hurting ourselves trying to get to him."

SAM NAHEM: "The more Ben Chapman and the guys insulted Jackie Robinson the better he played. It was an ironic twist that Ben Chapman, who was the leader of the racist business, had to tell them to stop getting on Jackie Robinson because he was killing us on the ballfield.

"I was very much for Jackie Robinson and at one point I tried to counter some of this racist stuff openly. One of the southerners was fulminating in the clubhouse in a racist way and I made some halfway innocuous remark defending blacks coming in to baseball. Boy, he went into a real tantrum and really came down on me. So I decided I would not confront anyone openly. Your prestige on a ballclub depends on your won-loss record and your earned run average. I didn't have that to back me. I only had logic and decency and humanity. So after that I would just speak to some of the guys privately about racism in a mild way.

"Once in '48 I was pitching against the Dodgers and facing Roy Campanella. He had come up that year and had been thrown at a lot, although there was absolutely no reason why I would throw at him. A ball escaped me, which was not unusual, and went toward his head. He got up and gave me such a glare. I felt so badly about it I felt like yelling to him, 'Roy, please, I really didn't mean it. I belong to the NAACP.'"

First-base coach Dusty Cooke had also been extremely tough on Robinson.

JOHNNY BLATNICK: "I'll never forget one day when we were playing in Brooklyn. I laid down a bunt and Jackie Robinson came over from second and covered first. I moved the runner up and they threw me out by about three steps at first. When I got down to the bag Jackie Robinson's foot was right across the bag. I could have stepped on him and put him out of baseball.

So I just jumped on over and didn't even try to touch the bag. When Dusty Cooke came into the dugout after the inning was over he just chewed my ass out saying, 'You could have cut his achilles tendon and then we wouldn't have to put up with him anymore.' Now, what kind of a person would do that."

Ben Chapman, for one, accepted Robinson as a ballplayer a lot easier than he accepted him as a man. One day in 1948, shortly before Ben was fired as manager, Curt Simmons and I happened to be following Chapman into the tunnel at Ebbets Field. Robinson had had a big day against the Phillies, helping the Dodgers sweep a doubleheader with seven hits and a couple of stolen bases. In Ebbets Field the runways from the two dugouts met underneath the stands and there was a common tunnel to the two dressing rooms. Chapman seemed to be waiting for Robinson in the tunnel and when Jackie passed by, Chapman blurted out, "Robinson, you're one hell of a ballplayer, but you're still a nigger." I remember thinking at the time that we would have had one whale of a battle if Jackie had lit into Ben. Both were big, broad, strong men who knew how to take care of themselves. But to Jackie's everlasting credit, he just looked at Ben and walked on by.

Jackie Robinson was a tremendous competitor who would do anything on the ballfield to win. But he also had a sense of fairplay that was exemplary, particularly considering what he had to endure when he broke into baseball. When we were in the Ebbets Field clubhouse in 1950 after we beat the Dodgers on the last day of the season, I looked up amid all of our celebration and saw Jackie going from locker to locker shaking hands and congratulating us on winning the pennant. It was an exceptional act by an exceptional individual, particularly given the Phillies' inexcusable treatment of him in 1947.

We had two memorable run-ins with Robinson after I joined the ballclub in June 1948. On one occasion Schoolboy Rowe was all over Jackie from our dugout and Jackie dropped his bat and walked over to the dugout and said, "Schoolie, come on out here, right now." Schoolie was 6'4" and a big guy but nothing happened and Robinson went back to the batter's box to hit.

Another time Jackie got into it with Russ Meyer, whom we called the Mad Monk because of his temper.

MEYER: "Jackie was on third base one night when I was pitching against the Dodgers in Ebbets Field, going up and down like he did, threatening to steal home. So I yelled over to him, 'Go ahead you nigger, try to steal.' Bad judgment on my part but I said it and I'm not going to deny it.

"Well, he did try to steal on the next pitch and Frank Dascoli called him safe. I made a real good throw, down, and he slid on the first base side and never did get the plate but Dascoli called him safe. The pictures in the newspaper the next day showed that he never did reach home plate and that Seminick had the plate blocked. Well, I charged Dascoli and I had him right up against the screen, right next to the fans. Ebbets Field was really small and the screen was very close. I grabbed him and he jerked away from me and buttons flew all over the damn place.

"Red Barber was broadcasting the game and he slid a microphone down the damn screen and what I'm calling Dascoli is going out over the air. I'm calling him a blind homer, a no good bastard, a sonuvabitch and worse, and apparently the Ebbets Field switchboard is lighting up like a damn Christmas tree.

"Well, anyway Robinson is over in the Dodger dugout laughing his ass off and I happen to glance over there and see him. So I walked over and really blasted him. I said, 'Come on you sonuvabitch, let's go, underneath.' The runways from the two dugouts met underneath the stands.

"So he said, 'Let's go.'

"I started to go into the tunnel and Bill Nicholson grabbed me and said, 'Monk, you don't want to do that.'

"When I got traded to the Dodgers in 1953 I was happy because the Dodgers were winning pennants and they were going to pay me well. But I got to thinking to myself, 'Sonuvabitch, I've got to walk into that clubhouse and face Robinson and those guys I've been battling all these years.'

"So when I did walk into the Dodger clubhouse the first guy that I bump into is Jackie Robinson. His locker is a little bit catty-corner from the entrance. He got up and walked over to me and he said, 'Monk, we've been fighting one another, now let's fight 'em together.' I want to tell you, talk about class.

"Jackie and I became good friends. He was a competitor, like I was. In '54, when the Giants beat us [the Dodgers] by two games, I was pitching against the Giants and Hank Thompson hit a home run off me. Monte Irvin was the next batter and I made a horseshit decision and I drilled him on purpose. It was stupid and to this day I regret that I did it, but I did, I drilled Monte Irvin. Monte had nothing to do with it. It was just bush. Anyway, I did it.

"So I came into the dugout at the end of the inning and Don Newcombe came up and said, 'What the hell you throwing at Monte for? He didn't hurt you.'

"And I said, 'Go screw yourself.'

"Jackie jumped up and said, talking to Newcombe, 'Hey, get off his ass. If you had half the balls he does, we wouldn't be in second place.'

"Jackie and I got to be very, very tight. We respected each other. He was a great guy and what a ballplayer. What a ballplayer. He was a helluva ballplayer. And Jackie Robinson was a class guy. He was a guinea pig and he took a lot of shit that a common, ordinary white guy would never ever have taken. But after he got established and was a star and everything then he dished it out, too."

I had the utmost admiration for Jackie as a player and as a person and consider it a privilege to have competed against him in the many battles the Phillies had with the Dodgers in those days. But sometimes good hard competition is misinterpreted by the media. One time years later, Howard Cosell and I attended a banquet, and Howard said to the head table, "Well, here is Robin Roberts, the man who disliked Jackie Robinson so much." Obviously Cosell had decided in his own mind that because I had competed so hard against the Dodgers I was somehow prejudiced or negative about Jackie Robinson. I had played and pitched hard against the Dodgers but no one had more respect for Jackie than I.

Although future Whiz Kids were beginning to speckle the Phillies' lineup, the 1947 team was still largely a veteran outfit. Old hand Emil Verban was the class of the league at second, hitting .285, leading all second baseman in putouts and assists, and making the All-Star team for the second consecutive year. Thirty-eight-year-old Dutch Leonard, acquired from the Senators, led the pitching staff with a 17–12 record and a 2.68 ERA. Thirty-seven-year-old Rowe was 14–10, and the staff ERA of 3.96 was fourth in the league, the team's best showing in many, many years.

The major bright spot for the Phils in '47, however, was Harry "the Hat" Walker. Sportswriter Stan Baumgartner nicknamed Harry "the Hat" because of his routine of tugging on and adjusting his cap between every pitch. In the minor leagues teammates called him "Cappy" because of the same nervous habit. Harry would step out of the box after every pitch and adjust his cap 10 or 12 times. Not only was this distracting to the pitcher, it was so hard on his caps that the Phillies had to order dozens for him.

The son of former major league pitcher Ewart "Dixie" Walker and younger brother of Brooklyn outfielder Fred "Dixie" Walker, Harry had hit .412 in the 1946 World Series for the Cardinals. He not only led both teams in the Series with six RBIs, he drove in Enos Slaughter from first with the winning run in the eighth inning of the seventh game, when Red Sox shortstop Johnny Pesky supposedly held the ball.

Although playing in all seven games of the '46 Series, Walker had batted only .237 for the Cardinals during the regular season and had trouble securing regular playing time behind the Cardinal outfield of Slaughter, Stan Musial, and Terry Moore. After Harry got off to a slow start with the Cardinals in 1947, the Phillies grabbed him on May 3 along with pitcher Fred Schmidt for outfielder Ron Northey and a sizable Carpenter check.

> **WALKER:** "I was playing pinochle with Red Schoendienst and Stan Musial before a game early in 1947 and somebody told me manager Eddie Dyer wanted to talk to me. When he told me I had been traded I was kind of shocked. I had been raised in the Cards chain and played in three World Series with them. They were almost like my family.
>
> "But Dixie talked to me. He had been traded around and told me that the trade was a big break for me. I was playing behind Terry Moore, Slaughter, and Musial and I was boxed in like a horse who has a chance to win the race but can't get out of the gate. Now I had a chance."

Ben Chapman immediately inserted Walker into the Phillies lineup, leading off and playing center field. Harry immediately got hot.

> **WALKER:** "When I got to Philadelphia, I had to borrow somebody else's glove and bat. My equipment had been shipped to Boston. I got hold of a Johnny Mize bat somehow. It was a big-handled bat, an old Rogers Hornsby model 36 inches long and weighing 36 ounces. I choked up three or four inches on it and hit with the barrel. Because the bat was so big, I quit

trying to jerk the ball to right. Shibe Park was a big park, and with the big monster wall out in right, I couldn't do anything going that way, so I learned to spray the ball and use my speed."

Walker stayed hot and won the National League batting title with a .363 average, a whopping 46 points ahead of second-place Bob Elliott of the Boston Braves, and 20 points ahead of American League batting champion Ted Williams. In addition, he led the league with 16 triples. Along the way he was named the starting center fielder for the National League All-Stars, together with Verban giving the cellar-dwelling Phillies two All-Star starters.

WALKER: "At the All-Star break I was leading the league at about .335. Dixie said, 'Harry, I believe you're going to lead the league.'

"I said, 'Aw, that belongs to somebody else, Musial and Williams.'

"He said, 'Well, I did it, I hit .357 to lead the league [in 1944 for the Brooklyn Dodgers] and there's no reason why you can't do it.'

"So we set up a schedule and I played by the week and not the season. If I went to bat 30 times I had to get 10 hits or better. If I didn't get 10 hits I'd push that week aside and start fresh. Starting fresh each week worked and I never went into a big slump. I went from .330 something to .363, so I hit pretty close to .400 the last half of that season."

Although Walker and Leonard gave the faithful something to cheer about, Del Ennis experienced some of the sophomore jinx, hitting just 12 homers and dropping down to .275 from his stellar rookie year. He did increase his RBI total by 8 to 81. Andy Seminick continued to do the bulk of the catching and led the team with 13 round-trippers. Blix Donnelly had a solid year as a reliever and spot starter, finishing 4–6 with a 2.98 ERA. Granny Hamner and Putsy Caballero each got yet another cup of coffee at the end of the year after productive seasons with Eddie Sawyer at Utica.

In May the Phillies acquired veteran left-hander Ken Heintzelman from the Pirates to shore up their pitching. Heintzelman, from St. Peters, Missouri, had been in organized baseball since 1935. He had pitched for mediocre Pirate clubs for several years and was known as a hard luck guy. His best year with the Pirates had been 11–11 in 1941 and he had battled injury and illness, in addition to losing three full seasons to World War II.

HEINTZELMAN: "I was kind of enthused about joining the Phillies. Pittsburgh was rebuilding and I probably wasn't in their plans. It certainly worked out to my advantage."

Ken was to become a solid member of the Phillies pitching staff until he retired after the 1952 season. In 1947 he won 7 and lost 10 while hurling 8 complete games.

While the Phillies' on-field performance in 1947 was disappointing, Carpenter and general manager Herb Pennock were continuing to build for the future with aggressive search and sign tactics for top young talent. The team on the field was meant to be competitive and hold the fort until the expanding farm system produced a pennant contender.

A broad hint of what was to come took place on the final day of the season. Curt Simmons, an 18-year-old, $65,000 bonus baby, hurled a complete game 3–1 victory over the fourth-place Giants in the Polo Grounds, striking out nine and giving up only five hits. The Giants, led by Johnny Mize, set a major league record that year with 221 home runs.

SIMMONS: "Mize and Kiner were tied with 51 home runs and Mize led off to get another at bat. He got a broken bat single to left field off me at some point but he didn't get a home run. He was one for five. I had them shut out until the ninth when they got a run.

"I was keyed up and a little nervous I'm sure, but I always had confidence in getting guys out because I had a good arm and I could throw. I never had trouble with guys really ripping me. I didn't want to walk too many and wanted to try to stay ahead of the hitters. I was more concerned about my control and just keeping my composure.

"Dick Koecher, another left-hander, had pitched the first game of the doubleheader and got beat and I pitched the second game. It was in the fall and it was cool. The shadows were coming in because it was the second game, so it was a nice set up for a hard-throwing left-hander who was a little wild."

Curt's victory assured the Phillies of a seventh-place tie with Pittsburgh, so at least they would have company in the cellar.

The signing of Simmons earlier that summer, perhaps more than any other event, signaled to the baseball world that the Carpenter-led Phillies should be taken seriously. A true high school phenom from the small

Pennsylvania Dutch community of Egypt, Curt began attracting major league scouts to the Lehigh Valley before his 16th birthday.

He pitched Whitehall High to three consecutive Lehigh Valley championships and during the summers pitched the Coplay American Legion team to two Pennsylvania state championships. In his senior year in high school he struck out 102 batters in 48 innings, allowing only 12 hits. Against Quakertown in the Lehigh Valley championship game, Curt whiffed 20 of the 21 hitters he faced. He also pitched for the Egypt town team in the Cement League (so-called because of the numerous cement plants dotting the countryside) and averaged about 15 strikeouts a game at each level, with a high of 23.

In 1945 Curt starred in a high school all-star game played in Shibe Park, striking out seven of the nine batters he faced in three innings of work. That led to the starting pitching assignment later that summer in an East-West American Legion All-Star game in the Polo Grounds. Babe Ruth managed Curt's East team against Ty Cobb for the West. After throwing four creditable innings, Curt shifted to the outfield, a position he played in high school when not pitching. He singled in a run and then, in the ninth, lashed a triple to drive in the run that gave his team a 5–4 win. For his efforts Curt was named the game's MVP.

> **SIMMONS:** "That first trip to New York was a real awakening for a small-town kid from Pennsylvania. I had never even ridden on an elevator before. All week we would practice in the morning and then they would take us sightseeing in the afternoon. We took a boat around Manhattan and went to the Empire State Building, where they showed us where that plane had crashed into the building.
>
> "Cobb was real serious about the game, very intense, but Babe was real loose, laughing and joking and giving Cobb a bad time, especially when we went ahead. He had a big wad of tobacco and called everybody 'kid.' I don't think he knew any of our names."

After the game, the Babe counseled Curt to switch to the outfield, commenting, "Anybody who can hit a low, inside pitch the way you did has no business wasting his time trying to be a pitcher." Of course, Ruth had started his career as an outstanding left-handed pitcher for the Boston Red Sox before switching to the outfield and making history. But luckily for the Phillies, Curt did not heed Ruth's advice.

By Curt's senior year, 15 of the 16 major league teams were reportedly vying for his services. Cy Morgan, a Phillies scout from nearby Allentown, had followed Simmons for several years and had become friends with Curt's parents. Cy helped arrange for the Phillies' exhibition game in Egypt, hoping it would give them an edge in the bidding war for Curt.

> **SIMMONS:** "The exhibition game in Egypt certainly helped the situation. My father was involved with booking the game. He was a cement mill worker and everybody was coaching him, telling him how to work this deal and all that. It was a real gamble on my father's part because there was a good chance I would get ripped or be real wild, but I pitched real well. I think I struck out 11 or 12. We had them beat 4–2 when our center fielder and right fielder ran together and it ended up 4–4. Then they called it because of darkness.

> "I'm sure the Phillie ballplayers weren't that happy about being in Egypt. You can imagine a big league team having to come to a small town and play a twilight game against some wild, skinny kid left hander. But that game increased my stock considerably, because at least the Phillies knew that I had legitimate stuff."

The bidding war for Curt ultimately came down to the Phillies, the Boston Red Sox, and the Detroit Tigers. Baseball's existing bonus rule, which required players receiving large bonuses to remain on their team's big league roster for two years, undoubtedly frightened other clubs from bidding too high.

> **SIMMONS:** "My parents and I told Cy Morgan that we would give him the last shot. We got an offer from the Red Sox for around $60,000, so we called Cy and told him we would sign for $65,000. He got authority from Herb Pennock and Carpenter and we signed."

Curt had just turned 18. The Phillies sent him to the Wilmington Blue Rocks of the Class B Interstate League, since under the bonus rule he could pitch in the minors his first year. He made his professional debut in Wilmington on June 21, 1947, and beat Lancaster 7–1, striking out 11, walking 4, and scattering 7 hits. In 18 starts for the Blue Rocks, Simmons won 13 and lost 5, with 197 strikeouts in only 147 innings of work. Although generally effective, Curt was plagued with bouts of wildness, once walking 13 in a game against Hagerstown.

After pitching in the league playoffs, Curt was promoted to the Phillies for his start against the Giants on the final day of the season.

I first saw Curt pitch the following spring, the first spring training for both of us. I reported about a week late because I was finishing up my degree at Michigan State. On the day I arrived it was too late for me to join the team workout so I just sat in the stands and watched. I was really curious to see Curt Simmons throw because he had signed for $65,000 and I had signed for $25,000. A tall left-hander was warming up. He had a good delivery and threw pretty well but was not all that impressive. I thought, "That must be Curt Simmons." And then another lefty started throwing. He threw about five pitches and then I knew which one was Curt Simmons.[1] Curt threw the ball harder and with more movement than anybody I have ever seen. It was easy to see why he got the bonus money he did.

Curt remained with the Phillies in 1948 and 1949 because of the bonus rule, but he had his troubles as wildness continued to plague him. It would all come together for Curt in 1950, though. Despite having his season disrupted twice and missing the World Series because of military call-ups, Curt would post 17 wins against only 8 losses and establish himself as one of the mainstays of the Whiz Kids.

Curt would go on to have a distinguished 20-year big league career, posting 193 wins. In 1964, at the age of 35, he would play a major role for the pennant-winning Cardinals, recording an impressive 18–9 mark and finally pitching in a World Series as the Cardinals defeated the Yankees in seven games.

Willie "Puddinhead" Jones, another vital cog for the 1950 pennant winners, made his first appearance with the club late in the 1947 season. Puddinhead (his nickname came from his North Carolina boyhood) was signed by Phillies head scout Johnny Nee in 1946 while playing for the semi-pro Palmetto League in South Carolina. He had played high school and American Legion baseball in Laurel Hill, North Carolina, before entering the Navy upon graduation in 1943. He eventually was able to play some ball in the service, where he reportedly hit .700 for one of his teams.

Upon his discharge in 1946 Willie hooked up with the semi-pro Bennettsville (South Carolina) Red Sox, where his .500 batting average and slick glove soon attracted scouts from the Dodgers, Giants, Yankees, Ath-

---

1. The first lefty was Dick Koecher, who had a solid career in the minor leagues but never did stick in the majors.

letics, Tigers, and Browns in addition to the Phillies. Willie was so impressive with the glove that Pie Traynor, until that time the finest third baseman ever, announced, "He's better than I was."

The Phillies signed Jones for a $16,500 bonus, quite sizable for the time, but Willie must have enjoyed his newfound affluence a little too much that winter. When he reported for spring training in 1947, he was horribly out of shape and about 25 pounds overweight. Chapman remarked, "He must have trained on corn pone and beans." And while Willie was generally a very easygoing, affable, and likeable person, sometimes his sense of humor got him into trouble.

> **SEMINICK:** "Puddinhead came into his first spring training with a beat-up glove and an old pair of spikes. Ben Chapman gave him a brand new pair of featherweight Spalding shoes, which then were the best baseball shoes available. After the workout, Willie was sitting in the clubhouse all sweaty and Chapman came in and asked Puddinhead, 'How do you like those shoes?'
>
> "Puddinhead looked up at him and said, 'How do you like 'em?'
>
> "Chapman said, 'Well, they're a good shoe.'
>
> "Willie said in his South Carolina drawl, 'Well jam them up your ass, nothing good will hurt you.' That was what Puddinhead, a rookie, said to the manager. The next day he was gone to Terre Haute, Indiana, in the Three-I League."

On another occasion, Puddinhead's directness produced a different result. In 1946 Willie accompanied a scout to a hotel in Bennettsville, South Carolina, where he was playing semi-pro ball. Willie took one look at the pretty young front desk clerk, Carolyn Goodson, daughter of the proprietors, and informed her, "Girl, I'm going to marry you." He was unaware that Carolyn was already engaged, but that did not stop him. They were married four months later.

Willie played himself into shape in Terre Haute and hit .307 with 107 RBIs in only 123 games before the Phillies recalled him late in 1947. He struggled with the big club, hitting .226 with only one extra-base hit in 62 at bats. But the talent was there and the Phillies regarded Jones, along with Hamner, as their infield of the future. By 1949 Jones had won a starting job and was on his way to becoming one of the premier fielding third basemen in the league.

EDDIE SAWYER: "Puddinhead had been a shortstop at Terre Haute, but not a very good one. With Hamner coming along we moved him to third base and he played there for me in Toronto in 1948 before I got the Phillies job. He became just an outstanding third baseman. When we played Brooklyn in those years the top attraction, outside of seeing Roberts and Newcombe pitch against each other, was watching Jones and [Billy] Cox play third base. Those two guys could really play third. They made all the tough plays with no errors. It's funny, but I can't remember Puddin' ever making an error."

BUBBA CHURCH: "I thought that there were two third basemen in the league, Puddinhead and Billy Cox. And I'd take Pud' every day. I don't think anybody walking could come in on a slow hit ground ball down the third base line and throw the guy out like he could."

Brooks Robinson was the best third baseman I ever saw, but Puddinhead was very close to Brooks. Pud' was exceptional.

SEMINICK: "Puddinhead played the shallowest third base of anyone in the National League. He had excellent hands and, though he didn't have the great arm, he got the ball to first base very quickly and accurately. He was a pretty good breaking ball hitter and a good clutch hitter. He could move runners around and hit the ball to right field. He walked like his feet hurt all the time, like he was walking on eggs."

STAN LOPATA: "The only problem with Willie was his feet. Unbelievable. He had the worst feet I've ever seen. Between games of a doubleheader in the summer when it was hot and humid he would get Unk Russell, our clubhouse guy, to get him a bucket of ice water. He would soak his feet in the bucket, socks and all. Boy, his feet killed him. But once he got on that ballfield, he was fine. He was a tough man with that glove."

When asked if his feet bothered him, Willie once replied, "They only hurt when they touch the ground." Although hampered by those chronically painful feet, Puddinhead held down the hot corner for the Phillies for over a decade, until the club swapped him to Cleveland during the 1959 season. During that time, Willie led the league's third sackers in fielding five times (four consecutively) and led in putouts seven times. A dangerous hitter with long ball power, he would slug 25 home runs, drive in 88 runs, and score 100 while playing every game for the 1950 pennant winners. After a stint with Cincinnati in 1961, he finished his 15-year big league career with 190 homers, a .258 batting average, and a slew of fielding records.

> **RICHIE ASHBURN:** "Willie was a heck of a ballplayer. He was unlike any guy I've ever seen. Had a lot of talent. Great guy, southern boy, could charm a bulldog off a meat wagon. He really could. I don't think he was the most reliable person who ever lived. Somebody could write a book about Puddinhead."

Even with the disappointing finish in 1947, the Phillies believed that the Carpenter-Pennock plan was about to pay dividends. Sadly, however, tragedy struck the organization after the season when Pennock died suddenly of a cerebral hemorrhage on January 30, 1948, while attending baseball's winter meetings in New York. He was just shy of his 54th birthday. Bob Carpenter called it "the saddest day of my life."

> **SAWYER:** "We were together the night before Herb died, Bob Carpenter, Shag Shaunessey, the president of the International League where I was going to manage Toronto, Herb, and me. We all went to Al Schacht's for dinner. The next morning was a big meeting at the Waldorf-Astoria. Bob and Herb were rooming together at our hotel and they met me in the lobby. They wanted me to go to the Waldorf with them but I had a meeting with Pete Campbell, president of the Toronto club, so I couldn't go and that is when Herb died. He died going through the revolving doors at the Waldorf-Astoria, just about 15 minutes after I talked to him."

Although Pennock did not live to see the fruits of his labors, he surely was one of the principal architects of the 1950 Whiz Kids. Under his leadership, the Phillies developed strong scouting and farm systems and spent about $1.25 million aggressively bidding for and signing the country's top young talent.

> **McDONNELL:** "Herb Pennock's death really hurt our ballclub. He was the guy who brought the scouts in from all over and signed all our great young players. He also brought in good minor league managers like Eddie Sawyer to develop the kids. And Bob Carpenter never interfered with Herb. They had a beautiful relationship. If Herb had lived I think we would have won three or four pennants in the 1950s. His death left a large void."

Between 1944 and early 1948 the Phillies had signed, under Pennock's guidance, Richie Ashburn, Curt Simmons, Granny Hamner, Willie Jones, Bubba Church, Stan Lopata, me, and several others to bonuses. In addition, he had in place solid baseball organization men, including head scout Johnny Nee, farm system boss Joe Reardon, and, waiting in the minor league wings, future manager Eddie Sawyer.

Chapter 5
CY AND ME

My first spring training was 1948 with the Phillies in Clearwater, Florida. I never met Herb Pennock, although I did correspond with him after I signed with the Phillies. I was trying to finish my degree at Michigan State and needed permission to report to spring training a week late. Michigan State was on the quarter system and the winter quarter ended about two weeks after spring training began. Herb Pennock wrote me in January giving me permission to report late. Unfortunately, by the time I actually received the letter Herb had died.

When I did report I immediately began having trouble with my legs. I experienced slight muscle pulls and twinges just running in the outfield and, as a result, I could not run full speed. While finishing school in the snow in Michigan, I had not worked out much, other than playing a little basketball. Once in Florida my legs had trouble adjusting to the soft, sandy turf.

One day, while I was still struggling with muscle pulls, I happened to be walking behind owner Bob Carpenter, unbeknownst to him. I overheard him say, "Looks like I blew another $25,000." Of course, that was the amount of my bonus and I knew that he was talking about me. I had not yet pitched and Bob's comment was upsetting, particularly since I thought I was there to pitch, not to run.

I was so new to the club that I did not have anyone with whom to share my troubles. Later I was sitting by my locker feeling sorry for myself and Cy Perkins, one of the Phillies coaches, came over and said, "They're on your ass, aren't they kid?"

I said, "Yes sir, they're all over me."

And Cy said, "Wait till you pitch, they won't be on your ass anymore." With that, he walked away.

Now I am not sure why Cy had such confidence in me. He had only seen me throw once before, when I worked out for the Phillies in Wrigley Field in Chicago the previous September. Although I did not know who he was then, I heard him say after I threw for a while, "Don't let that kid get out of the park." I know Cy did not say that for my benefit, but it was the first time that I really thought about being a major league pitcher.

Cy Perkins, whom we often called Duke, was a tremendous baseball man and a wise, warm, and compassionate person. Beginning in 1915, he had caught for Connie Mack's Philadelphia Athletics for 15 years before finishing his playing career for the Yankees in 1931. He then began his coaching career for the Yankees before moving on to coach for the Tigers in 1934 under Mickey Cochrane. He loved to talk baseball and had a knack for telling stories about the baseball legends he had played with. He told any number of stories about Babe Ruth, including Babe's theory of hitting. According to Cy, a bunch of the Yankees were discussing how to hit one day when Babe said, "It's not very complicated. Try to hit that white thing before it crosses home plate."

Cy told us that Babe's home runs were very high and just seemed to keep going until they left the ball park. If Babe hit a homer and sat next to Cy when he came back to the bench, Cy would say, "Nice hitting, Babe." Babe would reply, "Cy, can the Baby hit them?" Even late in his career the Babe was like a little kid who just loved to be complimented.

Cy also had a great respect for Ty Cobb as a ballplayer. When he was a young catcher, Cy had blocked the plate on Cobb without having the ball. The next day, Cobb came up to Cy before the game and told him, "Young man, you give me six inches of the plate or I'll rip your leg off."

Cy had a tremendous influence on me and regularly let me know that he never doubted my ability. He was always supportive and knew just when to say the right thing.

For example, while I was warming up for a game in spring training in 1950, Cy said, "Kid, I want to tell you something." He always called me "Kid." "I've been in baseball for 35 years and the five best pitchers I've ever seen are Walter Johnson, Lefty Grove, Herb Pennock, Grover Cleveland Alexander, and you." I just thanked him and chuckled to myself. My lifetime record at that time, after all of a year and a half in the major leagues, was 22 wins and 24 defeats. He went on, "I'm not kidding. You throw harder easier than anyone. You've got the best delivery I have ever seen. You are our next 300-game winner."

Cy never tried to tell me how to pitch. He would simply say, "Do it your way, kid." Cy appreciated my talent and wanted me to be in the frame of mind to get the most of it. He knew that I was a good pitcher because of a physical gift. If I got knocked out early in a game he would say, "Don't worry about it. Those guys on the other team are getting paid, too. Some days they are going to get their hits." Or he would tell me, "Remember, it's a long career."

One time I got knocked out of a game in the first inning. We left town after the game and I was in a compartment on the train feeling really down. Cy knocked on the door, came in, and asked, "How are you doing?"

I said, "Cy, how can I be doing?"

Cy sat down and started to reminisce off-handedly about his years with the Athletics. He talked about a big game Lefty Grove pitched against the Yankees. Warming up, Grove was throwing as hard as he ever had. The A's failed to score in the top of the first and Lefty took the mound. The Yankees proceeded to rip him for seven runs in the bottom half of the inning, finally forcing Mr. Mack to take him out of the game. Cy told me they were all astonished because no one, not even the Yankees, were supposed to hit Lefty Grove like that.

With that Cy left. And I began to feel less sorry for myself. I thought, "Lefty Grove got knocked out in the first inning so what the hell am I worrying about." Of course, that is exactly the message Cy intended me to have. He wanted me to think about it on my own and put my debacle into perspective.

When I won I never saw or heard from Cy. He thought that I had the ability to win, that I should win. But if I lost he was always there. He knew that I took losing very hard, that I had trouble sleeping and would walk the streets at night after losing. So Cy would often be there after a loss to make sure I kept things in perspective and did not become too morose.

In the spring of 1948 I finally pitched in an exhibition game against the Cardinals' "B" team, about a week after Cy had first come over to me in the locker room. In three innings I got nine consecutive outs, struck out four, and hit a triple. Of course, that was the first time I pitched for the Phillies, and afterwards everybody was very excited about my outing and nobody was worried about my legs anymore. I was sitting in the clubhouse after the game feeling very good about my performance when someone tapped my arm. I looked around and Duke just gave me a wink and walked on by.

That spring was the beginning of a wonderful baseball friendship. I believed in Cy totally and I knew that he was completely behind me. We did not socialize off the field and our conversations were almost all between starts and after I lost a ballgame. But his quiet, low-key manner had a remarkable way of keeping me believing in myself and my God-given talent.

I was not really a pitcher as a kid growing up just outside of Springfield, Illinois. I mostly played third base in high school and in the sandlots, along with some outfield and first base, and pitched only when the regular pitchers needed a rest. I also played a lot of basketball and football as a kid and playing sports was about all I thought about.

My dad was a Welsh coal miner who had immigrated to Springfield in 1921 with my mother and oldest brother and sister in search of work in the coal mines in central Illinois. I came along in 1926, the fifth of six children. Although we did not have much when I was growing up, we never thought about it. We were close knit and got along well together.

My first exposure to baseball was at home. We used to take my dad's Bull Durham tobacco sack and fill it full of grass. For some reason Dad had brought a cricket bat with him from Wales and we used it to hit the Bull Durham sack.

I went to a small two-room rural grade school called East Pleasant Hill. When I entered the fifth grade a new teacher, C. B. Lindsay, arrived. He was an energetic, enthusiastic teacher who loved sports and had a great influence on me. In school we played softball and basketball, and at home I followed the Chicago Cubs because we could get their games on the radio. I would put the radio in a window and stand outside and play the game along with the Cubs. When the Cubs were in the field I would put my glove on. When they came to bat I would bat. If Stan Hack was hitting I would get up left-handed; if Billy Herman was hitting I would bat right-handed. I would do that every day.

My mother was a big baseball fan as well and would listen to the games. It was dinnertime at our house when Gabby Hartnett hit his famous "homer in the gloamin'" against Mace Brown of the Pirates to catapult the Cubs into first place in 1938. Mom got so excited that she dropped a dish of potatoes that she was serving us.

In eighth grade we had a sports banquet near the end of the school year. Mr. Lindsay asked former Phillies great Grover Cleveland Alexander, who was staying in Springfield, to speak at our banquet.

"Ol' Pete" was the greatest pitcher in Phillies history and one of the greatest pitchers ever to play the game, with an incredible 373 lifetime wins. He began with the Phillies and pitched for them from 1911 through 1917, winning 20 or more games every season but one (when he won only 19). In 1915 he pitched the Phils to their first pennant with 31 wins. That year he threw an incredible four one-hitters while pitching half of his games in the bandbox Baker Bowl. Alexander followed 1915 with two more 30-win seasons before Phils owner William Baker, strapped for cash, sold him to the Cubs after the 1917 season.

Alexander suffered from epilepsy and had a terrible drinking problem that had kept him down and out for most of his adult life. The owner of the St. Nicholas Hotel in Springfield, John Connor, was allowing Alexander to stay at his hotel, which is why he was available to us. When he got up to speak at our banquet you could have heard a pin drop, the room got so quiet. I will never forget what he told us. He said, "Boys, I hope you enjoy sports. But I will warn you about one thing: Don't take to drink, because look what it has done to me." Then he sat down. That was all he said.

Sitting at that banquet, of course, I had no idea that I would, in about 12 years or so, become the first Phillies 20-game winner since Grover Cleveland Alexander. Or that I would help pitch the Phillies to their first pennant since 1915, the year Alex won 31 games. Or that, in 1976, I would become the second Phillies pitcher elected to baseball's Hall of Fame, following Ol' Pete.

Thanks to Cy Perkins, I heard a lot of stories about Alexander during my early years with the Phillies. Cy would tell me how Alexander stayed ahead of the hitters and what a tough competitor he had been. Cy's phenomenal knack for telling stories made me appreciate Alexander's greatness even more.

Alexander had won 190 games as a Phillie to set the team record and I remember what a thrill it was for me when I won my 191st game in 1958 to set a new team record. After the game I thought back to that eighth-grade banquet at East Pleasant Hill when Alexander had come and spoken to us.

Bob Carpenter invited Alexander to the 1950 World Series to commemorate Alex's role with the 1915 club. Ironically, Mr. Lindsay, my old grammar school teacher, bumped into Alexander on the sidewalk outside of Yankee Stadium after the last game of the series. Mr. Lindsay went up and introduced himself and reminded Alex of their previous acquaintance in Springfield. Sadly, Alexander died about a month later in a motel room in Nebraska.

I had another brush with a future Hall-of-Famer in my youth in Springfield. In 1936 Bob Feller, who was then the teenage phenom of the Cleveland Indians, came to Springfield to throw out the first ball for the final game of the Illinois State Amateur Baseball Championship. I was in the stands and managed to meet him and get his autograph before the game. But, as a typical 10-year-old, I somehow lost the autograph at the game and never got home with my precious piece of paper.

I attended Springfield High for two years with no great athletic success (although I did play first base for the varsity baseball team) before transferring to Lanphier High, also in Springfield, for my last two years of high school. At Lanphier my athletic career blossomed. I played end on the football team, fooled around with the shot put, and started at forward for our basketball team. In fact, basketball was the sport I was best known for in high school. I also played baseball, starting at third base my junior year and pitching and playing third as a senior.

The war was still on when I graduated in 1944, and I had thoughts of becoming a fighter pilot. I qualified for the Air Force Cadet reserve program and was sent to Michigan State University in East Lansing, Michigan. Late that fall I was accepted into the regular Air Corp beginning in March, and I was released from the reserve program. Our army basketball team had scrimmaged the Michigan State varsity, and when Ben Van Alystyne, the Michigan State coach, discovered that I was going to be out of the service for three months, he asked me and Joe Krakora, another cadet and a close friend, if we would play for Michigan State for those three months. January to March was the winter quarter under Michigan State's quarter system and so the timing worked out well.

After basketball season in the spring of 1945, I was ordered to report for basic training at Shepard Air Force Base in Wichita Falls, Texas. But with the end of the war nearing the Air Force's preflight training was suspended. I was then assigned to Chanute Field, Illinois, where I was discharged from the service on November 1, 1945, shortly after the war ended.

I returned to Michigan State in time for the basketball season. We had a solid team and I was named the outstanding college basketball player in Michigan by the *Detroit Free Press* for the 1945–46 season.

That spring I decided to go out for the baseball team. I just showed up for practice one day. The baseball coach, John Kobs, was surprised to see me because, though I was pretty well known as a basketball player, no one at Michigan State knew that I could play baseball.

Coach Kobs asked me, "What position do you play?"

"What do you need?" I replied.

"Pitchers," he said.

"Then that's what I am," I said. "A pitcher."

Now, I had pitched only my senior year in high school and in the sandlots when my team ran out of pitchers. But I had a good arm. I could throw hard and throw strikes. And I figured I might as well go out for what the coach needed, because I wanted to play and not sit on the bench.

As it happened, the team was leaving for its southern trip two days after I first worked out. I did not go on the trip but worked out on my own. Coach Kobs must have seen something because when the team returned he put me into some games rather quickly. I was hit hard in my first start against Western Michigan, but I ended up with a first-year record of 4 wins and 2 losses. My first win was a no-hitter against the Great Lakes Naval Training Station.

Our last game of the season was against the University of Michigan, a game that proved to be a turning point in my career, even though we lost 2–0. Immediately after that game Ray Fisher, a former big league pitcher and UM's baseball coach, invited me to pitch for his Montpelier, Vermont, club in the Northern League, which was a top college summer league. So I called my folks to tell them that I would not be coming home for the summer and went to Vermont.

That first summer, 1946, I had some success and finished with an 11–8 record. I had one memorable outing late that summer against the Keene (N.H.) Yankees. We were battling for the league championship and I was fortunate enough to pitch a no-hitter. I was not fortunate enough to win, however. Late in the game I walked a Keene batter, Joe Andrus. He stole second and scored on two infield outs. I lost 1–0 without giving up a hit. Keene's pitcher that day was future New York Knickerbocker basketball star Carl Braun.

I returned to Michigan State and again played basketball and baseball. I had a solid year on the mound for the Spartans with 6 wins and 4 losses and 86 strikeouts in 91 innings. I even beat the University of Michigan twice before returning to Vermont for another summer with Ray Fisher. That second summer, 1947, we had a fine ballclub and I really came into my own as a pitcher.

One day I was pitching very well in Montpelier, and I had sense enough to ask myself, "What am I doing now? Why am I so good today?" I could feel a good hip action opening up and everything working together and from that moment on I could throw a baseball hard with a very comfortable, easy motion. I just found my motion and knew what I could do with it. From then on I had those proper mechanics that, as Cy Perkins put it, allowed me to throw harder easier than just about anyone.

Pitching for Ray Fisher was a real pleasure and certainly helped my career. Ray had pitched in the big leagues with the old New York Highlanders and later the Cincinnati Reds. In fact, he had pitched for the Reds in the 1919 World Series against the infamous Black Sox, who had thrown the Series. He had actually been shut out 3–0 by Dickie Kerr in the third game of the Series. We asked Ray if it had looked like the White Sox were throwing the Series. Ray, who had a great sense of humor, told us, "Well, there were a lot of funny things going on. But I'll tell you one thing, I pitched against the only guy who was trying."

Ray, like my later manager on the Phillies, Eddie Sawyer, allowed us to play and did not try to make the game too complicated. In the middle of that second summer when I was pitching really well, Ray said to me, "Well, Robin, one thing I can tell you about pitching. Don't pitch anyone high and away because I can hit that pitch." Later on in my career, if I got one high and away and a guy hit the ball nine miles, I would often remember that Ray had told me not to throw it there.

When I went home to Springfield after the college summer league season was over, I pitched a game for a local team, as I had the previous summer. After a couple of pitches, my catcher from high school, Bob Cain, came out to the mound and asked me, "What happened to you? You've never thrown the ball like that before!" He hadn't said anything like that to me the previous year after I pitched in Vermont.

That summer I was 18–3 and we won the pennant. Because of my success, big league scouts began to show some real interest in me. A Phillies scout, Chuck Ward, who had watched me pitch all summer long in Vermont, wanted me to work out for the club.

Chuck later told me that he was most impressed with me on a day when I was struggling a little bit. The other club had a runner on first and he took off to steal second. After delivering the pitch, I turned to watch the play at second. When I did, the catcher hit me right in back of the head with the ball, something I have never seen happen again. The throw knocked me out but I finally came around and stayed in the ballgame. Although I had been in constant trouble before getting clobbered, afterwards I retired about 12 straight and we won the game. Ward said to me, "I wanted to sign you right then. I knew anybody with that hard a head would be a whale of a pitcher."

Other teams were interested as well after my second summer in Vermont, and I received invitations from the Yankees, Red Sox, Tigers, Athletics, and Braves to try out in September. I mapped out a schedule to work out for all of those teams after I returned to Springfield from Vermont. The Phillies happened to be first. I traveled up to Chicago to throw while the Phillies played the Cubs in a three-game series in Wrigley Field.

After I worked out (and overheard Cy Perkins telling the club not to let me out of the ballpark) the Phillies offered me a $10,000 bonus to sign. I knew that the Phillies had signed Curt Simmons for a huge bonus the previous June, but I did not have any real understanding of negotiating for large sums of money. I really did not believe that I was in line for a large bonus. I was just anxious to get into professional baseball and would have signed with a team for $2,000.

But I told the Phillies that I could not sign yet because I had promised other teams that I would work out with them. In addition, I planned to return to Michigan State to play basketball. They brought me back to throw the following day and upped their offer to $15,000. My commitment to the other teams was wavering, but I still held firm. The club brought me back a third day, the last day of their series with the Cubs. After that workout, Babe Alexander, the Phillies' traveling secretary, raised the team's offer to $25,000.

At this juncture, the Phillies really had my attention. As a kid, my parents had often fussed at me for playing so much baseball and not helping my brothers with the chores more. Lou Gehrig was my hero and I had read about him buying his mother a house with his baseball earnings. When I was growing up, I told Mom that I would do that for her someday.

So when Babe Alexander offered me $25,000 to sign I asked him, "That would buy a nice house, wouldn't it?"

"It sure would," he said.

"Okay, then," I said, "Let's go."

So I never did work out with the other clubs, even though I have often wondered how high the bidding might have gone if I had. The major league clubs were paying some large bonuses after the war. But I have never regretted signing with the Phillies.

After I signed, I did buy Mom and Dad a house right away. It cost about $19,000. Then I bought myself a car and a couple of suits and thought I was on top of the world. Unfortunately, I was very unsophisticated, particularly about income tax. When it came time to pay my taxes, I had no money and had to borrow from my father. Sadly, it took most of his life savings. So, although everyone assumed I had more money than I knew what to do with, I ended up in debt to my father. I was not able to pay him back for more than two years. In 1950 I turned over most of my World Series check to settle the score.

I returned to Michigan State for my senior year after signing with the Phillies. I was captain of the basketball team and very much looking forward to playing my last year. Chuck Ward had told me that my signing would not be effective until the following March so that I could compete in basketball. I was certainly naive and did not think there was anything wrong with this arrangement.

When I got back to school I found that my signing with the Phillies was somehow public and was reported in the *Detroit Free Press*. As a result, I was ineligible to play basketball because college eligibility rules then prohibited anyone who had turned professional in one sport from competing in any sport at the collegiate level. Watching the Michigan State basketball team play without me made for a very long winter. I went to the games and cheered on my teammates but had a lump in my throat all season.

I missed getting to play with Bob Brannen, who had transferred to Michigan State from the University of Kentucky after returning from the service. In those days, returning servicemen were allowed to transfer, and Kentucky had another star at center, Alex Groza. As a result, Brannen joined us at Michigan State and went on to a professional career with the Boston Celtics. I was left with trying to work out my frustrations by playing in the city league in Lansing. It was a sad time for me.

Once I got to spring training and got over my early leg miseries, I pitched well. After my first outing against the Cardinal "B" squad, I pitched four shutout innings against the Washington Senators and got the win. I had several more successful appearances, including a game against Cincinnati in Clearwater that I lost in the ninth inning on a home run to Hank Sauer, after relieving Ken Heintzelman in the fourth.

Babe Ruth visited our training camp one day while I was warming up. The Babe was talking to sportswriter Stan Baumgartner and it occurred to me that my mother would really appreciate an autographed ball from

The 1950 Phillies. The Whiz Kids had some adults among them.

I celebrate with Eddie Sawyer *(center)* and Dick Sisler *(right)* after we won the pennant in Brooklyn on October 1, 1950. (*Courtesy of Ted Silary*)

Left to right: Sam Nahem (who resurfaced with the Phillies in my first year in 1948), Walter "Boom Boom" Beck, and Johnny Podgajny in spring training, 1942, comparing spectacles.

The 1943 Philadelphia Phillies, who survived a tumultuous season to finish in seventh place with a 64–90 record. Bottom row *(left to right):* Glen Stewart, Jim Wasdell, Chuck Klein, Freddie Fitzsimmons (manager), Buster Adams, Benny Culp, Roger McKee. Second row: Reds Miller (trainer), Newt Kimball, Dick "Kupie" Barrett, Johnny Podgajny, Lynwood "Schoolboy" Rowe, Bill Lee, Jack "Tex" Kraus, Ron Northey. Third row: Dale Matthewson, Coaker Triplett, Ray Hamrick, Merrill "Pinky" May, Andy Seminick, Al Gerheauser.

Andy Seminick in 1943.
Andy was never that young.
(Courtesy of Andy Seminick)

Granny Hamner *(left)* and Putsy Caballero in 1944, ages 17 and 16, respectively.
(Courtesy of the Philadelphia Phillies)

Herb Pennock *(left)* and Ben Chapman. They were the brass.

Andy Seminick, Blix Donnelly, Ben Chapman, and Frank McCormick read about the unexpected success of the 1946 Phillies. Andy once really did have hair on top. *(Courtesy of Andy Seminick)*

Wonder why these 1946 Phillies were so happy? They are *(left to right)* Roy Hughes, Tommy Hughes, Del Ennis (behind Tommy Hughes), Benny Culp, Emil Verban, Vance Dinges, and Andy Karl. *(Courtesy of Andy Seminick)*

Jackie Robinson and Ben Chapman pose for photographers on May 9, 1947, after Chapman was censured for his racial baiting of Jackie. We'll take him on our side, Ben. *(Courtesy of Temple University Archives)*

Jackie Robinson sliding back into first against the Phillies in 1949, while Dick Sisler waits for the ball. Jackie did make an out occasionally.
(Courtesy of Temple University Archives)

Harry "The Hat" Walker. The Hat could hit.

Ken Heintzelman. Goober was a delight.

Curt Simmons shortly after signing with the Phillies. Lefty threw BBs. *(Courtesy of Curt Simmons)*

Left to right: Lou Possehl, Homer Spragins, and Dick Koecher, whom I first thought was Curt Simmons. *(Courtesy of Rich Westcott)*

(Top Left) Here I am pitching at Michigan State. I really wanted to play third base, but they needed pitchers. *(Courtesy of Michigan State University Sports Information Office)* **(Top Right)** Cy and me — a mutual admiration society. **(Above)** Babe Ruth *(left)* and Curt Simmons when Babe visited spring training in 1948. Babe Ruth died that August. *(Courtesy of Curt Simmons)*

Left to right: Walt Dubiel, Eddie Oswald, me, Charlie Bicknell, and Richie Ashburn in spring training, 1948, at Clearwater, Florida. Good kids having some fun.
(Courtesy of Charlie Bicknell)

Eddie Sawyer *(center)* with his two catchers at Utica in 1945, Joe Antolick and Richie Ashburn. I guess Joe was a better catcher than Richie. *(Courtesy of Eddie Sawyer)*

Johnny Blatnick, my first roomie in the big leagues. *(Courtesy of Johnny Blatnick)*

Dick Sisler when he signed his first professional contract with the Cardinals. The young Big Cat is flanked by his proud father, Hall-of-Famer George Sisler *(left)* and Cardinals president Branch Rickey *(right)*. *(Courtesy of Dot Sisler)*

Ruth, since she was such a baseball fan. So I got a brand-new ball out of the ball bag and asked to borrow a pen from Baumgartner. I asked Babe to sign the ball and he said, "Sure, kid," with his raspy voice. Of course, Babe's visit was in March and he died that August of throat cancer.

My mother was thrilled to get that baseball, and we still have it in the family. In all my years in baseball, that is the only time I ever asked anyone to sign a ball for me.

One day that spring, just before we broke camp in Clearwater to play our way north for the season, Ben Chapman came over to me and said, "Hey, kid."

I said, "Yes, sir."

He told me, "You are the best pitcher I've got."

"Well, thank you."

Chapman said, "Kid, they tell me you're too young for me to keep you up here. But I'm taking you to Philly. I don't care what they say."

So I thought I was going to start the season with the Phillies. A few days later I was behind 5–4 before being lifted for a pinch hitter in a game we eventually lost 7–4. After the game, Babe Alexander came up to me in the hotel and said, "Hey Rob, can I buy you a milkshake?"

I said, "Sure, Babe, that would be fine."

So while I'm drinking the milkshake Babe said, "Robin, we're sending you to Sumter, South Carolina, to join the Wilmington Blue Rocks club."

"No, no, no," I said, "The skipper said I was going with him to Philly."

"Well," Babe said, "Bob Carpenter says you are going to Wilmington." And Babe was correct. The owner said I was going to Wilmington, so I went to Wilmington.

The next day, a Wednesday, I packed my bags and headed for the train station to join the Wilmington Blue Rocks in Sumter. While I was waiting for my train, none other than Dick Sisler got off the same train. The Phillies had just traded for him from the Cardinals and he was reporting to his new team. It was the first time that I had met Dick, and little did I know then that we would both play such important roles on the last day of the 1950 season.

I arrived at the ballpark in Sumter on Thursday and immediately reported to Jack Sanford, the Wilmington manager. Sanford, who coincidentally was Ben Chapman's brother-in-law, asked me, "How are you feeling?"

I said, "Fine."

He said, "How about pitching tomorrow?"

"That would be fine," I said.

So I pitched the next day, Friday, and won a great ballgame, 1–0 in 10 innings. On Saturday I reported to the ballpark and Sanford began screaming at me, "What are you trying to do, get me fired? Carpenter is so mad at me."

I said, "Why? What is wrong?"

He said, "You didn't tell me you pitched six innings on Tuesday."

"But you didn't ask me," I said.

"Oh," he said, "they are so mad at me for pitching you with two days rest."

The Blue Rocks turned out to be a very good team and one that I thoroughly enjoyed playing for. We had two fine catchers, Eddie Oswald and Jack Warner; future Whiz Kid Mike Goliat played first; Charlie Dykes (son of long-time major league player and manager Jimmy Dykes) played second; Rudy Rufer was the shortstop; Red O'Connell was at third; and in the outfield we had Barney Lutz, Jack Lorenz, and Frankie Whalen, a great defensive player.

I pitched opening day and won 19–1 with 17 strikeouts. We continued to win, and I was having so much fun that I never gave a thought to going up to the Phillies. I lived in a private home with my catcher Eddie Oswald, and we were all just having a great time playing ball. Eddie, who had gone to St. John's University, was a superb defensive catcher who was an absolute delight for a young pitcher like me to throw to. He quickly became a good friend. Despite his defensive skills, however, he never made it to the big leagues. Tragically, Eddie's life was cut short by cancer when he was in his early 30s.

I won most of my starts in Wilmington and pitched one memorable 15-inning game against Harrisburg that ended in a 2–2 tie. I struck out a bunch of hitters but also struck out six times myself against opposing pitcher Joe Muir. I was very pleased later when Muir made it to the major leagues with the Pirates in 1951. Although Joe's big league career was brief, I would hate to think that any pitcher who had struck me out six times in one ballgame was not major league material.

Bob Carpenter's parents lived in Wilmington and were big Blue Rock fans. They had seats right behind our dugout and were enthusiastic rooters. After I would leave the diamond with a good performance they would yell down "Nice pitching, Robin." Of course, Curt had pitched for Wilmington in 1947 and I often wondered if the Phillies had sent us to Wilmington so that Mr. and Mrs. Carpenter could keep an eye on us.

By mid-June the team was in first place and I was rocking along with a 9–1 record, averaging 12 strikeouts a game. We were winning, I had a great catcher in Eddie Oswald, and I really fit in with all the guys. I later learned that Chapman even skipped a Phillies game once to watch me play.

> **PUTSY CABALLERO:** "One night in June we didn't have our manager, Ben Chapman. Although we didn't find out until the day after, Chapman and Bob Carpenter had taken a ride down to Wilmington because Roberts was pitching that night."

On June 18 we were in Hagerstown, Maryland, the morning after playing a night game. I was still in bed about 10 in the morning when I got a call in my room from Jack Sanford, the manager. He said, "Robin, what are you doing?"

"Well," I said, "I'm still in bed."

He said, "Come on down to the lobby. I want to see you."

So I quickly got dressed, wondering what I had done wrong, and went down to the lobby. There I found the whole club waiting for me. Sanford said, "Congratulations Robbie, you've just been called up by the Phillies." Then he gave me a pen and pencil set that was inscribed "Robin Roberts, Philadelphia Phillies."

Needless to say, I was really touched by this wonderful farewell, which was totally unexpected. After saying goodbye and thanking everyone I went back to Wilmington to collect my belongings. The next day I took the train to Philadelphia and checked into the Bellevue-Stratford Hotel at about 4:30 that afternoon. After checking in, I reported to Ben Chapman at the ballpark about 6:00. Chapman said, "How are you, Roberts?"

I said, "I'm fine sir."

"Can you pitch tonight?" Chapman asked.

"Yessir," I said.

"Fine," Chapman said, "You'll be pitching."

So I took my duffel bag and walked from Chapman's office into the clubhouse. Unk Russell, the clubhouse man whom I knew from spring training, motioned to me and said, "Wait a minute, Robin." He had me stand sort of out of the way. I could see another player was in the clubhouse cleaning out his locker, obviously the guy whom I was replacing. He finished filling his duffel bag and started to walk out the door. Then he saw me, stopped and walked over to me.

He said, "Are you Roberts?"

I said, "Yessir, I am."

"Well," he said, "I hope the hell you are a better pitcher than I am." Then he walked out the door.

That player was Nick Strincevich. He never returned to the major leagues. His number with the Phillies was 36, so that became my number for my entire career with the team.

About two hours after reporting I was on the mound for the Phillies against the Pittsburgh Pirates. It was only a little more than two years since Coach Kobs at Michigan State had asked me what position I played.

I was so nervous facing the first batter, Pirate shortstop Stan Rojek, that my knees were shaking. I threw him four very wild pitches and promptly put him on first base. I was still nervous going to a 3–2 count on the second hitter, third baseman Frank Gustine. I threw him a high fastball and he chased it for strike three. Fortunately, that strikeout got me over my nervousness.

In fact, I was only nervous one other time in my big league career. In 1955 I had a no-hitter against the New York Giants with one out in the ninth. Pitching to Alvin Dark, I had the same unsettled, nervous feeling that I had experienced pitching to Stan Rojek in 1948. Dark proceeded to get a base hit, ruining my no-hitter.

I think much of the reason nerves never bothered me when I pitched, except for those two occasions, was that I was able to concentrate so well on the mound. I just stood out there in total isolation, focused on throwing the ball as well as I could. Nothing bothered me and I was oblivious to even the batter. When I was throwing well, I would only see the bat when he swung, my concentration was so centered on the catcher. As far as I was concerned the ball was going to the catcher, not the batter.

Of course, sometimes I was wrong. I saw a lot of full swings, mostly on home run pitches. Those were often caused by my not finishing my delivery properly, although sometimes good hitters would just hit good pitches.

When I first came up Leo Durocher, like a lot of managers in those days, and coached third base. He was much like Ben Chapman in that he would really get on the opposing pitchers, calling them bushers or worse to try to distract them. I could hear him when I was in the dugout watching someone else pitch, but when I was pitching I concentrated so hard that I did not ever hear him hollering at me. One day I was beating the

Giants in the Polo Grounds pretty soundly, and as I was coming off the mound toward our third-base dugout, Durocher waited for me. He said, "Kid, I really bother you, don't I?"

I looked at him and just kind of smiled. From then on Leo changed tactics and I was the greatest pitcher who ever lived. He continually tried to butter me up. Leo never gave up. If one tactic failed to work, he would just try another. But bench jockeying was never a problem for me because my concentration was such that I just did not hear it.

The Phillies played a lot of big ballgames in the early 1950s, often against the Dodgers with Don Newcombe and I opposing each other. After one such game I asked my wife Mary, "Was there a big crowd tonight?"

She said, "It was jammed, over 30,000 people in the stands."

Not once, warming up or pitching the game, would I look at the crowd, nor did I ever hear them. That is how intense my concentration was.

As strange as it sounds, I felt that I belonged in the big leagues right away, even during that first ballgame. I just knew that I could throw hard and that I could put the ball where I wanted it. And, of course, I knew I had Cy Perkins in my corner.

Nevertheless, I lost that first game to the Pirates 2–0. Elmer Riddle pitched a five-hit shutout against us and the Pirates, who were in first place, scored a run in the third on two hits and a force out and another run in the seventh on a Wally Westlake home run. I pitched eight innings and gave up five hits before Harry Walker pinch hit for me in the ninth.

I got my first victory in my next start on June 23 against the Reds, beating ex-Phil Tommy Hughes 3–2. In the second inning, Andy Seminick hit a double off the right field wall to send Granny Hamner, who had walked, to third. I then got my first big league RBI by sending a high bounder to second baseman Benny Zientara, who just missed getting Granny at the plate. Ashburn then singled to center to score Andy. In the fourth, Richie manufactured another run by walking, stealing second, and scoring on a single by Walker.

It was a good thing he did because Hank Sauer connected off me in the sixth for a home run to make it 3–1, and another former Phillie, Danny Litwhiler, hit a round-tripper off me in the ninth to close it to 3–2. Ironically, I had struck both out twice before their home runs. I was already giving up the long ball, but happily with no one on base. For the game, I gave up seven hits in going the distance, striking out nine and walking two.

My next start was against the Cubs on June 27 in the second game of a doubleheader. It was a special game for me, not only because it was my first game against my boyhood team, but also because I would pitch against my favorite player from listening to Cub games on the radio as a kid, Bill "Swish" Nicholson. Bill was a slugging outfielder for the Cubs who had led the National League in RBIs and home runs in 1943 and 1944. He was to become my teammate after the 1948 season when the Phils traded Harry Walker for him.

We lost the first game 6–2 before I won the nightcap 7–4 in a game called after eight innings because of the Sunday curfew law then in effect. Del Ennis, who had a baby boy born just two days before, led the way for us with a double, a home run, and four RBIs while I got my first major league hit and second RBI off Cubs pitcher Cliff Chambers.

I struggled on the mound, giving up 10 hits in eight innings while striking out five and issuing two walks. Nick, my old boyhood hero, was two for four against me. Needless to say, I was happy with the win.

I pitched next on the Fourth of July against the Boston Braves, again in the second game of a doubleheader. After Blix Donnelly won the opener 7–2, I again scattered 10 hits to win 5–2 and run my record to 3 wins and 1 loss. I had to pitch out of several jams because I allowed five walks in addition to all those hits. Richie, Harry Walker, and third baseman Bert Haas were the hitting stars while I was helped by several good catches by Ashburn and terrific defense by Andy Seminick.

Unfortunately, I did not fare so well in my next start, July 9 against the Braves in Boston. In my first outing away from Shibe Park, I could not get through the second inning, when the Braves scored five runs on four hits. After Braves pitcher Johnny Sain, a good hitting pitcher, doubled with the bases loaded to clear the bases, Manager Chapman came out to get me.

"Kid," he said, "you don't hang that curve up here." With that he directed me to leave the mound. My successors did not fare any better and we lost the game 13–2.

According to the *Philadelphia Inquirer,* a Boston sportswriter had approached Chapman before the game, remarking how the Braves' recent loss of Eddie Stanky to a broken ankle would hurt their pennant chances. Ben reportedly replied, "What do you mean a chance for the pennant? Whoever said you had a chance for the pennant? By this time next month you'll probably be down in fourth place." At this juncture Boston was in first place by 2¹/₂ games while the Phillies were in sixth place, 6¹/₂ games behind.

The Boston writer immediately relayed Chapman's remarks to Braves' manager Billy Southworth, who called his team together to tell about Ben's opinion of them. According to the *Inquirer,* "It was the spark that the Braves needed to make them forget the loss of Stanky and drive them to their easy triumph."

Whether true or not, the Braves swept the three-game series with us and went on to win the pennant by 6¹/₂ games over the Cardinals, immortalizing the phrase, "Spahn and Sain and pray for rain."

I did not pitch again until July 18, after the All-Star break and after Ben Chapman was fired in St. Louis. Interim manager Dusty Cooke started me in the first game of a doubleheader against the Cubs in Wrigley Field, where I had heard so many games broadcast as a kid and where, about nine months before, I had tried out for the Phillies.

The game turned out to be a heartbreaker. We took a 2–0 lead in the fourth on a double by Blatnick, a single by Ennis that was knocked down in the infield, a sacrifice by Dick Sisler, and a two-run single to left by Hamner. The Cubs tied it in the bottom of the sixth on a single to right by future teammate Eddie Waitkus, an RBI double to left by Phil Cavarretta, and a single by Andy Pafko, driving in Cavarretta.

The game remained tied until the bottom of the ninth. With one out Cubs southpaw pitcher Johnny Schmitz singled. Andy then made a fine play in front of the plate on a ball topped by Hank Schenz to force Schmitz at second. With two out and a runner on first it looked like I was out of trouble. But Waitkus singled to put two runners on and then for some unknown reason I got wild. I plunked Caverretta in the midsection to load the bases and then on the very next pitch hit Pafko in the ribs to force in the winning run.

So my first start in Wrigley Field ended in disaster. As I started walking to the dugout with the game over, Pafko, who was upset because I had hit him, acted like he was going to charge the mound. The Cubs' first-base coach was a tough character called Hard Rock Johnson. He grabbed Pafko by the shirt and said, "You dumb SOB, he wasn't throwing at you, he just lost the game."

Years later Chicago newspaper columnist Mike Royko wrote a column about the dumbest things he had seen in his life. One of the things he mentioned was the time Pafko had started to charge the mound after I had hit him and lost the game.

I always had a hard time accepting defeat, even early in my career. After a loss, it really helped me to walk. I would walk back to the hotel from the ballpark or just walk around the city after the game to unwind, sometimes to the wee hours of the morning. I replayed the game in my head over and over, thinking of what I had done wrong. But if I did not go walking, I had a tough time sleeping after a loss. After a tough loss like my first outing in Chicago, I just needed to unwind.

McDONNELL: "Robbie was a lot of fun in the clubhouse. But when he was pitching, no one went near him. For an hour or an hour and fifteen minutes before the game we left him alone, never went near him. He concentrated so much. He would sit by his locker concentrating and we would just leave him alone.

"After the game if we were on the road and he lost he would say to me, 'Stay.' I would stay and we would have a beer in the clubhouse. Then we would walk back to our hotel, no matter where it was. We never took a cab or the bus back. When we played in Milwaukee in later years, we would walk back seven miles to the hotel. We would stop occasionally to get a beer and he would go over every pitch for the whole game. 'Why did I throw this pitch or why did I do that?' The whole game.

"Then we would get back to the hotel and it might be 3:00 in the morning and we would go to our rooms. Then he would call me sometimes, 'You still awake? Come on over.' It would take him five or six hours to unwind, if he lost. If he won he would join the gang, but not if he lost."

Although I realized that the competition was stiff (as Cy would sometimes remind me), I had confidence in my ability and thought that if I did what I was supposed to, my team should win. So when we lost, I assumed it was because I had not done my job properly and it bothered me.

Once, early in my career, Mary's two sisters and their husbands had come down to Chicago from Wisconsin to see me pitch and go to dinner after the game. We were playing a doubleheader and I pitched and lost the first game, a tough loss in a close ballgame. The second game was close also and Eddie got me up in the bullpen and brought me in to relieve in the ninth inning. The Cubs had runners on second and third and we were clinging to a one-run lead. I intentionally walked Smokey Burgess, the first batter, to load the bases and set up a force at any base.

Phil Cavaretta, the Cubs player-manager, pinch hit and hit my first pitch for a grand slam home run.

So after losing the first game and contributing substantially to our loss in the second game, I was supposed to go to dinner with Mary's sisters and their husbands, none of whom I knew very well at that time. I did manage to make it through the dinner but it certainly was not one of my better meals. I am sure I was not very good company.

> **STEVE RIDZIK:** "Robbie was a hard loser. Oh, he was a tough loser. I lockered next to him and he would come in after a tough loss and sit there. I would kind of peek over at him out of the corner of my eye and he would have tears running out of his eyes, he was so damn mad that he'd got beat. He was so wound tight with the game itself. One day he was pitching at Cincinnati and Bobby Adams hit the first pitch of the game for a home run in the left field seats. Robbie got so mad that he retired the next 27 guys.
>
> "He was a great competitor. We used to laugh that we could go out and have a few drinks the night before Robbie pitched because we knew we weren't going to pitch the day he was pitching. He had 27 or 28 straight complete games at one stretch."

I managed to shake off my rookie-year debacle in Chicago and win my next start in Cincinnati 6–1 with the aid of a fourth-inning triple play. With Ted Kluszewski and Danny Litwhiler on base and no one out, Virgil Stallcup twice tried to sacrifice. With two strikes, he hit a torrid line drive to Putsy Caballero at third. Putsy dove to his left to make a great catch and threw to Granny at second to double off big Ted. Granny then relayed the ball to Dick Sisler at first to get both runners and allow me to escape the inning unscathed.

The win over the Reds was the first of a personal three-game wining streak. In my first start after Eddie Sawyer took over the managerial reins, I beat the Reds again 8–5 in a come-from-behind win. Two errors by 'Bama Rowell at third led to four runs for the Reds in the top of the second, but we came back thanks to two home runs by Seminick and an inside-the-park round-tripper by Ashburn.

My third consecutive victory came on August 7 in Philadelphia, where we beat St. Louis 6–2 to stop a five-game Cardinal win streak. I was shaky for the first five innings, walking six and allowing two runs on five hits.

But Eddie Sawyer stayed with me and I finished strong, retiring the last 12 batters in a row.

That ballgame was particularly memorable for me. In the seventh inning I hit my first major league home run, over the right field wall by the Shibe Park scoreboard, off of Gerry Staley. In fact, it was my first home run since high school. After I touched second base and headed to third, Cardinal shortstop Marty Marion said, "What the hell's going on here?" I took it as a compliment, even though Marty probably did not mean it to be.

At this point in the season, I was feeling pretty good about my performance. I had 6 wins against 3 losses and eight complete games in nine starts. Although I had lost a couple of tough ballgames, I had only been knocked out once. But little did I know that my rookie year was only going to get considerably more difficult.

On August 14, I lost to Sheldon Jones of the Giants 3–1 on a two-run single in the fourth by Giants' rookie left fielder Don Mueller. Then on August 18, in my first start against the Brooklyn Dodgers, I lost a heartbreaker 1–0. Fireballing Rex Barney allowed only one hit, a clean single to center in the fifth by Putsy Caballero. Putsy stole second and Seminick slammed a ball to left that looked good for at least extra bases. But Dodger left fielder Marvin Rackley made a nice catch at the wall to end our only real threat.

I had given up a cheap run in the first when Rackley led off with a single. He moved to second on a Jackie Robinson ground out and I gave him third due to a bad pick-off throw to second. I fanned Snider but threw a wild pitch to Reese, allowing the run to score. Due to Rex's masterful performance, that, unfortunately, was the ballgame.

After a couple of no-decisions in close ballgames, I lost to the Cardinals 4–2 and got rocked by the pennant-bound Braves 13–2. Following two more no-decisions, my final victory of the year came on September 20 against the Pirates. I beat Pittsburgh ace Bob Chesnes 5–2 thanks to a homer by Del Ennis and the first major league home run by Puddinhead Jones, who had just been called up. I had an RBI and two hits myself, one over the third base bag and one over first base. Afterwards Cy said to me, "Boy, that is good hitting kid, when you can hit them down both lines."

Late in the season I was invited to a party in honor of Connie Mack, who, at 86 years of age, was still managing the Philadelphia Athletics. I went to the gathering with Cy, who had been an A's catcher under Mr.

Mack for 15 years beginning back in 1915. It was a thrill for me just to be there, and I went up to the honoree and said, "Mr. Mack, I'm Robin Roberts. I pitch for the Phillies."

He looked me straight in the eye and said, "You don't have to introduce yourself to me, Mr. Roberts. I've seen you pitch." I was greatly flattered and have always wished that I could think of things to say like that.

I ended the season with two starts against the Dodgers. They beat me 5–1 on September 26 as Ralph Branca pitched a five-hitter against us. The Bums knocked me around for five runs and eight hits in five innings, including a home run by Roy Campanella. My last outing, on October 2 in Ebbets Field, was even worse. The Dodgers chased me in the first inning, thanks to three hits and three errors, including a throw at first that I dropped. Although we came back to tie the game before losing 5–4, I had all winter to think about that first inning of my last outing.

I finished my rookie season with 7 wins and 9 losses in 147 innings. I completed 9 of my 20 starts and ended with a 3.19 ERA. It was not a bad beginning, pitching for a sixth-place club, although that last outing against the Dodgers rankled me the entire off-season.

Cy Perkins continued to play an important role in my baseball career, with his wise counseling and words of encouragement, always perfectly timed. In his quiet way, he was a great help to others like Del Ennis and Granny Hamner. We all had tremendous respect and affection for him. And, of course, Cy and I just seemed to have a perfect chemistry, right from that day in Wrigley Field when I was trying out for the Phillies.

In September 1954 Cy came up to me one day and said, "Kid, they're getting rid of me." I thought he was kidding at first, but he was serious. I knew that Bob Carpenter had no appreciation of Cy's importance to the team, so the next day I went to see him.

"Mr. Carpenter," I said, "Cy Perkins tells me that you are letting him go."

"Cy's getting old," he said.

"I don't think you have any idea how important he is to us." I said.

"You're kidding," he said.

I said, "How much does he make, Mr. Carpenter?"

"About $7,500. Why?"

"I'll pay his salary," I said. "That is how much he means to me."

But Bob Carpenter could not understand why Cy was so important to us and got rid of him anyway.

While Cy left at the end of the 1954 season, I pitched for the Phillies through 1961. Mayo Smith became our manager in 1955 and he brought in a new pitching coach, someone who had been a fine big league pitcher. I kept rolling along that year, winning my 20th game on August 18 against the Dodgers by a score of 3–2. Afterwards, the pitching coach, in congratulating me, said something that was very sobering. He said, "Congratulations, Robin. I don't know how you do it." I realized I had gone from a coach who said I should win 300 games to one who didn't know how I did it. In seven years I had won 157 games and the guy who did know how I did it was out of a job. I knew that baseball would never be quite the same for me.

In 1960 we had a weak team and winning was a struggle. I started the season with a 1–7 record. After I warmed up for my next start I went to the dugout to towel off. Just then I heard a familiar voice say, "Hi, Kid. You're throwing fine." Cy had come to the ballpark just to watch me warm up and to see if he could help. I won that day and won 11 and lost 9 the rest of the season. But that was the last time that I ever saw Cy.

The Phillies sold me to the New York Yankees in the fall of 1961. The Yankees released me right before the start of the '62 season and I went home, very unsure of my future. I was 35 years old.

After I got home, the phone rang. It was Cy. I had not spoken to him since the previous year.

"What are they trying to do to you, Kid?" he asked.

"I don't know," I said.

"Don't let them run you out of the game. You'll be pitching shutouts when you're forty," he said.

"Thanks Cy," I said.

"I'm telling you, Kid, don't you dare quit. There's no way you can't keep pitching."

So I signed with the Baltimore Orioles, pitched another five years in the big leagues and won 52 more games, thanks to Cy's phone call.

Cy passed away in 1963, but he influenced me until the end of my career. I was released by the Cubs at the end of 1966 and was recovering from arm surgery. In the spring of 1967 I asked the Phillies to let me pitch for Reading in the Eastern League until June 15, to see if a big league club would pick me up. I won 5, lost 3, and pitched a shutout. When nobody picked me up by June 15, I retired. Driving home that night, I thought about Cy and what he had said to me in 1962. I thought, "Cy, you old son of a gun, you told me I would pitch a shutout when I was forty, but you didn't tell me what league it would be in."

Of course, Cy had also told me early in 1950 that I was the next 300-game winner. And I did win 300 games: 9 at Wilmington, 286 in the majors, and 5 at Reading. But I am afraid even Cy would not let me get away with that one.

Cy Perkins contributed so much to the Whiz Kids team. He was a special coach and friend for me.

Chapter 6
PHENOMS, THE HAT, AND THE BABE RUTH OF CUBA

Although reeling from the sudden death of Herb Pennock, the Phillies went into spring training in 1948 believing that the team would be improved over 1947's disappointing outfit, which finished 32 games behind the pennant-winning Dodgers. Bob Carpenter had decided to fill the role of general manager himself, having worked closely with Pennock the preceding four years.

On February 7, Carpenter began his new role by trading outfielder Johnny Wyrostek to the Cincinnati Reds for veteran shortstop Eddie Miller, hoping to plug an infield gap that had existed for many years. With the addition of Miller, and the All-Star Emil Verban still at second, the Phils were thought to have the finest keystone combination in the league. Del Ennis and batting champion Harry Walker were considered fixtures in the outfield, as was Andy Seminick behind the plate. While other positions such as first base and third base were up for grabs, the Phillies had a core of top-notch major league performers upon which to build.

I was just one of a number of young pitchers in the 1948 training camp, and, at least initially, I expected to spend the year in the minor leagues. As usual, the Phillies pitching was considered a major question mark. Veterans Schoolboy Rowe and Dutch Leonard, along with Blix Donnelly and Ken Heintzelman, formed the core of the pitching staff. Curt Simmons, coming off of his strong performance on the last day of the 1947 season, was thought to be a sure-fire starter.

In addition, we had another bonus baby in camp, 19-year-old Charlie Bicknell from Plainfield, New Jersey. Bob Carpenter had signed Charlie to a sizable bonus the previous year and he had gone on to post a 6–3 record in half a season with Wilmington. Because of baseball's bonus rule, Charlie, like Curt, would have to be kept on the big league roster for two years or the Phillies would risk losing him to another team.

BICKNELL: "That rule really hurt me because I was not ready for the major leagues, that's for sure. I was green as grass."

One of manager Ben Chapman's tasks during spring training was keeping his players in line off the field.

LOU POSSEHL: "We had about 40 guys in camp. One night we came in after midnight and got on the elevator in the hotel in Clearwater. The elevator operator was a black man named Buster. He had a brand new baseball and was asking all the ballplayers who got on the elevator to sign it. The next day in the clubhouse Chapman had the ball and it had about 36 names on it. He started reading all the names and we wondered what he was getting at. He told us these were the guys who had come in after curfew, which was 12:00 a.m. He had given the elevator operator some money to get the ball signed. Chapman said, 'The other four of you guys must have taken the fire escape.'

"That to me was brilliant, the way he trapped us. That was trickery and deceit by brutal Ben. He fined us 25 bucks. I think they took it out of our meal money."

The first sign that the Phillies' preseason plans might go astray came when batting champion Harry Walker held out for more money.

WALKER: "When I held out I got in the doghouse with them because I asked for more money. I was making $10,000 when I went there. They said, 'Don't ask for a raise, you're making more than any of the other guys.' I said, 'I'm not arguing about that, I didn't even bring it up. But if I do the job then I get paid more next year.' So after I led the league they offered me a $2,500 raise. I said, 'Aw, you're kidding.' So I went up with Ben Chapman and spent the whole day with Bob Carpenter.

"They had given $40,000 to a fellow out of high school named Radcliffe who never got out of the minor leagues and had signed Simmons and Roberts, who were unknowns at the time, to big bonuses. These were people who had never played pro ball. So now they are offering me a $2,500 raise when they are spending

$25,000, $40,000, and more on unknown quantities. So I told Carpenter, 'We drew and you can afford to spend money on those guys, then I ought to get paid for what I did.'

"I asked for $30,000. [Ewell] Blackwell made about $30,000 and he had just one good year after coming out of the Army [Blackwell was 22–8 with a 2.47 ERA and a league-leading 193 strikeouts for the fifth-place Reds]. I finally signed a contract for $25,000. Twenty-five hundred of that was a bonus if we drew a million people."

By the time Walker finally signed a couple of weeks of spring training had passed. In that time a fleet-footed young outfielder from Nebraska named Richie Ashburn had arrived on the scene.

ASHBURN: "I went to spring training without a contract, too. Up until 1948, Utica in Class A was the top Phillies farm club. For 1948 the club had signed a Triple A agreement with Toronto of the International League and that was the contract I was supposed to have signed. I didn't sign it because I was holding out. My first year with Utica I made $300 a month. I hit .312 and got a $50 raise; I went from $300 to $350. Now, I hit .362 and I'm going to Triple A Toronto and they wanted to give me $500 a month. I wanted $900 a month, which was quite a bit of money in those days.

"When I got down to spring training, Harry Walker was a holdout, coming off of leading the National League in hitting. Charley Gilbert, another center fielder who had been with the club in 1947, had a severe muscle pull. So they were without a pure center fielder and when the exhibition games started I was in center field.

"I never particularly liked spring training, but I was excited in 1948 because I was playing with a major league club. Robin and I roomed together that first spring and neither one of us had a plug nickel, but we were so happy and thrilled to be there. And I had a tremendous spring. I must have hit close to .400 and I was hitting for extra bases. The old spring training park in Clearwater, Florida, had a short right field fence so I was also hitting quite a few home runs. In one stretch of five or six games I got hits that won games. They couldn't get me out and I was catching everything in sight in the outfield.

"It was the greatest spring training I ever had, but it still didn't look like I would be signed to the major league roster. Of course, I was down there not signed to anybody's roster. Ben Chapman said to me one day, 'I know what you're doing down here, but we do have the National League batting champion in Harry Walker and you'll probably go to the minor leagues.'"

So Walker was still considered the team's center fielder, even though he was off to a late start due to his holdout.

WALKER: "I had noticed with the Cardinals that players who were late reporting stayed out late for extra hitting to try to catch up. The day I reported in 1948 Schoolboy Rowe stayed late to shag for me and Maje McDonnell said he would throw some so that I could get extra batting practice. I hit a few balls when Chapman came out and said, 'Let's get one thing straight: he's a rookie on this team. Everybody has got to make this team and he is like everyone else. If you throw another ball, Maje, you can pack up and go home. If you don't get off the field Rowe, it will cost you $500.' So I was in the doghouse for holding out.

"Ashburn came up and was doing a good job, but I had led the league and really wasn't given much of a shot to get into ballgames."

ASHBURN: "Near the end of spring training the Phillies had a meeting to decide who was going to make the club. In the meantime, Harry Walker had signed finally but he was behind everybody in training so he wasn't playing much. I wasn't privy to what was said at the meeting but I did hear later that Benny Bengough had stated about me, 'If you don't sign this kid and bring him north after what he has done down here, I quit. I don't want anything to do with this organization.' I heard that kind of put me over the top. Of course, the rest is history. I stayed and I think I vindicated Benny Bengough, anyway.

"I took over center field and they moved Harry Walker to left field. And I'll say this about Harry Walker. I had help from a lot of people in this business and he helped me as much as anybody. Harry Walker and I hit a lot alike and pitchers pitched to us about the same. I had never seen any of these pitchers before so Harry would draw me aside and tell me what how this guy was going to pitch to me today. And he was always right. He was a good friend and a lot of help to me."

Johnny Blatnick was another spring training phenom in 1948, and he ended up displacing Harry Walker as the regular left fielder.

BLATNICK: "Harry Walker's wife and my wife were real good friends and I replaced him. You'd think there would be some hard feelings, but he was the nicest guy in the world. I've always respected Harry because he didn't show any hostility towards me or Richie. In fact, he helped us out and encouraged us."

Ashburn actually started the season in left field before shifting to center when Blatnick took over left. Ben Chapman also experimented with Ashburn at third base for a couple of games late in spring training. The day before the season opened, however, Ashburn gave everyone a scare in an exhibition game against Villanova University. Chasing a foul ball, he tripped over a spectator, turned a complete somersault and knocked himself unconscious.

Fortunately, he was not seriously injured and played in the Phillies' opener the next day in Boston. Ashburn was one for five in his debut as the Phillies beat Johnny Sain and the pennant-bound Braves 3–1 behind Dutch Leonard. The next day Richie went three for six as the Phillies rallied to beat the Braves 4–3 in 13 innings, followed by a two-for-five performance as the Phils lost the series finale 10–4.

After three games Richie was hitting a lusty .375. He went on to have a stellar rookie season, batting .333, second only to Stan Musial in the National League. During one stretch he hit in 23 consecutive games, getting 43 hits in 98 trips to the plate during the streak. He was named the starting center fielder for the National League All-Star team and led the league in stolen bases with 32, despite fracturing a finger sliding into second in late August and missing the rest of the year. After the season he was named Rookie of the Year by the *Sporting News*.

Ashburn was the Phillies' center fielder for 12 seasons, until he was traded to the Cubs after the 1959 season. A lifetime .308 hitter, he won batting titles in 1955 and 1958 and finished second twice. He was named to the All-Star team four times and had more hits than any other National Leaguer in the decade of the 1950s. In addition, Richie was one of the finest defensive outfielders of all time, establishing a variety of records for most putouts.

Richie was the quintessential leadoff man, leading the league in walks three times. His great speed and slashing hitting style continually put him among the league leaders in triples. One of the best contact hitters to ever play the game, Richie once fouled off 14 consecutive pitches thrown by the Cincinnati Reds' Corky Valentine.

> **ASHBURN:** "But I think my record was against Sal Maglie when he was still with the Giants. One afternoon I fouled 18 or 19 pitches off of him on a 3 and 2 count. He had excellent control and so did I. After a while he just started laughing. Then he would throw me another pitch and I would foul it off. That was the only time I ever saw Maglie laugh on a baseball field."

Maglie finally just lobbed one to the plate and Richie hit a two-hopper back to the mound. By this time they were both laughing.

> **BLATNICK:** "One night in Philadelphia there was a loudmouthed guy who was on one of our players, but I can't remember who it was. Rich told our man, 'Point him out to me.' Richie went up to bat and hit the guy in the chest about five or six rows up in the stands with a line drive foul ball. That's a true story."

Another time Richie reputedly hit a woman in the stands with a foul ball and then, while they were carrying her out on a stretcher, hit her with another foul ball.

Richie was a tremendous competitor and hustler throughout his career.

> **SEMINICK:** "Ashburn was one of the fiercest competitors on the ballclub. I never saw Ashburn give up on a ground ball he hit right at somebody. He ran hard every step of the way. He always thought he was going to beat it out and often he did. He put pressure on the infielders. One day in 1948 he hit a ball right back to the mound against Thornton Lee of the Giants. They had just gotten Lee from the White Sox and he just casually turned and threw to first and Ashburn was already across the bag. I guess the Giants hadn't told him about Ashburn.
>
> "Richie hated it when he made an out. He would come into the dugout and berate the pitcher, yelling out stuff like, 'You ain't got nothing.' It was kind of comical in a way. He never swore and he drank milk when he first came up and, coming from a small town in Nebraska, he had his own way of saying things."

McDONNELL: "Richie was a battler, a tremendous competitor. When he came to the ballpark, he came to play. He thought nobody could get him out. He would scream and yell at the pitcher if he got him out. 'How can you get me out with that stuff?'

"We would say, 'Hey, Richie, sit down.'"

ASHBURN: "I never went to bat thinking I would make an out. Ever. I don't care who the pitcher was—Koufax, Gibson, or you name him. I did yell at the pitcher a lot when I made an out. It was probably pretty foolish because I don't imagine the pitchers appreciated it much. I don't think pitchers liked me very much and I certainly didn't like them."

PUTSY CABALLERO: "When Richie came up in 1948 the only shortstop in the league who could throw Richie out on a ball hit into the hole was Marty Marion. Nobody else in the league could get him. All the shortstops had to start playing him in a few steps to have a chance to throw him out. We called him the White Flash in the minor leagues. Every play at first was a close play with him running. He never dogged it. He hustled all his life."

Often overlooked is Richie's durability. From June 7, 1950, through the end of the 1954 season he played in 730 consecutive games, the fifth-longest streak in National League history. The streak was broken on opening day of 1955 because Richie had been badly shaken up in a frightening outfield collision with Del Ennis while chasing a fly ball hit by Mickey Mantle in an exhibition game in Wilmington, Delaware, a few days before. But in the 10 seasons from 1949 to 1958 Richie missed only 22 games. The Phillies retired Richie's number 1 in 1979 and he was elected to the Philadelphia Baseball Hall of Fame the same year. His election in 1995 to the National Baseball Hall of Fame in Cooperstown, New York, was certainly much overdue and is most deserved.

Richie and I roomed together our first spring training with the Phillies in 1948 in the Phoenix Hotel in Clearwater. Although we both eventually made it to Cooperstown, that was the farthest thing from our mind that spring.

Ashburn was born and raised in Tilden, Nebraska, a farming community of just over 1,000 people in the northeastern part of the state. As a kid, he and his twin sister Donna were the fastest runners around, winning all the races at the county fairs and fall festivals in the area. His father, a blacksmith and later a machine shop operator by trade, was a semi-pro player on the town team. Richie also had an older brother who played, so Richie began on the local midget team at a very early age.

ASHBURN: "My dad started me as a catcher. He used to pitch to me and my brother would stand up there and swing the bat and intentionally miss it so I would get used to catching the ball with a guy swinging the bat. He also put a bat on my left shoulder, but we never really talked about it. He certainly knew it was two steps closer to first base from the left-hand side of the batter's box."

At the tender age of 13 Richie joined the American Legion team in neighboring Neligh, where he played with kids several years older. For the next few years he played in the spring for the Tilden High team and in the summer for the Neligh American Legion outfit, playing some outfield but mainly catching. His Legion team was one of the finest in the state and generally battled a team from Omaha or Lincoln for the state Legion championship.

By his senior year in high school, Richie was the outstanding prospect in Nebraska, even though he was only 16. Scouts began frequenting his ballgames and he signed with the Cleveland Indians before his graduation.

ASHBURN: "The contract with Cleveland was illegal because I hadn't graduated from high school. My dad and I didn't know much about the rules and what was right and what was wrong. I was called to Chicago by the Commissioner and I made a trip there on the train by myself to see Judge Landis. It was quite imposing to stand in his office and see him. He was very, very nice to me and asked me questions about my signing with the Indians. It was kind of like my grandfather was talking to me.

"What I remember most is that when I left he asked me, 'Son, do you think you're a major league ballplayer?' I said, 'I don't know, I've never seen a major league game.' So he just wished me luck and I went back to Tilden."

Judge Landis voided the contract and fined Cleveland $500 for signing a high school player. Later that summer Richie signed a minor league contract with Nashville in the Chicago Cubs' organization. That contract too was voided, this time by minor league president W. G.

Bramham, because it contained a clause guaranteeing Richie a percentage of the selling price when he advanced to the major leagues. As a result, Richie continued to play Legion ball in 1944 and was selected to play in an American Legion East-West All-Star game in the Polo Grounds in New York City.

> **ASHBURN:** "Going to New York to play in that all-star game is the only thing I've done in my baseball career that I regret. The reason I shouldn't have gone, and it bothers me to this day, is that our team was in the Nebraska state American Legion tournament. We had a good team, but I was the best player on that team and here I go traipsing off to New York City. Nobody ever told me that I shouldn't go. I have always felt that I shouldn't have gone.

> "But when you are 16 years old a trip like that seems like an awfully big deal. But it was still wrong and our team eventually got beat in the state tournament, without me. And I should have been there. If somebody, my dad or my coach, had said to me, 'Maybe you should stay home,' maybe I would have. But I should not have left my team and it has always bothered me that I did."

Richie's West team, managed by Mel Ott, was defeated by the East behind the pitching of future big leaguer Billy Pierce. Richie was disappointed that he did not start the game, but he did catch the late innings.

He returned to Tilden and, although pursued by a number of teams, including the Yankees and Cardinals, enrolled that fall at nearby Norfolk Junior College to study journalism and play basketball. His early exposure to journalism at Norfolk later paid large dividends. After his playing career he wrote a weekly column for the *Philadelphia Bulletin* for 19 years.

> **ASHBURN:** "I went to Norfolk on a basketball scholarship because there, unlike the big schools, you could play a sport even if you were a professional in another sport. And I was a good guard. I could play defense and I could shoot about as well as anybody."

That winter Richie signed with the Phillies.

> **ASHBURN:** "By this time we had gone through two contract signings that were both voided, so we were getting a little suspect of scouts. But Eddie Krajnik, who was the Phillies'

midwestern scout, was such a nice man and such an honest man and he had a lot to do with my signing with the Phillies.

"I didn't know anything about the Phillies except that they always seemed to finish last. I remember my dad saying, 'If you have the talent to be a major leaguer, that's a good place to go because they need ballplayers.' So I signed a contract with the Phillies for a small bonus, I think $3,500. But $3,500 was a lot of money in those days. But it wasn't really the money, it was the chance to start in pro ball."

The following spring, 1945, Richie joined Eddie Sawyer's Utica Blue Sox as a catcher. He had a memorable start in organized ball, batting .312 in 106 games, although his season was interrupted by the military.

ASHBURN: "I left the team late in 1945 when I was drafted. I went from Utica to Nebraska ostensibly to go into the Army. Then the draft board delayed my induction a couple of weeks so I went back to Utica to finish the season, which sticks in my craw a little bit because the Utica Blue Sox still owe me 75 bucks for my train fare. I never did get that. I reminded Bob Carpenter of that for years. And to this day I haven't received it. If you get compounded interest on $75 from 1945. . . ."

Late in the 1945 season Eddie Sawyer shifted Richie from catcher to the outfield, a move that ensured Ashburn of a big league career.

ASHBURN: "Although this might not have had a whole lot to do with Sawyer's moving me to the outfield, when I was catching and backing up the plays at first, I used to beat most of the runners down there even with all that equipment on. I can remember making a play at Utica while catching where there was a ground ball hit that pulled the first baseman off and the pitcher didn't cover. I made the putout at first from the second baseman. I really didn't think a lot about that because I could have done that quite a few times if I had been needed. But I think Eddie Sawyer had already realized that this would be a good move."

SAWYER: "Ashburn's best shot was his speed. He could run. He was always beating the runners down to first base, even with his catching gear on. He had great desire and was a guy who wanted to beat everybody. But if he caught very long his legs would go. And he couldn't throw. His arm was better from the outfield than it ever was catching. He wasn't a bad catcher, receiving the ball, except that he and the pitcher were fighting all the time. He was always yapping, back and forth, because the pitchers didn't throw the pitches where he wanted. And that doesn't help young pitchers any who are trying to develop. His temperament was not right for catching. When I put him in the outfield, he made great catches right away and I don't think he had ever played much there."

CABALLERO: "Richie and I roomed together for two years in Utica, and I can tell you, he didn't have the temperament to be a catcher. Richie would call for a pitch inside and if the pitcher, being young and in the minor leagues, would throw it outside, Richie would jump up and be indignant about it. 'Judas Priest, don't you see me on the inside?' he would yell. Richie never swore. 'Judas Priest' was about the strongest thing he said.

"Of course with his speed it made a lot of sense to switch him and Eddie Sawyer saw that, too."

ASHBURN: "I did always argue with pitchers and do to this day. There are only a couple of pitchers who I ever thought had any brains and one of them was Robin. Even now in the [broadcast] booth I probably overreact to pitchers. I also argued with the umpires a lot when I caught."

SAWYER: "I possibly made a mistake moving Ashburn to the outfield. I could have made an infielder out of him just as well. But we had a good infield and needed outfielders. And the outfield was a place he could exercise his legs."

ASHBURN: "I always kind of wanted to play second base. In fact, Casey Stengel let me play second base a couple of times that last year in New York [with the 1962 Mets]. I mean what did he have to lose, except another game. I think if I had played second base and had the same results offensively, I probably would have made the Hall of Fame sooner.

"But I loved center field. I never really had any trouble making the adjustment to the outfield. I do think after playing the outfield a certain number of games I picked up the ability to get the jump on the ball. I can remember one day it just seemed to kick in where I knew where the ball was going and I would be almost moving before the ball was hit. And I was blessed with tremendous eyesight. I could pick up the rotation on the ball very early, which of course was also a great help to me as a hitter.

"I didn't resist being moved from catcher. I was a kid and my manager told me what he thought. I mean Sawyer didn't ask me what I thought. He just said, 'Hey, you're going to be in the outfield.' I had no problem with it."

Richie's father, Neil Ashburn, had high hopes for his son in baseball and followed his career very closely. When Richie made the major leagues, Mr. Ashburn and his wife Genevieve actually moved to Philadelphia and ran a rooming house for some of the young single players, including yours truly. In 1945 Neil Ashburn made a trip east to Utica to see firsthand how Richie was faring in his first year of professional baseball.

SAWYER: "When Richie's father came to Utica he came into the clubhouse before a game, introduced himself, and said, 'Do you drink?'

"I said, 'Sure.'

"He said, 'I'll meet you at the hotel tonight and we'll have a couple of drinks.' So we played the game and Richie made a couple of plays in the outfield and got three or four hits. After the game I met Richie's father in the hotel bar. After a couple of drinks, he said, 'You know my kid was one of the best catchers in Nebraska.'

"I said, 'Was he? That's great, I'm glad he was. But I'll tell you, he'll never go to the major leagues as a catcher.'

" 'Well,' he said, 'Would that be because of you or because of him?'

"I said, 'Because of him, he can't throw.'

"Neil Ashburn said, 'Well, he didn't have any trouble throwing guys out in Nebraska.'

"I said, 'Wait a minute. There is not a single town in Nebraska in the major leagues. There are a couple in the minor leagues and maybe he'll make those. But we don't go by that.'

"So he said, 'Will he make the major leagues as an outfielder?'

"I said, 'I've only looked at him about a week, but he has got a pretty good chance now.'

"He thought about that a little and pretty soon he said, 'Mr. Sawyer, it has been nice talking with you. If that kid ever gives you any trouble, call me and I'll come east and knock hell out of him.' "

In late September 1945 Ashburn was finally inducted into the Army. He spent most of his 18-month hitch stationed in Alaska, where he played little baseball. Richie was discharged just in time to join Utica for the 1947 season, where he had a banner year. He led the league in hits with 194 and runs scored with 128 in 137 games, batting a robust .362, second only to the .375 of Wilkes-Barre's Joe Tipton.

Another spring training phenom for the Phillies in 1948 was Johnny Blatnick, who the Phillies drafted from the Cleveland organization upon Eddie Sawyer's recommendation. Playing for Wilkes-Barre the previous year, Blatnick had led the Eastern League in RBIs and had finished third to Tipton and Ashburn in batting with a .335 average. Signed illegally by the Indians during his junior year of high school in 1938, Blatnick had played four years in the low minors before going into the service in September 1942. Finally discharged in March 1946, Johnny had great years at Harrisburg and Wilkes-Barre before coming to camp in 1948 as a 27-year-old rookie.

Chapman had a slew of outfielders in camp, including veterans like Roy Cullenbine, 'Bama Rowell, Charley Gilbert, and Buster Adams. Even so, Blatnick started the spring slashing line drives and gaining more and more playing time in the exhibition games.

> **BLATNICK:** "We were playing the Red Sox down in Bradenton and I was taking batting practice before the game. Ted Williams was standing behind the cage and when I got done he called me over and said, 'Johnny, come on into the clubhouse, I want to talk to you.' So I followed him and he started giving me batting tips. He said, 'You've got good, quick wrists but you need to do one thing you're not doing. You're not getting your hip out of the way fast enough.' So I thought about that advice and I think that is what gave me my good hot start and helped me a lot."

Blatnick did go north with the Phillies but saw little action the first two weeks of the season as Chapman went with Ashburn in left field, Walker in center, and Ennis in right. Then on May 3, with Walker slumping and sidelined for a few days with the flu, Chapman moved Richie to center and inserted Johnny in left.

Blatnick immediately began hitting and on May 9 broke up a perfect game by Harry Brecheen of the Cardinals by barely beating out a slow roller to third baseman Whitey Kurowski with two out in the seventh. The following day Johnny was six for nine with 5 RBIs in a doubleheader sweep over the Reds. In Pittsburgh on May 13, before seven relatives from his hometown of Bridgeport, Ohio, John went four for four, raising his average to .444. After three weeks in the lineup, he was hitting around .400 and leading the league. John was still above .300 until the end of July, then tailed off to a final .260.

> **BLATNICK:** "All of sudden they must have found out my weak spot, high inside. When I look back, I must have been pretty dumb because when I took my stride I went in towards home plate instead of watching the ball and stepping out a little bit when the ball was inside."

On August 28 in Pittsburgh, the same day Ashburn broke his finger sliding into second base and was lost for the season, Blatnick threw a real scare into all of us.

> **BLATNICK:** "I was going real good when I passed out in the heat on a hot, sunny day in Pittsburgh in front of a lot of my hometown fans, since I lived only about 60 miles from Pittsburgh. About the third inning I came off the field into the dugout and keeled over.
>
> "I never had that problem after or before. I really laugh when I think about it because Schoolboy Rowe was pitching that day and it was so darn hot. How could a man his age [38] stand the heat and pitch the whole game and me, a rookie, keel over. Anyway, they kept me out of the lineup for a while and after that it seemed like I couldn't get back into the rhythm again."

In September Johnny had a memorable but dreadful day against the Dodgers.

> **BLATNICK:** "Maje McDonnell was the best batting practice pitcher that ever lived. He could throw them right down the pipe every time. On that night in Ebbets Field Maje threw me five pitches and I hit all five of them into the left field seats. So I thought I was going to have a pretty good night. Don Newcombe was pitching for the Dodgers. He struck me out five times and I never even fouled one off. After the fifth time I went

in the dugout, hauled off and clobbered a three-quarter-inch water pipe that was on the water cooler. That's how mad I was. Flooded the whole dugout. They fined me $90 to fix the cooler and I never even tipped one!"

Although considered one of the most promising Whiz Kids in 1948, Johnny could not make the club in 1949 and spent the year in Toronto, batting a solid .298. In 1950 he made the club out of spring training, but was traded to the Cardinals on April 27 for southpaw pitcher Ken Johnson to replace the injured Stan Musial. But Johnny appeared in only seven games for the Cardinals before they sent him down to the Houston Buffs in the Texas League.

> **BLATNICK:** "I was disappointed when Eddie Sawyer told me I had been traded. I liked the guys on the Phillies. They were a cohesive, fun-loving family. And I liked Philadelphia. The people there were good to me, even though if they don't like you there they could run you out. Plus, I thought those guys were going to go somewhere. They won faster than I thought they would. But I was down in Houston, Texas, pulling for them, even though I belonged to the Cardinals."

Johnny never made it back to the big leagues, one Whiz Kid whose potential went unfulfilled. He played with Rochester and Syracuse in the International League, first for player-manager Harry Walker and then against him, for six more years before retiring after the 1956 season.

One trouble spot for the Phils going into 1948 was first base. In spring training the club hoped that the likes of Al Flair, Howie Schultz, Roy Cullenbine, or Bert Haas would fill the bill but none of them proved consistently effective. So to shore up the position Bob Carpenter made one of the most successful trades in team history. On April 7, just a few days before the season opened, Carpenter sent young utility infielder Ralph LaPointe and $20,000 to the Cardinals for first sacker Dick Sisler.

Dick, son of George Sisler—arguably the finest first baseman ever to play the game—had an upbeat, easygoing personality and was a wonderful addition to the Phillies' clubhouse. He had been a disappointment to the Cardinals in 1947, hitting only .203 in 47 games. But when he joined the Phillies, Ben Chapman told him that the first base job was his.

> **SISLER:** "I was hurt when I was traded to the Phillies. I had grown up in St. Louis and the Cardinals were my hometown team. And it is hard to leave a ballclub where you know all the

guys and go to a new one. But it turned out to be the greatest break in my career."

Dick did take over first base in 1948 and dramatically improved his performance from the previous year with the Cardinals. In 121 games he hit a solid .274 with 11 home runs and 56 RBIs. Although he missed about three weeks of duty in late August and early September with a kidney infection that hospitalized him, Dick finished the season strongly. We all assumed he would be our regular first sacker in 1949 as well.

The Whiz Kids were a fun-loving bunch and none of us had any more fun than Dick. At the end of the 1948 season we came home from a road trip with only three or four days left in the season. Richie's mother had gone back to Nebraska so he and I moved out of the Ashburn's rooming house into the Adelphia Hotel downtown for the last home stand. Sisler was staying there as well, and one night I was in the lobby thinking about eating when Dick came by and asked me if I wanted to go eat. I said, "Yeah," and Dick said, "I'll see if I can go get us a sponsor." So off we go into the bar and order a beer. All of a sudden a well-dressed man came over and said, "Aren't you George Sisler's son?"

Dick said, "Yes, I certainly am."

The guy then went on for 20 minutes about what a great ballplayer George Sisler was and how great it was to meet his son. All of a sudden the guy said, "Have you eaten yet?"

Dick said, "No, we haven't." So we went into the dining room and had a nice steak dinner with the guy, who was really a ball fan. Of course, when the meal was over the guy picked up the check. After we said goodbye to the man and were walking out Dick said to me, "That's what I call a sponsor. If they want to talk about my old man, they got to pay for it."

Dick was just a great character. He had a great capacity to enjoy life to its fullest.

> **CABALLERO:** "Dick Sisler was a very, very funny guy. Dick was playing first base one time and I was playing second in the Polo Grounds. Now Dick stuttered a little bit. A fellow hit a high pop up between first and second. We both close on it and Dick is saying, 'I ga, ga, ga' and when the ball hits the ground he says, 'You take it,' with a big grin on his face."

Dick was not at all self-conscious about his speech impediment, which he always referred to as stammering. It rarely bothered him when he was in public or being interviewed on radio or television.

CABALLERO: "Dick told us a story about driving back to his home in St. Louis after the '51 season. He pulled into a gas station because he was low on gas and when he rolled down the window the gas attendant asked, 'H-H-H-H-How many gallons you want?'

"Dick said, 'F-F-F-F-Fill 'er up.'

"The attendant said, 'What are you, a wise guy?'

"Dick said, 'No, no, no. I'm that way too.' "

We sometimes called Dick "the Big Cat" because he was known more for his hitting than his fielding. He was certainly an adequate fielder, but he harbored no illusions about his defensive skills. When he would make a great play with the glove he would bound into the dugout saying, "Ooh, what leather!"

Dick had been a wonderfully versatile high school athlete in St. Louis, playing fullback for the football team and center for the basketball team, as well as competing in the high hurdles, high jump, shot put, and discus for the track squad. He also played a little baseball, particularly in the fast St. Louis Municipal League, where he attracted the attention of the Cardinals and other clubs. Dick, however, decided to follow the footsteps of his older brother George, Jr., and attend Colgate University in upstate New York. But after spending less than a year there, he signed with the Cardinals in the spring of 1939 at the age of 18.

He began in the low minors with Washington in the Pennsylvania State Association, hitting an impressive .319 with 86 runs batted in 95 games. His 16 homers led the league. In 1940 Dick played with Lansing in the Michigan State League and batted .322 with 83 RBIs in 105 contests. The next two seasons saw Dick achieve indifferent success in a variety of minor league settings. At one stop in 1942 with Asheville, North Carolina, in the Piedmont League, Dick was more successful off the field than on. One afternoon while swimming Dick met Dorothy Ann Campbell. They were married shortly thereafter, on September 19, 1942.

Dick was called into the Navy prior to the 1943 season. Eventually stationed at Bainbridge, Maryland, he was able to play a significant amount of baseball against current and future big leaguers. Batting against the likes of Bob Feller and future Whiz Kid teammate Jim Konstanty, Dick improved his baseball stock substantially during his almost three years in the service.

Shortly after Dick's discharge from the service in 1945, Cardinals owner Sam Breadon arranged for him to play for Mike Gonzales's Havana club in the Cuban Winter League. Breadon wanted Dick to reacclimate to professional baseball and learn to play first base, since the Cardinals had an abundance of outfielders, beginning with Stan Musial, Enos Slaughter, and Terry Moore.

Dick proceeded to become a legend in Cuba in three short months. He smacked 2 home runs in his first game and a few weeks later hit three round-trippers in one game. On another occasion, he clubbed a homer over a 450-foot barrier, the first ball hit out in that spot in 20 years. The stadium owner thereupon presented him with a $350 watch. All together Dick clouted 10 home runs in 35 games and batted over .400.

> **SISLER:** "My wife was not there at first and so I went over to our manager Mike Gonzales and told him I was going to go home. He said, 'Oh no no, don't you leave. Why do you want to go home?'
>
> "I said, 'Because I miss my wife.'
>
> "He said, 'Don't worry we'll pay for everything, we'll pay for everything for her to come down.' And they did."

Dubbed the Babe Ruth of Cuba, Dick was so popular that he and his wife Dot needed police protection wherever they went. The Cuban president presented Dick with a gold medal and fans showered him with gifts. He was offered $7,500 to jump the Cardinal organization and join the Mexican League, where a couple of Mexican baseball entrepreneurs were attempting to sign major league talent. When he turned down the offer, they threw in an expensive automobile, diamond watch, and diamond pin. His answer was still no, even though he had yet to make the big leagues.

While in Cuba, Dick became acquainted with Ernest Hemingway, a serious baseball fan. Hemingway was so impressed with Dick's exploits that he included him in his Pulitzer–winning novel *The Old Man and the Sea*. While most readers recall the old fisherman's frequent references to "the great DiMaggio," the old man also remembered "Dick Sisler and those great drives in the old park."

In the book, the boy who fishes with the old man says of Dick, "He hits the longest ball I have ever seen," most likely in reference to Dick's gargantuan blast in Havana in 1946.

The old man replies, "Do you remember when he used to come to the Terrace? I wanted to take him fishing but I was too timid to ask him. Then I asked you to ask him and you were too timid."

The boy then says, "I know. It was a great mistake. He might have gone with us. Then we would have that for all of our lives."

That spring Dick made the Cardinals. Because of his play in the Navy and in Cuba, the Cardinals sold their only true first baseman, Ray Sanders, to the Braves at the start of the season. Dick had a somewhat disappointing rookie season, batting .260 in 83 games and splitting time between first and the outfield, while Musial took over at first. Following his Ruthian winter in Cuba, he was able to hit only three home runs in 235 at bats. The Cardinals gave up on him after his even more disappointing 1947 season, where he hit no homers in 74 trips to the plate. The Phillies were happy they did because Dick became a key member of the Whiz Kids and hit the most famous home run in Phillies history.

The 1948 Phillies created some excitement of their own with the influx of new talent. After playing .500 ball the first month and a half of the season, the club got hot in early June, taking four straight from the Cubs in Chicago to pull within a game and a half of the lead with a 23–18 record. Ashburn extended his rookie record hitting streak to 23 games in the June 5 doubleheader sweep, upping his average to a lofty .380.

On June 6, however, the Phils came crashing down to earth, absorbing an 11–1, 2–0 doubleheader loss to the Cardinals in Sportsman's Park as Richie's hitting streak came to an end. In the first game Ben Chapman brought in 19-year-old bonus baby Charlie Bicknell to relieve Ken Heintzelman in the second inning, already down 5–1. Charlie pitched well, holding the Redbirds scoreless until the sixth inning.

> **BICKNELL:** "I was the mop-up man but I didn't do much mopping up, that's for sure. We'd had a bunch of doubleheaders so when Chapman brought me in he said, 'You're it for the day. Get somebody out.' I did okay until the sixth when Del Rice blooped a single to left and with one out, Erv Dusak hit a homer to left. Then Red Schoendienst, a banjo hitter, hit one on the roof in left. It was probably the first home run of his life. [It was actually Red's fifth homer in four years]. Musial was next, and if I could have gotten one over the plate he probably would have hit one, too. But I walked him, bringing up Whitey Kurowski.
>
> "Chapman came out to the mound at this point and told me, 'Knock the Polack on his ass.' So I knocked him on his ass. He knew it was coming. His bat went one way and his cap another.

"Larry Goetz was the umpire and he walked out to the mound from behind the plate and said, 'Look, don't do that again or it'll cost you 200 bucks.' It obviously was intentional, let's face it.

"So Goetz went back behind the plate and Chapman came out of the dugout and said, 'Knock the Polack on his ass, again.'"

"I said, 'You sure?'

"He said, 'Yep. I'm sure.' So I did and Goetz came running from behind the plate. For an old guy he could move pretty good when he wanted to. Chapman came charging out of the dugout and got in front of Goetz before he could get to me and they start going at it. They were about six inches apart arguing and everybody's got bad breath from chewing tobacco. So Goetz started backing up because every time Chapman opened his mouth he sprayed Goetz with tobacco. It was the first time I ever saw an umpire back up. Chapman kept spraying him and finally, Goetz just threw up his hands and went back behind the plate. I'm standing out there, 19 years old, and wondering, 'What am I doing here?'

"I finally got Kurowski to ground into a force at second but then Slaughter and Nippy Jones hit consecutive home runs off me, making it four in one inning. Marty Marion then hit a line drive right through the box. It was a rocket and I couldn't pick it up real quick because of the background. Everybody wore light colored clothing in Sportman's Park. I didn't pick it up until it was about 8 or 10 feet in front of me. I just cocked my head over to the side, just in time for that rascal to go by me. It would have laid me out.

"Chapman came out again and said, 'Go take a shower.'

"I said, 'Thank you, sir.' You had to go through the Cardinal dugout to get to the clubhouse because they had just one runway in Sportman's Park. As I walked through I heard a few of the Cardinals saying, 'Hang in there, kid.'"

The team began to fade in June when I was called up from Wilmington, and by mid-July we were mired in seventh place, although with a respectable 37–43 record. And though we were only 10½ games out of first place and only 2 games out of fourth, Bob Carpenter decided to make a change. So on July 16 he dismissed Ben Chapman in St. Louis even though we had beaten the Cardinals that day 3–1 on Del Ennis's sixth-inning two-run homer.

> **ASHBURN:** "I went to the All-Star game in St. Louis in 1948 and Ben Chapman went with me on the train from Philadelphia. On that trip Ben told me he wanted me to take more of a leadership role even though I was a rookie and had been in the league three months. The 1948 Phillies had a lot of veteran ballplayers and I wasn't going to go up to 'Bama Rowell, Bert Haas, Eddie Miller, Schoolboy Rowe and Dutch Leonard and tell them to shake their ass. But that is what Ben Chapman wanted me to do and he said, 'If somebody doesn't do something there are going to be a lot of changes on this ballclub.' He was talking about player changes but he is the guy who got fired."

> **CURT SIMMONS:** "I remember Chapman having a meeting in St. Louis in his hotel suite. He was raising heck about our bad play and running down everybody. He told us, particularly the veterans, 'If you don't straighten out, there are going to be some heads flying,' and then he got fired the next day."

Carpenter told the press that he was "dismissing" Chapman ("Please don't say I fired him") for "a multitude of reasons." He refused to elaborate except to say that he had been "disappointed for some time with the showing of the team." He was quoted in the *Philadelphia Inquirer* as saying, "I will not say it was Ben's fault. I can't say it was anyone's fault. But the club was not producing. In that case, any business must make a change."

Chapman responded by stating, "I wish that Mr. Carpenter would tell the public the real reason for my dismissal." He too refused to elaborate.

> **CABALLERO:** "Chapman told me one of the main reasons he was fired was because he had an attendance clause in his contract and since we were drawing well Carpenter didn't want to pay him the bonus money under that clause."

Chapman apparently was one of the highest-paid managers in baseball because the attendance clause in his contract coincided with the postwar baseball boom. After 1946, when Phillies attendance topped 1 million for the first time ever, Chapman's contract was reportedly modified. And after dismissing him in 1948, Carpenter honored Chapman's contract for the balance of the year.

One rumored reason for the firing was Chapman's refusal to play black players, a charge that Ben publicly denied. Although the Phillies sadly waited until 1956 to integrate (the last team in the National League to do so), it may be that Ben's general racial intolerance, which had offended a number of ethnic groups in Philadelphia, contributed to his departure.

> **SAM NAHEM:** "I got along okay with Chapman. Except he left me in once to take a real beating. When you're a racist you are also an anti-Semite. Some reporters asked him about it, whether he kept me in there for some reason other than the demands of the game. He denied that it was anti-Semitism. But Chapman's feelings towards me, whatever they were, were never overt and we got along."

At the time I knew very little about the politics that went into Chapman's dismissal. As a rookie, I was just worried about pitching. But many people later said that the principal cause of his firing was Ben's poor judgment and lack of discretion in criticizing Bob Carpenter. Shortly after Herb Pennock died the previous winter, Chapman was outspoken in his belief that the club needed another experienced baseball man as general manager. Carpenter, of course, took over those duties himself.

The day before the All-Star game in St. Louis, Chapman, who was frustrated by our lack of progress, again voiced his sentiments to a sportswriter friend in an off-the-record conversation. The sportswriter then unwittingly suggested to Carpenter that the team needed someone to succeed Pennock. Bob knew where those thoughts had originated and took them personally, since he regarded himself as a true baseball man. That continued insubordination, coupled with the fiery and bigoted Chapman's other problems, led Bob to make an immediate change.[1]

Even though Chapman rode us hard and criticized us often, we respected him as a good baseball man who was fair in his handling of us.

> **ENNIS:** "I was sad when Chapman got fired. I always liked Ben and I didn't know Sawyer from apples. So it was sort of strange because I was Chapman's boy. He liked me, too, and helped me a lot as a ballplayer."

---

1. In the 1953 team history entitled *The Philadelphia Phillies, Philadelphia Inquirer* sportswriter Stan Baumgartner reported that although Ben Chapman "never could make himself believe this explanation, it was exactly what had happened." It may be that Baumgartner was the sportswriter in whom Ben had ill-advisedly confided.

Chapman had been particularly rough on Andy Seminick both publicly and privately. As late as spring training 1948, Ben was telling the press, "I need a catcher."

SEMINICK: "Ben Chapman was an outstanding baseball man. He somehow knew that by getting on me I would respond. He would get on me quite a bit and I would respond to his criticism by trying to do better. Although I didn't realize it at the beginning, he just wanted me to do well and improve. So I give Ben Chapman a lot of credit for making me a better ballplayer."

POSSEHL: "Ben Chapman was very direct, He would tell you right to your face. There was no backstabbing with him. I loved the guy. He was my type of guy.

"After I beat Cincinnati in my first game, a couple of the coaches tried to change how I finished up. I fell off the mound to the left and my butt would be aimed at home plate. Chapman said, 'I don't care if he stands on his head, as long as he wins. What difference does it make how he finishes up?' He was a great guy."

BICKNELL: "Ben Chapman was a fiery rascal. Very fair. He didn't show partiality to anybody. Overall, he was a damn good manager. I hated to see him get fired. It was a surprise to everybody."

McDONNELL: "Ben Chapman would have been a very good manager with a good team. He was very sharp on the field, quick with moves. He knew his personnel well, baseball wise. But he wasn't very patient, especially with a young club."

Carpenter named coach Dusty Cooke interim manager while the press speculated about a permanent replacement. Cooke, a former Yankee teammate and close friend of Chapman's, managed us for 10 days while Carpenter sought a new skipper. Names mentioned included Mickey Cochrane, Mel Ott (recently fired by the Giants), Cardinal outfielder Terry Moore, Braves second baseman Eddie Stanky, Milt Stock (then a Cubs coach and later to play a key role as the Dodger third-base coach when we won the pennant in 1950), Billy Jurges (another Cubs' coach), Athletics coach Earle Brucker, and minor league managers Nemo Leibold and Jimmy Dykes.

BICKNELL: "When Dusty Cooke was interim manager he told me one night, 'You're starting against Pittsburgh tomorrow night.' Well, he should have never told me. I wore the toilet out that night. I kept Blix Donnelly [Charlie's roommate] up all night flushing that damn toilet.

"My first few pitches were up against the backstop. Then Kiner hit one about 16 hundred miles and that was the end of the day for me. But I appreciate Dusty Cooke giving me the opportunity."

That would be the only start in Charlie's brief big league career.

In a surprise move, on July 26 Carpenter promoted former college professor Eddie Sawyer to manage the Phillies from our Triple A Toronto Maple Leafs franchise. I knew Eddie from spring training that year and he had managed Ashburn, Caballero, Granny Hamner, and Stan Lopata at Utica. They all thought very highly of him. They turned out to be right.

ASHBURN: "I liked Ben Chapman but I was very happy when Bob Carpenter named Eddie Sawyer manager. I could see that things were changing in our organization. Of course, I knew about Robin Roberts and Curt Simmons. Robin was the best pitcher we had in camp in '48. I was surprised when they sent him down, but I think they thought that he needed some minor league experience. But I knew Robin would be back. So the club was changing a lot with the young kids coming in, like myself. We had Hamner, Del Ennis was still young, Putsy Caballero was there, Puddinhead Jones was on his way. We knew we were in a real transition period so I was very pleased that Eddie Sawyer was coming in and going to be put in charge of these young kids."

Eddie would prove to be superb at instilling confidence in the young players and in adding some key veterans such as Jim Konstanty, Eddie Waitkus, and Bill Nicholson. While Bob Carpenter, Herb Pennock, and Ben Chapman played important roles in assembling the Whiz Kids, it remained for Eddie Sawyer to put together the final pieces of the puzzle and to provide the stable leadership needed to take us to the pennant. Although we did not realize it at the time, July 26, 1948, was a decisive turning point for the Phillies.

Chapter 7
PROFESSOR SAWYER ASSUMES CONTROL

In some ways, Eddie Sawyer seemed like an unlikely choice to succeed Ben Chapman as our manager. He had never played, coached, or managed a game in the major leagues, although he had been in the Phillies organization managing our top minor league clubs since 1943. Richie Ashburn, Granny Hamner, Stan Lopata, and Putsy Caballero, who had played for Eddie at Utica, uniformly had the highest respect for him. He was, of course, responsible for moving Richie from catcher to the outfield and instilling confidence in Granny as a young kid after he had taken his lumps in short stints with the Phillies.

As we soon learned, Eddie was not a typical baseball man. He graduated with honors from Ithaca College, where he played halfback for the football team and pitched and played outfield for the baseball team. He also earned a master's degree from Cornell in biology and physiology and then taught biology at Ithaca for seven years during the baseball off-season, while helping to coach their football, basketball, and baseball teams. A remarkably intelligent man, Eddie is blessed with a photographic memory. While at Ithaca, he could call every one of the 1,500 students by his or her first name and knew each of their hometowns.

Originally from Westerly, Rhode Island, Eddie was a four-sport star in high school. After arriving with $20 in his pocket, he worked his way through Ithaca College in the heart of the Depression, tending furnaces, sweeping out gymnasiums, and serving as a short-order cook in a fraternity house. Ithaca gave him credit on his tuition and board and he was obliged to work it off each semester.

In 1934 he was signed to a professional baseball contract by the famed Yankee scout Paul Krichell while playing for a summer college league in Malone, New York. He broke in with Norfolk of the Piedmont League and led the team to a pennant, hitting a robust .361 with 143 hits in only 102 games. He followed with two more .300-plus years, mostly at Binghamton in the New York–Penn League, before moving up to the Oakland Oaks in the Pacific Coast League in 1937. There he severely injured his left shoulder while making a diving catch in the outfield.

Overall, Eddie had a rough few months in Oakland. In addition to his shoulder injury, he split a finger ramming into the outfield fence in an exhibition game against Seattle the day before the season began. The finger became infected because of fence paint lodged under his nail and swelled to twice its normal size. Then, early in the season he overran second base and dived back head first. An overzealous umpire attempting to get into position to call the play spiked Eddie on the back of his hand. Not surprisingly, Eddie played through both injuries.

The shoulder injury, however, failed to respond to treatment, forcing him back to Binghamton, where he nonetheless hit .345. After the season, Eddie decided to quit baseball. Although he was a fine hitter and possessed a strong throwing arm, his slowness of foot had retarded his progress as a player in the highly competitive Yankee organization. Now he had a painful shoulder that made it difficult for him to swing the bat.

That winter he began teaching at Ithaca with thoughts of earning a Ph.D. and entering academia on a permanent basis. But when spring came around the Yankees were short on outfielders at Binghamton and he decided to try baseball once again, with the idea of eventually becoming a manager.

> **SAWYER:** "I told my wife Polly that when I stopped hitting .300, I was going to try to go over to managing."

That year at Binghamton, with his shoulder still bothering him, he hit .299. The following year, 1939, Eddie began his managing career with Amsterdam of the Class C Canadian-American League. He continued to play and play well, leading the team to a pennant and leading the league in hits with 169 (in 122 games), doubles with 53, and RBIs with 103, with a .369 batting average. He was only 28 years old.

Eddie continued to serve as a player-manager in the Yankee farm system through 1943, each winter teaching and coaching back at Ithaca.

Then Eddie was hired to manage the Phillies' top farm team at Utica after the 1943 season because of his relationship with new Phillies general manager Herb Pennock.

> **SAWYER:** "After the '43 season we stayed in Binghamton. I taught and coached football at Binghamton North High School since Ithaca College was down to about 300 students, mostly women, because of the war. I was thinking of quitting managing and going back to school for another degree when Herb called. The Yankees wanted me to manage their second Triple A club in Kansas City, but I knew they weren't going to have a good team because their top Triple A team was Newark. The Yankees didn't like it when I turned the Kansas City job down so I figured I better change organizations or leave managing because the only place for me with the Yankees would be down."

While he was coaching football at Binghamton North High, Eddie's team ran up against a team with a star running back named Johnny Logan. Logan, who would be the Braves' shortstop for much of the 1950s, ran for five touchdowns against Eddie's club. In 1951, when Logan broke in with the Boston Braves as a highly touted prospect, Eddie told us, "If you think this kid can play baseball, you ought to see him play football."

At Utica, Eddie directed the Blue Sox to two pennants and a third-place finish in four years.

> **SAWYER:** "Each year at Utica it seemed to get better because with Bob Carpenter and Herb Pennock running things we signed a lot of good young players out of high school. Utica was only Class A but was then the Phillies' top farm team, so Herb and farm director Joe Reardon sent me most of the top prospects. The first year we finished third and then we won the pennant in 1945 with Ashburn, Caballero, and Hamner.
>
> "In 1946 Ashburn and Hamner were in the service and the organization sent several of my top players to Wilmington so they could win the pennant. They did, but we finished seventh. The next year we got Ashburn, Hamner, and Caballero back and Lopata caught for us. We won the pennant by a wide margin."
>
> **STAN LOPATA:** "We had a terrific team in 1947. Mr. Sawyer and Lefty Gomez, who managed Binghamton, were close friends and we really enjoyed playing against him. We started the '47 season with four games at Utica against Binghamton and then

four games at Binghamton. Before the week was out Mr. Gomez was eight games out of first place; we won all eight games!"

PUTSY CABALLERO: "We should have been playing Triple A ball but Utica was the top Phillies' farm club so we all played in the Eastern League and really dominated. Hamner and Ashburn would make great plays and our opponents would say, 'What are they doing down here, they ought to be in the major leagues!' "

Sawyer had a great knack for handling and developing young players and left an indelible mark on those who played for him at Utica.

ASHBURN: "I didn't realize until a few years afterwards how fortunate I was to play for Eddie Sawyer. One, he let you play. He'd stick your name in the lineup and just turn you loose and let you play. Now, if you did some things wrong, he would tell you. He wouldn't make it a big deal, but he would correct you.

"As good an example as any would be the time in the minor leagues when I was on first base one day and a ground ball was hit to the infield and I went into second to break up the double play. Well, it seemed to me that the best way to break it up was to jump up with both arms up in the air so the guy couldn't get the throw off. The shortstop, who was a veteran player, was so surprised to see me hurtling through the air that he didn't throw to first. I thought, 'Boy, I really did my job there.'

"When I got back to the dugout Eddie said, 'Hey kid, come here. We don't break up double plays like that, you'll get killed. Somebody will hit you right between the eyes.'

"He didn't scold me, he just told me. He knew I was inexperienced. I had never even seen a major league game. But Eddie knew that if we played enough, we were going to learn. And that's what we did.

"I never played for another manager like him. He was a very bright guy and when I was younger he was a father figure almost. But Eddie wasn't that old when we were at Utica. He had a young family with two daughters and we used to spend a lot of time at Eddie's home with Eddie and his wife Polly and the kids. He was really great for young guys like myself to play for early in our careers."

LOPATA: "Mr. Sawyer was a great manager and a very smart manager. He was very good with young ballplayers and really was like a second father to me. He could be strict if necessary but most of the time he was very gentle. But he could be very rough.

"We had always heard that he had really been a tough man back when he played. I understand his wife Polly wouldn't go to his ballgames when he played because he was so rough. He kind of settled down but if he had to be he was there. He wouldn't back down from anybody."

ASHBURN: "I understood that Eddie was under some sort of probation because he had belted a couple of umpires in earlier days. We heard that he would be barred for life if he ever touched another umpire. But he didn't give umpires that tough a time at Utica.

"One time at Utica a fan threw a beer in his face. There were a lot of gamblers in Utica, probably two-thirds of the people in the stands in those days were gamblers. We had blown a game and this guy made the mistake of throwing a beer in Eddie's face as he was walking off the field to the clubhouse. I don't know how many times Sawyer punched the guy before he hit the ground."

CABALLERO: "Eddie had this guy on the ground and we had to pull him off. I mean this was our manager, we usually did the fighting! Eddie was a quiet, professor type, and even though he was a big strong man we didn't expect that from him."

LOPATA: "I had caught the first game of a doubleheader in Utica and was in the bullpen for the second game. At the end of the game I ran back to the clubhouse under the stands so that I could get showered and changed quickly. We only had two shower nozzles in about a six foot by six shower room, and if you wanted hot water or to get changed fast you had to hurry to the shower.

"After everybody else filed in there was a knock on the clubhouse door and I opened it since I was the closest. I saw this guy standing there with blood all over his face with what looked like a broken nose. He said he wanted to see Mr. Sawyer, but I told him he better get out of there. I later learned that he was one of those Utica gamblers and had thrown beer in Eddie's face after the game."

ASHBURN: "I had seen Eddie with just words stifle one of the veteran players who was popping off in the clubhouse. Eddie walked over and told him in effect his next words might be his last. And the guy shut up.

"One night on a bus trip we had a pitcher who had been drinking and was in the back of the bus popping off about Sawyer. Eddie, who always sat in the front of the bus, walked back to the back of the bus and without a word picked this guy up off his feet and stuffed him in the luggage rack overhead. And this pitcher was a pretty good-sized guy. Then Eddie told him to shut his trap.

"That stuff was kind of impressive but it always surprised me about Eddie. He was a brilliant, scholarly man but he could also be very tough."

CABALLERO: "Eddie controlled the team and had our respect. He let us play because he knew that we were young kids and we would learn just by playing. He knew we would make mistakes and he would correct us, but he mainly just let us play to improve. If we repeated the same mistakes he would take us aside and talk to us about it. A couple of times a year Eddie would get upset at us and slam the clubhouse door and nobody would move. He knew how to get our attention, but mainly he just let us play."

LOU POSSEHL: "I loved the guy. He never tried to change anything with you as a ballplayer. But he had a knack for knowing when to pull a pitcher, when not to and how to build up confidence. He put me in a couple of tough games and I got through them. But I did it because he had the faith in me to do the job when I had to do it. He was a quiet man but a very good baseball man.

"It was very rare when Eddie flew off the handle. When he did, he meant it. He got a little mad at me once. He loved me and I loved him but he got mad at me one day in 1947. I had a one-run lead against Albany and Pinky May, the manager, was up. Eddie came out and said, 'You want to pitch to this guy or put him on base?'

"Naturally I said, 'I want to pitch to him,' and he got a base hit to tie the score.

"Eddie said, 'That'll teach you something, you dumbie.'

"The next year at Toronto we were playing at Newark and the same situation came up with Ken Silvestri coming up. Eddie said, 'You want to pitch to this guy?'

"I said, 'No, I want to put him on.' I knew damn well he remembered from the previous year, so just to satisfy him I said, 'I'll put him on.'"

To this day, Eddie asks about Lou and whether Lou wants to put any men on base or not.

Just before Herb Pennock's death in 1948 the Phillies entered into a working agreement with a Triple A franchise, the Toronto Maple Leafs of the International League. Not surprisingly, Herb and Bob Carpenter selected Eddie to manage the team. Stan Lopata followed him to Toronto to catch while Puddinhead Jones was promoted early in the season from Utica to play third base. In Toronto, Eddie first encountered pitcher Bubba Church, a young World War II veteran from Birmingham, Alabama, who threw a nasty curve, and journeyman right-hander Jim Konstanty, who had failed to stick with both the Cincinnati Reds and Boston Braves. All four would play important roles with the pennant-winning Whiz Kids, with Konstanty setting the standard for relief pitching and winning the National League's Most Valuable Player Award.

When Eddie took over the Phillies from interim manager Dusty Cooke on July 26, Toronto was in third place with a 48–47 record.

SAWYER: "I had known that eventually I was going to get the Phillies job because Herb Pennock had that in mind all along, but I didn't think it would come along so soon. Of course, it was something I had hoped for for a long time. I had managed in the minors for ten years, a pretty long apprenticeship.

"I think Bob Carpenter wanted to go another direction and as the club started to bring the young players up, I think they wanted me because I had managed a lot of the kids and they had had success under me. Ben and I were pretty good friends, but I don't think Ben had the patience for the young guys. They really took a lot of patience."

CABALLERO: "After Eddie was named manager of the Phillies we always kidded him, 'You made us big league ballplayers in the minor leagues, you got us up here. Now we're bringing you up to the major leagues with us.'"

In an unusual move, Eddie kept all three of Ben Chapman's coaches, Dusty Cooke, Benny Bengough, and Cy Perkins. In addition, George Earnshaw, former star hurler with Connie Mack's great Athletic teams of the late 1920s and early 1930s, was with us in a number of roles during the late 1940s. He scouted and sometimes coached for us, although by 1950 he was serving as a roving minor league pitching instructor for the organization.

> **SAWYER:** "All three were ex-Yankee ballplayers and I knew them all well. Also I had worked with them in spring training every year that I had been at Utica. We got along well and rather than go out and get other people, I just kept them all. They knew the major leagues better than I did. Dusty Cooke was one of Ben Chapman's best friends, but we got along great. I think they all knew the team had to make a change."

Chapman's three coaches all had vast major league experience. Cy Perkins had caught for 15 years with Connie Mack's Philadelphia Athletics. Cy was the A's regular catcher for six years until 1925, when a rookie named Mickey Cochrane came on the scene. Originally from New England, Cy ended his playing career with a stint with the 1931 Yankees. He had coached with the Yankees and Tigers and managed in the minor leagues before Ben brought him to the Phillies coaching staff in 1946. Cy's relaxed attitude and baseball wisdom fit in perfectly with Eddie's patient style.

> **BOB MILLER:** "Cy Perkins and Benny Bengough and Dusty Cooke really added a lot to our ballclub. I used to sit on the train with Robbie and some of the other young pitchers and listen to Cy tell stories about baseball in the 20s and 30s and about Connie Mack. He would talk and talk about pitching. He was a great advocate of good location and never letting the count get beyond one ball and two strikes. He had such an influence on me and on Robin. The coaches were all fantastic."

Dusty Cooke was more outgoing than Cy. Chapman had brought Dusty to the club as the trainer in 1946 and made him a coach before the 1948 season. They had been close friends since their days as teammates on the Yankees in the early 1930s. In fact, the two had competed for the

Yankees' center field position, with Ben winning the job and Dusty ending up with the Red Sox.

Once a top prospect with a strong arm and exceptional speed, Dusty's playing career was hampered by a broken collarbone and a leg fracture. He played for the Sox from 1933 through 1936, hitting .291 in 119 games in 1933 and .306 in 100 games in 1935. After returning to the minors in 1937 (where he hit .345 at Minneapolis) he spent a year roaming the outfield in Cincinnati before playing out the string for four more years with Jersey City and Rochester in the International League.

Dusty Cooke was a large man, standing six feet two and weighing over 200 pounds, and was very strong. He was also quite good-natured. According to Bill Werber, Dusty's former teammate and roommate on the Yankees and Red Sox, the two of them played a lot of bridge on the train. One evening in 1930 while they were traveling on a Pullman, Babe Ruth began pestering Dusty while he was playing cards. Despite several friendly warnings, the Babe kept needling and agitating Dusty. Finally, Dusty laid down his hand, bodily picked up Ruth and stuffed him into an upper berth, with the Babe laughing all along.

Dusty had no particular expertise to be a trainer when Ben hired him for that position. The story was that all the equipment Dusty had in his training room was a bottle of rubbing alcohol and a roll of tape. But he must have been somewhat effective. I was told that Granny Hamner once had some boils on his back and Dusty cut them off with a razor blade and poured alcohol over them. Ham said, "It hurt like hell, but they never came back."

By the time I joined the club in 1948 Dusty was coaching first base and Frank Wiechec was the trainer. Frank was a college-educated physical therapist who had spent a number of years as the trainer for Temple University. Bob Carpenter rightly thought that to get someone with that type of background could be a real help to the club. Frank did not know too much about baseball when he joined us, but he learned and was a very effective trainer.

Frank was very enthusiastic but sometimes his lack of background in baseball became quite telling. His normal routine was to always loosen and stretch the arm of the starting pitcher. One day in spring training he worked on Curt Simmons, who was starting that day. After Frank finished, he patted Curt on the shoulder and said, "Good luck, Curt." Curt looked at him and said, "Frank, I'm left-handed." Frank had loosened up Curt's right arm.

After Frank became our trainer, Dusty coached first and served as our hitting instructor. His theory of hitting was quite simple: move your hands forward and just "ping" at the end. Dusty knew that hitting was largely a natural skill and he simply honed in on the basics with us.

Dusty was an enthusiastic rooter and had the loudest voice I can remember in baseball. As I mentioned earlier, when I pitched I had the ability to concentrate so that I never heard crowd noise or players hollering. But Dusty had one of the few voices I ever heard on the mound while I was pitching. I can still hear Dusty yelling to me when I was in a tight spot, "Reach back and get it, Robbie, reach back and get it."

Benny Bengough, the third coach that Chapman brought to the club in 1946, was a holler guy, very positive and vocal. He had starred in football, basketball, and baseball at his hometown Niagara University. A catcher like Cy, he signed with Buffalo of the International League in 1917, right out of college. Initially only the bullpen catcher, Benny threw out four baserunners in his first start, after, the story goes, his mother went to the manager and insisted he give her son a chance. Ironically, in that game Benny threw out the speedy Burt Shotton, later the manager of the 1950 Brooklyn Dodgers, three times. After five full seasons with the Bisons, he caught on with the powerful New York Yankees in 1923, but appeared in only 19 games for the pennant winners.

Benny caught for the Yankees from 1923 through the 1930 season, backing up first Wally Schang and then Pat Collins. In 1925 he became the regular Yankee catcher the same day Lou Gehrig replaced Wally Pipp at first base. Although hitting .258 in 95 games and leading the league with a .993 fielding average, Benny's stint as a starter did not equal Gehrig's.

Arm trouble that would not respond to treatment relegated Benny to backup status the next year. Late in the season his arm improved and manager Miller Huggins put him back into the lineup. Unfortunately, shortly thereafter Cleveland pitcher George Uhle hit Benny with a pitch on that same sore arm, breaking a bone above the wrist. He was not able to return to play until August 1927 but managed to catch 31 games for those legendary '27 Yankees and appear in two World Series games as the Yankees swept the Pirates. The following season he hit .267 in 58 games and then caught all four games of the World Series as the Bronx Bombers again swept the Series, this time defeating the Cardinals.

A fine fielding catcher, Benny's lifetime batting average was a respectable .255. He remained an important cog in the Yankee wheel through the 1930 season. Surprisingly, he went to bat 1,125 times in his big league career with nary a home run.

After leaving the Yankees, Benny spent two years with the St. Louis Browns before beginning a minor league managing career in 1934 with Washington in the Pennsylvania State League. He served as a player-manager there and with Joplin of the Western Association (where he hit .340 and .329) through 1937. After Benny coached with Newark of the International League, Bucky Harris brought him back to the majors as a coach with the Washington Senators in 1940. Benny stayed with the Senators until going into the service in 1943. After the war, his old Yankee teammate Ben Chapman hired him to coach for the Phillies.

Benny was a jolly, bald-headed man who always kept us loose. He was kind of the team spirit, and his enthusiasm and constant encouragement were very helpful to our young team. He frequently warmed up the pitchers and made us believe we had great stuff through his excitement and because of his old catching mitt. That glove made the loudest popping noise in the history of the game when a ball hit right in the pocket. As a result, when Benny warmed us up we always *sounded* like world beaters, even if our stuff was mediocre that day.

Benny often warmed up young pitchers who were trying out for the Phillies. We joked that his old glove had cost Bob Carpenter thousands of dollars over the years. That loud popping noise made every kid sound like Walter Johnson.

Benny always hit pregame infield practice for us and was the originator of our shadow infield. We used the shadow infield when we played exhibition games during the season in minor league towns. Benny would begin with regular infield practice, hitting grounders to third, shortstop, and the like. Then he would slip the ball into his pocket and pretend to hit the ball to Puddinhead Jones at third. Willie would pretend to field it and throw to Dick Sisler at first and so on around the infield. Dick, who was not a particularly adept first baseman, would make the greatest plays in shadow infield anyone ever saw. He liked to make fun of himself by calling himself the Big Cat, and he was as good in shadow infield as his dad George, who was one of the all-time best fielding first baseman.

The end of regular infield practice is when the coach hits a pop fly to the catcher. In our shadow infield, Benny would pretend to hit a high pop foul to Andy Seminick. Benny and Andy were both very bald and Andy would bump into Benny going after the phantom pop up, knocking both of their caps off and sending them both sprawling, bald pates exposed. The minor league crowds loved it and so did we.[1]

Eddie also kept a young coach, 28-year-old Robert "Maje" McDonnell out of Villanova University. Maje was to become one of my closest friends on the Phillies. He had served 40 months in the infantry in the European theatre and emerged from the war with a Bronze Star, a Purple Heart, and five battle stars. A basketball and baseball star in college, Maje returned to Villanova after the war to finish his education.

McDONNELL: "Villanova always played the Phillies in an exhibition game right before opening day. My senior year, 1947, I pitched for Villanova against the Phillies. I pitched the whole game and got beat 7–6, but I pitched a good game. I struck out about seven and the Phillies were impressed with me. Herb Pennock invited me down to the Phillies' offices the following Monday and asked me about going out and specializing in relief and maybe coming up with another pitch or taking a job with the big league club as the batting practice pitcher and working with the team year round in the front office. I was 5' 6" and 125 pounds, so I took the batting practice pitching job.

"I started with the Phillies the day after I graduated from Villanova. I was the batting practice pitcher in 1947 and Ben Chapman really took a liking to me. I was the youngest nonplayer on the field and worked very hard, but of course I enjoyed every minute of it. Cy Perkins, Benny Bengough, and Dusty Cooke were all considerably older and they couldn't do much physical work, so I did a lot of it. I was young and could work morning, noon, and night. If anybody wanted extra hitting I would go out at anytime. Whatever they wanted, I would do. Ben Chapman appreciated that.

"I pitched to Harry Walker, who won the batting title that year, an additional 5 or 10 minutes beyond his normal batting practice every day. I kept him in a groove all year and he was very grateful. At the end of the 1947 season Harry Walker went

---

1. Benny was the narrator in *The Team*, one of the three baseball novels written by Frank O'Rourke in the late 1940s and early 1950s in which the Phillies were very thinly disguised as the Philadelphia Quakers. *The Team* was loosely based on the 1948 Phillies, as told by coach Benny. The center fielder was Robbie Ashton, the right fielder Del Anderson, the left fielder Johnny Blatik, etc. The other two books were *Bonus Rookie* (1950) and *Never Come Back* (1952).

to Ben Chapman and told him that I should be one of his coaches. So Ben Chapman called me in and made me a coach. At 28 I probably was one of the youngest coaches ever in the major leagues."

Maje continued as a tireless batting practice pitcher for us for many years, in addition to his coaching duties. He was always willing to do whatever he could to help us win, and with his supportive attitude he was an important part of the Whiz Kids. Because we shared a common interest in sports of all kinds, we spent a lot of time together on the road, attending boxing matches or going to movies.

Maje was also a frequent companion on my long walks after a tough loss. One time in 1955 I lost a 13-inning ballgame in Milwaukee when Chuck Tanner hit a home run. Afterwards Maje asked, "What are you thinking?" We decided we would walk back to the Schraeder Hotel from County Stadium. It was about seven miles and we sat and chewed the fat in a city park and just took our time getting back. It was one of those nights when I knew I was not going to get any sleep and Maje was nice enough to stay up with me. We got to the hotel at about 7:00 in the morning. We walked right into the coffee shop to have breakfast because we were quite hungry. Mayo Smith, our manager, was in there eating breakfast and thought we were just up early.

That night in Milwaukee was an example of the kind of special friend that Maje was. I always appreciated that he was around like that when I was struggling after a tough game.

Maje served as an assistant basketball coach at Villanova in the off-season for nine years and coached in three NCAA tournaments back when only 16 teams were invited. He may be the only person in history to coach in a World Series and an NCAA Basketball Tournament.

In addition, after the 1951 season Maje organized our off-season Phillies basketball team, which toured around in the winter playing pro teams, town teams and high school faculties. Our competition ranged from not very good to quite good and we did not lose many games. Curt Simmons and Del Ennis always played, and occasionally in later years retired NBA stars like Paul Arizin, Tom Gola, and Ernie Beck played with us. Then we really were invincible.

McDONNELL: "Most people don't know that Robin was a very fine basketball player. He was one of the best pure shooters I've ever seen. I played with him 17 years in the off-season and he must have averaged 22 points a game during that time. And we played a lot of good clubs."

Perhaps not surprisingly, Sawyer's coaches quickly developed great respect for the new manager.

CABALLERO: "Dusty Cooke told me, 'I've played and coached with a lot of managers, but Eddie is one of the smartest managers I've ever seen.'"

McDONNELL: "Sawyer was tremendous with the young ballplayers, very patient. He was a good man, knew the game, and just let the boys play. And they played relaxed. They were putting out physically, but they were relaxed mentally. He was very sharp, walked softly with a heavy stick. You knew when he walked into the room that he was in charge. He was a leader of men. I was under six managers and he was the one fine leader of men. He had that gift, some people have it, a lot don't.

"Eddie was the same every day. You couldn't tell whether we had won or lost."

Eddie came in and changed very little for the rest of the 1948 season. He wanted to get to know us as players so he just observed us and let us play. All the while, he was making decisions about who could help us in the future and who he wanted to get rid off. He did sell Emil Verban to the Cubs in early August so that Granny Hamner could play second base, and he brought up Willie Jones and Stan Lopata from Toronto late in the season to get a taste of the big leagues.

We played even more poorly after Eddie took over than we had for Ben, winning 23 while losing 39 to finish in sixth place, 25½ games behind the Boston Braves.

We all liked his low-key approach, which contrasted with Ben Chapman's more volatile nature. We did not have team meetings and Eddie said very little to us except to occasionally correct something we had done wrong. He gave the coaches a lot of responsibility and we had more contact with them than we did with Eddie.

SIMMONS: "Eddie Sawyer was the professor. He was very quiet spoken. He would sit and twirl a cigar and say very little. He wasn't a holler guy for sure. We had very few meetings. It was very simple baseball, you know, let's go. I really liked playing for that type of manager who just said 'Hey, let's play.' He was kind of like Walter Alston who came along later with the Dodgers."

ENNIS: "Sawyer was a very different type of manager than Ben Chapman. He was mild mannered, a professor. He grew on us. We learned a lot of baseball under Eddie Sawyer."

I personally did not have any kind of conversation with Eddie for almost a year after he became our manager, except to say hello or goodbye each day. He never talked to me before I pitched. Most of the time I would read in the paper that I was starting so I would go get a ball and warm up and go pitch the game. Occasionally Ken Silvestri or Cy Perkins would mention when I would next be pitching, but I never heard from Eddie.

Finally, one day in Pittsburgh in July 1949, Eddie was in the coffee shop of the hotel where we were staying when I walked by. He motioned me over and said, "Robin, you think you are a big league pitcher, don't you?"

"Yessir, I do," I said.

"Well so do I," he said.

That was the first real conversation we had, almost a year after he became manager. It was also the only conversation I can remember having with Eddie. He managed through his coaches and, except for pleasantries, we just did not talk. The only time he said anything to me before a start was that last day of the 1950 season in Ebbets Field when, about an hour before the game, he tapped me on the shoulder, handed me a new baseball and wished me luck.

ASHBURN: "I asked Eddie a few years after I played for him why he didn't talk to us much. And he said, 'I didn't have to talk to you. I never worried about you guys. The only guys I talked to were the players I had doubts about.' Although that makes sense, I never played for another manager like Eddie."

Unlike most managers then and all managers now, Eddie did not have pregame meetings to go over how to pitch to the opposing lineup. Eddie wanted to keep the game simple and let the pitchers throw to their strengths, which, as a young pitcher, I appreciated.

SAWYER: "I never believed in meetings to go over the hitters. I let Andy Seminick or whoever was catching call the game and position the players. I thought it was a waste of time to talk about the hitters. You might be talking about how a batter can't hit a curveball when your pitcher doesn't even have a curveball. I believed that the pitcher should throw his best pitch."

CHURCH: "Eddie was a pleasure to pitch for. He wasn't vocal but you knew what your job was. Eddie never second-guessed a pitcher. I didn't know what second-guessing a pitch was until I went to Cincinnati in 1952. I had never been second-guessed. I never heard Eddie second-guess anybody. When you went out there to pitch a ballgame, it was your ballgame. He expected me to pitch as well as I could. But I never had to look over my shoulder when Eddie was the manager.

"Eddie was the same every day, very low key, win or lose. He just never made any waves. We didn't even have meetings to go over the hitters."

SEMINICK: "I called all the pitches. I can't remember Sawyer or any of the coaches ever calling for a certain pitch or a pitchout. And not one time did any of them ever second-guess any pitch that I had called. I am sure that I gave them plenty of reason to second-guess me sometimes but they never did. Sawyer and the coaching staff just let the guys play the game and never second-guessed any of us or asked, 'Why did you do that?' They would correct you when you made a mistake but that was all. Eddie Sawyer was just great to play for."

Eddie very seldom came to the mound during a game. If he came to the mound, he generally was going to take you out. Occasionally we would have a conversation on the mound, but it would be very short. One time he came to the mound in an extra-inning game I was pitching against the Dodgers. I had two outs but Brooklyn had a man on second. Jackie Robinson was the next batter, followed by Roy Campanella. Eddie ran out and asked, "Who would you rather pitch to, Robinson or Campanella?"

I said, "It doesn't matter to me, Skip."

Eddie said, "It doesn't matter to me either," and ran off the field.

Looking back, it is amazing how low-key Eddie was with us. I cannot remember ever seeing Eddie emotionally upset over anything that happened to us on the playing field. He was the same in July 1948 as he was on October 1, 1950, when we finally won the pennant. The way he acted in the clubhouse never changed.

Eddie was truly a ballplayer's manager. We performed without any undue pressure, although we knew Eddie expected our total effort to win. There was no question that Eddie was in charge, but he never did anything that would make us doubt ourselves. Eddie and Cy instilled confidence by simply letting us play the game to the best of our abilities.

The only doubts I ever had in my early years with the Phillies came after losses. A good night's sleep was generally sufficient to restore my confidence and I was ready to go again. Home runs generally did not bother me much, unless one cost me a ballgame. My philosophy was to throw strikes and stay ahead of the hitters, and I knew I was going to give up some home runs with that kind of approach.

Under Eddie, the game was quite simple. He picked the players and by and large let them run the ballgame. He did not try to complicate the game with a lot of strategy. Even our signs were simple.

CABALLERO: "H, hat, was for hit. S, shirt, was a steal. Belt buckle, B, was a bunt. Anyone could remember those signs. Of course, we had a take-off sign, so Eddie could put a sign on, take it off, and put it back on, several times if he wanted to. But our signs were that easy. Eddie thought that baseball should not be complicated. He didn't want to have signs that would fool or confuse his own players."

SIMMONS: "We didn't really have many tricks. We didn't pitch out or hit and run that much. Our signs were so simple that I'm sure the other team had them."

SAWYER: "Our signs weren't complicated because I didn't want to confuse 'em. We didn't hit and run all that much because we didn't have the guys to do it with. We really ran more in the minor leagues because I had faster teams down there. But good, sound baseball was the best approach as far as I'm concerned. I did have individual signs with a few of the guys. Nobody else knew them and if we traded one of those guys you didn't have to change signs.

"But I never believed in too much confusion. If they thought they had our signs we could always change them. One day later on I said to Ken Boyer, 'Do you have our signs?'

"Ken said, 'Oh yeah, had them for a long time.'

"I said, 'Good. If we change them you're stuck, aren't you?'

"We almost took his hat off one night at third base. He thought we had the bunt sign on and Hamner hit a rope right by him.

Ken died a tough death but he could have could have died that night. Hamner spun his hat right around his head.

"That's what we used to do with Durocher. He loved to have your signs, so we would make sure he had them quick. Then when we changed them he was in trouble."

Like some of my other teammates, I did not fully appreciate Eddie Sawyer as a manager until much later in my career. When Bob Carpenter fired Eddie in June 1952 and replaced him with Steve O'Neil, I was pretty noncommittal about the whole thing. We were not playing very well for the second consecutive season and it was fairly obvious that Eddie was not getting along particularly well with Carpenter, so it was not much of a surprise to me when it happened.

Right after Eddie was let go, Richie and I were discussing the change and I told Whitey that I thought Steve O'Neil would be fine. I still remember Richie saying, "Loyalty, Robin, loyalty." I guess the guys who had played for Eddie in the minor leagues had more reason to appreciate Eddie than someone like me who had just met him in the big leagues. He had not talked to us a whole lot anyhow and it was difficult for me then to fully appreciate how he handled us and what a great player's manager he was.

ASHBURN: "I don't think Robin thought that much of Eddie Sawyer after he became manager of the Phillies. I'm sure he liked him because Eddie was a very likable guy, but I don't think he thought Eddie was a very good manager. I think Robin later discovered that Eddie Sawyer was a very good pitchers' manager. And a very good judge of pitchers. He had a good feel for pitchers. I think later when Robin had played under a couple of different managers after Sawyer left, he realized how good Sawyer was.

"Sawyer was a hands-off manager for the most part. He wasn't a back-patter. He wasn't a screamer or yeller if you did something wrong. I think Robin in the beginning would have liked to have seen more reaction out of Eddie Sawyer. Well, Eddie Sawyer didn't miss anything. If he thought something ought to be talked about he would talk about it. He didn't bother the people that played hard. He never said a word to those guys because he didn't think he had to. He'd get on some people but it would be in his office or somewhere private."

Richie, of course, is correct about my feelings for Eddie. As I looked back on that time later on it was obvious that Eddie was a great manager to play for. I wish I could have played for him all 18 years. It would have been a pleasure.

Toward the end of 1948 Eddie brought up a journeyman pitcher, 31-year-old Jim Konstanty from Toronto, where they had begun the season together.

> **SAWYER:** "I had Konstanty in Toronto only because he was on the Toronto roster when the Phillies entered into the working agreement with the Maple Leafs. We had to supply as many players as we needed for the club, but they also had some of their own and he was one of them. At Toronto, I started Jim in the seven-inning games when we played doubleheaders and he did an excellent job for me. And then I decided to use him for relief and he wanted to start the short games, too. He pitched real well and was in a lot of games.

> "We got along all right because I didn't pay any attention to him and every time he looked for me I always had something to do. I'd always say, 'The only time I am free is Tuesday,' and that is the day we would travel.

> "We could bring up our own players from Toronto, like Stan Lopata, but we had to pay Toronto for their players, $25,000 for the first player and $5,000 each for any others we wanted. Now Konstanty and Pete Campbell, the Maple Leafs' president, didn't get along. The reason they didn't get along is that they were both the same. So we wanted to take two players, Konstanty and Jocko Thompson. Pete Campbell thought that was fine. He was glad to get rid of Konstanty but he said, 'Take him as a second player, don't make him think he is a $25,000 player. Take Jocko as the $25,000 player and pay $5,000 for Konstanty.' "

Jim was a tall, solidly built right-hander who, because he wore glasses, looked like a college professor himself. He was a very clean-living family man who lived a very ordered life. Jim seemed to have a routine for everything he did. He took his pitching very seriously and worked hard at it. Dick Sisler, who was great at coming up with nicknames, called Jim "Yimca" because he looked and acted like a YMCA instructor.

Sawyer's use of Konstanty in relief at Toronto turned his career around and turned out to be a key to the ultimate success of the Whiz Kids, much like his shifting of Ashburn to the outfield at Utica had been. After appearing in a league-leading 46 games with the Maple Leafs in 1948, Jim pitched in relief in six games for us at the end of the season, winning one, losing none, and giving up only a single run in 10 innings of work. We had no idea then what an important role Jim would play in our future.

Jim was born in Strykersville, New York, in 1917 and endured a difficult childhood, losing his mother when he was nine years old and moving frequently around New York State. While Jim was in high school in Arcade, New York, his father moved to Buffalo in search of steady work in the mills, leaving Jim and his younger brother John to fend for themselves. They had to rent a room from the town drunk and Jim worked long hours at the local Borden milk factory to get them by financially. In spite of all this, Jim played high school baseball, basketball, and football. He excelled at basketball in high school and, like me, managed to get a college basketball scholarship, in his case at Syracuse University.

Jim worked his way through college, waiting tables and washing dishes. A fine athlete, he became only the second Syracuse student to letter in four sports: basketball, baseball, boxing, and soccer. His college coach did not think much of his pitching so he played third base and, his senior year, first base. After graduating in 1939 with a degree in physical education (also my major), Jim wanted to play baseball professionally. He was able to hook on as an outfielder in the semi-pro Northern League in 1939 and 1940, where I later pitched for Montpelier during my college days at Michigan State. Jim earned his living in those years as a physical education teacher and coach at St. Regis High School in upstate New York. There he met his future bride, a young history teacher named Mary Burlingame. (My wife is also named Mary, and when I met her she was an eighth-grade history teacher in my hometown, Springfield, Illinois.)

While playing for Massena in 1940 Jim convinced his manager George Miner to give him a shot at pitching. He did quite well and the following spring was signed by the Syracuse Chiefs in the International League. He was already 24 years old.

The Chiefs sent him to Springfield of the Eastern League to pitch under the tutelage of the famous old shortstop, Rabbit Maranville. There he had a rough first year in professional baseball, winning 4 and losing 19. While sharing mound duties with roommate and future great Early

Wynn, Jim pitched in hard luck all year. He lost his first start on April 25 to Hartford 7–6, the first of 13 one-run losses he would endure. Five of those losses were by 1–0 scores. His ERA was an unimpressive 4.55, however, and he allowed 197 hits in 170 innings.

The following year, 1942, Syracuse kept Jim but barely allowed him to pitch. He got into only five games all year, but his one victory, late in the year over Newark, carried the Chiefs into the International League championship playoffs. In 1943, Jim pitched regularly for the Chiefs but without particular distinction, finishing with an 8–12 won-loss record. His ERA was a solid 3.42 and he allowed only 144 hits in 166 innings of work.

Nonetheless, Jim was discouraged about his future in baseball and over the winter of 1944 was prepared to quit and teach and coach high school sports full-time. Syracuse general manager Leo Miller changed Jim's mind with a raise in salary and an indication that the Cincinnati Reds, with whom the Chiefs had a working agreement, had shown an interest in him. As a result, Jim decided to retire from teaching so that he could give baseball his full-time attention.

With the benefit of a full spring training for the first time in 1944, Jim pitched well for Syracuse, winning 8 out of 14 decisions with a 3.21 ERA. With the wartime shortage of pitchers, the Reds did indeed purchase him in mid-season. Pitching his first game against the Cubs, he allowed three straight singles on fastballs. Future Whiz Kid teammate Bill "Swish" Nicholson, then the leading slugger in the league, was next. Jim struck Bill out on four changeups, beginning a pitching pattern that would ultimately lead to great success. At age 27, Jim went on to post an excellent rookie season with a 6–4 record and sparkling 2.79 ERA in 20 games and 113 innings.

He lost the 1945 season to the Navy but reported to the Reds' 1946 spring training camp in Tampa with high hopes. But the Reds had a strong staff coming back from the war with Johnny Vander Meer, Ewell Blackwell, Joe Beggs, and Bucky Walters, and they traded Jim with cash on opening day to the Boston Braves for outfielder Max West. Jim's stay with the Braves was brief. He pitched ineffectively in 10 games before being shipped back to the International League, this time with the Toronto Maple Leafs, to make room for a rookie southpaw named Warren Spahn.

Jim's departure from the Braves was hastened by some bad advice from one of his Reds' teammates, who told him to ask for more money when he reported to his new team. At the time the Mexican League was attempting to lure major league players south of the border with large contracts (sometimes called "the great Mexican hayride") and some players were using that as leverage to extract more money from their clubs. Jim immediately approached Braves manager Billy Southworth and general manager John Quinn about an increase, making him all the more expendable when he failed to pitch well.

With Toronto for the balance of 1946, Jim could win only 4 games while losing 9. His career seemed in a tailspin and he seriously considered going back to teaching and coaching, especially when Toronto offered him a sizable pay cut.

During this period Jim became friends with an undertaker named Andy Skinner, who was a neighbor in his off-season home of Worcester, New York. This unlikely friendship was to be one of two important turning points in Jim's career.

> **SKINNER:** "Jim's wife Mary was brought up right across the street from me in Worcester. Jim and I just hollered to each other across the street one day and that is how we met. Nobody introduced us, we introduced ourselves."

Jim was playing semi-pro basketball in Utica and Skinner often rode with him to the games. They naturally talked baseball and pitching and before spring training Jim began throwing to Andy, working on his slider and a palm ball, a new pitch he had picked up from Ted Kleinhans, an old southpaw. Although Skinner had not played baseball since high school, he had a very analytical mind that loved to find solutions to problems.

> **SKINNER:** "I had always bowled a lot and I was a pretty good bowler. If you watch a bowling ball you can see how it spins, whether it curves or backs up or whatever it does. Well, I got to thinking about it. If you turn your hand upside down you make a baseball do the same thing.
>
> "I would catch him before spring training down in the high school gym and try to figure out why the spins on a baseball would make it do different things."

Skinner scrutinized Konstanty's slider and palm ball, both of which were inconsistent. He suggested different grips and spins, and as a result Jim became more consistent with his breaking pitches. He decided to resume his career with Toronto. He pitched there for the entire 1947 season, going 13–13 with a solid 3.47 ERA in 197 innings of work.

SKINNER: "We had gotten to be very good friends so I went up to Toronto a couple of times during the summer to watch him pitch and got more involved with his pitching. One night they even gave me a Toronto suit. I put it on and took batting practice. I couldn't hit the ball to go to heck."

LOU POSSEHL: "I never saw the undertaker when I was pitching at Toronto with Jim, but I heard Jim talk about him. After he would have a bad outing he would say, 'I've got to see the undertaker' or 'I've got to call the undertaker tonight.' I thought he was always joking until I read about it in the newspaper."

Skinner became Jim's private pitching coach while he was in Toronto. Whenever Jim got in a slump, he called Andy. In fact, Jim always claimed that Skinner played an important part in our pennant in 1950. In early July Jim, who was nearly unhittable early in the year, began having trouble getting batters out. His strikeouts were down, and then on the Fourth of July he blew a game to the Braves. The Phillies had struggled back from a 7–0 deficit to lead 9–8. Jim pitched scoreless seventh and eighth innings but gave up a grand slam home run in the ninth to Sid Gordon to lose 12–9.

Jim decided he had lost the bite on his slider and called Skinner in Worcester. The next day Andy showed up before the game at Shibe Park in street clothes. In the bullpen Skinner took off his coat and rolled up his sleeves and began to catch Jim. According to Jim, Skinner noticed his release point was wrong, among other things.

The session must have worked. Two days later Jim relieved me in the eighth inning of a 1–1 game with the Dodgers in Ebbets Field, after I was taken out for pinch hitter Dick Whitman in the seventh. Konstanty got the Dodgers out on seven pitches in the eighth and four pitches in the ninth in a game we won 4–1, thanks to Bill Nicholson's three-run homer in the top of the ninth.

SKINNER: "Jim would just call me whenever he wanted some help. So I would go meet him in Ebbets Field or the Polo Grounds or Shibe Park, wherever the Phillies were playing. One day I went to New York to the Polo Grounds for a game. Somebody had died so we took the hearse so we could pick up the body afterwards. After the ballgame, I told Jim I'd give him a ride back to his hotel. Roberts, Simmons, and Meyers came along with him. There wasn't room so they had to ride in the back end where the caskets ride. So the three of them got in the back end and we pulled up in front of the Commodore Hotel and the three of them got out of the back end. Everybody on the street pretty near died right there.

"Sawyer asked me to go to spring training with the Phillies after the World Series. Had my own uniform. Of course, the catchers hated me down there. They didn't like anybody like me sticking their nose in baseball. It caused a little disturbance."

SEMINICK: "Jim had a lot of confidence in Andy Skinner. One time I was warming Jim up on the sidelines and Jim kept asking, 'How was that one, Andy?' I would answer him, but it turns out he was talking to Andy Skinner, who was standing behind me. But I wasn't upset about it or anything. We just laughed about it."

POSSEHL: "After Jim had those great years in the big leagues I saw him and said. 'Where does your undertaker live? I'd like to go talk to him.' Course my arm was shot by then."

Of course, Konstanty's second big break was pitching under Eddie Sawyer at Toronto at the start of the 1948 season. Eddie had a knack for recognizing how players could best contribute to a winning ballclub. His shift of Konstanty to relief and Ashburn to the outfield are two leading examples.

POSSEHL: "You could look at Konstanty from the bench when we were with Toronto in '48 and figure they would hit him all over the lot. He didn't have a great year. He did have a good year. I think he was 10 and 10 [with a 4.06 ERA]. I could probably throw 90-plus. Then Eddie would bring in Konstanty, who had the same arm motion as me and the same arm speed as me. But his ball got up there with about half the speed as mine, so the hitters were way off. His palm ball, with good arm speed, would just die when it got to the plate.

"Eddie saw that and brought him up even though he didn't have that great a year. And Jim was over 30 when Eddie brought him up. But Eddie saw something in him and you know the results."

Our sixth-place finish with 66 wins and 88 losses in 1948 certainly did not suggest that we were about to become pennant contenders. We ended up only a game and a half ahead of Cincinnati and two games in front of the cellar-dwelling Cubs.

Nonetheless, more of the pieces were falling into place. Ashburn had a tremendous rookie year, batting .333 and leading the league in stolen bases with 32, even though he missed the last month of the season. Del Ennis, who had suffered through much of 1947 with a back wrenched sliding into base, got back on track with 30 homers (the most for a Phillie since 1932), 95 RBIs and a rock-solid .290 batting average. Granny Hamner finally cracked the starting infield, ousting all-star Emil Verban, and hit .260, driving in seven runs in one game against the Cardinals. Willie Jones was again called up late in the season and played exceptionally well, batting .333 in 60 at bats. Jones would be primed to take over third base in 1949. Dick Sisler contributed at first base with 11 home runs and a .274 average, but Andy Seminick tailed off to .225. Johnny Blatnick and Putsy Caballero played their only seasons as regulars, and defending batting champ Harry Walker, although losing his starting position to Ashburn, still hit .292 in 112 games. Six-time All-Star shortstop Eddie Miller, acquired before the season in a trade from Cincinnati for outfielder Johnny Wyrostek, put in his last season as a regular, batting .246 with 14 round-trippers.

Our pitching was less than stellar, with a 4.08 team ERA. Dutch Leonard was our staff ace with a sparkling 2.51 ERA and only a 12–17 record to show for it. Schoolboy Rowe won 10 and lost 10 while Walt Dubiel went 8–10. Sam Nahem from Brooklyn appeared in 28 games with a 3–3 record but a 7.02 ERA. Sam was a very different kind of ballplayer, having graduated from Brooklyn College and St. John's University School of Law.

> **NAHEM:** "I had a tryout with the Brooklyn Dodgers during college. Casey Stengel was the manager and asked me to throw batting practice. Van Lingo Mungo, the pitcher, was hitting against me and I hit him in the butt. At the end of my tryout, Casey Stengel said, 'We're going to sign you up. If you can hurt that big son of a bitch, you must have something on the ball.'"

Sam started one game for the Dodgers in 1938, going the distance to beat the Phillies 6–3.

> **NAHEM:** "The Phillies had three runs in, bases loaded and nobody out in the first inning. I looked over to the bullpen and nobody was warming up. I thought, 'My God, I could be here

the rest of my life.' Luckily the next batter lined into a double play and I got the next hitter to get out of the inning. I was throwing as hard as I could and not getting anybody out so I decided to ease up a little. The ball started moving a little and I think I only allowed two hits the rest of the game."

Sam then pitched in the minor leagues while going to law school in the winter. In 1941 he made the St. Louis Cardinals, compiling a 5–2 record with an impressive 2.98 ERA. He pitched for the Phillies in 1942 after the club purchased him in the off-season. After three years in the military, Sam decided his pro baseball days were behind him. But he had good success pitching semi-pro ball after the war and the Phillies invited him to spring training in 1948.

Well-educated and a left-wing political activist, Sam sometimes had trouble relating to other ballplayers.

> **NAHEM:** "Andy Seminick really put me in my place once. He said to me, 'Sam, we all know that you went to college and that you're a lawyer from New York. For heaven sakes, Sam, I come from a coal mining family.' Then I realized that I had a condescending attitude toward them. It was arrogant of me. That wasn't right because everybody is interesting in their own way and I hadn't been pursuing that. So I was well chastised."

Although Sam had pitched in the big leagues before, he never seemed comfortable on the pitching mound. Shortly after I joined the club and had pitched a couple of games, Sam came up to me and said, "Kid, you're really scared out there, aren't you?"

I said, "No, I'm, not."

He said, "That is what really pisses me off. I'm scared stiff out there."

One time Eddie brought Sam in to pitch relief against the Cardinals and he had to face Red Schoendienst, Enos Slaughter, and Stan Musial. He retired Schoendienst and then called Dick Sisler over from first base. We all saw Dick laughing while he trotted back to first. After the inning was over Dick said that Sam had told him, "I got the first guy, you want to try these next two?"

Sam's comeback ended late in 1948 when the Phillies released him.

> **NAHEM:** "I didn't do well in my abortive comeback. My fastball was hard enough but it was straight and my slider, which had

been my money pitch was just about gone. I often wish that God had given me movement on my fastball, but He didn't. One time I was throwing with all my might and I was really being battered. I asked my catcher Andy Seminick, 'Don't I have anything on the ball?'

"Andy said, 'Yes, the balls that reach me have plenty on them.' So my conclusion was that my pitches were breaking a little late."

I finished my rookie year with 7 wins, 9 losses, and a 3.18 ERA, while Curt Simmons, hampered by control problems, won 7 while losing 13 in his first full year. Blix Donnelly started 19 games and pitched pretty well, although he had only a 5–7 record to show for it. Kenny Heintzelman struggled to a 6–11 record and a 4.29 ERA, with small hint of his fine 1949 season to come.

Over the winter Eddie would begin to fill in the missing pieces with trades and would begin to put his imprint on the club. By the end of the 1949 season, little more than a year after Sawyer took over, we would be bona fide contenders.

Chapter 8
NEAR TRAGEDY

Eddie Sawyer moved quickly after the season, trading Harry Walker to the Cubs for veteran slugger Bill "Swish" Nicholson, my boyhood favorite, just before the World Series. With the emergence of Richie Ashburn, Harry had become the odd man out. Like Richie, Harry was mostly a line drive singles hitter while Bill at 34 was still very much a long ball threat. He had hit 45 home runs the previous two years for the Cubs.

> **SAWYER:** "We just couldn't have Ashburn and Walker in the same outfield and Nick was a good outfielder with some pop still left in his bat, so we made the deal."

Nick was born and bred in Chestertown, on the Eastern Shore of Maryland. In high school he made all-state in football and played basketball and competed in track. He attended Washington College in his hometown and ran track his first two years. The school did not begin a baseball program until Bill's junior year, so he played for a town team until then.

Bill graduated from Washington with a math degree in 1936 and was signed by the Philadelphia Athletics. They sent him to Oklahoma City in the Texas League where he struggled, hitting only .167 in 48 at bats with no homers. The A's still called him up at the end of the 1936 season and he promptly went 0 for 12.

After that inauspicious beginning, Bill spent the next three years playing for Portsmouth, Williamsport, and Chattanooga in the minor leagues. At each stop he hit over .300 and hit 20 or more home runs. Connie Mack never gave him another shot, however, and the Chicago Cubs purchased him outright in midseason 1939 for the hefty sum of $35,000. At the time he was hitting .334 with 23 homers and 85 RBIs in only 105 games at Chattanooga.

In one of his first games with the Cubs he hit a home run to beat the Cincinnati Reds 1–0. I listened to that game on the radio in Springfield and from then on he was my boy.

For the balance of 1939, with me listening to virtually every game, Bill batted a solid .295 for the Cubs in 55 games. The following year he firmly established himself as a big league slugger, with 25 round-trippers, 98 RBIs and a .297 batting average. That began a stretch in which Bill was the preeminent slugger in the National League. From 1940 through 1944, with me following his every move, he averaged 27 home runs a season while making the All-Star team four times. (Bill's own boyhood hero was another slugger from Maryland's Eastern Shore, Hall-of-Famer Jimmie Foxx. Just as Nick became my teammate, he also got to play with his idol when Foxx joined the Cubs in 1943 and 1944.)

Nick was able to play through the war years because his colorblindness made him 4-F. He led the league in both homers and RBIs in 1943 with 20 and 128, respectively, and again in 1944 with 33 and 122. In 1944 Bill hit four consecutive home runs (three in one game) in a doubleheader against the Giants at the Polo Grounds. For the day he clouted five homers and a single in seven at bats.

Nick tailed off somewhat in 1945, but his Cubs won the pennant before losing to the Tigers in seven games in the World Series. Although he hit only .219 in the Series, he drove in eight runs in the seven games.

Bill was usually Nick to his teammates, though he was known to the fans as "Swish." Nick had the habit of taking some healthy practice swings each time he came to the plate before stepping into the batter's box. In Brooklyn, the fans began yelling "swish" after each cut. It soon caught on all over the league; everywhere Nick went the fans would holler "swish" when he took a cut.

Nick's lusty swings, coupled with his inherent strength, produced some unusual results from time to time. On one occasion he hit a pop up so high in front of home plate that he ended up with a triple when the infielders lost it and it bounced off the catcher's shinguard. Another time with the Cubs, Nick nailed a low line drive against Carl Hubbell that the second baseman almost caught. The ball landed in the right-center field bleachers at the Polo Grounds, about 440 feet from home plate.

During the war years Nick earned such respect as a slugger that the Giants, leading 9–6, actually walked him intentionally with the bases loaded.

It was a great thrill for me when Nick became my teammate before the 1949 season. And I was not disappointed when I got to know him personally. He quickly earned the respect of the entire organization, for Nick was the consummate professional ballplayer, willing to give advice if asked but mainly leading by example. In 1949 Nick was our regular right fielder much of the year, although a shoulder injury limited him to 98 games and curtailed his effectiveness. He served mainly as a pinch hitter during our pennant year, winning two games with dramatic home runs, until diabetes forced him into the hospital late in the year. But Nick had played on a pennant winner and knew what it took to win. His mere presence was a steadying influence on our young team in 1950.

STEVE RIDZIK: "When I finally made the ballclub in 1950, I was standing in the outfield by myself one day during batting practice and here come Nick and Eddie Waitkus to stand with me. Nick had that big chew in his mouth and he said, 'Hey, these guys all put their pants on like you do. Don't be afraid, you're a major leaguer now. If they give you any problems, knock them on their butt. I'll be the first guy there to help you if you're in trouble.'"

SEMINICK: "Being with Nick was a real pleasure. He had a lot of class. He always had a smile on his face and a big chaw of tobacco. He was a tough man at the plate."

PUTSY CABALLERO: "We all respected Bill Nicholson. He had been through what we hoped to go through. He was on the quiet side but when he said something we listened. He knew the pitchers in the league and would tell us what to expect in certain situations. He was a man's man."

DICK WHITMAN: "Bill Nicholson and I sat on the bench together a lot in 1950. If we were one run behind, Nick would pinch hit because he could hit the ball out of the park. If we were two runs down then I would pinch hit first, hoping to get on base and then Nick would hit the ball out of the park.

"One time on the bench I asked Nick why he hit a certain pitcher so well. Nick said, 'Well, he always used to pitch me inside. So every once in a while I had to double off the wall with my forearm. That would get him to throw the ball out over the plate.' I thought he could hit the wall with his forearm too, because it was like a tree trunk.

"Bill had to take insulin even back then. He would be walking down the street and would go, 'Oh.' Then he would stop, reach into his pocket, pull out a needle, give himself a shot right through his pants and keep on walking."

Several years ago Eddie Sawyer, Curt Simmons, Maje McDonald, and I traveled to Chestertown, where Nick lived until he passed away. The community honored Bill by unveiling his statue in the town square and we were all invited to join in the festivities. It was a particularly nostalgic day for me. I had gone from a kid listening to Nick play baseball on the radio to playing first against him and then with him to seeing his town dedicate a statue of him.

One week after the Walker-for-Nicholson trade, Sawyer acquired another Cub, 25-year-old Russ Meyer, to shore up our starting pitching. The purchase of Meyer was actually the second part of the deal that had sent veteran infielder Emil Verban to the Cubs the previous August. Russ had compiled a 10–10 record with a respectable 3.65 ERA for the cellar-dwelling Cubs in 1948. The Cubs likely were willing to part with him because of his legendary temper, which often erupted while he was on the mound, leading the press to refer to him as "The Mad Monk" and "Russ the Red."

It sometimes seemed that Monk was simply in the wrong place at the wrong time. While with the Cubs, he broke his right ankle in 1947 in a collision with the Phillies' Jack Albright at first base and his left ankle late in 1948 sliding into third after slugging a triple. On another occasion, he said something to offend a pretty young blond woman in a Chicago bar and she responded by biting Russ on the nose so hard that it left a scar.

Once, after joining us, Monk was approached by a guy selling diamonds on a New York City street.

MEYER: "I had met some people for dinner at Toots Shor's on West 51st Street. Traffic was terrible and I couldn't get a cab and couldn't get a cab. Their car was about five blocks away in a parking garage and so I decided to walk back to the hotel since it was only about nine blocks away. So it's about 9:30 or 10:00 and I'm taking my time walking back to the hotel. I walked by a men's store that was closed and I hear this guy in the entryway say, 'Hey buddy, come here.' He was dressed halfway decent. He said, 'Hey, you want a good deal?'

"I said, 'What the hell are you talking about?'

"He said, 'I got a hot diamond here.' Then he shows it to me and its beautiful, about a two-carat job.

"I said, 'Where the hell did you get it?'

"He said, 'Never mind where I got it. Let's just say its hot.'

"I said, 'Well, what do you want for it?'

"He said, 'It's worth about fifteen hundred bucks but I'll take a hundred for it.'

"I said, 'A hundred bucks! You gotta be kidding me. If I had a hundred bucks, I wouldn't be talking to you. How about 50?'

"He said, 'Okay, I'll sell it for 50.' So I peel off 50 bucks thinking I've just made the steal of the century.

"So I walk into the lobby of the hotel and four or five of the guys are sitting in there, including Bill Nicholson, Eddie Waitkus, and Maje. So I told them, 'Boy, you wouldn't believe the deal I just made.'

"Nick said, 'What? What did you do?'

"I said, 'I just bought a hot diamond for fifty bucks.'

"Nick said, 'Let me see that diamond. You won't mind if I scratch it on the floor.' So he took it and put it on the floor and ground it with his heel. The damn thing immediately disintegrated. It was friggin glass and now it's just powder on the floor. So I am raging mad. Fifty bucks down the tube.

"Our next trip into New York I'm walking down 42nd Street towards Broadway and I'm about to go into a steak-and-egg joint to get breakfast at about 11:00 in the morning. We were playing that night. I'm alone and I stop to buy a couple of newspapers at a little newsstand when I see this guy who sold me the damn ring walking towards me. I mean this is New York City and there are millions of people there but I happened to pick this guy out of a crowded sidewalk. Well, I grab this sonuvabitch in front of all these people and I'm screaming at him, really letting him have it.

"And he said, 'What's the matter with you, what's the matter?' and he's yelling, 'Help, help, help!'

"Anyway a cop came by and I said, 'This guy sold me a ring for 50 bucks that he said was a hot diamond that turned out to be glass.'

"The cop said, 'This guy did that?'

"I said, 'He sure did.'

"The cop said, 'Are you going to give this man his $50 back?'

"The guy said, 'Yeah, yeah, I'll give him his $50 back.'

"The cop said, 'I think you ought to give him 25 more for all his trouble and embarrassment.'

"The guy said, 'Okay,' and he gave me an extra $25 and the cop let him go.

"So I made 25 bucks on the deal. Can you imagine the odds on that happening? When I went back to the hotel Nick was the first guy I saw. When I told him what had happened, he said, 'You've got to be kidding me. You have got to be the luckiest bastard alive.'

"To top everything off, I was pitching that night against the Giants in the Polo Grounds and I pitched a helluva game and we won 2–1 or 3–2."

McDONNELL: "I roomed with Russ for four years after he joined the Phillies. I roomed with his bags most of the time when he was still single. But the night before he was going to pitch he was always in. Russ had a very good heart. He was always bringing something to me in the room, a sandwich or a beer, no matter what time he came in.

"Russ was a good-looking guy and probably the best-dressed ballplayer in the National League. He won the award once or twice and then lived up to it. When we would go on a 16-day road trip he would have 15 suits, 7 sport coats, 7 pairs of slacks, 15 pairs of shoes. I'd say, 'Monk, do you mind if I put my two suits in the closet?'

"Of course, Monk had a terrible temper on the field. He would just blow up and effectively take himself out of ballgames. But he wasn't that way off the field. He was a generous, kind, good-hearted guy."

Russ really did have trouble controlling his temper on the field, in part because he was such a tremendous competitor. But Russ's temper brought him a good deal of grief. He injured himself kicking the pitching rubber in anger, once just missed the clubhouse attendant when firing a bar of soap across the room, and broke a toe kicking a steel locker.

MEYER: "One night in Philly I got bounced around early and got knocked out about the third inning. It was a wet, drizzly night and I came in the clubhouse and got undressed and tore the clubhouse up a little. Finally I decided I might as well take a shower. I can't explain this but I started into the shower holding one of my baseball shoes. I said to myself, 'What the hell is this,' and I turned and threw it at the ceiling. And would you believe it, it was the best fastball I threw all night. It stuck in the damn locker room ceiling. My baseball shoe stuck in the ceiling.

"I wanted to get it down but, hell I couldn't get it down. Finally they got it down after the game but the mud from my baseball spikes was up there in the clubhouse ceiling for I don't know how long."

Monk was socked with suspensions at least three times for run-ins with umpires. He got 10 days when he grabbed Frank Dascoli and popped the buttons off the ump's jacket while protesting Jackie Robinson's steal of home. Early in 1950 Monk disputed a call at first base in which umpire Al Barlick called the Braves' Earl Torgeson safe on a swinging bunt. Monk lost it and charged Barlick, bumping him a couple of times. Teammates separated them but Monk returned for more, finally throwing the ball down in disgust. Unfortunately, it hit Barlick in the shin, drawing a seven-day suspension and a $200 fine, a substantial amount in those days.

MEYER: "I threw the ball on the damn ground and it bounced up and hit Barlick in the leg and he threw me out of the damn game. Barlick said, 'You threw the ball at me.'

"I said, 'I didn't throw the friggin' ball at you. I threw the ball on the ground in disgust at your call, but I didn't throw the ball at

155

you. You don't think I'm that damn goofy, do you?' And I was good friends with Al. He's from Springfield, Robbie's hometown, close to Peru, my hometown.

"But Al said, 'Well, I made the call now and you're out of here.'

"I said, 'That's just great. Here I am in a tight ballgame and you're throwing me out of the damn ballgame.'

" 'Well,' he said, 'I got a little bit excited.'

"I said, 'Excited my ass.'

"So Al told me he would make it easy on his report to the league office. So I got suspended for a week and fined 200 bucks. The next time I saw Al I said, 'You gonna pay me the 200 bucks?' I said, 'It must have been a nice report you wrote.' "

Monk's most famous confrontation with an umpire occurred on a Sunday afternoon in 1953 in Philadelphia, soon after we had traded him to the Dodgers.

MEYER: "The first game I pitched for the Dodgers against the Phillies I pitch against Robbie in Connie Mack Stadium [formerly Shibe Park]. It was the Game of the Week on national television. Augie Donatelli was back of the plate. We're in a helluva game, zip-zip going into the seventh inning. I got the bases loaded, two men out, and Richie's up. I went 3–2 and I threw him a helluva breaking ball and he just bowed to it. Donatelli calls it ball four. Forces in the go-ahead run.

"Well, I went bananas. I came charging off the mound. Campy [catcher Roy Campanella], who never said anything unless he knew he was right, even turned around and was jumping up and down. I'm telling Donatelli, 'You homer, you sonuvabitch. Squeeze the shit out of me, that's right.'

"He said, 'What did you say?'

"I said, 'I called you a damn homer.'

"He said, 'You're out of here.'

"I said, 'That's great. For your damn mistake now throw somebody out of the damn game. Cover your ass.'

"So I go back to the mound. I ain't leaving. I ain't going. [Dodger manager Charlie] Dressen comes over and said, 'Hey, he threw you out of the game.'

"I said, 'I don't give a shit, I ain't going.'

"He said, 'You gotta go. Come on, you gotta go.'

"Somewhere I got ahold of the resin bag. How, to this day I can't tell you, I don't know. So I said, 'Oh, screw it,' and I start walking off the mound. As I did, I just flipped that resin bag up into the air. I'm walking. I'm walking fast now and of course the Philly fans, they're in seventh heaven now. They're loving this. So I'm walking and the resin bag is up in the air somewhere. After I took about five fast steps, that bag came down and hit me right in the middle of my damn cap on my head. White powder went everywhere. As pissed off as I am, even I had to laugh.

"I got into the damn dugout, starting down those concrete steps, and I had to give Donatelli one last shot. I knew I was going to get fined. I knew I was going to get suspended. I was going to get my money's worth. So I yelled, 'Nice going Augie, you sonuvabitch.' Then I said, 'Here. This is for you,' and I grabbed my crotch.

"Unbeknownst to me they got the cameras on me. The Game of the Week had a camera in the dugout on me. So all this went out over T.V. So I guess the switchboard in the office lit up like a Christmas tree, from what Maje told me. Mothers were calling, priests were calling. They wanted to bar me from baseball.

"For about 10 years or so after that they had the Meyer rule in baseball, no television cameras were allowed in dugouts."

Russ was right about the consequences of getting thrown out of the game. He was fined $100 and suspended for three days.

ASHBURN: "Russ was a good pitcher and a good competitor. I remember once batting against him with the bases loaded and I started fouling off pitches. Finally he yelled in and said, 'Try and foul this off,' and he hit me in the back, forcing in a run."

MEYER: "I had a big lead and it was late in the game, about the seventh or eighth inning. There were two outs and that little shit fouled off about seven or eight in a row so I drilled his ass and said, 'Here, foul that sonuvabitch off.' "

For all of his antics, Russ was a very good pitcher, possessing a good fastball, curve, and an excellent screwball. He would become the premier right-handed pitcher in the National League in 1949, winning 17 while losing only 8 with a 3.08 ERA in 213 innings.

Russ grew up in Peru, Illinois, and was a product of one of the best youth baseball programs in the country. He pitched Peru to the finals of the 1941 National Baseball Congress and attracted the attention of the Cubs, White Sox, and Yankees. He signed with the White Sox and spent 1942 at their Superior (Wisconsin) Blues farm club in the Class D Northern League, winning 7 and losing 8 in 184 innings of work.

Shortly thereafter Russ was drafted by the Army, where he experienced the first and most serious of his physical ailments. While stationed at Fort Leonard Wood, Missouri, Russ pitched a good deal for his camp team. In midsummer he started the third inning of an exhibition game against the St. Louis Browns, facing the Browns' Walt Judnich. After one pitch, he collapsed on the mound, the victim of a ruptured appendix. Peritonitis set in and caused a heart murmur. Russ spent 13 weeks in the hospital, much of it under an oxygen tent, and lost 35 pounds. He received a medical discharge because of the damage to his heart and was told by Army physicians not to try to play baseball for at least two years.

But after gaining some of his weight back over the winter Russ was eager to try professional baseball again. He was declared a free agent because of the demise of the Northern League and signed with his favorite team from his boyhood, the Chicago Cubs. The Cubs sent Russ to Nashville in the Class AA Southern Association, where he learned the screwball from former Cub pitcher Hy Vandenberg. Monk pitched for Nashville for three years, steadily improving each year and earning late season call-ups to the Cubs in 1945 and 1946. He made the big league club as a reliever in 1947 and pitched well with a 3–2 record before a broken ankle ended his season prematurely.

Monk's strong 1948 season established him as a solid starting pitcher. He came within one out of a no-hitter against the Cardinals in Wrigley Field that year. Whitey Kurowski lashed a two-out single and Russ settled for a one-hitter. Although Russ came to us with little fanfare, he would become an important part of the success of the Whiz Kids.

Surprisingly, Eddie Sawyer made a third deal with the Cubs on December 14, 1948, acquiring pitcher Hank Borowy and first baseman Eddie Waitkus for veteran pitchers Dutch Leonard and Walt "Monk" Dubiel. One would not expect to help build a pennant contender by making three trades with the last-place team, but that is exactly what Eddie did in 1948.

Although Dick Sisler had played first base in 1948 with modest success, Eddie wanted to acquire a better defensive first baseman to allow Dick to compete for an outfield job, his more natural position.

SAWYER: "I went to talk to Mr. Wrigley about the deal and said, 'I am very interested in [Cub first baseman-outfielder Phil] Cavarretta,' and he said, 'Mr. Sawyer, so am I. He is going to be my next manager.'

"Since they planned to keep playing Cavarretta, they made Waitkus available and he filled out our infield well, with Hamner and Puddinhead coming along. I really hated to give up Dubiel because the scouts liked him and he was a pretty good pitcher who had pitched for the Yankees.

"Dutch Leonard was still a pretty good pitcher, too. In fact, I took him to the All-Star game in 1951 after we traded him. But none of our catchers could catch his knuckleball. But Chicago didn't have anybody to catch him either so I traded him to them. After we traded Leonard, Andy Seminick came in and said, 'Hey skip, I ought to kiss you.'"

Wrigley was true to his word; Cavarretta did manage the Cubs from 1951 through 1953. Dubiel had gone 13–13 in 1944 and 10–9 in 1945 for the Yankees, then slipping to the minor leagues before making the 1948 Phillies. He went on to indifferent success with the Cubs, posting losing records in 1949 and 1950 before bowing out of the big leagues in 1952.

In Hank Borowy, Eddie acquired a veteran pitcher who had some outstanding years pitching for the Yankees during the war years, going 15–4 as a rookie in 1942, followed by 14–9 and 17–12 records. In 1945 he was 10–5 for the Yanks when he was abruptly sold to the Cubs on July 27 for $97,000. Hank went on to pitch the Cubs to the pennant, compiling a sparkling 11–2 record with a league-leading 2.13 ERA.

Hank had tailed off in subsequent years due to recurring blister problems and a shoulder ailment. He would record a solid 12–12 record for us in 1949 in 28 starts. Although Hank would make our ballclub in 1950, he would appear in only three games before being sold to the Pirates in early June.

The acquisition of Waitkus was a key move; it helped solidify the infield and stabilized first base for us, long a troublesome position. The Phillies had fielded a different player at first for a dozen years prior to

The powerful 1947 Utica Blue Sox. Stan Lopata is in the second row, far left; Granny Hamner is sixth from the left, first row; Richie Ashburn is fourth from the left, first row; Eddie Sawyer is sixth from the left, first row; and Putsy Caballero is third from the right, first row. They won the Eastern League pennant by a wide margin. *(Courtesy of Eddie Sawyer)*

Eddie Sawyer flanked by three of his former Utica players, Putsy Caballero, Granny Hamner, and Richie Ashburn, shortly after Eddie was named manager of the Phillies in 1948. Putsy said they brought Eddie to the majors.
(Courtesy of Rich Westcott)

Dusty Cooke. "Reach back and get it, Robbie."

Benny Bengough. I can still hear that old catcher's glove popping.

Maje McDonnell, as good a friend as a guy could want. *(Courtesy of Ted Silary)*

Our off-season Phillies basketball team. Del Ennis and I are in the middle of the back row. Curt Simmons is on the far left and Maje McDonnell on the far right of the front row. We were even better when Paul Arizin joined us.
(Courtesy of Curt Simmons)

Eddie Sawyer talking to his Toronto pitching staff in 1948. Jocko Thompson
is in the second row, left, and Jim Konstanty is kneeling, second from right.
(Courtesy of Mary Konstanty)

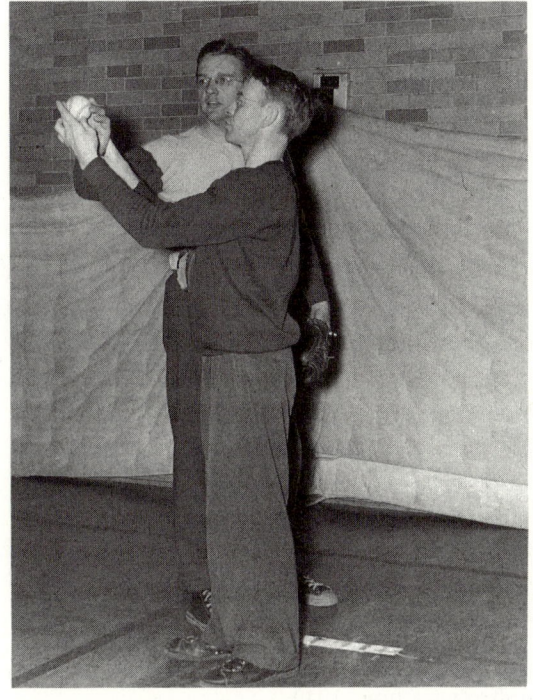

Jim Konstanty working with
his private pitching coach,
undertaker Andy Skinner.
I needed Andy's help later
on in my career.
(Courtesy of Andy Skinner)

Bill "Swish" Nicholson after joining the Phillies in 1949. My hero became my teammate.

Russ Meyer, the Mad Monk.

Bob Carpenter with *(left to right)* Eddie Waitkus, Dick Sisler, and Hank Borowy in spring training, 1949.

Bill Nicholson *(left)* with fellow outfielders Stan Hollmig and Jack Mayo.
The old and the new. *(Courtesy of Rich Westcott)*

Stan Lopata.
Lop became a fine catcher.
(Courtesy of Stan Lopata)

Andy Seminick *(left)* and Richie Ashburn
signing baseballs for kids from orphanages in 1949.
(Courtesy of Temple University Archives)

Schoolboy Rowe — a great athlete. *(Courtesy of Rich Westcott)*

Eddie's arrival, with the exception of 1941 and 1942 when Nick Etten held forth at the bag. Sawyer believed Eddie could end that revolving door. He had hit .295 and made the National League All-Star team with the Cubs in 1948. In addition, Eddie had blistered the ball in Shibe Park, batting .478 against us in 11 games.

A lean, left-handed six-footer, Eddie played first base with style and grace and indeed would be our regular first baseman for three full seasons and substantial parts of two others. He could pick 'em with the best of them, scooping low throws with seeming ease.

PAUL STUFFEL: "If it wasn't for Eddie Waitkus playing first base, our infielders would have had a lot more errors on balls they threw in the dirt. Waitkus was incredible. He never made a bad play."

McDONNELL: "Waitkus is the best fielding first baseman I've seen here. Very classy. He was beautiful on thrown balls. He had such grace."

At the plate, Eddie was a line drive hitter with an excellent eye. He would hit .284 as our leadoff man in 1950, contributing greatly to our dash to the pennant. Of course, 1949 would prove to be a tumultuous year for Eddie because of a bizarre incident that would rock all of sports and ensure his place in history.

Waitkus was from Cambridge, Massachusetts, where he grew up sneaking into Braves Field in Boston. The summer after his high school graduation he led a semi-pro team from Lisbon Falls, Maine, to the National Baseball Congress tournament in Wichita. There he hit .500 in nine games, attracting the attention of pro scouts. He signed with the Cubs when they offered a small bonus, turning down college scholarship offers from Holy Cross and Duke.

The Cubs sent Eddie to Moline, Illinois, in the Three-I League in 1939 and he performed well, hitting .326 in 122 games at first base. He advanced to Tulsa in the Texas League in 1940 and again had an outstanding year, batting .303 in 162 games. He blasted 39 doubles and 16 triples to lead the league.

Eddie actually made the Cubs after a good spring training in 1941. But he hit only .167 in 12 games and the Cubs shipped him back to Tulsa where he came in at .293. He had a banner 1942 with the Los Angeles Angels in the Pacific Coast League, with a fine .336 average, 40 doubles, 8 triples, and 9 home runs in 175 games.

Although Eddie appeared to be on his way, military service intervened, costing him the 1943, 1944, and 1945 seasons. Eddie served with the amphibious Army engineers, and unlike many of his baseball contemporaries in World War II, was unable to play any baseball in the service. He did not throw a baseball for 32 months while earning battle stars in the New Guinea, East Indies, Solomon Islands, and Philippines campaigns.

When Eddie arrived at the Cubs' spring training at Catalina Island in 1946, he was the longest of long shots to even make the team. Not only had he not played a lick of baseball for almost three years, but the Cubs had Phil Cavarretta entrenched at first base. Cavarretta had led the Cubs to the 1945 pennant, hitting .355 to win the batting title while earning the league's Most Valuable Player award. And, of course, 1946 was the year when all the war veterans returned to the majors, most after playing service ball.

But Eddie picked up where he left off in 1942 in the Pacific Coast League and made the team. Bill Nicholson started slowly at the plate, and in early May Cubs manager Charlie Grimm moved Cavarretta to Nick's spot in right field and inserted Eddie at first. Waitkus quickly established himself as one of the top fielding first basemen in the league. He hit .303 for the year, the only Cub regular over .300, and rivaled the Phillies' Del Ennis for Rookie of the Year honors.

Eddie continued to perform well for the next two seasons, hitting .292 in 1947 and .295 in 1948 with often spectacular play at first. Luckily for us he became available because the Cubs wanted to move the aging Cavarretta back to first and had some youngsters coming along such as Dee Fondy and Chuck Conners, later of *Rifleman* television fame.

Waitkus, like Nicholson, was a real professional and an intense competitor, as illustrated by an incident early during his rookie year. The Cubs were hosting the Dodgers and their fireballing right-hander Kirby Higbe. Eddie was at bat with two men on when manager Leo Durocher visited the mound and told Higbe, "Wake this busher up."

Higbe proceeded to blow a fastball in high and tight, sending Eddie sprawling in the dirt. Kirby fired the next pitch on the outside corner, a classic pitching pattern to a batter who has just been knocked down and should be a little gun shy. But Waitkus clubbed a line drive triple into the gap, clearing the bases.

After the Dodgers got the Cubs out, Durocher strolled to the first base coaching box, where a warm-up throw "eluded" Eddie at first and almost nailed Leo. Eddie supposedly gave Durocher a tongue-in-cheek apology.

Waitkus doubled to right center his next at bat, after which Durocher asked, "Who is that busher." On being informed, Leo reportedly said, "After this, let him sleep."

Eddie was one of the few bachelors on the Phillies and was, along with Monk Meyer, one of the sharpest dressers on the team. He was often seen in the company of beautiful young women and his attraction by the opposite sex would become all too telling later in the summer.

RIDZIK: "Older guys never hung around younger players in those days and I was only 18 or 19 years old. But many a night in spring training I would be standing out in front of the hotel and Bill Nicholson and Eddie would come by and see me and call me over. 'Hey, Steve, come here. You eat yet?'

"'No.'

"'Come with us.' So we would get in a cab and go over to the Beachcomber Restaurant on the beach side. I'd have a beer with them, one beer, and we would eat dinner. They wouldn't let me pay for anything. They always picked up the tab. We would finish eating and they would put me in a cab and say, 'You go on home. You go back to the hotel now, we're going out.'"

BUBBA CHURCH: "Eddie Waitkus had a big influence on me. He had a great demeanor. He was the guy who always called time and came over to the mound to settle things down. He would say, 'Hey, sweets, lets slow that engine down just a bit. Let's get it back together.'"

Eddie was always upbeat in the clubhouse, although not particularly loud or talkative. His favorite expressions were "how goes the battle" and "keep the faith." On seeing me, he would say, "How goes the battle, Robbie?" At the time I was a young guy with a good fastball, not worried about anything, and I used to think to myself, "Just what the hell is the battle, Eddie?" But as I grew older I began to understand what he was talking about.

Eddie Sawyer quickly put his imprint on the first spring training in which he was in charge, emphasizing running, throwing, and hitting rather than calisthenics and team meetings, often called skull sessions. As the spring wore on, Willie Jones asserted himself at third base and Waitkus took over at first as expected. The starting outfield was set with Nicholson, Ennis, and Ashburn.

Two rookie outfielders, Stan Hollmig and Jack Mayo, also showed promise. Stan, from Hondo, Texas, was the son of a former minor league pitcher who named his son after his favorite player, Stanley "Bucky" Harris, the "Boy Wonder" manager of the Senators in the 1920s (and manager of the Phillies for part of 1943). Hollmig had starred in football, basketball, and baseball at Texas A&M and had impressed scouts with 400-plus-foot home runs. The Phils outbid a number of major league teams to sign him to a $25,000 bonus and sent him to Wilmington in 1948, where he hit .303 with 11 home runs in 84 games.

Jack Mayo was a fleet-footed, left-handed hitting outfielder whom the Phillies had signed out of the University of Notre Dame. Jack had played against me in the Vermont collegiate summer league in 1947. Originally from Illinois, he had never played baseball before college. Jack was an excellent defensive player who many thought was faster than Ashburn. He had played at Utica in 1948, earning a late season call-up to the Phils, where, after an impressive big league debut, he batted .229 in 35 at bats.

With Hollmig and Mayo, 28-year-old Johnny Blatnick was the odd man out in the outfield. Because of the bonus rule, the Phillies had to keep Hollmig, a right-handed hitter, on the big league roster or risk losing him to another organization. Despite hitting almost .400 for the spring, Blatnick, also a right-handed batter, was farmed out to Toronto.

Eddie Sawyer surprised the sportswriters covering the team when, late in spring camp, he announced that the Phillies' regular catcher for 1949 would be Stan Lopata. Andy Seminick had slumped to .225 the previous year and had led the league's catchers with 22 errors (he also led in putouts and assists). Some thought that his difficulties handling Dutch Leonard's baffling knuckleball had affected his overall play.

Eddie brought six catchers to spring training and, although Stan was one of them, he was thought to be a year or two away from the majors when camp opened. But working with Cy Perkins, Stan improved dramatically behind the plate and became our opening-day catcher.

Stan grew up in a Polish section of Detroit and played on the same American Legion team as future Whiz Kid teammate Bob Miller. Stan was always a catcher and was first noticed by Tiger scout Wish Egan in 1941. (The Detroit sandlots of that era produced an inordinate number of big league catchers, including, in addition to Stan, Hobie Landrith, Harry Chiti, and Joe Ginsburg.)

> **LOPATA:** "He [Egan] asked me to come down and catch batting practice for the Tigers during the summer vacation time when school was out. They paid me my bus fare and it was really quite a thrill. I would catch batting practice for guys like Charlie

Gehringer, Hank Greenberg, Billy Rogell, and Mickey Cochrane, who was my hero as a catcher. They had a good ballclub with pitchers like Schoolboy Rowe and Eldon Auker. I would catch for them almost every day of the week when they were home and then I would take the bus home when the game started."

The Tigers tried to sign Stan when he graduated from high school in 1943 but, on the advice of his American Legion coach, he turned down their offer of a $500 bonus and assignment to Pulaski, Wisconsin. He went into the service in December of that year and served with the 14th Armored Division in the European Theatre, earning a Bronze Star and a Purple Heart.

LOPATA: "After I got out of the service I played about two or three games with a semi-pro team in the Detroit Federation when Eddie Krajnik of the Phillies [who also signed Ashburn] came along and signed me for $15,000, which was pretty good money in those days. I knew they didn't have too many catchers and I just wanted to make the major leagues, so I was happy to sign with the Phillies organization.

"I paid off my parents' mortgage with my bonus and bought them some furniture, including a refrigerator and television. My dad was from Poland and was never interested in baseball. He was a cake oven operator and was happy to have a job. Dad had worked all of his life and that is all he knew. He never thought that people could get paid this kind of money for playing baseball. But he started to get interested in baseball after I took care of the mortgage and bought furniture. He became very excited about my career."

The Phillies sent Stan to Terre Haute, Indiana, in the Three-I League, where he hit a solid .292 in 67 games and earned a promotion to the Phillies' top farm team at Utica. There in 1947 under Eddie Sawyer, Stan had a banner year, hitting a lusty .325 with 88 RBIs in 115 games and earning the league's Most Valuable Player award. In 1948 he moved with Eddie to Toronto in the International League, where he batted .279 with 15 home runs and earned a late season call-up to the Phillies.

Overall we had a very successful spring training in 1949, winning 20 and losing only 9 games before losing our traditional preseason city series with the Athletics two games to one. Puddinhead and Stan emerged as regulars. Granny Hamner had really come on and was regarded as the top shortstop prospect in the league. He succeeded in nailing down the job and moving the veteran Eddie Miller to second base. With Waitkus at first our infield appeared set to go with our strong outfield. Dick Sisler had hit .400 in Florida and was counted on as a most capable reserve at first base and in the outfield.

Our pitching was considerably more unsettled. Curt Simmons was still struggling and Jim Konstanty had yet to assert himself. Ken Heintzelman, Meyer, Borowy, Simmons, and I were the starters, but none of us were coming off of particularly good years. We also hoped for contributions from Schoolboy Rowe, Blix Donnelly, Ken Trinkle, and Jocko Thompson.

My most memorable outing that spring occurred when I pitched against the Red Sox at old Recreation Field in Clearwater, where the right field fence, although fairly high, was only about 280 feet from home plate. The first time I faced Ted Williams I ran the count to 3–2. I then threw him a slow curve, a pitch I did not use much, and he took it for strike three. As Williams walked back to the bench, he glared at me, letting me know his displeasure at that last pitch.

On his next trip to the plate Williams hit a ball off me that not only cleared that short right field fence, but cleared the ground behind the fence and the street running outside the park before landing in the parking lot across the street. Ted could get even in a hurry.

In spite of our successful spring, we really did not view ourselves as pennant contenders. At this juncture my young teammates and I were simply glad to be playing in the big leagues. We let Eddie, the coaches, and the sportwriters worry about predictions of how high we might finish.

We began the season in fine fashion, beating the defending National League champion Braves in Boston 4–0 behind Kenny Heintzelman. Unfortunately, the following day, April 19, the worm quickly turned as the Braves swept a doubleheader from us, 4–3 and 11–2.

The first game was a particularly devastating loss. Going into the bottom of the ninth we led 3–0 against Warren Spahn. Curt Simmons had pitched brilliantly, shutting the Braves out on one hit. In the ninth Eddie Stanky and Alvin Dark singled and Curt walked Earl Torgeson, loading the bases. Eddie brought in Ken Trinkle to stem the tide, but disaster struck quickly. Ken walked Bob Elliot to force in a run and Jim Russell slashed a single to tie the score. A wild pitch got Elliot to third, and Tommy Holmes drove in the winning run by flying out to Richie in center. A certain victory suddenly ended in defeat and Curt came up empty after being almost unhittable.

After losing the nightcap, we lost another tough ballgame the next day, 6–5. Although Puddinhead tied a major league record with four doubles, the Braves scored two runs in the eighth to break a 4–4 tie. Willie's fourth double drove in Nick with a run in our ninth, but we left him stranded to lose the season opening series one game to three.

Our pitching, with the exception of Heintzelman, continued to disappoint, and by April 29 we had lost 8 of the first 11 games. I had lost to the Dodgers 8–6 and to Spahn and the Braves 2–0. At the start of a three-game series in Brooklyn, Eddie inserted Andy Seminick into the lineup at catcher. Stan had done a good job but at that point Andy was a much more seasoned backstop with the experience necessary to help get our pitching turned around.

We immediately swept the Dodgers in Ebbets Field with Andy clouting a key home run in the third game. In fact, we won six of seven with Andy catching and, although somewhat forgotten in spring training, he had won his job back. Lopata would see a lot of action in 1949 and 1950 but Andy would continue to be our regular catcher until he was traded to the Reds after the 1951 season. Stan would not become our regular catcher until 1955, although he would catch a lot of games for us in the early 1950s. In 1956 he would have one of the most productive seasons by a catcher in Phillies history, stroking 32 homers, driving in 95 runs, and scoring 96.

With improvement in our starting pitching, we hovered close to the .500 mark for the first two months of the season. Heinz continued to pitch superbly and I got untracked with four wins. In addition, Hank Borowy, Russ Meyer, and Curt pitched some good ballgames.

> **McDONNELL:** "As the season went on in '49, you could tell we were going to be a pretty good club with our youth and carefree attitude. I remember that we worked out one day in late May or early June on an off day. Cy Perkins, who was a beautiful baseball man and very sharp, said to me, 'Maje, these kids are going to win it next year.' He told me that in May of 1949."

On June 2 our offense flexed its muscle in a memorable game against Cincinnati in Shibe Park, shaking a team batting slump that had hampered us for two weeks. We trailed 3–2 going into our eighth inning against lefty Ken Raffensberger. By the time the Reds got us out we led 12–3 and had broken or tied nine major league records. During the inning we rocked three pitchers for 10 runs and 8 hits, including 5 home runs, tying the record for circuit clouts in an inning. Del Ennis, Willie Jones, and Schoolboy Rowe each homered, and Andy Seminick hit two in the inning, also tying a major league record. Andy had also homered in the second and so had three for the game. In that incredible eighth inning, Granny Hamner missed a home run by about a foot, doubling off the left field wall, and Puddinhead came within inches of another homer, tripling off of the top of the wall in right. So we were about 15 inches from seven home runs for the inning.

That win brought us into a fifth-place tie with the Reds, one game under .500. Andy hit another homer the next day to beat the Cubs 1–0 behind Heinz's shutout pitching. On June 8, I pitched my first big league shutout, blanking the Pirates 2–0 in Shibe Park, thanks to Stan Hollmig's second major league home run in the sixth inning against Ernie Bonham.

We broke into the first division the next day, only three games behind the league leading Dodgers, by beating the Pirates 4–3 in a thrilling 18-inning ballgame. Konstanty pitched nine shutout innings in relief of Russ Meyer. Murry Dickson had held us to only three hits in 10 innings of relief until the 18th. Then, with one out, Del singled to left. Andy followed with a ringing one-hop double off the left field wall, sending Del to third. Jack Mayo then took two strikes before flying to Wally Westlake in center field. Del tagged up and just slid under catcher Eddie Fitzgerald's tag to win the ballgame.

We split a four-game series at home with the Cardinals (I won my fifth straight and seventh of the year) before taking the train to Chicago to begin a 15-game western road trip. Russ Meyer beat the Cubs in the series opener 9–2 on June 14, spoiling Frankie Frisch's debut as the new Chicago manager.

That evening I went out to dinner with an old Army buddy of mine named Bob Silvers who lived in Chicago. The next morning, about 10, I got a phone call from him, asking me, "How's Waitkus?"

I said, "What do you mean, how's Waitkus?"

He said, "Eddie Waitkus was shot last night." And that was the first I had heard of it.

Eddie had come in from a dinner with Russ Meyer and his folks and found a note in his room that said:

> It is extremely important that I see you as soon as possible.
> We're not acquainted, but I have something of importance to
> speak to you about. I think it would be to your advantage to let

me explain it to you. As I am leaving the hotel the day after tomorrow, I'd appreciate it greatly if you could see me as soon as possible. My name is Ruth Ann Burns, Room 1279-A. I realize that this is a little out of the ordinary, but, as I said, it's rather important.

Eddie called her on the telephone and asked what she wanted. She told him that she did not want to discuss it over the phone and asked if he would come up to her room. Eddie's mistake was in agreeing to do so.

Eddie went up to her room, knocked on the door, and went in when she said, "Come in for a minute."

He asked her, "Just what do you want?" When she stepped aside, Eddie walked across the room to the window. He turned around to see her coming out of the closet with a .22 caliber rifle in her hands.

She said, "I have a little surprise for you. You're not going to bother me anymore," and shot Eddie once in the stomach.

As Eddie slumped down he asked, "Oh baby, what did you do that for?"

The girl, who turned out to be 19-year-old Ruth Steinhagen of Chicago, returned the rifle to the closet and called the hotel switchboard to say that she had just shot a man. That call probably saved Eddie from bleeding to death.

CABALLERO: "Eddie told us in the hospital, 'Putsy, you won't believe it. I remember falling down and her stepping over me and going to the phone.' She called the front desk. That is what saved his life."

MEYER: "My mom and dad and my fiancée had come up from Peru to see me because I pitched that day. I got them a suite at the Edgewater Beach Hotel where we stayed. After the game Eddie went to dinner with all of us and then we had a couple of drinks in the hotel."

McDONNELL: "About 1:30 or 2:00 in the morning this girl called our room and asked to speak to Russ Meyer. Russ was a little upset because she woke us up. He said, 'What do you want? What do you want?'

"She said, 'How's Eddie?'

"He said, 'I don't know how he is. Call and ask him.'

"She said, 'No Monk, he's been shot. It's just come over the news that Eddie Waitkus has been shot.'

"We jumped up and called some other rooms and in the next 15 minutes a bunch of us met down in the lobby with Eddie Sawyer and the coaches. He was close to death.

"Eddie told me later, 'Maje, I think I had a smile on my face when she shot me. I thought Bill Nicholson or someone was in that closet and the whole thing was a practical joke.'"

SEMINICK: "Eddie Miller and I were asleep when the phone rang about 2:30 in the morning. Eddie answered and it was a friend of his from Philly telling him that Eddie Waitkus had been shot. Eddie, of course, got excited and when he got off the phone and told me I actually fell out of bed."

Eddie was seriously wounded and near death with a bullet lodged near his spine. In the weeks that followed, Eddie gradually improved. Although one early report suggested he could return to us in a month, the bullet had pierced a lung and Eddie would have to undergo four operations. He would be out for the year. Only by undertaking a vigorous rehabilitation and conditioning program under our trainer Frank Wiechec over the winter in Florida would he be able to come back in 1950.

CABALLERO: "Several months later Ashburn, Bill Nicholson, and I went to see Eddie in the hospital. Eddie roomed with Bill. They were real close friends. Both of them had played with the Cubs. Eddie is laying in bed with a big hole in his chest and Nick looked at him and said, 'Eddie, do you realize that you've been shot at and hit and everybody in the world knows your name now. Eddie Waitkus! Eddie Waitkus! How many times do you think I've been shot at and missed and no one even knows about it. You got shot at one time and hit and your name is all over the country.'

"Eddie was laughing so hard it was making him hurt.

"He wasn't the same after. You could put your fist in his back where they had operated to take the bullet out. When the weather changed he had trouble bending over to tie his shoes."

SEMINICK: "One day before the season was over Waitkus visited us in the clubhouse before a game. He looked like a skeleton. He was nothing but skin and bones. His eyes were way back in his head. It shook us all up to see him."

Ruth Steinhagen, it turned out, was a mentally unstable young woman who had been obsessed with Eddie while he was with the Cubs. Beginning in 1947, she sat behind first base in Wrigley Field, watching Eddie's every move. Although she always stood by the players' gate after the ballgames, she never spoke to Eddie or asked him for his autograph. She apparently decided that she could never have Eddie, so no one else should either. She shot Eddie the first time she ever met him.

> **MEYER:** "They said that this girl had a picture of Eddie blown up to like 4 by 6 feet and had it up on her wall in her room. All along her walls and ceiling were pictures of Eddie in Wrigley Field."

Miss Steinhagen was found mentally incapable of standing trial and spent three years in a mental institution. She dropped from sight after she was released.

Chapter 9
The First Division

Although we were all shocked by Eddie Waitkus's shooting, we had to play the Cubs in a doubleheader that day. Surprisingly perhaps, we were able to concentrate on our jobs and we actually beat the Cubs twice, 4–1 and 3–0, behind the pitching of Ken Heintzelman and Hank Borowy. Fortunately, we had Dick Sisler to take over first base and he immediately contributed with three key hits in the first game. I relieved Hank in the second game with one out in the ninth and runners on first and third. After walking Rube Walker to load the bases I managed to get Frank Gustine to hit into a double play to end the game.

In baseball you have to play every day. We did not have much of a chance to dwell on events, even traumatic ones, because there was always another ballgame to play. We were stunned by what happened to Eddie but we were forced to get right back into our routine.

The next day we were down 3–0 in the eighth inning and scored four runs with two outs to again beat the Cubs 4–3. Eddie Sawyer allowed Jim Konstanty, pitching in relief, to bat in the eighth with the go-ahead run on third. Jim repaid Eddie's confidence with a two-strike, two-out single over second baseman Emil Verban to drive in Bill Nicholson and win the ballgame.

We continued our winning ways the following night in St. Louis in a game that was special to me. More than three busloads of friends and family from Springfield, including some of my high school teammates from Lanphier High, my high school coach Ted Boyle, and my parents and brothers and sisters, came down to watch me pitch. I sent them all home happy, pitching my second big league shutout to beat Cardinal ace Harry Breechen 8–0 and send us into third place. Dick Sisler hit his first home run of the year and had three hits to raise his average to .333. He was 8 for 18 since taking over for Waitkus at first.

My parents usually came down to St. Louis to watch me pitch during my early years with the Phillies, since St. Louis was only 105 miles from Springfield. I would then drive home with them after the game and stay overnight. A couple of years later, in 1951, I won my 20th game in St. Louis, beating the Cardinals 2–1. After the game my Dad said to me, "Bud, do you mind if I don't go anymore?"

I said, "No, Dad, you don't have to go."

He said, "They drive me crazy." So after that he stayed home and listened to the games on the radio. Mom told me that if I got men on base he would turn the radio off and take a walk. Then he would come back, turn the radio back on and if I was still pitching, he knew I had gotten out of the jam. If I was not still in the game, he had not missed anything he would have wanted to hear.

In contrast, my mother really enjoyed the games, laughing and saying hello to everyone. I am sure she worried about whether I won or lost, but only because she knew how much it meant to me.

The 1949 season marked the second year in which Richie Ashburn's parents, Neil and Genevieve, ran a rooming house for some of the young guys on the Phillies who were still single. Neil Ashburn had sold his machine shop business back in Nebraska and moved to Philadelphia the previous year after Richie had clinched his position with the ballclub. The Ashburns simply wanted to be able to enjoy watching their son play.

> **ASHBURN:** "My parents had never seen me play major league ball. They just wanted to take a summer and see the games. They came back and rented a place on the Main Line. We were all young and single then, so what better place to stay than with my mother and dad. My mother is still one of the all-time great cooks. Players are interested in eating, of course. So four of us just moved into this nice house and paid them rent each month to take care of the groceries. I'm sure they didn't make any money on the deal, but they really enjoyed taking care of us and going to all the home games."

The Ashburns' boarding house started right after I joined the club in June and it worked out beautifully. The first year the Ashburns rented a house in suburban Bala Cynwyd and Richie, Curt Simmons, Charlie

Bicknell, and I lived with them. The four of us generally shared a ride to the ballpark and, if we had a night game, we often shot pool or occasionally went swimming. We also spent time just sitting around relaxing and talking.

Mrs. Ashburn was a great cook and prepared wonderful pregame meals for us. The pitchers who were not pitching would work out first and sometimes I would feel a little sluggish working out because Mrs. Ashburn cooked so well and we ate so much. Sometimes she would bake a cherry pie, knowing it was my favorite.

> **SIMMONS:** "We would sit down to eat at around 3:00. We would eat like we were going to go out and work the farm for 10 hours. Then we would go to the ballpark to work out and do our running maybe an hour after eating this huge meal. But we were kids and it didn't bother us a bit.
>
> "It was great for us. Mrs. Ashburn was a great cook and Mr. Ashburn would do the patting on the back and talk baseball with the guys."
>
> **BICKNELL:** "That was the first time I had ever been away from home in my life and Mr. and Mrs. Ashburn made everyone feel at home. They were mighty fine folks."

For the 1949 season the Ashburns rented a house in Bryn Mawr, also a Philadelphia suburb, from some schoolteachers who were away for the summer. The previous year a Philadelphia newspaper article had given the exact address of our house, resulting in the frequent ringing of our doorbell by young fans. The move to a new neighborhood was in part designed to provide us with some privacy.

We were still young kids ourselves, however, and we frequently played stickball in the street with the neighborhood kids. One local teenage girl presented Richie with a cocker spaniel puppy, which we naturally called Philly. If Richie had a bad day we would call the puppy Utica—as in "Here Utica, here Utica"—to suggest to Richie where he might be heading.

Jack Mayo joined Richie, Charlie, Curt, and I in the Ashburn rooming house in 1949. When Jack broke his ankle late in the year Mike Goliat was called up from the minors and moved in while Jack recuperated back in Youngstown, Ohio.

Several of us got married after the '49 season but the Ashburn rooming house provided us with an ideal, almost idyllic setting those first two years. All we had to worry about was playing ball.

We continued to play well immediately after the Waitkus shooting and by June 25 we were firmly entrenched in third place, nine games above .500 and only two games behind the league-leading Dodgers. We then lost a doubleheader to the second-division Reds 4–3 and 5–2 and could win only 4 of 14 games leading up to the July 12 All-Star game. We ended the first half of the season in fourth place, only three games above .500.

Andy Seminick, who had lost his regular catcher's job in spring training, was voted the National League's starting catcher by the fans, beating out Roy Campanella and Walker Cooper. In a nice gesture, Eddie Waitkus was named an honorary All-Star. The Philadelphia press and fans, however, were very upset that neither Ken Heintzelman nor I were selected to the All-Star pitching staff by manager Billy Southworth. Kenny was 10–5 and I was 9–6 at the break.

Our teammates were also upset at our omission. Russ Meyer, never at a loss for words and never one to understate a case, was quoted as saying, "That is nothing but rank injustice. . . . It was unfairness of the worst sort. I hope the American League beats them 45 to 0."

Heinz was probably a little more deserving than me since he was a veteran pitcher who was having a good year. It was the first time that I was under consideration for the All-Star team and I was certainly hopeful of being named. It was a little disappointing but was really not that big a deal. I was fortunate enough to make it the next seven years, so I ended up with plenty of All-Star experiences, all of which I enjoyed immensely.

The American League did win the 1949 game, 11–7, a see-saw affair in the only All-Star game ever played in Brooklyn. Who knows, maybe Kenny and I would have let in a few fewer runs.

After the break we continued to play about .500 baseball, alternating between fourth and fifth place but effectively dropping out of the pennant race. We dropped below .500 to 50 wins and 51 losses on August 4 by losing another Crosley Field doubleheader to the seventh-place Reds, 8–5 and 9–1. Monk Meyer started the first game and blew sky high in the first inning as the Reds batted around.

Sawyer started out to get Monk after Jimmy Bloodworth, who would join us early in 1950, doubled to score Johnny Wyrostek with the fourth run of the inning. Monk responded by slamming the ball down against the pitching rubber. It bounced almost to the first base foul line. In those days, before air conditioning, we would have a bucket of ammonia water iced down in the dugout to help keep us cool from the summer heat. Monk stormed off the mound and, when he reached the dugout, gave the water bucket a hard kick. He immediately fell to the dugout floor, rolling around in great pain. They took him to the hospital where X-rays showed a break, so the doctor put a cast on Monk's foot.

> **MEYER:** "I was ticked off and frustrated and they had this big damn water bucket in Crosley Field. I think it was made out of cast iron. I tried to kick a hole in it and the minute I did, boy oh boy. My ankle just swelled up about twice its size."

It seemed certain that Monk was through for the season. Even though injured, he was to finish out the road trip with us before returning to Philadelphia to recuperate.

A couple of days later in Pittsburgh, Monk told Bill Nicholson, "Nick, my foot doesn't hurt that much anymore."

Nick said, "Your old break probably showed up on the X-ray. Go get that checked again. You're probably all right." Nick was Monk's teammate in Chicago and knew that Monk had broken his ankle a couple of years before.

So they took the cast off and sure enough there was no new break.

> **MEYER:** "They sent me to Temple University Hospital and took X-rays. Sure enough one of those old breaks had showed up. I thought I was through for the season. In fact, I was scared shitless to be honest. Bob Carpenter had said, 'If he's out for the year, he's not going to get paid either.' I had injured it in my line of employment but not the way I should have."

Russ, who was about to go home for the season with an 8–6 record, was pitching again in a week and ended up winning 17 ballgames for us. He won 9 and lost only 3 after kicking that bucket and had the best season of his career.

The day after our doubleheader loss to the Reds we hit rock bottom. Schoolboy Rowe lost a tough 1–0 game to Bill Werle and the Pirates in Pittsburgh. Eddie had not been pitching Schoolie much and Schoolie had been pestering Eddie to let him pitch. Finally Eddie said, "Okay, you can pitch today." And Schoolie, who was a 17-year major league veteran, pitched a great ballgame. With two outs in the bottom of the ninth, Schoolie had a two ball two strike count on Danny Murtaugh, the Pirate second baseman, with Ralph Kiner on third. Murtaugh slapped a ground ball to the right of Granny Hamner at shortstop. Granny made a fine pickup but threw low to Dick Sisler at first. Dick tried to scoop it but the ball bounced out of his glove as Kiner scored the winning run.

Schoolie was so upset that he hurled his glove about 50 feet in the air, almost reaching the stands. Umpire Babe Pinelli picked it up and handed it to Schoolie, but he dropped the glove to the ground and kicked it as hard as he could, sending it flying again.

Dick thought that Schoolie was showing him up and confronted him in the dugout. They were both big guys and we were afraid they were going to tangle but Schoolie made his peace with Dick and nothing happened.

That ballgame turned out to be one of the last that Rowe pitched in the big leagues, and it was sad the way it ended with Schoolie so upset. A few weeks later the Phillies released him outright. I was in the outfield shagging balls before the game when Schoolie walked out in his street clothes and motioned to me. "Kid, I've just been released," he told me.

"I'm sorry to hear that, Schoolie," I said.

"Just one thing," he said. "You're tipping your curveball. I can tell when it's coming."

I always thought it was funny that Schoolie never told me that when we were on the same pitching staff. But after he was released and my performing well could no longer affect his role on the team, he walked out to the outfield in his street clothes to let me know that I was tipping my curve.

Schoolie was an exceptional athlete from Eldorado, Arkansas, tall with a beautiful pitching delivery. While still in high school, he had pitched and won an exhibition game against the White Sox, allowing only six hits. A writer covering the game reported "[a] schoolboy beat the White Sox today," forever after providing Schoolie with his nickname.

Schoolie once told me about a deal he struck as a kid pitching in a semi-pro league in Arkansas where he was to get paid by the strikeout. The problem was that Schoolie did not trust the team's owner, who kept the official score for the game. So every time he would strike someone out he would put a rock behind the mound. At the end of the game there were 15 rocks there, so he went to collect for 15 strikeouts.

He had started in the big leagues with Detroit in 1933 and led them to the 1934 pennant with a 24–8 record. That year he won 16 consecutive games, tying the American League record. During the 1934 World Series he was giving an interview on radio when all of a sudden he asked his sweetheart, Edna Mary Skinner, "How'm I doin', Edna?" It quickly became a catch phrase that fans all over the country repeated and made famous.

Cy Perkins was with the Tigers as a coach when Schoolie was having his great years there. He told me that he would almost have to beg Schoolie to get to the mound. Schoolie would throw up in the clubhouse and even in the dugout, he would get so nervous before starting a game. Even with us, late in his career, if he would come in from the bullpen to relieve, he would first go down into the dugout and throw up.

> **SAWYER:** "Mickey Cochrane managed him in Detroit and told me that he never let Schoolie know when he was pitching. If he knew, he would come to the ballpark looking awful. But he said he was a great pitcher once you got him over the white line."

Early in his career Schoolie was overpowering, but a serious arm injury in 1937 had forced him to become a knuckleball and slider pitcher with us. The Phillies purchased him in 1943 after Brooklyn and Detroit had given up on him. Interrupted by service in World War II, Schoolie went on to win 52 games for us over five seasons. Schoolie was also an exceptional hitter and had a career .263 average with 18 home runs. With the Phillies in 1943 Schoolie led the league with 15 pinch hits.

After Schoolie lost the heartbreaker to the Pirates we rebounded by winning the final three games of the series to go two games over .500. We went home only to run into the Dodgers, who were in a dogfight for the pennant with the Cardinals. They beat me 8–1 in Shibe Park and swept a three-game series from us.

Sawyer was not happy with our performance and decided to lay down the law the next day after we traveled to New York for a series with the Giants. Eddie seldom had meetings but he called one for 12 noon on August 12 in the Commodore Hotel, where we stayed in New York. Eddie told us in no uncertain terms that we were sluggish and in some cases not hustling all the time. He advised us that if we did not change our ways and take better care of ourselves on and off the field we were headed for the second division again. Apparently he had spotted some of us eating huge meals and was upset about some of the guys getting sunburned at the beach during an off day a few days before.

So he imposed a curfew, barred our wives from traveling with us, and changed our system for eating on the road. Previously we just signed for our meals at the hotel, but Eddie decided to give us six dollars a day meal money instead. He required us to pick up our meal money each day by 8:30 in the morning from our trainer, Frank Wiechec. So from then on there we were, a bunch of grown men, lining up every morning at Wiechec's room to get that day's meal money.

SAWYER: "Some of the guys were taking advantage of just signing for their meals and were overeating, sometimes before games. They were young and some of them just didn't have much discipline yet. But it wasn't really that big a deal. The press sort of blew it out of proportion at the time."

A lot of us groused about the new rules, but for some reason we did begin to play better. We beat the Giants that day 2–0 behind Granny's homer and Hank Borowy's shutout pitching, before losing a double-header to the Giants the next day. We then moved to Ebbets Field, where we returned the favor to the Dodgers, sweeping them in a three-game series in their own backyard. Heintzelman won a remarkable 12-inning, 2–1 game in the opener against Don Newcombe when Richie drove a ball against the center field wall to score none other than Heinz from second base. The Dodgers were so loaded with right-handed power with Jackie Robinson, Carl Furillo, Gil Hodges, and Roy Campanella that it was unusual for southpaws to even pitch in the bandbox Ebbets Field. But Goober not only pitched, he threw a 12-inning seven-hitter to beat them.

We won the second game of the series 11–7 by scoring five runs in the eighth inning against Erv Palica to break a 5–5 tie. Buddy Blattner, who was with us that year as a reserve infielder, led the way with a two-run homer and Del Ennis slammed a two-run double off the wall to go with his earlier home run. The next day we won 9–5 by scoring eight runs in the sixth and seventh innings behind another homer by Del and one by Puddinhead Jones. Konstanty saved the game, relieving Borowy in the ninth with no outs, the bases loaded, and one run in. He retired the next three hitters, allowing only one more run to cross the plate.

After sweeping Brooklyn, we returned to Philly on August 19 to play the Giants on Eddie Waitkus Night. Eddie had endured four operations in recovering from his gunshot wound and looked frail and gaunt when he visited the clubhouse before the game. In a pregame ceremony, Eddie received a new car, a television, golf clubs, luggage, other gifts, and a bronze four-leaf-clover plaque. Dick Sisler presented Eddie with a bronzed first baseman's mitt mounted on a stand with all our signatures etched upon it. Eddie was clearly moved by all the festivities in his honor and promised to get back into the lineup as soon as he possibly could.

I pitched the ballgame and beat the Giants and old nemesis Dave Koslo, who had a lifetime 10–0 record against us, 7–1. Richie had four hits and Dick had three, raising his average to .304, to lead our attack. The win pushed us into a fourth-place tie with the Braves, only a half game behind the third-place Giants. The next day we were down 3–0 to the Giants in the seventh when we exploded for seven runs against Monte Kennedy and Kirby Higbe. We went on to win 9–3 behind Del Ennis's perfect four-for-four day, including his 19th homer of the season, to vault into third place.

Our doubleheader the next day, August 21, against the Giants began well with Heinz pitching a 4–0 shutout for his 15th win of the year. The second game, however, was quite another story. We were trailing 3–2 with one out in the top of the ninth when all hell broke lose. With Giant first baseman Joe Lafata at bat, Willard Marshall, who had opened the inning with a single, stole second and went to third on Stan Lopata's wild throw. On the next pitch Lafata lashed a low liner to center field. Ashburn raced in, caught the ball a good eight inches off the ground, rolled over and threw the ball into second. I was out in the bullpen and could see that Richie caught the ball almost knee high. Unfortunately second-base umpire George Barr, who must have had his view of the play blocked, ruled that Richie trapped the ball. Marshall scored from third to make it 4–2. Richie immediately charged in to protest, followed shortly by Del Ennis, Granny Hamner, Willie Jones, and Eddie Sawyer. Meanwhile the crowd of almost 20,000 booed and hissed and began to throw fruit, bottles, and anything else they could find.

When Eddie and company finally gave up trying to convince Barr the error of his ways and returned to their respective positions, a new barrage came from the stands, also laced with bottles. After several near misses all the players retreated to the dugout. All the while our public address announcer, Dave Zinkoff, kept telling the crowd that the umpires would declare a forfeit if the pelting continued, but he was largely drowned out by the boos.

The groundskeepers were able to clear the debris after a few more minutes and the umpires ordered play to resume. Schoolboy Rowe, who had pitched the entire game for us, threw a few warm-up pitches and was about to pitch to Bill Rigney, the Giants next batter, when the fans around home plate began another barrage. Home-plate umpire Al Barlick was hit in the back with a tomato and third-base ump Lee Ballanfant was grazed by a bottle and hit by a pear. That was it. The three umpires quickly met at home plate and simultaneously declared a forfeit.

> **SAWYER:** "I wasn't as unhappy with Barr as I was with Ballanfant and Barlick. I thought Barr had been blocked out on the play by someone but they could see the play and wouldn't

overrule Barr. But you had to know George Barr. He was always the man in charge. But there was a lot of question in the league about how well he could actually see. We had our share of problems with him over the years.

"Because of the blue laws then in effect we couldn't play after 7:00 on Sunday. So when we played a Sunday doubleheader we often had to finish the second game the next night or the next time the opposing team was back in town. So time was running out while the fans were throwing things. But we could have finished the game on the Giants' next trip except the umpires called a forfeit.

"The fans in the upper deck were throwing bottles and cushions and stuff that were landing in the box seats, because they couldn't reach the field from up there. People down there had umbrellas up and were getting out of the way any way they could. It's a miracle somebody wasn't seriously hurt. It was really a mess. I know it was my worst day in baseball."

That ballgame was the last time refreshments were ever sold in bottles in Shibe Park. Other parks around the league shortly followed suit and pretty soon bottles were banned in both leagues.

After an off day, we again showed our ability to bounce back from adversity by beating the Reds 4–3 in 13 innings on August 23. I relieved Jim Konstanty, who had pitched $3^2/_3$'s scoreless relief innings, in the 13th and won when Blattner, batting for me in the bottom of the inning, doubled against Kent Peterson, sending Andy Seminick to third with one out. Richie drove in Andy for the winning run with a long fly to center, giving me my 12th victory of the year.

After another off day we split an August 25 doubleheader with the Pirates. We lost to Murry Dickson in the first game 5–1 before I pitched and won the second game 4–2 for my 13th win and second in three days. Dick Sisler cracked a homer and Andy and Mike Goliat, recently called up from Toronto, each had two hits. I was up 4–0 in the eighth when the Pirates touched me for two runs. With two out and the tying runs on base I had to face the dangerous Ralph Kiner, who would lead the league in home runs. I quickly fell behind him 3–0 before getting him to pop to Granny for the final out of the inning.

It was not unusual for me to relieve between starts in 1949. Eddie used me in relief 12 times that year, even though I started every fourth day for most of the season. It certainly did not bother me to pitch between starts. I usually threw in the bullpen on the second day after a start anyway. My attitude was always to just take the ball when Eddie handed it to me and do the best I could. I never worried about the number of pitches or innings or games I threw. My motion was so fluid and smooth that I could pitch a lot without bothering my arm. I guess it went back to what Cy Perkins observed when I first came up—I could throw harder easier than just about anybody else in the game.

> **SAWYER:** "I was trying to get Robin established in the big leagues because he had so much talent and was such a great competitor. I always believed that the best way to learn to pitch was to be on the mound. Robin hadn't been a pitcher very long and I wanted to get him more used to the mound. In fact, I had all my starting pitchers pitch batting practice because I wanted them on the mound facing live batters. They threw a lot of batting practice without screens in front of them because I wanted them to be able to field their positions as well. As a result we had good fielding pitchers."

We lost the last two games of the series with Pittsburgh to drop to only a game over .500 before taking two out of three from the Cubs to conclude our homestand. The last game was an exciting 6–5 come-from-behind victory, thanks to eighth-inning homers by Lopata and Seminick off of Bob Muncrief. I had started but left for a pinch hitter after six innings, losing 4–1. Our eighth-inning rally put us up 6–4 going into the ninth with our ace Konstanty on the hill. But Jim got into trouble, gave up a run to make it 6–5, and had runners on second and third with two outs and the dangerous Hank Sauer at bat. Hank seemed to own us; he had a real knack for winning games against us with big hits.

This time he topped a ball off the end of his bat toward shortstop that looked like trouble. Neither Jim nor Willie Jones at third could get to it but Granny raced in from shortstop, scooped the ball and threw it to Dick Sisler at first in one motion, just nipping Sauer and saving the ballgame.

Those two wins over the Cubs started us on a great streak that solidified our hold on third place. From August 28 through September 9 we won 12 out of 15 games to improve our record to 72–64, four games ahead of the fourth-place Braves. Unfortunately, we were still 13 games behind the first-place Cardinals, who were locked into a tight two-team pennant race with the Dodgers.

We opened a series with the Braves in Boston September 10 and I lost a tough 1–0 ballgame to Warren Spahn. The Braves touched me for a run with two outs in the first on a single by Jim Russell and a double by Marv Rickert, and that turned out to be the ballgame. In our eighth both Sisler and Ennis singled, but Braves right fielder Tommy Holmes made two great catches on long drives to rob Lopata and Stan Hollmig and preserve Spahn's shutout. We again bounced back from that difficult defeat to sweep a doubleheader from the Braves the following day, 3–1 and 6–3.

A couple of days later I won my 15th (and, it turned out, last) game of the season, beating the Pirates 12–4 at Forbes Field in Pittsburgh behind home runs by Hamner, Goliat and, in his first big league at bat, rookie Eddie Sanicki. We then split a two-game set with the Reds in Cincinnati before moving on to St. Louis for three games with the league-leading Cardinals.

Unfortunately, we ran into George Barr again in the first game of the series. It was Dick Sisler Day and before the game Dick, who was from St. Louis, was given a new car, television, luggage, and other gifts. That was the only highlight of the afternoon for us.

I started the game against the Redbirds' George Munger and was leading 2–1 going into the bottom of the third. Red Schoendienst led off the inning with a double and scored on Marty Marion's single to tie the score. Stan Musial singled off Granny's glove to put runners on first and second. Enos Slaughter was next and I worked the count to 3–2. With the count full the Cardinals sent the runners and I threw one right down the middle. Enos never took his bat off his shoulder and Andy threw to third to nail Marion coming from second.

It looked like we had gone from no outs and two on to two outs and a man on second. But Umpire Barr, who was behind the plate, called ball four. The pitch was right down the pipe and I just could not believe he had called it a ball. Eddie Sawyer raced out to argue and, for one of the few times, got thrown out of a ballgame, as did Russ Meyer who was hollering from the bench. Barr even ran Cy Perkins out of the game the following inning when Cy kept complaining.

Cy had a lot to complain about. Instead of almost being out of the inning we had the bases loaded and no one out. Ron Northey was the next hitter after the rhubarb finally died down. He hit my first pitch on the roof in the right field pavilion for a grand slam homer to make the score 6–2. It was downhill from there and we lost 15–3, our most lopsided defeat of the year.

But once again we bounced back the next day to beat the Cardinals 4–3. Rookie Jocko Thompson pitched a complete game for his first big league win and Eddie Sanicki again homered to trim the Cards' lead over the Dodgers to a game and a half.

> **MEYER:** "A bunch of us were up in the Steeplechase Club in the Chase Hotel in St. Louis during our last series there, having something to eat and having a few beers. Bill Nicholson, Dick Sisler, Del Ennis, and Hank Borowy were all there and we got talking, and we all agreed that we had a good shot at winning the whole thing in 1950."

We went on to clinch third place on September 26 by beating the Dodgers 5–3 in Ebbets Field in another thrilling comeback victory. Down 3–1 in the eighth, we rallied for four runs off Jack Banta on a clutch two-run single by Dick Sisler and a two-run circuit clout by Andy Seminick. The win did severe damage to Brooklyn's pennant hopes, putting them a game and a half behind the Cardinals with only four games left in the season. It also assured us of the highest finish by a Phillies team since 1917, a span of 32 years. Although we were well out of the tight pennant race between the Cardinals and Dodgers, we took real satisfaction in knowing we would finish ahead of the Braves, the 1948 pennant winners.

After beating the Giants 2–0 in a single game, we ended the season with two games against the Dodgers in Shibe Park, with the pennant hanging in the balance. Going into the weekend series the Dodgers were one game ahead of the Cardinals, with two to play for each club. St. Louis had lost three in a row to lose their lead, while Brooklyn had won two straight. The Dodgers needed one win over us to clinch the pennant.

The Dodgers jumped in front 3–0 with single runs in the second, third, and fifth innings off starter Ken Heintzelman. Kenny was not himself, allowing nine walks and six hits before Eddie brought me in to relieve after Goober walked the bases loaded in the fifth. I managed to get out of the inning with only one run, a sacrifice fly to Richie by Pee Wee Reese to score Roy Campanella.

We came back to score a run ourselves in the bottom half of the inning off of Dodger starter Ralph Branca when Willie Jones doubled Bill Nicholson home. Eddie had Buddy Blattner hit for me to try to get Puddinhead in, but Buddy fouled out and left fielder Louis Olmo made a nice catch on Richie's looping fly ball to end the inning.

We did considerably more damage in the sixth when Dick led off with a triple against the scoreboard in right and Del followed with his 25th home run, an upper deck clout to left, to tie the score. With that Carl Erskine relieved Branca. Andy greeted Ersk with another home run (his 24th) to left to put us into the lead 4–3.

Brooklyn tied the score against Curt Simmons in their eighth on a single by Furillo to drive in Reese. Curt, who had relieved me in the sixth after Blattner hit for me, had pitched well before running into trouble. With two runners on, Eddie brought in Konstanty, who got out of the inning on two comebackers to the mound.

Dodger manager Burt Shotton was using his entire staff to try to win the pennant, and he brought in ace southpaw Preacher Roe to pitch the eighth. With one out, Sanicki worked Preacher for a walk on a 3–2 count. Puddinhead then stepped to the plate and launched an 0–1 fastball into the left field stands to win the game 6–4. Konstanty retired the Dodgers in order in the ninth to preserve the victory.

The Cardinals lost to Chicago and the seldom-used Bob Chipman 3–1 for their fourth straight loss, so the Dodgers could still win the pennant outright by beating us on Sunday. St. Louis had to defeat the Cubs and hope we could again beat Brooklyn to gain a tie for the pennant and force a playoff.

Our ballgame on Sunday turned out to be a classic. It would be the first of three consecutive years that we would play an extra-inning game on the last day of the season against the Dodgers with the pennant on the line for them. Only in 1950, however, would the pennant be on the line for the Phillies as well.

Russ Meyer and his eight-game winning streak started for us against the Dodgers' big rookie right-hander Don Newcombe, who already had 17 triumphs against only 8 losses in his first year. Brooklyn again jumped out in front, scoring five runs in the third to chase Monk. After the first three runs scored, Eddie brought me in to try to stem the tide. Two men were on and Eddie had me walk Campanella to load the bases and bring up Newcombe. Newk, who was an excellent hitter,[1] slashed a single to left to score runs four and five before I could get us out of the inning. The 5–0 Dodger lead seemed insurmountable, particularly the way Newcombe was throwing.

---

1. Newcombe would hit .271 lifetime with 15 home runs. He was so good that he was used as a pinch hitter 87 times during his 10-year career. His best year at the plate was 1955 when Newk won 20, lost only 5, and batted .359 with 7 home runs.

Newk continued to mow us down in our half of the third and I pitched a scoreless fourth. In our half we started to fight back with some offensive fireworks of our own, as we had so many times late in the season. With one out and Del and Nick on base, Puddinhead sent a booming home run to the stands in left to suddenly bring in three runs. Goliat followed with a single and Hollmig, batting for me, slammed a double over second to send Mike to third. That was all for Newk, and Dodger coach Clyde Sukeforth waved flame-throwing Rex Barney to the mound. Richie hit a shot to right that looked like it would fall in, but Furillo made a fine play to catch up to the ball and pull it in. Goliat came in on the play for our fourth run. Although Granny bounced out for the third out, it was now 5–4 and we were back in the ballgame.

Brooklyn came right back with two more runs in the fifth off of Curt, who took over the pitching for me. Campanella had the big blow, a two-run double off Konstanty after Eddie replaced Curt with two on and no one out.

We rallied again in the bottom half, scoring a run to make it 7–5, thanks to Nick's run-scoring blast off the scoreboard to plate Del, who had walked. We finally managed to tie it up in the sixth off of Barney. Johnny Blatnick, up from Toronto and hitting for Konstanty, singled to right with one out and went to second when Furillo fumbled the ball. It was John's only major league hit of the year. Richie fouled out, but Granny delivered with a clutch two-out single through the pitcher's mound to score John. Sisler followed with a single, moving Hamner to second and sending Barney to the showers. Jack Banta came in for the Dodgers and was greeted by Del's hard shot past Reese at shortstop to score Granny with the tying run. Andy struck out to end the inning, but we had finally evened the ballgame.

Sawyer brought in Heintzelman to pitch, who twice worked out of tense jams to keep Brooklyn scoreless. Meanwhile we could do little against Banta. In the bottom of the ninth, Dick led off with a walk but we could not advance him, sending the game into extra innings.

Heinz was immediately in trouble in the top of the tenth when Reese hit a looping single just in front of Del in left. Eddie Miksis sacrificed Pee Wee to second, bringing Duke Snider to the plate in a situation remarkably similar to one that would occur exactly a year later.[2] Just as

2. Here Duke was batting in the top of the tenth with one out and the potential winning run on second. The October 1, 1950, game was at Ebbets Field and Duke would bat in the bottom of the ninth with no one out and the winning run on second.

he would the following year, Duke came through with a single to center, this time on the first pitch. Unfortunately, Richie, unlike a year later, had no chance to throw the runner out and Pee Wee scored the go-ahead run.

We walked Jackie Robinson intentionally before Louis Olmo sent a shot through third that Willie Jones could not come up with, scoring Snider. Eddie brought Ken Trinkle in to face the right-handed hitting Furillo, who grounded into a double play. But the damage was done.

Mike Goliat gave us some hope in the bottom of the tenth by singling sharply to left with one out. But Eddie Sanicki, hitting for Trinkle, struck out and Richie flied to Olmo in left to end the game and the season, and we watched the Dodgers mob Jack Banta. Banta, who one week before had blown a game to us that looked like it would cost Brooklyn the pennant, had pitched four scoreless innings of relief to send the Dodgers into the World Series.[3]

Watching the Dodgers celebrate their pennant in our ballpark was certainly bittersweet. But we felt very good about our year. We had played the Dodgers extremely tough in the last weeks of the season when they were desperately trying to win the pennant. We had finished the year strong, we were young, and we had gained confidence. We were coming and the rest of the league knew that they would have to reckon with us.

> **ASHBURN:** "After that last ballgame against the Dodgers, Eddie got us all in the clubhouse and said, 'We are going to win it all in 1950. Come back next year ready to win.'"

---

3. The Cardinals had beaten the Cubs 13–5 in a game that ended just before ours did. The Dodgers thus avoided a playoff by defeating us in 10 innings and finished a single game ahead of St. Louis. In the American League, the Yankees beat the Red Sox 5–3 to win the pennant by a single game over the Red Sox, thus ending two of the most thrilling pennant races in baseball history.

Chapter 10
Spring Training 1950: The Whiz Kids Give Notice

I was anxious for the 1950 season, and not only because we were now a first-division club with a chance to compete for the pennant. I had finished 15–15 after going into the All-Star break with 9 wins and 6 losses, and I was eager to prove that I could be a consistent winner in the big leagues. After that crazy game in St. Louis where Ron Northey hit the home run after our rhubarb with George Barr, I had started only one other game during the stretch run. I lost to the Cubs 9–6 on September 21 after blowing a 5–2 lead in the sixth and seventh innings.

After that we had a lot of off days and Eddie used me in relief while starting Ken Heintzelman and Russ Meyer, who were both pitching well, almost exclusively. But for the second consecutive year the season had ended on a down note for me personally and I was chomping at the bit to get started in 1950.

MAJE McDONNELL: "We came on strong in '49. If Waitkus hadn't been shot, we might have had a shot. We were coming, boy oh boy, we were coming. Good pitching, the kids were hitting and fielding. The attitude was terrific. We had such a good clubhouse. Good teams have good clubhouses. We had a lot of fun. We kidded each other, got on each other. The Whiz Kids had that at the end of '49 and in '50.

"That was the first time the Phillies had finished in the money in a lot of years. We all got our check for our World Series share just before Christmas. It was about $800 a person and, boy, we were on cloud nine."

In spite of our strong finish in 1949, we still had some holes to fill going into spring training. Willie Jones, who had hit a hard .244 with 35 doubles, 19 homers, and 77 RBIs in his first season at third, and Granny Hamner, who had played every game at short, formed the most promising left side of an infield in baseball. First base seemed to be in fine shape between the resurgent Eddie Waitkus, who had worked hard all winter with trainer Frank Wiechec in Clearwater, and Dick Sisler, whose strong hitting (.289) had helped key our success in '49.

Second base, however, was a big question mark. The veteran Eddie Miller, a four-time National League All-Star shortstop, had played quite a bit of second for us in '49 after Granny took over at shortstop. But Eddie had hit only .207 and appeared near the end of the line. Buddy Blattner was a possibility; he had contributed several timely hits and clubbed five homers in limited action the previous year. Putsy Caballero had spent much of '49 at Toronto, where he hit .318, and at 22 still had great potential. But Eddie Sawyer was counting on Mike Goliat to take over the keystone sack.

Goliat was a tough kid from Yatesboro, Pennsylvania, who had come up the hard way. During and after high school he had worked in the western Pennsylvania coal mines, following in the footsteps of his father. At 19 he joined the Army and, while stationed in Japan, played baseball with some minor ballplayers who were fulfilling their service commitment. Mike more than held his own and decided that baseball could be his escape from the mines. When he was discharged from the service, he traveled to Vandergrift, Pennsylvania, only 12 miles from his home, to ask for a tryout with the Phillies' Class D farm club there. After a couple of workouts, the team signed him and he was installed as the regular third baseman. In his first year in professional baseball, 1947, Mike hit an impressive .370 with 133 hits and 86 RBIs in only 94 games.

In 1948 Mike was my teammate at Wilmington in the Class B Interstate League, before I was called up to the Phillies in June. Mike, playing first base as well as third, hit .315 with 17 homers and led the league in runs scored. That earned him a 1949 promotion to Toronto, where he was hitting .286 when summoned by the Phillies in late July.

Surprisingly, Mike had played only a few games at second base before his promotion. When the Phillies sent word to Toronto manager Del Bissonette to send Goliat up, the Maple Leafs were in the middle of a night game with the Rochester Red Wings. Between innings Del told Mike, who was playing second base, that he would be going to Philadelphia right after the game. On the second play after the Maple Leafs took the field, Mike was hit covering second by former Phil Ralph LaPointe, and he was trying to break up a double play. The collision severely wrenched Mike's knee, and he literally limped into Philadelphia.

Frank Wiechec treated Mike's knee daily and Eddie Sawyer quickly worked him into the lineup. Playing with pain, Mike consented to have his knee X-rayed only if the club would agree to keep him in the lineup no matter what the X-rays showed. "It was too hard getting up here in the first place," according to Mike.

Goliat moved into the Ashburn's rooming house with us for the rest of 1949, replacing Jack Mayo who had broken his ankle and returned home to Ohio to mend. Mike had a tough start at bat, with only 3 hits in his first 46 times up. His knee not only limited his mobility in the field but hampered him at bat. But Mike's confidence, at least outwardly, never wavered. He told Mr. and Mrs. Ashburn that he would start hitting and he did. Mike got some key hits in our late season surge and raised his average to .212 in 55 games. And although Mike was not exactly nimble at second base, he was gritty and determined and had a very strong arm. He had shown that he could get the job done.

Our outfield also posed some problems heading into 1950. Richie Ashburn had encountered some of the so-called sophomore jinx and had tailed off to .284 from his .333 average his rookie year. His stolen base total had dropped from a league-leading 32 in 1948 (where he missed the last month of the season due to injury) to 9. Although Richie still had a solid year in 1949, it did not meet the expectations set by his banner first year.

Eddie Sawyer, in what must have been in part a psychological ploy, announced to the press before spring training began that Eddie Sanicki would go into camp as the club's center fielder. Richie would have to win his job back. Sanicki was a 24-year-old long ball hitter from Clifton, New Jersey, who had belted 121 homers in four minor league seasons. He had 33 circuit clouts at Toronto in 1949 before a late season promotion to the Phils. With us he had 3 hits in 13 at bats, all of which were home runs. In addition to his long ball potential, Sanicki was a natural center fielder, fast and with a strong throwing arm.

Del Ennis was, of course, a lock in left field. He had emerged as a premier power hitter, putting together his finest season in 1949, with 25 home runs, 110 RBIs, and a .302 batting average. Del had finished the '49 season on a tear, thanks to switching from a 34- to a 42-ounce bat during the dog days of August. He claimed that the heavier stick enabled him to hit the ball where it was pitched rather than pulling everything. It certainly must have worked as Del raised his average from around .270 to his final .302.

Del always treated his bats with great care.

> **ENNIS:** "I used to hang out at a gas station in the off-season called the Gas House. We were the Gas House Gang. I used to take a dozen bats home at the end of each year. I would fill up one of those big drums with linseed oil at the station and leave the bats laying in the drum all winter. They would get to be about 40 to 42 ounces. Then when I would get to Florida for spring training I would put them in a dryer where they dried the uniforms. That would get them down to about 36 ounces and make them harder. Seminick and I used the same bat all year in '50."

Bob Carpenter knew how valuable Del was to the team and rewarded him accordingly. Del's salary for 1950 was $30,000, at the time the highest ever paid a Phillie.

Going into camp, right field was a trouble spot and wide open. Bill Nicholson was coming off of an injured shoulder and had played sparingly late in '49. He was 35 years old and, although still a valuable ballplayer, could not really be counted on to play every day. Stan Hollmig had started off hot in 1949 but had later cooled off considerably. Although hitting .255 for the year, he had not nailed down right field while Nick had been injured. Dick Whitman, picked up on waivers from the Dodgers, Johnny Blatnick, and Jack Mayo were also in the picture as were rookies Charles Hood and William Loos.

Eddie Sawyer, of course, had several possible outfield scenarios. If Sanicki took over center, he would move Richie to left and Del to right, his more natural position. And Dick Sisler, if he continued to hit like he did the last half of 1949, would demand considerable playing time, either at first or in the outfield.

Our catching appeared to be in fine shape with Andy Seminick and Stan Lopata. Andy had bounced back from a subpar 1948 season to become the starting catcher in the All-Star game. He finished with a career-high 24 home runs and 68 RBIs in 109 games. Although Stan had shown great promise in his rookie year, hitting .271 in 240 at bats, Andy was expected to be our number-one catcher.

Our bullpen catcher would again be Ken Silvestri, whom Eddie had drafted from the Yankee organization after the 1948 season. Hawk, as we called him, had broken into organized baseball in 1936 and made the White Sox in 1939. The war, where he earned three battle stars and a bronze star in the Pacific, cost him four full seasons. Afterwards, he served a couple of years as a backup catcher for the Yankees before spending 1947 and 1948 in Triple A.

Hawk played sparingly for us, appearing in only four games in 1949. He would get into only 11 ballgames for us in 1950, and in 1952 he would not appear in a single game although he was on our active roster the entire year. He would officially become a Phillies coach in 1953.

Although Hawk rarely played, it is hard to describe how important he was to the Whiz Kids. He would warm us up in the bullpen like it was the seventh game of the World Series. He just had wonderful, infectious enthusiasm, all of the time. Hawk would hold his glove low and on the outside corner and if you hit it warming up, he would get excited and yell, "That a boy Robbie! They'll never touch you today with that stuff."

He was that way every day of the week. And even though Hawk was an active player, he would come in early and pitch batting practice to the pitchers. I would get two batboys to shag in the outfield and Hawk would throw me a hundred pitches when there was no one else in the park. He did the work of about eight people, all with his unbridled enthusiasm.

Our pitching staff finished 1949 with a collective 3.89 earned run average, third best in the league. Even so Eddie believed we had holes to fill and brought 18 pitchers to camp. Ken Heintzelman and Russ Meyer had each won 17 games and were counted on as starters, along with Hank Borowy, a 12-game winner, and me. But Kenny had worn down the previous year and Hank had suffered with a sore arm late in 1949; they both were likely to need more rest between starts.

Curt Simmons, although beginning his third full season in the big leagues, was still only 20 years old. He had finished strong in '49, pitching mostly in relief, and looked like he might have turned the corner.

> **SIMMONS:** "My first couple of years I was just trying to get it going. I would beat myself because I was so wild. I would win one and then get off track. We used to ride the trains and the Pullmans were the old curtain jobs with upper and lower berths. Rookies and utility guys on top was the system. At one point I won two or three in a row and they put me in a lower berth. Then I lost a game and I'm back in the upper berth.

"In '49 I started some games early but I was shaky so Sawyer put me down in the bullpen. My motion was herky jerky, I would stride toward first base, I wouldn't open up like a pitcher is supposed to, and I wasn't smooth. George Earnshaw was kind of a roving pitching coach; he would be with the Phillies for awhile and then he would work with our pitchers in the minor leagues for awhile. He harped at me about my legs, trying to get me to square up, and I tried. So I'd think about my legs and not be able to throw the ball.

"I wanted to win a lot of games, too, so I'm willing to try whatever they suggest. They're my coaches and I'm 18 or 19 years old. I didn't realize I was that herky jerky. I thought I was fairly smooth. I had no idea. There was no video camera. I just concentrated on getting the hitter out, throwing strikes. Until they brought it to my attention I just rared back and fired.

"So finally in 1950 spring training Sawyer and Cy Perkins said, 'Hey kid, do it the way you did in high school. Just throw it the way you did back in Egypt.' And it worked, I started doing better."

Cy Perkins was never happy that the other coaches were fooling with Curt's delivery. He would tell me that Connie Mack used to say, "Never fool with a pitcher below the belt. He's been throwing all his life that way and don't think you can change him."

SAWYER: "Curt had a herky jerky motion and threw across his body. I think everybody in the world had told him he couldn't be successful in the big leagues throwing across his body that way. But he got everybody out before and the Phillies gave him a lot of money when he was throwing that way, so I told Earnshaw and our other coaches to leave him alone. I never thought a right-hander could tell a left-hander how to pitch anyway, because they throw so differently. Anyway I said to Curt, 'You go right back to pitching the way you pitched in Egypt, Pennsylvania,' and he got a big grin on his face.

"The only other thing I did was in spring training ask Lefty Gomez to go down in the bullpen and work with Curt to help him hide the ball, which he didn't do very well. Even though Curt threw very hard, the hitters could pick up the ball pretty early and have a good wack at it when Curt threw it over the plate. Of course, at that time Curt didn't throw too many over anyway. Lefty worked with him for two days for about 20 minutes a time on hiding the ball and came back and said, 'He's all right.' Other than that I just let him pitch."

Eddie's philosophy with Curt would pay dividends in 1950, but in spring training he was still very much a question mark.

In the hopes of bolstering our starting pitching, Sawyer had purchased Milo Candini from Oakland of the Pacific Coast League and Ed Wright from the Braves organization. Milo, a 32-year-old veteran from California, had broken into the major leagues in 1943 by winning his first 7 decisions before finishing 11–7. He pitched for five years with some success with weak Washington Senator teams, losing 1945 and most of 1946 to the service, and had won 15 games the year before with Oakland. Ed Wright had won 12 games for the 1946 Braves and, after slipping to the minors, showed promise of regaining his earlier form.

> **SAWYER:** "I'd had Candini in the minor leagues, He had a good arm and had won 11 games for Washington one year. Anybody who had done that well with Washington was worth a shot. The usual question was whether Washington would win 11."

Jocko Thompson, a lean southpaw from Massachusetts with a Warren Spahn–like leg kick, was our leading southpaw prospect after Curt. He had appeared in eight late season games for us in '49 after going 14–5 at Toronto. Breaking into professional baseball in 1939, Jocko had lost four complete seasons to the military. He emerged one of the most highly decorated paratroopers in World War II. He was twice wounded and was awarded seven battle stars, the Silver Star, the Bronze Star with cluster, and decorations from the French, Dutch, and Belgians, among his many honors. In the process he was given a battlefield commission during the Battle of the Bulge and at the war's end served as an aide to General James Gavin in the occupation of Berlin. We understood that Jocko still carried around a considerable amount of shrapnel in his body.

Rookies Bob Miller, Steve Ridzik, Jack Brittin, Paul Stuffel, and Emory "Bubba" Church were other pitching possibilities, as was 35-year-old Blix Donnelly.

A Minnesotan, Blix had broken into organized baseball in 1935 and had pitched in the minor leagues for nine years before sticking with the Cardinals in 1944. He starred in the 1944 World Series against the Browns, pitching six scoreless innings and allowing only two hits. After throwing two shutout innings in relief of Mort Cooper in a losing cause in game one, he relieved Max Lanier at the start of the eighth inning of game two. He proceeded to strike out seven in four innings and was the winning pitcher thanks to Ken O'Dea's pinch hit single in the bottom of the 11th inning.

The Phillies purchased Blix from St. Louis in July 1946, making him one of the most senior Whiz Kids. Never a star, Blix was a valuable spot starter and relief pitcher for us. For some reason, he was a world beater against the Braves, and Eddie would always pitch Blix in Boston. In addition, Blix was a solid citizen who often gave good advice to the young kids on the team.

> **BICKNELL:** "Blix Donnelly was my roommate when I was with the Phillies. He smoothed over a few things for me, especially with the sportswriters. Frank Yeutter had an article in the Philadelphia paper that said, 'How Bicknell ever got carfare for a tryout in Philadelphia amazes me.' Typical Frank Yeutter. Blix Donnelly told me, 'Look. These guys are going to write a lot of things that you don't like. Ignore them and stay away from them.'"

Steve Ridzik had pitched professionally since he was 16 and now, still only 20, had his first real shot at the big leagues.

> **RIDZIK:** "In 1945 I was away from my home in Yonkers, New York, working out with the Pittsburgh Pirates. They were ready to sign me but my father passed away and I came home for the funeral. A Phillies birddog, Fred Mathews, who had been scouting me in Yonkers, came to the funeral and I ended up signing with the Phillies. I was 16 years old, a sophomore in high school. It was legal then to sign before you finished high school, although they changed the rule two years later.
>
> "My brothers were in the service and I told my sisters, 'Just don't say anything, I'm going down to play ball.' I went down to Greensboro, North Carolina, in the Carolina League, and that was quite an experience. I was really too young at 16 to compete at that level. I thought I was a real sensation until I got down there and played with the big boys. They made me a believer in a hurry. Johnny Allen, the old pitcher, was my manager and he was a tough guy. He was from the old school and I really learned a lot from him.

"I came back and pitched in my junior and senior years in high school. I pitched the school to three city championships. I came back chewing tobacco and knocking guys down.

"After my junior year I waited until the high school year was over and then played at Schenectady in the Canadian-American League. Lee Riley was my manager there, Pat Riley's father. Pat was three or four years old and used to be around the ballpark all the time.

"But no one found out I was a pro until I was out of high school. My high school coach was a great guy and was really upset with me. He had basketball and baseball scholarships lined up for me when I told him I was playing in the pros. It was a tough thing."

After going 9–3 with Schenectady in 1947 and leading the league in earned run average, Steve was invited to spring training with the Phillies in 1948 at the age of 19. He started the year with Toronto under Eddie Sawyer.

RIDZIK: "We were playing in Baltimore when the Phillies called Robin Roberts up from Wilmington in June, and Eddie Sawyer told me they were sending me to Wilmington to replace Robbie. I thought this was a real demotion and I told Eddie, 'The hell with it, I'm going home,' and I packed my bags and jumped on a train and went home to Yonkers. I had worked my way up from the buses to the trains and all of a sudden they wanted me to go back to the buses. But I needed some time to cool off.

"The following day Mr. Carpenter called me and said, 'They're fighting for the pennant down there and we want someone with some experience to replace Robbie. You can go right to the Phillies from Wilmington, just like Robbie did.'" So he made me feel a lot better and it worked out real well for me. We were tied for the pennant the last game of the season and Jack Sanford, the manager, called me in and said, 'Well, this is what we brought you here for.' I was very fortunate. I won the game and we won the pennant."

The Phillies had signed Jack Brittin, from Morrisonville, Illinois, near my hometown of Springfield, after an outstanding career at the University of Illinois. Jack was two years older than me and had his college career interrupted by three years in the Navy, where as an ensign he participated in the invasion of Okinawa. Back for his senior year in 1947 he had pitched the Illini to the Big Ten championship before losing to New York University 2–1 in the College World Series. Some sportswriters compared Jack's motion and mannerisms to mine, and we had actually been teammates one summer on an all-star team after his family moved to Springfield. Jack followed me by one year to the Wilmington Blue Rocks, where in 1949 he posted a sparkling 21–7 record and won the league's Most Valuable Player award.

Paul Stuffel was a flamethrower from Canton, Ohio, who had signed right out of high school in 1945. He first served in the military before beginning his professional career in 1947 with Bubba Church at Salina, Kansas. At Terre Haute, Indiana, in 1949 he had struck out a startling 288 batters in 252 innings while compiling a 13–13 record.

> **STUFFEL:** "My second year back from the service the Phillies sent me to Terre Haute in the Three I League. Ray Brubaker was the manager and we really hit it off. He was like a father figure to me. He'd pat you on the back and let you blow a little smoke. The first ballgame I pitched, he died of a heart attack. He died right on the bench in the dugout. Hard to believe, but we finished the ballgame. Of course, we didn't know that he had died until later."

Thanks to the emergence of Jim Konstanty in 1949, our bullpen looked pretty solid going into 1950. Jim had become one of the top relievers in the league in '49, going 9–5 with a 3.25 ERA in 53 appearances. Little did we know that Jim would so dominate in 1950 that the rest of our bullpen would get little work. Our 1950 staff would hurl 57 complete games. Jim appeared in 74 of the remaining 97 games. In most of those games, he was the only pitcher used in relief.

The winter of 1950 was an eventful one for me. In December I married Mary Ann Kalnes, who was teaching school in my hometown of Springfield. Mary is from McFarland, Wisconsin, and is a graduate of the University of Wisconsin. She studied there about the same time that I was at Michigan State. I played at Wisconsin with the MSU basketball team and Mary remembers going to the game, but she does not remember me. I guess I failed to make much of a first impression.

After Mary graduated she applied for teaching jobs in Denver, Colorado, and in Springfield, because of her love of Abraham Lincoln. She got a job in Springfield and taught sixth, seventh, and eighth grade history at the Dubois School.

When I went home to Springfield in 1948 after my rookie season with the Phillies, it was the first time I had spent much time there since high school because I had been in the service, gone to college, and played ball in Vermont. My sister, Nora, had a good friend who taught at the Dubois School. One day she asked Nora, "Why doesn't Evan [everyone calls me Evan in Springfield] call this young teacher from Wisconsin who really doesn't know anybody here?"

So I called Mary and we went out and from then on she was the only girl I ever dated. In fact, I wanted to get married that spring and take her to spring training with me but Mary was not quite ready for that, so we got married the next winter.

When the Phillies reported to Clearwater on February 28 to start 1950 spring training, Mary and I were still in Wisconsin, staying with her parents. Although it was difficult to be up in the snow when spring training began, we remained in the north because I was unhappy with the contract Bob Carpenter had offered me. I had made $9,000 in 1949 and I wanted $20,000 for 1950 because I believed I had established myself as a big league starting pitcher. Bob Carpenter offered me $18,500, which I did not think was enough.

About a week into spring training I went down to Clearwater to sit down with Bob face-to-face. I signed on March 7 after Carpenter offered an attendance clause. In addition to my $18,500 base salary, I was to be paid for each fan we drew over 800,000 for the year. Of course, since we won the pennant and drew over 1.2 million fans, that attendance clause turned out great for me. I ended up making $22,500, more than I was asking for in spring training.

Andy Seminick and Ken Heintzelman also held out that spring. Heinz signed the same day I did but Andy took the train home to Elizabethtown, Tennessee, after three unfruitful meetings with Bob Carpenter. Andy finally signed a week later on March 15.

Eddie Sawyer, following his tightening of the reins the previous August, wanted spring training to be without distractions so that we focused on nothing but baseball. He forbade wives, families, and automobiles in camp, requiring everyone to live at the team hotel and walk back and forth to practice.

The Phillies' wives, who were already unhappy with the skipper for banning them from road trips the previous season, were incensed that

Eddie was depriving them of their annual trip to Florida. I brought Mary to Clearwater when I came down to negotiate with Bob Carpenter, only to find that Mary could not stay with me in the team hotel. Mary stayed in a rooming house close to the team hotel for two weeks before heading back to Wisconsin for the rest of spring training.

Spring training got off to a rocky start when, a couple of days before I signed, Steve Ridzik fractured his kneecap in an intrasquad game. Steve had won 15 games the year before for a last-place Utica team and was thought to have a good chance of sticking with us.

RIDZIK: "I was hit on the knee by Bill Nicholson while pitching batting practice early in spring training. I shook it off and didn't think anything about it. A couple of days later I was pitching in an intrasquad game. I went into my motion, popped that leg up and there was a loud crack and down I went. They said it sounded like a gunshot. They flew me to Philadelphia that day and I was operated on the next day. They put two clips in it.

"The evening I was injured Mr. Carpenter called my family in Yonkers and he talked to them for about a half hour, reassuring them that I was going to be fine. I thought that was a class act. My family really appreciated that he took the time to do that. The Phillies treated you like a family."

SAWYER: "I had a rule in spring training that nobody could work out until they had signed a contract. Bob Carpenter came to me and said, 'Ridzik and these guys are not getting in shape just sitting around.'

"I said, 'You've got to sign him. I'm not going to play him until you do. What are you going to pay him if he gets hurt?' Well, the odd part of it was that he signed Steve Ridzik at the hotel that day and called me at the park and told me. Steve had been throwing on his own, so I had him pitch batting practice and he got hit by a line drive and hurt the day he signed a contract."

Six weeks later Steve joined us in Philadelphia to work with trainer Frank Wiechec. He stayed with us for a month, pitching batting practice and getting his knee in shape. When he was ready to pitch, the Phils sent him to Toronto where he won eight games before being called up around Labor Day.

RIDZIK: "I signed with the Phillies just before they started handing out those large bonuses. I signed for $150 a month with no bonus. So when I got to the Phils late in 1950 Mr. Carpenter came over and shook hands and handed me a $1,000 check. He said, 'Here. You're a big leaguer now. Go on out and buy yourself some clothes 'cause you got to dress like a big leaguer.' That was a lot of money. That was more than I made the whole season before."

Although Steve would get into only one late season game for us in 1950, he would go on to become a solid major league relief pitcher for the Phillies, Giants, Indians, and Senators. In 12 big league seasons he would win 39 and lose 38 while posting a steady 3.79 ERA.

In addition to Steve's injury, we lost four of our first five spring games, reaching our nadir in a 23–6 pasting by the World Champion Yankees on March 15 in Clearwater. Later we blew ninth-inning leads on successive days, giving up three and then eight runs to lose to the Tigers and Red Sox.

But we soon turned it around. As camp wore on it became clear that we could hit. We won six of our last seven games in Florida by scores of 13–3, 13–4, 13–8, 21–6, 10–2, and 10–3. We were hitting a robust .318 as a team when we entrained for our two-week trip north at the end of spring training.

Our solid play enabled Eddie to plug some holes from the year before. With a sensational spring, Mike Goliat established himself as the regular second baseman, both in the field and at bat. Putsy Caballero, who was not even on the roster at the start of spring training, hit .379 and earned a reserve infield spot. As a result, the club released the veteran Eddie Miller.

When it became clear that Eddie Waitkus could reassume his position at first, Sawyer began playing Dick Sisler in the outfield. Dick worked hard to improve his fielding and burned up the Grapefruit Circuit with his bat, hitting .437 in Florida. It became more and more apparent as the spring wore on that Dick had played himself into the starting lineup. Bill Nicholson also hit over .400 in Florida in limited action, but at age 35 he continued to have nagging injuries. He caught his spikes, injuring an ankle just before we left Florida, and missed most of our trip north. Nick was also battling chronic shoulder and knee problems.

Ashburn quickly rebounded from his disappointing sophomore season and reestablished himself in center, hitting at a cool .409 pace in Florida. Eddie Sanicki, who just a few weeks earlier Sawyer had touted (at least to the press) as our new center fielder, had trouble making contact at the plate and was farmed out to Toronto before the season began. Although he would have a cup of coffee with us in 1951, he never stuck in the big leagues.

SAWYER: "Richie had taken the job away from Harry Walker and I think he thought it was his for life. I just wanted to show him it wasn't. But Richie perked up and he played well.

"Sanicki was an excellent center fielder. He could run and throw. He was a good long ball hitter but he swung at too many bad pitches. But when he hit the ball he hit it good. When I had him in Toronto I hit him eighth against right-handed pitchers and fourth against left-handers. He could hit any ball breaking into him but he had trouble with any ball breaking away from him.

"I had the idea that he might play better ball in the major leagues than he had in the minors but it just didn't happen. He didn't get too much of a chance to play and when I did play him he didn't look too good. I think that was because I didn't play him much. He was a slow starter in the spring and we sent him down to get playing time. He had a chance to be a pretty good player, but once he didn't make it with us he kind of gave up and he never really hit his stride again."

Dick Whitman, late of the Dodgers, came from nowhere to win a spot as a reserve outfielder. He hit .438 to lead the team in Florida and showed that he could run and field well. Dick was a 29-year-old graduate of the University of Oregon who would prove to be a valuable addition to our club in 1950. He had broken into professional ball in 1942 and spent three years in the infantry in World War II, surviving the Battle of the Bulge and earning a Bronze Star and Purple Heart in the process. In 1946 he made the Dodgers straight out of the Army and batted .260 in 265 at bats. For much of the next three years, he was shuttled back and forth between the Dodgers and their Montreal farm club.

WHITMAN: "About August of 1948 Branch Rickey called me into his office and said, 'Son, you're doing a pretty good job for us, but we are going to have to option you to Montreal.'

"I was hitting .291 for the Dodgers at the time and told Mr. Rickey, 'Gosh, I didn't expect that this year.'

"Mr. Rickey said, 'Now don't jump to any conclusions. Let me talk.' When Branch Rickey talked, you listened.

"And he said, 'We have a ballplayer in Montreal that I'm sure you know, named Duke Snider. He is going to be one of the next great ballplayers. We have a deal with Montreal that we will not take a player off of their roster unless they are satisfied with the player we send down in his place. And they will take you.'

"I said, 'Well, what does that do for me?'

"He said, 'We are going to give you a $3,000 raise right now which will go on your contract this year and next year.'

"I said, 'Where is the ticket.' Mr. Rickey even arranged for Duke and I to trade our houses.

"The Dodgers were in third place and Montreal was leading the International League. We won the International League and the Little World Series and I got some extra money off that as well. I thought I had made a pretty smart deal until the major league baseball pension started and I realized I had missed that time in the big leagues towards my pension."

Dick spent the entire 1949 season with the Dodgers and appeared in the World Series as a pinch hitter.

WHITMAN: "After the '49 season I was going home and stopped off to see a friend in Bend, Oregon. He said, 'Well, how do you feel about being traded?'

"And I said, 'To whom?'

"He said, 'To the Phillies.'

"I said, 'The Phillies. Who are the Phillies?' I hadn't seen a paper in days, driving across the country to get home. And I had never dreamed that I could be traded to the Phillies.

"I didn't really know why they had purchased me because they seemed to have a lot of outfielders with Ashburn, Ennis, Nicholson, and Sisler. There wasn't a lot of room. When I got to spring training, Eddie Sawyer took me in his office and said, 'We purchased you for the sole purpose of challenging Richie Ashburn. He didn't have a very good year last year and we think you can play well enough to push him to improve.'

"And that spring I tore the cover off the ball. I was always a great hitter in the spring."

Whitman would lead the National League in 1950 with 12 pinch hits, including several game-winners.

After a slow start in spring training our pitching began to take shape by the time we left for the north. After a couple of rough outings, Curt seemed to find himself against the Cards on March 29, pitching six impressive innings in a 10–2 victory. Eddie's hands-off approach seemed to be paying early dividends as Curt regained his confidence. The rest of the staff seemed to be rounding into shape as well and it looked like two rookie pitchers, Bubba Church and Bob Miller, would stick and be able to help us.

Our first stop after breaking camp was Birmingham, Alabama, Bubba Church's hometown. Bubba had shown a fine curveball in Florida and Eddie picked him to start in his own backyard against the Birmingham Barons of the Southern Association. He proceeded to pitch our first complete game of the spring, allowing seven hits as we won 10–4. After that performance it was pretty clear that Bubba would make the ballclub.

Bubba, who got his nickname because that was as close as his little brother could come to saying "brother," served 27 months in the Burma Road sector of India during World War II. He had dropped out of high school to enlist at age 17, lying about his age in the process. In India he and other GIs hacked baseball fields out of the jungle and created the "Tea Patch League." Bubba usually pitched because he was the only guy on his team who could throw a curveball.

Discharged in 1945, Bubba immediately finished high school and played summer baseball well enough to attract several big league scouts. He was advised by his amateur coach, Charley Chappell, to go on to Mississippi State on a baseball scholarship and not to sign professionally until Ben Chapman, also a Birmingham resident, returned home from managing the Phillies at the end of the baseball season.

> **CHURCH:** "After 27 months in India I was looking for a little more excitement than Starkville, Mississippi, had to offer. I also realized that if I stayed in school and graduated I would be 26 years old before I could get started in professional baseball. So at Christmas break I went to see Ben Chapman about signing with the Phillies. Ben Chapman called Herb Pennock and Herb said, 'Bring him to spring training.'
>
> "Ben asked me, 'How long do you think it will take you to get to the majors?'

"I said, 'Three years. If I'm not there in three years, I'm back in school.'

"Ben said, 'If you're not there in three years, you ought to be back in school.'

"Although I was 22, Ben told me, 'You're 21 years old.' Twenty-two was a little old to start a professional career and so Ben told me to be 21. And so I was 21. I think my wife Peggy and I had two kids before she found out how old I really was."

After Bubba got to spring training in 1947, the Phillies could not decide if they wanted him to pitch or play the outfield. Bubba was an excellent athlete and good hitter and Chapman wanted him to play every day. Pennock thought that with his arm and curve ball he should be a pitcher. Finally, they decided to send Bubba to Salina, Kansas, in the Class C Western Association and let him try both.

CHURCH: "The first half of the season I would pitch one game and play three games in the outfield. I loved it. I was just having a blast. Early on they told me not to steal any bases. Halfway through the season I was 9 and 6 as a pitcher and hitting about .320. Then the order came down from Philadelphia that I would not play the outfield any more. So I won 12 games and lost 3 the rest of the year to wind up 21 and 9."

The following year Bubba jumped all the way to Triple A under Eddie Sawyer in Toronto and struggled, finishing with a 5–9 record and a 5.52 ERA. After some soul searching in the off-season while attending Louisiana State University, Bubba had an outstanding 1949 season in Toronto, winning 15 and losing only 8 while leading the International League with a 2.35 ERA. In 211 innings he gave up only 152 hits. His performance earned him a real shot at making the Phillies in 1950.

CHURCH: "I had a lot of help in Toronto. Hal Wagner, a veteran catcher who had caught in Boston and Detroit, worked and worked with me. I was into throwing sliders and sinkers and sailers and Del Bissonette, who succeeded Eddie Sawyer at Toronto, told me, 'Bubba, you've got a good fastball and a good curveball. Take something off of both of them and you'll have four pitches.' So I did. And that was the way I pitched, right into the major leagues.

"I wanted to be on that Phillies ballclub in 1950 so bad I could taste it. With Toronto we would go right through Philadelphia on the train on our way down to play Baltimore. You could actually see Shibe Park from the train and sometimes some of the guys would go over there, if we had time between trains. But I had made up my mind that I would never go into Shibe Park until I was on that big league roster, and I didn't until I came north with the Phillies in 1950."

After the ballgame in Birmingham we continued our swing through the south, visiting New Orleans and Shreveport before heading for Texas, where we sandwiched two games against the Fort Worth Cats around a game against the Dallas Eagles of the Texas League. In the second game against the Cats, 23-year-old rookie Bob Miller relieved Russ Meyer at the start of the fourth inning, after Monk had been rocked for seven hits and five runs in three innings. Entering the game trailing 5–0, Bob held the Cats to one run on five hits the final six innings as we came back to win 10–6 on two homers by Granny Hamner and one each by Del Ennis and Willie Jones.

That sterling performance cemented Bob's improbable jump from Class B Terre Haute of the Three I League to the Phillies. Bugger, as we called him, had had a superb year at Terre Haute, compiling a 19–9 record with 28 complete games and a 2.72 ERA in 255 innings. He had pitched well against us that August when the Phillies played an exhibition game in Terre Haute and had earned a late season call-up, pitching three shutout innings.

MILLER: "Dale Jones, our minor league pitching coach, came to my house in January, 1950. He had the Phillies' roster and he told me, 'Bob, you're going to be one of their starters this year. They think the world of you.' I sort of believed him but I didn't really think that I could make the jump from Class B ball to the big leagues. I thought I would be going to Utica, which was our A club in the Eastern League."

Bob was from Detroit and as a high school pitcher had twice lost to future Tigers and Indians pitcher Art Houtteman in the Detroit Catholic High School championship game in Tiger Stadium. As a 16-year-old he had played American Legion ball in the summer with future Whiz Kid teammate Stan Lopata. Immediately after graduation from high school in 1944, Bob was drafted into the Army although he had received a basketball scholarship at the University of Detroit.

For the next two and half years Bob served in the military, including 18 months overseas where he saw combat in Northern Luzon in the

Philippines. After the war he was stationed in Japan, where he was able to play some baseball. Discharged in the fall of 1946, Bob enrolled at the University of Detroit and pitched quite successfully for the baseball team in the spring of 1947. That summer he pitched and won three complete games in five days in a national amateur tournament in Youngstown, Ohio, and first attracted the attention of Phillies scout Eddie Krajnik.

Bob resisted signing right away and pitched another year in college. He did sign with the Phillies the following spring for a $2,500 bonus, choosing us over the Tigers, who already had local prospects such as Billy Pierce, Ted Gray, and Houtteman under contract. The Phillies sent him to Terre Haute in late June 1948, where Bugger pitched pretty well, compiling a 6–5 record and a solid 3.51 ERA in 118 innings of work in his first professional year.

As a bonus player, the Phillies had to call Bob up in 1949 or risk losing him to another organization for the waiver price. With Curt, Stan Hollmig, and Charlie Bicknell already on the big league roster, the Phillies did not have room for another bonus player. Fortunately, however, no other club drafted Bob in 1949 and he forced his way onto the Phillies' roster with his 19 wins at Terre Haute.

Bob was a strapping 6'3" with a physical appearance and pitching style reminiscent of a young Dizzy Dean. He threw a sizzling fastball and an effective sinkerball and would prove to be a vital addition to our 1950 pitching staff. Without the emergence of Bubba and Bob, the Whiz Kids could have never won the pennant in 1950.

Charlie Bicknell, who had been with us in 1948 and 1949 under the bonus rule, was one casualty of the strong spring showings of Bubba, Bob, and Curt. As we left Texas the Phillies put Charlie on waivers and the Braves claimed him for the $10,000 waiver price. In his two seasons with the Phillies he had pitched only 54 innings, compiling an 0–1 record.

> **BICKNELL:** "I was relieved when the Braves bought me. The Phillies couldn't put me down in the minor leagues where I needed to be. I knew I needed experience and I got it in the Braves' system. I had some good years in the minors and won a couple of pennants.
>
> "With the Phillies, I just sat back and took the whole thing in. I thought to myself, 'What the hell am I doing here?' I knew I shouldn't have been there. I think the other guys knew it, too, but they tried to smooth things over. But I didn't really feel a part of the team.

"They fit you for a uniform in spring training. Everybody gets fitted the way they want. When we got to the clubhouse in Philadelphia after spring training, everyone had two white uniforms and two gray for the road in their lockers. But I had one of each. I never said anything or told anybody, but that hurt.

"If you ever notice the 1948 team photo you'll see that I'm not in that picture. I'm not in it because I didn't want to be. I told the team I had somebody sick back home on picture day.

"I was a mop-up man. I didn't get to pitch much and when I did they usually knocked my jock off. So I was happy to go to the Braves and pitch in the minors."

We traveled to Little Rock after our Texas swing to play the Travelers of the Southern Association. I held the Travelers to three hits and one run in a 9–1 game halted after six innings by rain. I had pitched pretty decently in Florida after my late start, and now on our trip north I began throwing really well.

The following day Curt held the Memphis Chicks hitless in six innings while striking out six in a 9–0 win. Thanks to Eddie Sawyer's hands-off policy, Curt was beginning to find himself.

> **SIMMONS:** "I had gone through two big league seasons and I just started having a little more confidence and started getting guys out. I was really pitching well on our trip north in 1950. I was getting the ball over and I was really nailing down those high minor league teams. That got me going."

In the Memphis ballgame, Mike Goliat slugged two home runs and a single to drive in five runs. Mike, free of injury, looked like he was going to be a star at second base. He had fielded flawlessly all spring and was hitting for average and with power with 7 homers and 35 RBIs. Stan Baumgartner, who covered the Phillies for the *Philadelphia Inquirer*, wrote that Goliat was the best second baseman in Florida, superior even to Red Schoendienst of the Cardinals.

Our final stop was Louisville before heading to Philadelphia for our traditional three-game City Series against the Athletics. I was pitching batting practice there to my old roomie Johnny Blatnick when Eddie Sawyer hollered out, "That's enough, Robin."

I said, "Just one more, Eddie." I threw one more pitch and Blatnick nailed me in the calf with a line drive. Although painful, I ended up only with a bad bruise and it appeared I would be able to pitch against the Dodgers in our opening series. Needless to say, Eddie Sawyer had a few choice words about "just one more."

Snow flurries and cold reduced our City Series to two games, canceling the first meeting. Eddie started me the next day and I gave up three runs in four innings as we lost 7–4 in 46-degree weather, despite Goliat's eighth round-tripper of the spring. Curt, aided by two innings of relief from Bob Miller, beat the A's 11–2 the following day to split the series and propel us into the regular season on a winning note.

> **MILLER:** "The first pitch I threw in the City Series was against Sam Chapman, the old outfielder for the A's, and he hit it over the scoreboard. I said to myself, 'Whoa, maybe I'm in the wrong league here,' but after that I got them out."

We headed into the season confident that we were a good ballclub. Our pitching, after a slow start, had come on strong. I was throwing good and Curt appeared ready to fulfill his considerable potential. Konstanty looked as if he would continue his outstanding relief work from '49 and the emergence of Church and Miller promised to give us depth that we had not previously enjoyed.

Heintzelman and Meyer had not pitched particularly well in the spring but had each won 17 games in 1949. They had been our best pitchers the last two months of the season and were counted on to lead our staff in 1950. Two top prospects, Jack Brittin and Paul Stuffel, would be waiting in the wings in Toronto, where they would be joined by Steve Ridzik when he recovered from his knee injury. Thus, overall we believed our pitching had a chance to be outstanding.

We tore the cover off the ball all spring, ending our swing north hitting a vigorous .335 as a team. Of course, the games in our southern swing were against minor league opposition, but we knew we could hit. Ashburn, Ennis, Nicholson, Sisler, and Whitman, all outfielders, hit over .400. Ashburn had reclaimed center field with a vengeance, Dick Sisler had forced his way into the lineup, and Whitman had forced his way onto the ballclub.

Our infield was set and looked very strong. Our catching promised to be sound as Lopata again challenged Seminick for playing time. Waitkus was ready to resume his place at first and Goliat had nailed down the second base job with his exceptional spring. Hamner and Jones had both hit well above .300 and had done nothing to dispel the notion that they were the best young shortstop and third base combo in the league.

Granny now had two full seasons under his belt and had started every game at shortstop in 1949, leading the league in at bats and assists. At 22 he had become a vital part of our ballclub. Granny, a cocky, outspoken guy, had become something of a team leader, although I am not sure there was anyone necessarily following.

> **ASHBURN:** "Granny was a tough ballplayer. He was never intimidated on or off the field. But he did like to stay up and play cards half the night."

> **CHURCH:** "Granny had a problem sleeping. Granny couldn't sleep. When we were in Philadelphia, Granny would go to the shore and stand in water up to his hips fishing most of the night. And on the road Granny would want to go out and move a little. I walked the streets with Granny Hamner till 3:00 in the morning in every National League city.

> "Granny was a great fellow. He loved baseball. Played hard. Played hurt. Played."

That spring we had impressed none other than Branch Rickey, president of the Dodgers. Rickey had watched us clobber the Fort Worth Cats, a Dodger farm club, during our swing through Texas, and he picked us to finish second behind Brooklyn.

During that spring sportswriters first began referring to us as the "Whiz Kids." Bob Carpenter had jettisoned "Blue Jays" as an official team nickname over the winter. In six years it had never really caught on. Whiz Kids, in contrast, quickly took hold because of our youth, our fast finish in 1949, and our impressive spring.

Harry Grayson, sports editor of the Newspaper Enterprise Association Service (NEA), was generally given credit for first using the nickname. In covering the major league camps that spring he had made our Clearwater base his headquarters, and we had apparently impressed him. He was probably the only national writer to pick us to win the pennant.

No one seemed to know whether Grayson took the name from the University of Illinois basketball team of the early 1940s, who were known as the Whiz Kids because of their youth, or, as some have suggested, as a takeoff on "The Quiz Kids," a popular radio show from the 1940s that featured precocious children showing their brilliance by answering obscure questions. But during the summer Babe Alexander, our public relations man, arranged for us to present Mr. Grayson with a lighter inscribed "In appreciation to Harry Grayson, the man who named us the Whiz Kids."

Going into the season, we knew we faced stiff opposition. Brooklyn and St. Louis, the two league powers in 1949, both had good starting pitching, great hitting, and solid defense. We knew they would both be tough. Boston had the same nucleus that had won in 1948, including pitchers Warren Spahn, Johnny Sain, and Vern Bickford. In addition, the Giants had added Sal Maglie to their pitching corps and, under Leo Durocher, appeared to be a contender.

Although we knew we were talented, I am not sure many of us really thought we could beat the Dodgers or the Cardinals for the pennant over the long haul. But, as we later found out, our skipper had more confidence in us than we did in ourselves. One day during a rain delay the first week of the season Eddie was alone in his office evaluating the upcoming pennant race.

> **SAWYER:** "We had a pretty good spring training and had really come on strong the year before, when we finished third. I was going over the lineups to see who we had to beat and the Dodgers seemed to be the main obstacle. We had played the Dodgers pretty even most of the time. We played each other 22 games a year, 11 in each place. The Dodgers played better in Philadelphia and we played better in Brooklyn. I went over the other teams and I figured that if we played the way I thought we should we would win by 10 games. So I wrote on a slip of paper that we would win the pennant by 10 games. Then I stuck it in the drawer in my desk and forgot about it.

> "After the season was over I was in my office looking in that drawer for a cigar. Frank Yeutter, who was the writer for the *Philadelphia Bulletin,* was sitting there with me when I pulled this slip of paper out of the drawer. So he made a big deal out of it. It turned out I was only eight games off."

Chapter 11
A Tense Pennant Race

As the 1950 season opened some sportswriters predicted that we would challenge the Dodgers for the pennant. On the morning of our April 18 opener against the defending champion Brooklyn Dodgers, Stan Baumgartner wrote in the *Philadelphia Inquirer,* "What promises to be the greatest season for the Phillies since the pennant-winning days of 1915 will get under way at 1:30 P.M. at Shibe Park today," referring to us as "Eddie Sawyer's astonishing Whiz Kids." Our success during the last half of 1949 and our strong showing in spring training had created an uncommon amount of anticipation in Philadelphia.

To add to the excitement of the new campaign, we broke out sharp new red pinstripe uniforms, complete with red caps and stockings, on opening day.

> **SAWYER:** "I actually designed the pinstripe uniforms. I thought the old uniforms were terrible looking big league uniforms. And Bob Carpenter agreed to change them. I worked for Wilson Sporting Goods and so I told them that I wanted pinstripe uniforms like the Yankees, only in red. I thought that the Yankee blue pinstripes were good looking uniforms.
>
> "But Wilson did not want to make them. They said they could not make uniforms with pinstripes for anybody but the Yankees. But I knew that wasn't true because Red Rolfe [former Yankee third baseman] was coaching at Yale and had pinstripe uniforms there. So even though I was with Wilson, I told them, 'I

have a lot of good friends at MacGregor. They'll make them for us any way we want them.' So Wilson decided to make the uniforms for us.

"We were still using the old uniforms in spring training. But after a game against Detroit in Clearwater we had Jack Mayo, who was about 6'2" and a real handsome guy, model the new uniform outside the clubhouse in front of a whole lineup of women, scouts, and some of the front office people. Bob Carpenter's wife Mary said, 'This really isn't fair. Jack Mayo would look good in anything.' But they all liked them and we had them made up for opening day."

Eddie tapped me to open the season against the Dodgers. That first series was important because we knew we would have to beat the Dodgers if we were to win the pennant. The first game was significant to me not only because it was my first opening day start but because I had not yet beat the Dodgers. In my first year and a half I had gone 0–5 against them, losing some close ballgames and getting knocked around in some others. In fact, Bob Carpenter had brought that up in our contract negotiations when I held out earlier that spring. And he was right.

My opponent was Don Newcombe, who had burst on the scene in 1949 with a 17–8 record and was already considered one of the top pitchers in the league. A crowd just shy of 30,000, the largest opening day gathering in our history, showed up on a cool, clear day. I always liked pitching in cool weather because the ball felt smaller in my hand, making it seem like I had a little extra pop on my fastball.

After I retired Brooklyn in order in the first, it took us only two pitches to score off of Newcombe. Richie Ashburn lined Newk's first pitch to left for a single. Granny Hamner, a well-known first-ball swinger, rifled the next offering past Duke Snider in deep right center, scoring Whitey for our first run. After Newk got Eddie Waitkus to pop to Pee Wee Reese at short, Del Ennis worked the count to 2–2 before ripping a shot off the top of the left field wall to drive in Granny.

We scored three more in the second to chase Newcombe, two in the third, and one in the fourth to make it 8–0. We went on to win 9–1 as I scattered seven hits to finally beat the Dodgers. We clobbered five Dodger pitchers for 16 hits, including 4 by Mike Goliat and 3 each by Hamner and Waitkus.

ANDY SEMINICK: "We had already scored five runs off Newcombe in the opener by the time Jackie Robinson came up to the plate for the first time. Jackie said to me, 'What do you guys think you're going to do, win the pennant?'

"I said, 'Yessir, we're going to do it this year. You bet.'"

Throughout his brief career Goliat would hit Newcombe like he owned him. One year later, on opening day in 1951, Mike tagged Newk for a home run. As he came to home plate after rounding the bases he asked me facetiously, "What's the home run record in this league anyway?" Unfortunately, by June of that year Mike was back in the minor leagues, never to return.

Although Brooklyn beat Russ Meyer the next day 7–5, our opening thrashing of the Dodgers and their ace was a great psychological boost to us to start the season.

We then traveled to Boston for four games against the Braves. The initial contest ended in a 2–2 tie, called in the eighth inning due to sleet and freezing cold. The following day Curt Simmons hooked up in a great pitching duel with Warren Spahn and led 2–1 in the eighth, thanks to Del's run-scoring triple and single.

But history did repeat itself. The previous April, Curt had taken a one-hitter and a 3–0 lead into the ninth at Braves Field, only to lose 4–3. Many, including Eddie Sawyer, thought that game had destroyed Curt's confidence and ruined his season. Now, in the bottom of the eighth Curt walked Sam Jethroe, who was sacrificed to second by Willard Marshall. Curt then got two strikes on the dangerous Bob Elliot, the Braves third baseman. Elliot worked the count to 2–2 and then connected on a high outside fastball, sending it far over the fence in right for a 3–2 Braves victory.

We split a doubleheader with the Braves the next day, losing 4–3 and then winning 6–5 to break a three-game losing streak. The nightcap was my second start of the year. I could not hold a 4–2 lead, falling behind 5–4 in the fifth due in large part to Sid Gordon's two-run homer. Jim Konstanty relieved me after six innings and held the Braves scoreless as we tied the game in the seventh on Willie Jones's double and Dick Sisler's pinch single and won it in the eighth. With one out against the Braves' Bob Hogue, Waitkus singled and Del doubled him to third. Puddinhead then drove in the winning run with a long fly to center.

Konstanty, helped by fine running catches in the ninth by Dick Whitman and Del, gave notice of his MVP season to come by throwing three perfect innings for the first of his 16 victories in relief.

In spite of the come-from-behind win against the Braves, we continued to struggle early. On April 26, we lost a tough 5–4, 10-inning contest to Brooklyn in Ebbets Field when the umpires failed to call fan interference on a long fly to left by Roy Campanella. Sisler leaped at the wall for the ball and missed it when a fan leaned over and deflected the ball. Umpire Babe Pinelli ruled a ground-rule double over the heated objections of Eddie Sawyer, who officially protested the game. The decision put runners on second and third and allowed the Dodgers to score the winning run a couple of batters later. Our record fell to 2–5.

Fortunately, I continued to pitch well against Brooklyn, beating the Dodgers 9–2 the following day as our offense came to life behind Dick Sisler's four-hit day and Willie Jones's four RBIs. We returned home and Curt again faced his nemesis, the Boston Braves. This time Curt pitched a masterful three-hitter, overpowering the Braves 6–1. After struggling for two years, it looked like Curt had arrived as top-notch starting pitcher. In spite of our slow start, our chances to be in the pennant race improved dramatically with Curt's emergence.

Mike Goliat broke an 0-for-26 slump in Curt's win with a double in the fifth, his first hit since the second game of the season. Puddinhead stroked a two-run single to run his hitting streak to 10 games. He was hitting a robust .400 with 13 runs batted in.

Our prospects for 1950 got even brighter the next day when Bob Miller made his first major league start a success, pitching us to a tense 2–1 complete game victory over Boston. Leading in the ninth, Bob retired the first two batters before walking Tommy Holmes and allowing a double to Sam Jethroe. At this juncture, with the tying run on third and the go-ahead run on second, Eddie Sawyer visited the mound. The skipper stayed with Bob, who proceeded to walk Buddy Kerr unintentionally to load the bases.

Eddie started out to the mound again but changed his mind and went back to the dugout to let Bob pitch to Earl Torgeson, the next batter. Torgeson ripped Bob's second pitch deep to right field, but we all breathed a sigh of relief when Del made a nice catch to end the ballgame. Eddie had shown uncommon confidence in a rookie starting his first game, but, as a result, it looked like we had another solid starter.

SAWYER: "I had seen Bob pitch in Terre Haute and he pitched well late in games. In fact, I thought he might make a good relief pitcher because he had good control. But when we started him he pitched pretty well. His best pitch was a curveball. He got more fellows out on a 3–2 curve than anybody I ever saw in my life. And of course I wanted to build up his confidence if he could get them out. So I decided to leave him in there. Then he went on to win eight straight games."

MILLER: "The ninth inning was almost a disaster for me. I had two outs but then I guess I started overthrowing and walked a couple and they loaded the bases. Earl Torgeson, their number-three hitter, came up and hit a line drive right at Del Ennis. It went off the bat and the next second it was in Del's glove and the game was over. Three or four feet either way and I would have been a losing pitcher instead of a winning pitcher. I was very excited and jumped off the mound. The first thing I wanted to do was call my mom and dad in Detroit. I owed them so much, they were always behind me. When I called them I think they were more excited than I was."

The emergence of Curt and Bob was very timely because Russ Meyer and Ken Heintzelman were struggling and Hank Borowy was battling a sore arm. Monk managed to get himself suspended for seven days for hitting umpire Al Barlick with the ball and bumping him while protesting a close play at first in the third inning of a game against the Braves on April 30.

Eddie certainly thought we could use more pitching because that week he traded Johnny Blatnick to the Cardinals for 27-year-old southpaw Ken Johnson.

SAWYER: "Johnny Blatnick was having a tough time. He had come up in 1948 and looked like he was going to break the league wide open. In fact, I had recommended him to Herb Pennock when John was in the Eastern League. He came in and played very well for Ben Chapman. But then he had really struggled. The Cardinals wanted a right-handed hitter and we needed a left-handed pitcher because some teams were really susceptible to lefties. Kenny was kind of flakey but he had a great arm and one of the best curveballs I've ever seen, although he couldn't always throw it for strikes. But I liked John and I was sorry it didn't work out for him."

BLATNICK: "We were coming back from New York on the train when Eddie Sawyer asked me to come over and talk to him. He told me they had traded me to St. Louis for Ken Johnson and that the Cardinals wanted me to report right away because Stan Musial had gotten hurt the day before and they needed somebody to play the outfield the next day. So I went right out to the airport when we got to Philadelphia and flew into Pittsburgh where the Cardinals were playing and went right to the ballpark. I had to borrow shoes and a glove and everything else because I had left it all in Philadelphia.

"So I put the new uniform on and in the first inning I batted and drove in Enos Slaughter from second base with a single. But I wasn't there too long before they got Johnny Lindell from the Yankees and sent me down to the Houston Buffs in the Texas League. It was so hot and miserable down there that they had us wear shorts for our uniforms.

"I liked the guys on the Phillies and was disappointed to leave. They were a fun-loving, cohesive bunch who could really play baseball. So I was down there in the heat all summer rooting for the Phillies to win the pennant even though I belonged to the Cardinals."

Ken Johnson was signed in 1941 by Branch Rickey of the Cardinals as an 18-year-old playing American Legion ball in Topeka, Kansas.

JOHNSON: "I convinced Branch Rickey that I needed some money to go to school at KU [Kansas University] because my parents couldn't afford to send me. So I got a signing bonus of $5,000 and I thought after that there wasn't any money left in St. Louis."

Ken spent three years in the Army during World War II and played a lot of service ball while stationed in the Philippines. After the war he continued to be plagued by wildness and bounced around the Cardinal chain before earning a call-up late in 1947. On September 27, his first big league start, Kenny threw a complete game one-hitter to defeat the Cubs 3–1. He began 1948 with Rochester and was again promoted, this time in midseason. Still troubled by wildness but with great potential, he pitched sparingly for the Cardinals in 1948 and 1949 before his trade to the Phillies in 1950.

JOHNSON: "We were in Pittsburgh when [Cardinals manager] Eddie Dyer told me I had been traded to the Phillies. I was a little sad to leave the Cardinals because I got along well with my teammates there and I didn't know anyone on the Phillies except Dick Sisler. But the fellows on the Phillies were good guys also. Eddie Sawyer told me he wanted to spot start me against some of the teams that had a lot of left-handed hitters and that is what he did. The trade certainly worked out fine for me."

Five days after the trade, Ken beat the Cubs 5–2 in Wrigley Field, pitching into the ninth inning before tiring. His performance was remarkable considering he had pitched very little for the Cardinals since his elevation to the major leagues in the middle of 1948.

Eddie Sawyer had Ken Silvestri behind the plate for Johnson because he wanted a veteran catcher and Andy Seminick was away from the club just then because of the death of his mother.

> **SAWYER:** "I told Hawk not to worry about pitching to spots. I just wanted Kenny to get the ball over the plate. So I said to Hawk, 'As he goes to the mound each inning tell him to throw every ball through the center. We don't care if they make a hundred hits. What we don't want is 10 walks.'"

Hawk did as he was told and Kenny scattered 12 hits but gave up only two bases on balls. Ken would go on to play an important role for us as a spot starter, winning four games against only one loss in eight starts.

Ken's victory over the Cubs on May 3 evened our record at 7–7. We had won five of seven after our slow start, thanks to our newfound pitching depth. We continued to play extremely well, winning seven of our next eight games, including six in a row. We moved into second place behind the Dodgers on May 7 by sweeping a doubleheader from the Reds in Cincinnati 6–0 and 6–4. The following day we came from behind to again beat the Reds 6–5, thanks to a two-run seventh-inning rally spearheaded by Dick Whitman and Richie Ashburn. Newcomers Miller and Johnson again provided the winning pitching.

Although we were rained out the next day in Pittsburgh, we took over first place as the Reds beat Brooklyn 4–0 behind former Phil Ken Raffensberger's three-hit shutout. I then pitched against the Pirates, looking for my fourth win. We jumped out to a 3–0 lead, thanks to Puddinhead's three-run first inning homer off of Murry Dickson. I took a 3–1 advantage into the ninth but gave up base hits to the first two Pirate batters, Tom Saffell and Johnny Hopp, to put runners on first and second. That brought up Ralph Kiner, who already had seven home runs in the young season. After I fell behind on him 2–1, Ralph popped up a fastball to Granny at shortstop.

But I was not out of trouble by a long shot. Nanny Fernandez singled through the mound, scoring Saffell. Hopp, the tying run, took third on the play when Richie fumbled the ball in center. I now had to face pinch hitters Wally Westlake, another slugging outfielder, and Dale Coogan with the tying run on third and the winning run on first. I bore down and fanned Wally on four pitches for the second out and then whiffed Coogan for the final out send us back to Philly on cloud nine.

After that tense 3–2 win over the Pirates, we headed home having won 11 of 14 games on our western swing. We had started the trip in sixth place and were coming home in first, a game in front of Brooklyn and St. Louis.

Near the end of that tour Eddie added another infielder, purchasing 32-year-old Jimmy Bloodworth from Cincinnati. Jimmy had broken into organized baseball way back in 1935. After coming to the major leagues in 1939, he had played a lot of second base for the Washington Senators and Detroit Tigers. Following a stint in the minors in 1948, he had rebounded to become the Reds' regular second baseman in 1949. Jimmy was a good acquisition because of his versatility and experience, and he would come though with several clutch hits for us during the course of the season.

Curt overpowered the Giants on three hits in the first game of our home stand as we won 7–1 behind round-trippers by Dick Sisler and Del Ennis. After a loss to the Giants the following day to end our winning streak at six (the second game of the doubleheader that day was suspended because of the Sunday curfew law with us leading 9–7 after eight innings), we prepared to open a three-game series against the Reds. I was to pitch the opener against Cincinnati ace Ewell Blackwell.

In those days, it was common for teams to pitch their aces against each other in the first game of a series, although I am not sure I qualified just yet. But it was for that reason that I pitched so many games against Don Newcombe and Warren Spahn over the years. Blackwell had dominated the league in 1947 with 22 wins (including 16 in a row), 193 strikeouts, and a 2.47 ERA. Known as the Whip, he was 6'6" tall and, with a right-handed sidearm delivery, absolute murder on right-handed hitters. Although he had suffered with a sore arm in 1948 and 1949, he was healthy in 1950 and looked ready to dominate again.

The game turned into a classic pitching duel. In our first Richie and Granny led off with infield hits. Waitkus walked to load the bases and Del Ennis grounded into a double play, scoring Richie. That scratch run turned out to be the only score of the ballgame. Ewell allowed only one more hit, but in the meantime I was shutting the Reds out on two hits in what was probably my best major league performance to that date.

After that ballgame, I had a feeling we were to be reckoned with and had a legitimate shot at the pennant. Beating one of the top pitchers in the league in a 1–0 game somehow demonstrated to me at least that we were for real.

The next day we rallied in the bottom of the ninth to beat the Reds 5–4 in another nail-biter behind another clutch pitching performance by Ken Johnson. We had fallen behind 4–3 in the fifth but tied it in the seventh and won it in the ninth when Eddie Waitkus led off with a triple off Reds starter Herm Wehmeier. Del was intentionally walked before Puddinhead laced an 0–2 pitch to center to drive in Eddie and end the ballgame in our favor.

Those ballgames against the Reds gave us a lot of confidence. Although we had a long season ahead, it seemed that someone was always coming through with a clutch fielding play, base hit, or pitching performance to win a close, hard-fought game.

On May 24 we scored six runs in the eighth to erase a 3–0 deficit against the Pirates in Bubba Church's second big league start. Sisler's three-run homer was the big blow and Konstanty, who relieved Bubba in the eighth, held the Pirates scoreless to record his second win of the year. We closed our home stand successfully the following day as Bob Miller won his third straight, scattering eight hits to shut out the Bucs 3–0.

Although we won 6 out of 10 on our first long home stand, we slipped a game behind the streaking Dodgers, who seemed to be winning every day. Dick Sisler was hitting a blistering .364 and he, Del, and Puddinhead were the top three in the league in RBIs. Our pitching continued to be steady behind Curt, Bob Miller, Ken Johnson, and me, and Jim Konstanty was regularly shutting the door when anyone faltered.

Our upcoming 18-game road trip was sure to test our staying power. I opened the trip on May 26 against the Giants in New York. We were tied 2–2 in the eighth inning of another tense, seesaw game when Eddie Stanky bobbled Sisler's grounder for an error. Puddinhead followed with a double to send Dick to third. Then our new acquisition, Jimmy Bloodworth, contributed to our cause by clubbing a sacrifice fly to Whitey Lockman in center to drive in Dick with the go-ahead run.

I survived a jam in the bottom of the ninth to record my sixth win and, in the process, matched my season high of 11 strikeouts.

The next day I got thrown out of my first big league ballgame, without even leaving the bench. With Curt pitching, Andy Seminick was on home-plate umpire Artie Gore all afternoon, fussing about ball and strike calls. One inning Andy came off the field and sat by me, still shouting at Artie. Finally, Artie walked over to the dugout and yelled, "Roberts, you're out of here."

I was sitting in the dugout, enjoying the bright Saturday afternoon sunlight and had not said a word all day. In fact, I was about half asleep since I had pitched the day before and knew I was not going to be used. I looked over at Eddie Sawyer and he said, "Go ahead, Robin."

So I trudged out to the clubhouse, which in the Polo Grounds was located in dead center field. When I passed Artie he said, "I had to throw out somebody and I knew they weren't going to use you."

While making that long walk, I thought about my mother reading that I had been thrown out of a ballgame and probably thinking that I had done something really bad. It occurred to me that I would have to get Artie Gore to write her a letter and explain the situation.

It was lucky for us that Artie let Seminick stay in the game because Andy laced three hits, including a grand slam home run off of Sheldon Jones to lead us to an 8–5 victory and into a tie for the league lead with the Dodgers. Curt got his sixth win with help from Jim Konstanty.

A couple of days later on May 30 we lost a doubleheader to the Dodgers in Brooklyn, 7–6 and 6–4, to fall to third place, a game and a half off the pace. I pitched the first eight innings of the opener, another close ballgame, and left down 6–5. We scratched out a run with two out in the top of the ninth on two walks, an infield hit by Granny, and a wild throw to tie the score. Brooklyn came back against Jim Konstanty in the last of the tenth. After two walks, a bad throw by Granny on Preacher Roe's slow-roller allowed Bobby Morgan to score the winning run from second. Russ Meyer, still unable to get untracked, lost his fifth straight in the nightcap.

By the beginning of June we were in the thick of a tight pennant race with the Dodgers and Cardinals. The Braves and Cubs were close as well, making it a five-team race. Rainouts had plagued us, as they had the league in general, and the resulting makeup games late in the season would play havoc with our depleted pitching staff. Eddie Sawyer already had a new slogan for the press, "The Kids, Konstanty, and Rain," a take-off on the "Spahn, Sain, and Pray for Rain" saying made famous by the 1948 Boston Braves.

Our kid pitchers and Jim Konstanty were carrying the load, winning 22 of our 23 victories to that point. Curt had arrived and was 7–2. I was 6–2, Bob Miller and Ken Johnson were both 3–0, and Konstanty was 3–1 and dominating the league in relief.

In contrast, our veteran pitchers were having their problems. By June 4 Russ Meyer and Ken Heintzelman, who had each won 17 games in 1949, were a combined 1–9, yet we were within a half game of the lead. In addition, Blix Donnelly was 0–2 and Hank Borowy, a 12-game winner in '49, had thrown only three innings and would be sold shortly to the Pirates.

Bubba Church gave notice that he could contribute as well, defeating the Cubs 6–2 on June 2 in Wrigley Field for his first major league win. Jim Konstanty closed with two and a third innings of hitless relief.

We returned home June 12 with an 8–7 record from our long road trip, in third place 2½ games behind St. Louis. We quickly lost two straight to the Cardinals to fall 4½ games out of the lead, our low point for the year.

We did not stay down for long, again exhibiting our remarkable resilience. The Reds followed the Cardinals to Shibe Park, and we swept a three-game series from them to climb back to 1½ games out of first place. After giving up a first-inning home run to Johnny Wyrostek to fall behind 2–0, I beat Blackwell again 5–2 in the first game for my eighth win. Simmons and Miller pitched complete-game wins over Cincinnati the next day as we won 4–3 and 4–2. Bill Nicholson, just activated from the disabled list, knocked in the winning run in the first game with a pinch single in the bottom of the ninth to secure Curt's eighth win. Bob Miller, the talk of the league, won his fifth straight with a seven-hitter in the nightcap.

After winning two out of three from the Pirates, including Meyer's first win and Miller's sixth straight, we were only a half game behind the first place Dodgers. Our record on June 23 was 32–22.

For the next three weeks, up until the All-Star break, we were never farther than one game out of the lead in the seesaw pennant race.
We grabbed the lead, by mere percentage points over St. Louis and Brooklyn, on June 27 when Simmons, aided by Konstanty, beat the Braves 3–2 in Boston. Spahn in defeat gave up only three hits, but one was Sisler's 10th homer with Willie Jones on base in the seventh inning. But following 3–1 and 3–2 losses to the Braves we were back in second place, a half game behind the Dodgers. The Braves, themselves contenders, were only two games out of the lead.

Sisler clubbed six hits in the two defeats to raise his average to a torrid .338 while Monk and Heinz continued to pitch in bad luck and fell to 2–7 and 1–6, respectively.

Heading into that Boston series we encountered the beginning of the bad luck that would plague us as the season wore on. On June 26 we were to play the American League Athletics in a city series exhibition game to benefit sandlot baseball in Philadelphia. Eddie Sawyer sent Bob Miller ahead to Boston, where he was to start the first game of that series against the Braves.

> **MILLER:** "I went to the 30th Street Station in Philadelphia to catch my train to Boston and was in plenty of time. But I tripped on the steps carrying my luggage. I didn't know it at the time but I threw my whole back out of joint. By the time I got to Boston I couldn't even walk. I was tilting way to my right side."

> **SAWYER:** "When we caught up with Bob Miller in Boston he was all doubled up with a bad back and couldn't pitch. He looked like he had slept in a bathtub."

> **MILLER:** "I missed a couple of starts in July but I think I may have tried to come back too soon. In September, I was in the middle of a tight game against Cincinnati and Ewell Blackwell, losing 2–0. When I went out in the seventh inning to take my warmup pitches I felt a sharp pain in my right shoulder. And I missed another three weeks with that.

> "Little did I know how much that back injury would hurt my whole career. Unfortunately I was never again really free of that back problem even though I pitched another eight years in the big leagues."

> **SAWYER:** "Bob was never the same pitcher after that. He sort of pushed the ball rather than really throwing it. It was a real shame because he was a fine pitcher until his back injury."

Bob was 6–0 at the time of his mishap. He struggled with his physical problems the rest of the season, but still managed to finish with an 11–6 record.

After the series in Boston we returned home to face the Dodgers in an important four-game series. I was again matched against Brooklyn ace Don Newcombe in the first game before 31,555 fans, the largest crowd of the year. Neither one of us was particularly sharp, but the Phillies broke in front 4–1 after five innings due largely to Mike Goliat's second-inning double and sixth home run in the fifth. Armed with that lead, I could not survive the sixth. Duke Snider led off with a homer to left and Jackie Robinson, Roy Campanella, and Jim Russell followed with consecutive hits to reduce our lead to one run.

Eddie decided that was enough for me and Konstanty came in to give up a game-tying single to Gil Hodges. Then, with the bases loaded and no one out, Jim got the side out with no additional damage to keep us in the ballgame. He did not allow a ball to leave the infield.

Hodges put the Dodgers in front in the eighth with a home run before we rallied in the bottom half of the inning. With one out, Puddinhead singled and Dick Sisler walked. Putsy Caballero ran for Sisler and Andy Seminick continued his hot hitting by blasting a shot to left to drive in Jones with the tying run. Goliat laced a drive off of Newk's wrist to load the bases and literally knock Don out of the game. The hit gave Mike a single, two doubles, and a home run off Newk in five trips to the plate for the year. Preacher Roe then came in to pitch for the Dodgers and Eddie sent Jimmy Bloodworth up to hit for Konstanty. Just as he had in a similar situation against the Pirates three weeks before, Bloodworth stroked a double to clear the bases and give us a hard-fought 8–5 win.

The win put us in the league lead, three percentage points ahead of the Cardinals, who had kept pace by beating Pittsburgh 9–4. We beat the Dodgers the next two days by identical 6–4 scores to send them $2\frac{1}{2}$ games off the pace. Bob Miller, struggling to recover from his back injury, won his seventh straight in the first game, again with help from Konstanty. Mike Goliat continued his hot streak with three more hits, including another homer and Puddinhead clubbed a round-tripper as well.

The second 6–4 win was the first game of a Sunday doubleheader that drew 35,118, breaking the attendance mark set in the first game of the series. With the scored tied 4–4 in the eighth, Bill Nicholson won it for us with a pinch-hit two-run homer off of Ralph Branca to give Russ Meyer his third victory.

Even though we blew an 8–0 lead in the second game of the doubleheader, which ended up an 8–8 suspended game because of the Sunday curfew rule, the series was a significant confidence builder for us. By beating Brooklyn in three consecutive games in the heat of the pennant race, we confirmed that the Whiz Kids were for real. Konstanty's remarkable performance further strengthened our conviction; he had relieved in all four games, allowing only one earned run in $7\frac{2}{3}$ innings.

St. Louis had kept pace as well, so we still only had a lead of a couple of percentage points after our series with the Dodgers. After dropping two of three to the Boston Braves in Shibe Park, we slid to second place on the Fourth of July, 1½ games behind the Cardinals and only a game in front of the surging Braves. But, again showing our resiliency, we won five of six against the Giants and the Dodgers to burst into the All-Star break a game ahead of the Cardinals, 2 games in front of the Braves with the Dodgers 4½ behind.

Although still laboring, Bob Miller won his eighth straight during that stretch, beating the Giants 9–6 behind home runs by Andy, Granny, and Puddinhead and with relief help from Konstanty. Curt then beat Brooklyn in Ebbets Field 7–2 for his 10th win before I was again matched against Dodger ace Newcombe.

This time we were both sharp. Billy Cox touched me for a home run in the first for Brooklyn's only run and Newk shut us out on three singles for seven innings. In the eighth, after Dick Whitman grounded out batting for me, Richie tied the game with home run over the screen in right field. Konstanty, as usual, came in and held the Dodgers in their half of the inning. In our ninth, Puddinhead doubled with one out. Andy was passed intentionally after Sisler popped up for out number two. At that juncture, with two on and two out, Eddie Sawyer surprisingly replaced Mike Goliat, who hit Newk liked he owned him, with Bill Nicholson.

With Nick coming up, the Dodgers immediately had a big conference on the mound, presumably to discuss how to pitch to Nick. Nick then laid into Newk's first pitch and clubbed it high over the scoreboard in right for a three-run homer and a 4–1 lead. Jim set the Dodgers down in order in the ninth for his seventh victory. It was the second time in a week that Nick had beaten Brooklyn with an eighth-inning pinch homer.

I have often wondered what the Dodgers were talking about when they had that mound conference.

> **SAWYER:** "The Dodgers had this big meeting about how to pitch to Nick. They met for about five minutes and called the outfielders in and everything. Then Nick hit the first pitch about 500 feet over the right field fence. We laughed and laughed and asked the Dodgers what they were meeting about."

Brooklyn finally beat us the following day 7–3, despite Andy's two home runs, to snap our five-game win streak as we headed into the All-Star break in first place with a 44–29 record.

I was 10–3 at the break and was thrilled when I was selected for the National League All-Star team along with teammates Willie Jones, Dick Sisler, and Jim Konstanty. Puddinhead had slugged 17 homers and was hitting .322, Dick was at .325, and Jim had already appeared in 36 games and had established himself as the top reliever in the league.

Of course we felt more of our teammates were deserving as well. Bob Miller was an amazing 8–0 and Curt had come of age and was 10–5. Del Ennis had 15 homers and was third in the league with 60 RBIs. Andy Seminick was hitting a lusty .316 with 9 home runs and Richie Ashburn, Granny Hamner, and Eddie Waitkus were all fielding superbly and coming up with clutch hits. The Whiz Kids were winning the close games with good pitching, fine defense, and timely hitting.

I was excited to be named to the All-Star team, but I was so intent on the pennant race and winning games that I had not really focused on it. The previous year I had been 9–6 at the break and many thought I should have made it then, so it was very gratifying to be selected in 1950.

The 1950 game was in Comiskey Park in Chicago and I was able to take Mary with me. My folks came up from Springfield, so it was even more special when manager Burt Shotton named me to be the starting pitcher. It was the first of five All-Star games that I was fortunate enough to start for the National League.

The game turned out to be a classic. In the top of the first inning Ted Williams made a great catch on a long drive by Ralph Kiner, crashing into the left field wall to rob Ralph of extra bases. Although Ted played until the ninth inning, he had fractured his elbow on the play and was lost to the Red Sox until the end of the season.

I faced Ted in the bottom of the first and we employed the old Boudreau shift against him, with the shortstop playing on the first-base side of second and the second baseman swung deep into the hole at first. Williams hit a line shot past Stan Musial at first that Jackie Robinson caught in his exaggerated position at second. It is unbelievable that Williams could hit a ball that hard with a broken elbow, but he did.

After a scoreless first, we touched American League starter Vic Raschi for two runs in the second on Robinson's ground single, Enos Slaughter's resounding triple off the wall in left center, and Hank Sauer's sacrifice fly. The American League got one back against me in the bottom of the third when Cass Michaels's hit bounced into the bullpen for a double, Phil Rizzuto beat out a bunt, sending Michaels to third, and George Kell drove him home with a fly to center.

Because of All-Star game rules, I was through for the day after those three innings. The American League scored two runs in the fifth inning off Don Newcombe to take the lead 3–2. Neither team scored again until the ninth inning when Ralph Kiner tied the game with a clutch home run against Art Houtteman to send the game into extra innings. Again neither team could score until the 14th inning, when Red Schoendienst won it for us with a dramatic homer off of Ted Gray.

Not only did the National League win one of the most exciting All-Star games before or since, but the Whiz Kids all contributed to the victory. In addition to my three-inning stint, Jim Konstanty threw a scoreless sixth inning, Dick Sisler singled to right as a pinch hitter for Don Newcombe in the same inning, and Willie Jones played the entire 14-inning ballgame, singling in the 13th inning and playing errorless in the field.

During the All-Star break the rest of the Phillies played exhibition games against the Rochester Red Wings and our own Toronto Maple Leafs. But Sawyer sent Waitkus home to Boston to rest and ordered Hamner, who had been nursing back and leg strains, to the Poconos for a three-day vacation.

Eddie and Granny must have benefited from the rest because on July 13 they combined for five hits, including Granny's first-inning homer, in our first game of the second half, as Curt pitched us over the Cardinals by a score of 3–2. Andy Seminick homered in the second and Dick Sisler hit the game winner, a solo homer in the sixth to break a 2–2 tie. Our lead was now two games and seemingly climbing.

My hometown of Springfield, Illinois, planned a testimonial for me before the next day's game in Sportman's Park in St. Louis. To add to the occasion I was to pitch against the Cardinals' crafty southpaw Harry Brecheen. Before the game the good citizens of Springfield gave me a savings bond and a diamond wristwatch. Adlai Stevenson, the governor of Illinois, even showed up, in addition to my mom and dad, my high school coach Ted Boyle, and the mayor of Springfield. A trim, young Harry Caray served as master of ceremonies.

Unfortunately the game did not go as well as the pregame. Granny, still benefiting from his three days off, got us ahead 2–0 in the third with another home run with Richie on base. But St. Louis tied it up in their fourth on a bad hop ground ball double by Schoendienst, a single to center by Musial, a pop fly single by Slaughter that Granny reached but could not hold, and a seeing-eye base hit through the infield by Bill Howerton.

232

We remained deadlocked until Howerton led off the sixth with a home run off the bleacher screen in right center. After Dick Whitman pinch hit for me in the seventh, Jim Konstanty uncharacteristically gave up another run. Gerry Staley shut us down in relief and we got beat 4–2. The loss was a frustrating one because we had runners in scoring position in five different innings after Granny's homer in the first but could not score.

That game seemed to catapult us into a slump in which both our hitting and pitching became suspect. The Cardinals again defeated us July 15, this time by an 8–6 score, and our lead was gone. We moved on to Chicago, only to get walloped in a doubleheader by the Cubs, 8–0 and 10–3, as Bob Miller finally lost in the second game. We were back in second place, a half game behind St. Louis.

The following day Brooklyn swept a doubleheader from the Cardinals and Boston beat the Pirates 8–6 while we were rained out with the Cubs. That combination of events on July 17 pushed us back into the lead by a half game and, incredibly, bunched the top four teams within one game of each other. The Dodgers, although in fourth place, trailed us by just a game while the Cardinals and Braves were tied for second place, only that half game behind us. The pennant race could not get much hotter.

After the rainout, we faced another doubleheader with the Cubs. I was hit hard in the first game, giving up 13 hits in six innings and losing 5–2 to Chicago's Paul Minner for our fifth consecutive defeat.

Between games, Eddie Sawyer decided to change the batting order to try to shake us out of our slump. He moved Waitkus, who had been struggling at the plate, from third to first in the order and moved Richie from leadoff to second. He dropped Granny, whose hitting had tailed off again, from second to sixth. Also looking for effective pitching, the skipper started Bubba Church in the second game.

> **SAWYER:** "We weren't hitting much, and if you don't hit in Wrigley Field you don't win. We didn't have too many options, so all we could really do was switch the batting order around. Waitkus was a good leadoff man and Richie hit in very few double plays and was an excellent bunter. He didn't strike out and could hit behind the runner. But I just wanted to shake things up a little."

The new order immediately paid dividends as we scored five runs in the first two innings of the second game to take a quick 5–0 lead. Bubba came through on the mound as well, scattering five hits to defeat our old nemesis Bob Rush by an 8–3 score. Bubba's clutch pitching performance was only his second big league victory and ended our five-game losing streak, which would be our longest of the year.

> **CHURCH:** "We had good pitching early on in 1950, and Bubba had to sit in that bullpen. I was used to pitching 200-plus innings in the minor leagues, and I wasn't pitching much at all, only an inning or two here and there. Cy Perkins and Ken Silvestri were real supportive in the bullpen and kept me involved in the ballgames, but I was nervous, fidgety, and grousing a little about not pitching more, although I wasn't making waves.
>
> "One day on the train Eddie Sawyer called me over to his seat and said, 'Quit worrying, you're going to get your shot. If we didn't think you could help this ballclub, you wouldn't be here.' And sure enough, right after the All-Star break I got my shot."

We moved on to Pittsburgh for our second doubleheader in two days on July 18. In the first game Curt and the Pirate southpaw Bill Werle hooked up in a memorable extra-inning duel that was deadlocked 1–1 in the top of the 11th. With one out, Bill Nicholson lifted a high pop up right in front of the plate for what looked like out number two. But Pirate catcher Clyde McCullough and third sacker Danny O'Connell collided and the ball ricocheted off Clyde's shin guards toward the stands. By the time the Pirates could recover the ball Nick was on third base with what must be one of the shortest triples of all time.

Putsy ran for Nick and Granny smashed Werle's second pitch over the left field screen into what was then called Greenberg Gardens for a game winning two-run homer. We needed both runs because Pittsburgh scored a run in the bottom of the 11th to make the final score 3–2. Jim Konstanty saved Curt's 12th victory in the 11th inning, retiring three straight hitters with the tying run on base.

That win was a big one because we were still struggling on that long road trip. We lost to the Pirates in the second game of the doubleheader 4–2 and again the following day 10–8, wasting three homers in the process, before Bubba Church again came to our rescue in the series finale to beat the Bucs 4–1 and pull us into a tie for the lead.

We got no break from the schedule and had to travel to Cincinnati for consecutive doubleheaders with the Reds in Crosley Field. I got us off to a good start in the first game, scattering four hits to shut out the Reds 2–0 for my 11th win. I even got a base hit off Reds knuckleballer Willard Ramsdell and drove in our first run with a long drive to left that scored Seminick from third. Unfortunately Ken Heintzelman's tough luck continued in the nightcap as Cincinnati beat him 6–1. His record fell to 1–8.

The split kept us in a tie with St. Louis, who divided their own doubleheader with the Braves, who themselves remained just one game back. The fourth-place Dodgers were all of a game and a half behind.

The following day we defeated the Reds twice before almost 30,000, edging ahead of the Cards, who beat the Braves 8–4 but still slipped a half game back. In the opener we exploded for 12 runs on 15 hits, including two home runs by Puddinhead and one each by Del and Andy, as we coasted by the Reds 12–4. Curt won his fifth straight and became the first hurler in the league to register 13 wins.

Russ Meyer won the fight-marred second game 7–4, defeating the tough Ewell Blackwell with help from Konstanty, a five-for-five game by Eddie Waitkus, and two hits and two RBIs from Mike Goliat. In the top half of the third Willie Jones slid hard into Reds second baseman Connie Ryan trying to break up a double play. Ryan was spiked on the play and took a swing at Puddinhead. While the two of them wrestled both benches emptied, although no other fights broke out.

Puddinhead and Connie were both ejected, but the fight seemed to spark us and we were able to rough up Blackwell for 12 hits in his seven innings of work. Connie's reaction was predictable; it was the second time that season that Puddinhead had spiked Ryan with an aggressive slide at second base and, in addition, we had won 12 of our 14 games with the Reds. We were not Cincinnati's favorite opponent.

Ironically, Ryan would become our teammate after the 1951 season, coming over to us from the Reds with catcher Smoky Burgess and pitcher Howie Fox in a trade for Andy Seminick, Dick Sisler, infielder Eddie Pellagrini, and pitcher Niles Jordan.

I, like a lot of ballplayers, was never too anxious to get into fights on a ballfield. I was always afraid that I would break my hand. Stan Musial expressed my sentiments a few years later when we got involved in a donnybrook with the Cardinals. Both teams raced out onto the field and Stan grabbed my arm and said, "Robin, we're making too much money to get hurt in something like this."

Instead of a travel day to return home after our long road trip, we had to go to Pittsburgh for a makeup game. For our trouble, we suffered a tough 2–1 loss to the Pirates in a game called after six innings because of rain. Waitkus hit a two-run homer in the top of the seventh to put us ahead 3–2, but then the rains came and the game reverted back to the previous completed inning.

The Cardinals were idle so we returned home from our longest road trip of the season in a virtual tie for the lead, two percentage points behind St. Louis. We had played in every rival park in the league except Boston and New York and had finished with a 9–10 record, surviving that five-game losing streak.

July 25 marked our first home appearance since July 7 and turned out to be a turning point in our season. We opened our 16-game home stand with a doubleheader against the Cubs with Bubba and I pitching before the season's largest crowd, almost 33,000. Bubba was masterful in the opener, needing only 88 pitches and allowing only three hits to blank Chicago 7–0 and run his record to 4–0. We routed Cubs starter Johnny Klippstein with four runs in the top of the first, due in large part to Dick Sisler's two-run double. Del Ennis drove in three runs in the game and slammed his 18th homer of the year.

I was opposed again by Bob Rush in the nightcap and we hooked up in a memorable pitching duel, with the game still scoreless going into the bottom of the ninth. We had wasted several golden scoring opportunities, but had not been able to dent the plate. In the fifth I singled and Waitkus doubled me to third with no one out, but we could not score. In the seventh, I again singled and Eddie drilled a single to right with one out, taking second on the throw to third, but we again came up empty. In the eighth, Granny belted a two-out triple to deep center field. Andy Seminick then smashed a hard grounder down the third base line, but Chicago third baseman Bill Serena made a great backhand stop and threw Andy out to end the inning.

I retired the Cubs in the top of the ninth and we went out to try to get to Rush once more. Goliat grounded to third to start the inning and then Eddie let me hit, perhaps because I was already two for three. I managed to coax a walk, much to the displeasure of Cubs manager Frankie Frisch, who protested the ball four call and was ejected from the game. Eddie then sent Caballero in to run for me, which surprised a lot of folks since he had let me hit.

Of course Putsy was a lot faster than I and Eddie immediately ordered a hit and run with Waitkus at bat. Eddie rolled out to first but Putsy, running with the pitch, made second easily. We had two outs, but Richie came through with a clutch single to center to drive in Putsy with the only run of the game.

After I won that second game Bubba came up to me in the clubhouse and said, "I can't believe you did that to me."

I said, "What do you mean, Bubba?"

He said, "I pitch a three-hit shutout and I can already see the headlines tomorrow and then you come along and pitch a shutout and win 1–0 in the second game. I don't think that's fair." Of course, Bubba was joking and we had a good laugh over it.

> **CHURCH:** "Eddie Sawyer paid Robbie and I a great compliment after that doubleheader. He told the press that we had pitched the two best baseball games he had seen in the major leagues."

Our double shutout of the Cubs was two years to the day since Eddie Sawyer had taken over as manager of the Phillies. It vaulted us into first place, a half game ahead of the Cardinals, who defeated Brooklyn 9–5 in a single game. Since mid-May we had been in and out of first place six times. This time we had a lead we would not again relinquish, although we would come very close.

We fell behind the Cubs the following day 4–0 after five innings. Monk Meyer started but was thrown out in the fifth when he protested a balk call by pushing umpire Lon Warneke in the chest. Milo Candini came in and got us out of the inning and blanked Chicago in the sixth. In the bottom half of the sixth we came back to score six runs, thanks in large measure to six walks, including five in a row, handed out by Cubs' starter Monk Dubiel. Ironically, Dubiel did not walk a batter in his other seven innings on the mound. Cubs manager Frankie Frisch refused to even warm up a relief pitcher while Dubiel struggled in the sixth, telling the press that he was tired of his starting pitchers "peeping out to the bullpen to see if a reliever is ready." For our part, Konstanty relieved Milo and threw three scoreless innings, allowing only one hit, to wrap up our come-from-behind victory.

Since the Cardinals lost to the Dodgers that day, we stretched our lead to a game and a half. Candini was the winning pitcher, his only win of the year against no losses. After the season, Milo went to Bob Carpenter about signing for next season.

> **CANDINI:** "I was under the impression that if you were on a team that won the pennant you automatically got a raise. But Bob Carpenter didn't want to give me one so I told him, 'We couldn't have won the pennant without me.'"

SAWYER: "Milo had been a very good pitcher and he could still pitch. It was really my fault that he didn't pitch more in '50, but the way the year developed and with Konstanty there just weren't that many spots where I could use him."

Curt Simmons completed a four-game sweep over the Cubs the next day, July 27, pitching us to a 13–3 triumph behind a grand slam homer by Del Ennis, who drove in an amazing seven runs for the day. It was Curt's last start before joining his National Guard unit for two weeks of required summer camp at Indiantown Gap, Pennsylvania, although he would be able to take his regular turn when we were at home in Shibe Park.

The cellar-dwelling Pirates came to town next and we won our fifth straight in the series opener by a 4–1 score behind Bob Miller's complete-game pitching. The other three contenders all lost so we increased our lead to 2½ games over the Cardinals, 4½ over the Braves, and 5 over the Dodgers. Bugger extended his record to 9–2 and scattered eight hits in his best game since slipping on the steps at the train station. It was his first win since July 6 and his first complete game since June 22. Del continued his hitting tear with two hits and another RBI to take over the league lead from the Pirates' Ralph Kiner with 80.

Pittsburgh's Bill Werle stopped our winning streak the following day 7–4 as Bubba Church absorbed his first major league loss. Del sparkled in defeat, slugging his 20th home run of the year with Richie aboard in the third, to give him 82 RBIs for the year and us a short-lived 2–0 lead. The Pirates chased Bubba with two runs in the fourth and four in the fifth. But we remained 2½ games ahead of St. Louis, who lost to the Giants. Brooklyn, however, swept a doubleheader from the Cubs to come within 3½ games of the lead.

We got back on track the following day, July 30, sweeping a doubleheader from the Pirates. I coasted to a 10–0 victory in the first game, my third shutout in a row. I finished the game with 28 consecutive shutout innings, my best stretch of pitching in the big leagues to that point.

The second game proved considerably more difficult. Ken Heintzelman continued to pitch in tough luck and trailed Murry Dickson and the Pirates 2–0 when relieved by Konstanty. In our eighth, Puddinhead doubled and Dickson could not find the plate, walking two to load the bases. Del made him pay for his wildness by smashing a grand slam homer, his second bases-loaded clout of the week, to turn the game around and give us a 4–2 lead. Jim retired the Bucs in the ninth for his ninth victory in relief.

Del's grand slam gave him an incredible 41 RBIs for the month of July. He was on his way to a season in which he led the league by driving in 126 runs, hit 31 home runs, and bat .311 to finish fourth in the race for the batting title.

Ironically, Del, one of the Phillies' all-time greatest sluggers, was probably subjected to more booing by Philadelphia fans than any player in team history. It largely began in 1951, when Del slumped to 15 homers, 73 RBIs (the only season between 1949 and 1955 that he failed to drive in at least 100 runs), and a .267 batting average, mostly because of a back injury suffered early in the season.

ENNIS: "One time we were playing St. Louis with a one-run lead in the top of the ninth. Somebody hit a fly ball to right field. I'm sitting there waiting for it and it doesn't even hit my glove. It falls in front of me and two runs score to put them in front by a run. Thirty thousand people are booing me.

"Standing out there in right field I had a premonition that they were going to bring Gerry Staley in to pitch the bottom of the ninth. A couple of guys get base hits and in comes Staley to face me. I thought Staley would throw me a sinker and he does on the first pitch. It doesn't sink but is up in my eyes as big as a grapefruit. I hit it right over the roof. Thirty thousand cheered me right out of the park."

Del did that sort of thing more than once in his career.

RIDZIK: "I had come into a ballgame against the Dodgers in Shibe Park. It was the seventh inning and we were ahead by three runs but the bases were loaded with two outs. A fly ball goes out to Del and, with two outs, everybody is running. Damn if the ball doesn't hit him on the heel of the glove and he drops it. All three runs score and we got a tie ballgame. We had a packed house and those people started to boo him unmercifully. It was really terrible.

"The next inning when he went out to left field they booed and booed and booed. They booed him when he ran off the field at the end of the inning. Unmerciful. I looked over at him sitting in the dugout and he's got his hands clenched and he's just white. He's just livid. Here he is, a hometown guy and everything. I mean DiMaggio dropped them occasionally.

"He came to bat in the last of the eighth inning with the score still tied and two outs. The fans just booed and booed and all our guys on the bench are just hotter than a pistol. We were ready to go fight the thirty-some thousand. He didn't deserve that. So Del hits one up on top of the roof and as he's rounding the bases the people go crazy. They cheered and cheered and cheered. They were standing and wouldn't sit down. They wanted him to come out of the dugout. But he wouldn't move. He just sat there white as a ghost, mad as hell.

"When he went out for the ninth inning the fans stood up and applauded again. I had to step back off the rubber a couple of times because they wouldn't sit down.

"That was one of the greatest thrills of my career, watching something like that happen to somebody else. It was beautiful."

ENNIS: "In 1955 I took my boy to the ballgame on his birthday. We beat the Cardinals 7–2 and I hit three home runs and drove in all seven of our runs. I popped up the fourth time with runners on base and the fans liked to boo me out of the park."

On another occasion Del popped up with runners on base and the boo-birds took after him. They were still on him when he next came to the plate, this time with the bases loaded. Del quickly turned them around, smacking the first pitch into the upper deck for a grand slam home run.

ENNIS: "The Phillie fans were really tough on me. Part of it was because of I was from North Philly and the South Philly fans would get on me just because of that. But after a while I wouldn't let it bother me. I figured I could play ball or go home and I wanted to play ball. I just made sure I always gave 100 percent."

Del was a fine ballplayer who was very underrated. He was quiet and low key but he played every day and often played hurt. He was an excellent fielder who had a rather effortless style in the outfield, in stark contrast to Richie's more conspicuous approach in center field. To some it may have appeared that Del was somewhat lackadaisical, and when he did occasionally boot one the fans would really get on him. But I never saw Del fail to run hard on a ground ball, even one back to the pitcher. I once mentioned to Del that I had never seen him dog it running to first base. He told me, "It's only 90 feet."

That statement really typified Del's makeup and his approach to the game. He came to the park everyday ready to play and play hard.

> **SAWYER:** "Del was a good outfielder and he had a good arm. He wasn't the slowest guy either. He could run pretty good. He was a made to order right fielder. Del was quiet but he was always ready to play. I can't remember him ever out of the lineup. I never heard him say, 'I don't feel good' or 'I'd like to get out for a day.' He was just a true professional ballplayer."

One time Del broke a small bone in his left foot. He was able to play through the injury, getting his foot taped every day. Del had a tendency to lunge at the plate, but because of the injury to his front foot he was forced to stay back while batting. As a result he hit like gangbusters while his foot was broken. In fact, after the bone healed Del started lunging a little too much again. We threatened to break his foot again, but we never did.

Over the years, Del made some of the greatest catches in the outfield that I have ever seen. In 1952 against the Giants in the Polo Grounds, with the score tied in the bottom of the 10th, Willie Mays clubbed a ball high and deep to left center. It looked like it was going to land close to the 455-foot sign and might well be a game-ending inside-the-park home run for the fleet-footed Mays. Del was off with the crack of the bat and was about to reach for the ball when he tripped over our bullpen mound, which in the Polo Grounds was on the field of play. As he was going down he reached up at the last possible moment and snared the ball barehanded with his right hand.

During the 1950 season, Jackie Robinson hit a shot to right center like a two iron off of me. Del ran over, but when he got to the ball he was off stride. So he reached up and caught that ball barehanded, as easy as could be. He just threw the ball in like it was a routine catch. Jackie couldn't believe it and ran right past first base to right field and yelled at Del, "How did you ever catch that ball?"

> **ASHBURN:** "Ennis reached up and caught that ball barehanded on the dead run, just like picking an apple off a tree. He never cracked a smile, just like it was routine play."

Del was sometimes prone to long batting slumps, which also would get the boo-birds going. He was an excellent clutch hitter and a consistent run producer over the years, driving in over 100 runs seven different years, but somehow the fans expected him to deliver every time up.

When the fans were on Del one day, Cy Perkins said to me, with typical wisdom, "You know, the only time they will appreciate him is when he is gone."

When the Phillies traded Del to the Cardinals after the 1956 season he drove in 105 runs to finish second in the league. Meanwhile, we were never as good a club afterwards. Del left a real vacuum in our cleanup hitter position that we could not fill.

Although the Phillie fans failed to appreciate Del, we would not have won the pennant in 1950 without him. Thanks in large part to Del's sizzling July, we entered the dog days of August three games in front of Boston, who beat the Cardinals on July 31 to take over second place. We got a much needed day off on the last day of July and so began August with a 58–39 record and our largest lead of the season.

The Whiz Kids had won 13 of 18 since Eddie Sawyer had shuffled the batting order in Chicago. Eddie Waitkus had come alive in the leadoff slot, batting .333 since the switch. Richie put together a 17-game hitting streak in the number two spot, hitting .400 over that span. Although Del had remained in the cleanup slot, he had hit .355 over the same time period.

We were still in a four-team race, with St. Louis 3$\frac{1}{2}$ games back and the ever dangerous Dodgers only 4 games out. But we were in the early stages of a long home stand, were relatively healthy, and were on a roll. We had begun to believe we could really win this thing.

Chapter 12
AUGUST: THE WHIZ KIDS TAKE COMMAND

Off the field, the month of August did not start well for the Whiz Kids. On August 1 we learned that Curt Simmons's National Guard unit would be called to active duty within about 30 days. Although the call would cut short Curt's two-week summer camp by a few days and enable him to return to the ballclub for the time being, he would be lost to us for the stretch drive in September. His division would train at Camp Atterbury in Indiana, making it impossible for him to commute to the club to pitch every fourth day.

> **CHARLIE BICKNELL:** "In '49 Bob Carpenter asked Curt Simmons and me to join the National Guard in Philadelphia, which was part of the 28th Infantry Division. The way he put it we had no choice. He was trying to protect his investment. So we both joined the National Guard and then the Korean War broke out. At that time there were two National Guard Divisions that could be activated, go through basic training, and be ready for combat within a short period of time. They were the 28th and the division down in Oklahoma. So they activated our whole division. Of course, by that time the Phillies had sold me to the Braves on waivers."

Since Charlie was in the minor leagues, Curt was the first major leaguer to be called to active duty during the Korean War, just as about 10 years previously another Phillie, Hugh Mulcahy, had been the first big leaguer drafted for World War II.

SIMMONS: "Frank Powell, our traveling secretary, would talk to me and say, 'We're going to get you an extension. You're not going. Don't worry.'

"I'd say, 'I hope not. I don't want to go. I want to be right here for the rest of the season.'"

On the field the news was considerably brighter. We split a double-header with the Reds on August 1 to retain our three-game lead. Trailing 4–1 in the fifth inning of the first game, we rallied for four runs to forge into the lead, behind Del Ennis's two-run single and Andy Seminick's game-winning base hit off of the Reds' Frank Smith. Bob Miller struggled to his 10th win, allowing 13 hits and giving way to Jim Konstanty in the ninth.

Curt flew in from Indiantown Gap to pitch the second game but did not have it and was knocked out in the fourth inning of a 4–1 defeat. Our only bright spot against Ewell Blackwell was Stan Lopata's first home run of the year.

The following day, Bubba Church pitched a masterful three-hit shutout to win a tight pitching duel against the Reds' Willard Ramsdell by a 2–0 score. Bubba even drove in Granny Hamner for the first run in the fourth with a line single to left, before Del slugged his sixth homer in eight games to close out the scoring in the eighth. We were 3½ games ahead of Boston and Brooklyn. The Cardinals lost to the Braves 4–3 and slipped to fourth, four games out.

After rain washed out our final game with the Reds, the Cardinals came to town for an important five-game series. Although St. Louis had started to fade a little, they had an 8–5 season series advantage over us and had a real chance to get back to the front of the race if they could handle us successfully.

I started the first game, going for my fourth straight shutout and 14th victory of the year. After three scoreless innings, we broke in front 2–0 against southpaw Howie Pollet when Del, his blazing bat continuing, slashed a triple to the right field corner. Dick Sisler slammed a double down the same line just over first baseman Rocky Nelson's reach to score Del. After Granny sacrificed Dick to third, he scored on Andy's long fly to center fielder Bill Howerton.

My scoreless string ended abruptly in the Cardinal sixth. With two outs I walked Stan Musial, bringing up Enos Slaughter. Enos could really hit breaking balls and I was primarily a fastball pitcher. But I got behind in the count and, trying to be too smart, threw him a curveball. It did not take me long to realize that I should have thrown him a fastball. He jumped all over it and homered over right field to tie the score and end my scoreless string at $32^2/_3$ innings.

I had good stuff and got back to pitching like I knew I should, and we remained tied until the bottom of the eighth. With two outs, Del squibbed a hit to center for his third hit of the game. Dick Sisler then smacked a ball over second to send Del to third and bring up Granny. Redbird manager Eddie Dyer decided against walking Granny intentionally, probably since Hamner had struck out, sacrificed, and popped to the catcher in his previous trips. This time, however, he laced Pollet's second pitch off the right field fence, barely a foot above Slaughter's outstretched glove, for a two-run triple and a 4–2 lead. I got the Cardinals out in the ninth for our 10th win in 12 games.

Russ Meyer, with ninth-inning help from the ever-present Konstanty, eked out a 2–1 win over the Redbirds the following day, August 5, to stretch our lead to four full games over the Braves, who lost to the Cubs in 13 innings. Our game was scoreless until the bottom of the fifth when Granny blooped a fly ball behind first for a double. With one out, newly-wed Mike Goliat came to the plate to face St. Louis pitcher Gerry Staley. Mike had surprised all of us by heading off to Reading after the game the day before to marry Eleanor Dalpra, his fiancée from Cleveland.

Mike gave himself a wonderful wedding present by clubbing Staley's first pitch over the wall in deep left center field for a two-run homer. The Cards scrapped together a run in the seventh and Monk guarded a 2–1 lead into the ninth. With one out, an error and a single to center by Rocky Nelson, who took second on Richie's throw to third, put runners on second and third. Eddie Sawyer brought in Konstanty to pitch to Cardinal pinch hitter Tommy Glaviano who, on a 3–2 pitch, popped to Puddinhead Jones at third. Jim then got our old teammate Harry Walker to pop to Granny in foul ground behind third to secure another thrilling win for us.

The Cardinals sent Harry to Rochester in the International League right after the game. He was hitting only .203 in limited action. Harry would get only a few more at bats in the major leagues. He would go on to have some outstanding seasons in Triple A, winning a batting title and several pennants as a player-manager. He later had a successful big league managerial career, piloting the Cardinals, Pirates, and Astros for a total of nine years.

The Cardinals brought us back to reality the next afternoon, sweeping a doubleheader 7–1 and 2–0. Still, our lead over the Braves was three games, with the Dodgers another game and a half back. The Redbirds, who had slipped to 6½ games off the pace, got back even with Brooklyn.

We had one more game with St. Louis to conclude our long home stand, and Eddie decided to start Ken Johnson against his former teammates. It was his first start since getting knocked out early against the Braves on the Fourth of July. He had pitched very little since getting hit on his throwing hand while pitching batting practice shortly thereafter.

Ken had an exceptional curveball. If he could get it over, no one was going to hit it. Most big league hitters can hit the breaking pitch, but Kenny could make hitters look very bad trying to hit his.

> **SAWYER:** "If you didn't tell Ken ahead of time that he was going to pitch he would do all right for you. If he had time to think about it he could be awful. He had a lot of ability, one of the best curveballs I've ever seen, although he couldn't always throw it for strikes. But when I saw Musial and Slaughter and those guys try to hit against him, I was glad he was on our side.
>
> "That night against the Cardinals, Ken didn't know he was pitching. His wife was having a baby and he was at the hospital. And we didn't know she was having the baby either. He came waltzing in just about game time and told me his wife just had a baby and that everything was fine. So I said, 'Well, you're pitching.' That was the best way to tell Ken anyway, but he was so late that day I was starting to look around to see who I could pitch."

All Ken did to celebrate the birth of his daughter was to pitch a two-hit shutout to lead us to a decisive 9–0 win against Harry Brecheen. He began by walking two and giving up a single to Musial to load the bases in the first. But Ken pitched out of that jam without damage before walking two more in the second. Again he escaped the inning without allowing a run. He walked only two more and allowed only a swinging bunt hit to Del Rice the rest of the way, retiring the last 14 Cardinals in a row.

Meanwhile Mike Goliat drove in four runs with a double and a base-clearing triple, and Puddinhead slugged a homer among his three hits. The Braves lost to the Giants 9–3, and our lead was back up to four games as we traveled to Brooklyn for a two-game series with the Dodgers.

I was again matched against Don Newcombe in the first game of the series on August 8. Although I struggled, giving up 12 hits in 8¹/₃ innings before Konstanty relieved me in the ninth, we hung on to win 6–5. Goliat continued to own Newk, going three for four with a game-tying double in the seventh. For the season he was an improbable 8 for 11 against Don. The victory was my fifth straight, making me 15–5 for the year. After beginning the year without ever having defeated Brooklyn, I was 3–0 against them for 1950.

The Braves lost 2–1 to the Giants that day, and suddenly we were five games in front of the pack. The ever-dangerous Dodgers were 5¹/₂ games behind.

> **SAWYER:** "Goliat just wore Newcombe out. Even though his average wasn't very high, he hit the better pitchers in the league. The ones that got him out were the lesser pitchers. Mike was a pretty good ballplayer but, of course, he was playing out of position. He did a reasonable job at second base for someone who hadn't played there. He was a first and third baseman but we needed a second baseman so we played him at second. But he helped us a lot, especially against the Dodgers."

We beat Brooklyn again the next afternoon, 5–4, in another nail-biter. Goliat was the hero again with a long eighth-inning sacrifice fly to drive in Puddinhead from third with the winning run. Konstanty, appearing in his 50th game in relief of Russ Meyer, worked out of jams in the eighth and ninth inning to secure the victory. It was our 9th win over Brooklyn in 14 games and our 14th triumph in our last 18 starts. We were continuing to win the close ones and beat the contenders.

Returning home to face the Giants on August 10 before a packed house of 33,000, we won our third straight one-run game, 6–5 in 10 innings, to boost our lead to six full games over the Braves. It was our 20th one-run victory of the year, against 9 losses by the same margin. Konstanty, making his third straight appearance and his fifth in six days, won his ninth game in relief. Goliat, continuing his hitting tear since his marriage, got his 10th round-tripper while Granny drove in four runs with three hits, including a homer of his own.

Sal Maglie stopped our four-game winning streak the following night, August 11, hurling the Giants to a 3–1 triumph. Curt Simmons, back with us while awaiting his call to active duty, gave up only four hits in defeat.

Our lead shrank to five as Boston's Vern Bickford pitched a resounding 7–0, no-hit victory over Brooklyn.

The Giants and the Phillies were intense rivals in those days. Earlier in the year, Eddie Sawyer had accused the Giants pitchers of intentionally throwing at our hitters and New York manager Leo Durocher had publicly complained about the aggressive manner in which Andy Seminick blocked the plate. Andy tended to wear the Giants out with his hitting as well and was not very popular in New York.

> **SAWYER:** "There were a lot of fights in baseball in those days, but most of them weren't too serious. A lot of ours began with close plays at the plate. Andy was really tough at blocking the plate. On a close play, you had to go through Andy. There was no way to do that because Andy wouldn't give an inch. Boy, was he strong back there."

Eddie Stanky, New York's intensely competitive second baseman who was known as "the Brat," had hit upon an idea for distracting batters in the Giants' series against the Braves immediately preceding ours. In their August 9 game, Boston's Bob Elliot had asked umpire Al Barlick to move out of his line of vision. Barlick did so but Stanky then moved into Barlick's old spot and succeeded in distracting Elliot, who was called out on strikes.

Stanky decided to try to bother Andy the same way in our August 11 game, moving over by second base and performing jumping jacks while Andy was at bat.

> **SEMINICK:** "Stanky's hop-straddles sure did distract me, so I stepped back and told Al Barlick, the umpire, 'He can't do that.'
>
> "Barlick said, 'Well, there's no rule in the book that says he can't.'
>
> "So I was really boiling about that. In addition, they had a history of throwing at me. Maglie, in particular, was always throwing at me or behind me, and in the eighth inning of that game he hit me in the elbow."

Maglie was called "the Barber" for a reason.

> **CHURCH:** "You would have thought a fly landed on Andy's elbow when Maglie hit him. He just ignored it and went down to first. But in the clubhouse that elbow got big. The next day it was all discolored and just looked terrible."

Eddie Sawyer also complained to the umpires about Stanky's gyrations and Durocher agreed, before the game the following day, to instruct Stanky to cease and desist until a ruling from league president Ford Frick could be obtained.

I started that August 12 ballgame against the Giants' Sheldon Jones and little did I realize that Andy was not finished with the Giants. I got in immediate trouble in the first, loading the bases with one out before striking out Wes Westrum and getting Bobby Thomson to roll into a force out to escape the inning unscathed.

The Giants did get to me for a run in the second, but we rallied in our half of the inning. With two outs Granny doubled to left and Andy worked Jones for a walk. While Andy was at bat Stanky made a big show at second of standing absolutely frozen.

> **SEMINICK:** "I was still upset from the day before, with Stanky's antics and Maglie's throwing at me, and I had decided that I had to do something about it. So when I got on base I had already made up my mind that I was going to run into anyone who was in my way."

It probably did not help Andy's mindset any when Jones threw a beanball at our next hitter, Mike Goliat, sending him to the dirt. Mike got up and took a step toward the mound before deciding to fight back with his bat. He hit the next pitch to left to score Hamner from second.

Andy rounded second on Mike's hit and never broke stride, heading for third. Just as Giant third baseman Henry Thompson reached for Whitey Lockman's throw from left, Andy slammed into him. Thompson went one way, the ball another and Andy got up and scored, beating Jones's throw to the plate from behind third.

> **SEMINICK:** "Usually I wouldn't have tried to go to third on a single hit right to the left fielder, but I went on into third where Hank Thompson happened to be. I guess I hit him pretty hard."

> **ASHBURN:** "Andy hit poor Henry Thompson with a forearm shiver and Henry's teeth looked like chiclets flying out of his mouth. He just cold cocked him. You really didn't want to mess with Andy Seminick."

> **SAWYER:** "Henry Thompson just flew through the air when Andy hit him. He was out cold. Durocher and Freddie Fitzsimmons, who was coaching for them, ran out and tried to

get Henry together, while our guys were yelling, 'You better call Jersey City [the Giants' top farm club].' Leo and Freddie were walking Henry around, one on each side, trying to bring him to. Finally Leo said, 'Henry, you ready to play some more?'

"Henry said, 'Mr. Durocher, I want to play some more, but not today.' They had to take him out of the lineup. It seemed like he had blood coming out of his nose and his mouth and he got cut on the side of his face somehow. He was in pretty bad shape."

I was the batter after they helped Thompson off the field. I managed to single to center to drive in Goliat, who had taken second on Andy's adventure at third, for our third run of the inning.

After the Giants got us out the game rocked along quietly until the bottom of the fourth. Jack Kramer had taken over on the mound for the Giants after Jones was lifted for a pinch hitter. With two outs Andy came to bat. Stanky, upset over the havoc Seminick had wreaked in the second inning, moved over behind second base, directly behind Kramer and in Andy's line of sight. On the second pitch he waved his arms over his head wildly and was promptly ejected by umpire Lon Warneke for "making a farce out of the game."

Durocher argued vociferously and officially protested the game. Bill Rigney replaced Stanky at second and Andy again walked. Goliat grounded to Alvin Dark at short and Alvin tossed over to Rigney, who was covering second for the force out. Andy barreled down the line and slid into second, bumping Rigney.

SEMINICK: "I didn't go out of the way, just slid right into the bag, but Rigney was close by and I bumped him. I didn't bump him real hard. I guess Rigney was upset with everything that had already happened and so he came after me. I'm still on the ground, so I grabbed him by his shirt, pulled him down and started popping him. I guess you could say I beat him to the punch. After a couple of punches, Rigney said, 'Turn me loose, you're killing me.'"

CHURCH: "Rigney fell on top of Andy and drew back to hit him. All of a sudden we see Rigney's body bouncing up about a foot and a half or two feet. Andy's just laying on his back, popping him. He was holding Rigney with his left hand and popping him with his right and Rigney would go up every time."

SAWYER: "Andy beat the life out of Bill Rigney and he was on the bottom. Rigney was up on top of him. Oh, he beat him awful."

SIMMONS: "I felt sorry for Rigney. He didn't have a chance against Andy."

Of course, everyone from both teams raced on to the field. I, along with Alvin Dark, Mike Goliat, Benny Bengough, umpire Lon Warneke, and others, tried to separate Andy from Rigney. But tempers were hot and several other fights broke out. Jimmy Bloodworth got into in it with Jim Hearn and Rudy Rufer and took a swing at Durocher. The Giants' Tookie Gilbert went after Andy, only to be intercepted by Dusty Cooke.

CHURCH: "I was looking for Tookie Gilbert because I knew Tookie. Tookie was going wild, so I decided to avoid him. Then I saw Durocher come storming out and I was bigger than he was, so I just threw my arms around him and heaved him out into the outfield. I got him before anyone else did. Then I looked up and saw Monte Irvin and we both had bats in our hands. Monte said, 'Don't do it, Bubba,' and I said, 'I won't if you won't, Monte.'"

SIMMONS: "Durocher was all mouth. He wasn't going to fight anybody. He was just out there woofing. Sawyer was out there mostly as a peacemaker but I think wanted to get at Durocher. Al Barlick was trying to push him away and Eddie told him, 'Al, get your hands off me, Al. Don't put your hands on me.' Sawyer was getting mad and he could be a tough guy."

ENNIS: "We didn't like Durocher. He would get us knocked down on 0–2 counts all the time. He was a gutless son of a gun. We were looking for him."

The umpires had a difficult time restoring order and the police came on to try to clear the field. All together the rhubarb must have lasted close to 10 minutes. At one point a policeman threatened to arrest Tookie Gilbert for abusive language and resisting an officer's command, but umpire Lee Ballanfant talked him out of it.

After order was finally restored, Andy and Rigney were both ejected (and fined $25 each).

ENNIS: "The next day Durocher said we'd have been playing Jersey City if they hadn't gotten Seminick out of there."

The game itself, even absent the fisticuffs, proved to be a thriller. I continued to struggle on the mound once play resumed. The Giants tied the score in the sixth and went ahead in the seventh on a Bobby Thomson home run. We came back to tie in the bottom half on an error, a ground single to right by Bill Nicholson (batting for me), and a run-scoring single by Eddie Waitkus.

Konstanty followed me on the mound and, as he so often did that year, held the Giants at bay until we could break the tie. In this game, that took until the 11th inning. Stan Lopata, catching after Andy's banishment, opened the inning with a booming triple to center off Dave Koslo, who had held us scoreless since the seventh. Koslo intentionally walked Goliat and Bloodworth to load the bases, but Waitkus drove home the winning run with a sacrifice fly to center.

Konstanty's win was his 10th in relief. After all the hubbub, we were 5 games ahead of the Braves, 6½ in front of the Cardinals, and 7½ in front of the Dodgers, who had lost to Boston.

We sometimes called Andy Seminick "the mad Russian" in deference to his heritage. Although Andy was quiet and somewhat reserved, he was so tough that he had all of our respect.

ENNIS: "Andy was really a hard-nosed, aggressive catcher. He was strong like a bull and everybody on the club listened to him when he spoke. He could sure get us going, though, because he played so tough and was so good at blocking the plate."

CHURCH: "Andy Seminick was the epitome of stability. I think he was born to be a catcher. And he knew us, knew how to handle us. I had a ballgame in Philadelphia where I charged the umpire, Larry Goetz. I was upset because he wasn't giving me the outside corner. I knew I had a piece of that corner. About the fourth or fifth time I thought, 'I'm not going to have this.' I went in to about 10 feet from home plate and Andy knew what I was going to do so he got out in front between me and Goetz. I heard Goetz say, 'Get back on that mound you bush sonuvabitch. I'll run you out of here.'

"Andy said, 'Get back out there, Bubba. Get back out there.'

"I said, 'Hell, he won't give me the outside pitch.'

"Well, Andy got me calmed down and said, 'Get back out there. No more. Don't say anything else.' It was early in the ballgame and Andy wanted to make sure I didn't get run. Goetz told me the next day that my follow-through, where I ended up way off toward first base, made it look like those pitches were strikes, but they really were outside. Andy confirmed it. He had just wanted to make sure I stayed in the game."

ASHBURN: "If there was a leader, I would have to say it was Andy Seminick. Although I don't think anybody ever said Andy was our leader, he commanded respect because of his toughness and his great work habits. He was like a fireplug blocking the plate. He was just immovable. Overall, Andy and Bill Nicholson were veterans that set great examples for the younger players.

"Andy was quiet, really a nice guy. The fans loved him. His teammates loved him. My wife loved him. He was a guy who didn't have a hair on his head and he wasn't Tyrone Power, but he had a presence that women just loved. He has his Andy Seminick fan club in Philadelphia to this day."

SIMMONS: "Andy led by example. We didn't ever worry about a batter charging the mound because we knew Andy would be there. And he was the best at blocking the plate. He was really a physical presence back there, although he was real quiet."

Andy's fan club was formed by two sisters, Anne and Betty Zeiser, and their friend Kitty Kelly in 1948, at a time when Andy was still having his troubles behind the plate. Anne had won a "favorite Phillies" contest in 1947 while still a schoolgirl by writing a catchy poem about Andy. The prize was a pass to the 1948 home games and a chance to meet Andy.

ANNE ZEISER: "Back then Andy Seminick was not the darling of the Phillies' fans, and we decided to start a movement that would help bring him into the good graces of the fans. We went to Babe Alexander of the Phillies and he gave us all the encouragement we needed. Andy was an underdog at the time and we had had enough of the unjust boos and wolf calls going in his direction.

"When we approached Andy with the idea and asked for his permission we coaxed a very reluctant okay from him. I really believe Andy did not think it would work out."

Andy's club was the largest and most active of the clubs that Phillies fans started for the different Whiz Kids, publishing a newsletter and holding days for Andy in 1949 and on July 30 during the 1950 season. It was probably mere coincidence, but Andy began coming into his own in 1949 about the time his fan club gave him his first special day. And Andy was loyal to his fan club.

ANNE ZEISER: "It was my sister's birthday on the day of Andy's big fight with the Giants, and Andy came to her birthday party that evening along with his wife and son and showed cartoons to the kids at the party. He told us that he never wanted to hurt anyone but that he had to stand up for his rights. But he was sure sore all over."

SAWYER: "Andy was a very quiet, hardworking ballplayer. Everything Andy accomplished he had to work hard for. At first I doubted whether he could throw well enough to catch in the major leagues. But he worked at it and got so he had a good arm.

"And Andy was tough and got into more scraps than just in 1950 with the Giants. For some reason Gene Hermanski of the Dodgers and Andy didn't like each other. One time in 1948 Hermanski went out of his way to hit Andy while crossing home plate in a close game in Brooklyn. There wasn't even a play on him and Andy was up in front of the plate. So they had words and Andy decked Hermanski. They had to carry him off. Dusty Cooke was yelling, 'Who's next?' And the funny part was that the umpire, it may have been Jocko Conlon, didn't throw Andy out of the game."

SEMINICK: "Since there was not going to be a play on Hermanski, I just took a couple of steps in front of the plate to let him by, as I always did if a runner was going to score without a throw. Hermanski just went out of the way and knocked the tar out of me, knocked me on my can. So I got up and hit him a couple of times before they broke it up. I thought he was out of line and so I let him know it."

ENNIS: "Gene Hermanski was a pretty big guy, but Andy grabbed him by his chest and threw him about 10 feet in the air. Boy, Andy was tough."

Andy had another encounter with Sal Maglie earlier in 1950. I had never seen Maglie pitch before because he had been suspended for jumping to the Mexican League in 1946 and I really did not know who he was. We were beating the Giants handily in the Polo Grounds and in came Maglie to relieve. He was an older-looking guy who needed a shave and I thought, "That is why they call him 'the Barber.'"

Andy came to bat, and after Maglie got ahead in the count he brushed Andy back with a high inside fastball. On the next pitch Andy pushed a bunt down the first base line, hoping to run over Sal when he came over to field the ball or cover first. Maglie never moved off of the mound and Andy just ran to first and got a base hit. The next day Maglie was quoted in the paper as saying, "I get paid to pitch, not to fight."

Maglie was one of the finest pitchers in baseball for several years in the early 1950s. His style was to work inside on the batters, although he did not throw at their heads. Sal was going to pitch the way he wanted to pitch, and Andy, equally as willful, was going to try to make Maglie pay for throwing inside. Maglie had good sense; he knew better than to tangle with Seminick.

Ken Johnson lost a tough 2–0 game to New York's recently acquired Jim Hearn the day after our ruckus with the Giants. We remained five games in front of the Braves, who lost to Brooklyn and were coming to town next for an important two-game series.

After an off day we broke out of a team hitting slump, plummeting Boston 9–1 in a night game August 15, as Curt recorded his 15th win with help from the ever-present Konstanty. The following night I pitched a three-hitter to win 5–1 and extend our lead to a wonderful seven games. I threw only 79 pitches, 54 of them strikes, and completed the win in one hour and 45 minutes.

After another off day we headed to the Polo Grounds for the start of a crucial 17-game road trip. We had won 18 of our last 24 and thought that if we could play well on the road we would coast to the pennant.

We played the opening game of the New York series on August 18, only six days after our brawl with the Giants in Philadelphia. Not surprisingly, the over 26,000 fans in the Polo Grounds that day greeted Andy with cascades of boos.

> **SEMINICK:** "I got a threatening letter a day or two after the fight in Philadelphia saying they were going to get me in New York. The fans were all on me at the start of the game, and a bunch of the Giants were waving white handkerchiefs from the dugout when I first came to bat."

Richie Ashburn suspended in midair while scoring against Pittsburgh, August 1949. Catcher is Phil Masi. *(Courtesy of Temple University Archives)*

Phillies leaving Philadelphia by train to head to 1950 spring training in Clearwater. Pictured are Benny Bengough, Curt Simmons, Traveling Secretary Frank Powell, Maje McDonnell, Del Ennis, and Bill Koszarck. The weather was better in Florida. *(Courtesy of Rich Westcott)*

Mike Goliat *(left)* and Eddie Miller tugging at second base in spring training, 1950. Goliat would win the job and the veteran Miller would be released. Mike could sure hit Newcombe. *(Courtesy of Ted Silary)*

Del Ennis signing his 1950 contract for a team record $30,000 with Bob Carpenter's assistance. Del was worth every penny. *(Courtesy of Rich Westcott)*

Ken Silvestri.
The Hawk was underpaid.

Milo Candini. We couldn't have won
the pennant without his win.

Jocko Thompson — a choir-boy look and a decorated paratrooper in World War II. *(Courtesy of Philadelphia Phillies)*

Blix Donnelly — one of our real veterans. He called us younger guys "humpties."

Me with my bride, Mary Ann Kalnes Roberts. *(Courtesy of Ted Silary)*

Steve Ridzik. A spring training injury knocked him out of the 1950 season, but he became a solid big league pitcher. *(Courtesy of Ted Silary)*

Three of our mainstays in 1950 *(left to right)*: Willie Jones, Del Ennis, and Eddie Waitkus. *(Courtesy of Ted Silary)*

Bubba Church. What a curve!

Bob Miller. Bugger looked like Dizzy Dean on the mound.

The starting infield for the Whiz Kids *(left to right)*: Eddie Waitkus (1b), Granny Hamner (ss), Willie Jones (3b), and Mike Goliat (2b).

Ken Johnson. Hooks could pitch, hit, and run.

Bill Nicholson (12) is greeted by me and the entire dugout after his three-run pinch homer on July 8 gave me a 4–1 lead. Andy Seminick (21) and Willie Jones (6) were on base when Nick slammed his game winner. And to think the Dodgers had a meeting at the mound on how to pitch to him.
(Courtesy of Andy Seminick)

The 1950 Phillies All-Stars *(left to right)*: Willie Jones, Dick Sisler, Jim Konstanty, and me. *(Courtesy of Rich Westcott)*

My hometown of Springfield, Illinois, threw a day for me on July 14 in St. Louis. A young Harry Caray is on the far left, next to Eddie Sawyer and Illinois governor Adlai Stevenson. On my right is my dad, Thomas Roberts, then Harry Eilson, mayor of Springfield, and Ted Boyle, my high school baseball coach.

Whiz Kids waiting for a train. Life is good when you're young and have the lead in the pennant race. *From left:* Blix Donnelly, Dick Sisler, Andy Seminick, Richie Ashburn, Jim Konstanty, Del Ennis, Bob Miller, and Mike Goliat. *(Courtesy of Rich Westcott)*

The Phillies–Giants fight on August 12. Several of us are in the middle trying to save Bill Rigney from Andy Seminick. In the top middle, Bubba Church is strong-arming Leo Durocher. These things happen in a pennant race. *(Courtesy of Andy Seminick)*

A classic example of the immovable Andy Seminick blocking the plate against Pee Wee Reese of the Dodgers. Look how far Pee Wee is from home plate. Wasil was the best. *(Courtesy of Andy Seminick)*

Anne Zeiser, Kitty Kelly, and Betty Zeiser in their official Andy Seminick Fan Club outfits at the Polo Grounds in New York. Were they ever loyal fans. *(Courtesy of Anne and Betty Zeiser)*

Left to right: Del Ennis, Andy Seminick, Bob Miller, and Jim Konstanty after our 6–4 win over the Reds on August 23. Del and Andy had homers while Jim saved Bugger's 11th (and final) victory in the ninth. *(Courtesy of Rich Westcott)*

Left to right: Dick Whitman, Curt Simmons, and Jimmy Bloodworth celebrating our 9–8 come-from-behind win over the Cardinals on August 30. *(Courtesy of Rich Westcott)*

In the face of all that, Andy came to bat in the top of the second and walloped Jim Hearn's first pitch into the upper deck in left field for a home run. By the end of the game the Giant fans were cheering Andy.

SEMINICK: "The last time I came to bat that day the Giant fans were cheering and clapping for me. It was quite a thrill to see that. It was very satisfying to hear them cheer me."

Unfortunately, the Giants won the ballgame 7–4, beating Monk Meyer. The Dodgers, starting to come on strong, had taken over second place by sweeping a doubleheader from the Giants on our off day. On this day the Dodgers closed to 5½ games, beating the Braves 8–3 behind Carl Erskine, recently recalled from their Montreal farm club; Boston remained 7 games back, and St. Louis was in fourth place 8 games from the lead.

Two days of rain forced postponements of two games with the Giants until our next visit to the Polo Grounds, which would be during the last week of the season. Those makeup games would result in our playing consecutive doubleheaders at a time injuries had severely depleted our pitching.

The rains let up on Monday, August 21, allowing us to play the last game of our series with the Giants. Curt was masterful, pitching a four-hit shutout for his 16th win as we defeated Larry Jansen 4–0. Puddinhead and Andy slugged homers and Del had three hits, driving in his 100th run of the season. Brooklyn also won, so we headed west to Cincinnati with a 5½ game lead.

In those days we still traveled by train and by necessity spent a lot of time with our teammates. A ballclub was like an extended family, and the Whiz Kids were a close-knit group. We enjoyed each others' company, and, of course, as a bunch of young kids fighting for the pennant we had a common purpose.

On train trips some of the guys, like Granny, Richie, Puddinhead, and Putsy would play cards by the hour. On our western road trips the poker game sometimes lasted for days. I usually lost when I played, so the card-players were always happy to see me coming. Maje McDonnell, our young coach and batting practice pitcher, and I were both sports fans and we often went to the fights or other sporting events together on the road.

When we were in another city groups of guys would go out to eat to-gether, or to the movies or, to shoot pool, or we would just sit in the ho-tel lobby. Sometimes our togetherness could get us into unusual predicaments. One incident that happened later, in 1955, is a good example. We were traveling north from spring training and were supposed to play an exhibition game in a small town in North Carolina. It started raining hard that morning, so Del, Richie, Earl Torgeson, and I started shooting pool at a local pool hall. We did not know if the game had been called or not, so we asked Jack Meyer, a rookie pitcher, to let us know if they called the game so that we could catch the team bus to the train station.

We were enjoying ourselves shooting pool when all of a sudden one of us looked up and found that Jack was not there. We stepped outside and the bus was gone, too. We soon discovered that the team had left town on the train heading north while we were still shooting pool.

We decided to call the local air charter service to see if we could fly to the next town and meet the train. On the phone the guy said that he could take four small guys. When we got out to the airstrip the pilot took a look at Ennis, Torgy, Ashburn, and me and said, "I can't take you guys. You're too big."

It was a cloudy, rainy day but we finally talked him into taking us. It cost us $20 each. We took off and followed the train tracks and pretty soon we could see the train. We landed at the next town after we passed the train and asked the pilot to wait for us in case we could not get to the train station in time to get on the train. We all piled into a taxi and, sure enough, when we pulled into the station, the train was there.

We all jumped on the train and sat down. Pretty soon our traveling secretary, who was then Johnny Wise, walked by and asked, "Where have you been?"

I said, "What do you mean? I've been right here."

Wise said, "I know you weren't on this train. I've been looking all over for you. Where were you?" But we just all sat there quietly and no one on the club ever did figure out what happened to us.

> **SEMINICK:** "When we got into a town and wanted something to eat, a whole group of us would go. It wouldn't be just two or three of us but would be practically the whole ballclub having something to eat or having a beer."

> **McDONNELL:** "The Whiz Kids were a very close, very tight group. We had a lot of fun, but togetherness was a big thing with us. We went everywhere together. If we would go out to eat it was nine or ten guys."

SIMMONS: "You kind of picked your group. We had guys in their late 20s or early 30s. We had the kids. I was 18 when I came up and 20 or 21 in 1950. I didn't drink any beer, just went to the movies and drank milk shakes. There weren't too many of those guys. But we all got along well and groups of guys would hang out together."

CHURCH: "Nobody was allowed to have a real bad day and leave the ballpark by himself. Somebody would hang around until he was ready to go and go with him. And if you had a good day you better not feel too good. Just don't feel too good because somebody is going to knock you down. Somebody is going to bring you back down to earth.

"The older ballplayers took care of the rookies. Guys like Eddie Waitkus, Bill Nicholson, and Blix Donnelly. They would come by and say, 'Come eat with us.' When we got to New York, Blix took me to the famous Oyster Bar in Grand Central Station. He took me by Brooks Brothers and taught me about bow ties.

"There were no egos on that 1950 ballclub. We were different but we respected each other and there were no egos. We didn't have anyone fussing at the manager or grousing or creating problems. And there were no cliques on that ballclub. We would all go eat together after a ballgame. And our wives were close as well. They would get together and play bridge or visit with one another while we were on the road."

LOPATA: "Our wives got along real well. We would go out on long road trips and our wives would get together with the kids. Our families weren't too large then so they would get the kids together to play and have lunch or dinner together. Then they would meet at someone else's house in a day or two."

MARY ROBERTS: "The Phillies' wives were a very close group. The team sat us in the same section, same rows every time we came to the ballgame. So we did get to know everyone. Those of us with children didn't get to the game very often, but when we did we caught up on all the news.

"Robin ate about 4:00 or 4:30 before a game and then went to the ballpark. As a result we didn't eat together very much. He would be hungry when he got home from the ballpark and would eat a scrambled egg sandwich or something light about midnight. Then he would sleep in and have a late heavy breakfast. So I never ate with him during the season and I was in the kitchen most of the day.

"When the guys were away we visited, because when the Phillies were in town it seemed like we were busy every minute of the day and we didn't have time to visit each other. So we would eat at each other's homes and talk and visit when the guys were on road trips.

"In 1950 we lived on Washington Lane in a very nice row house. The Joneses and Hollmigs were close by. When the guys were on the road Carolyn Jones, Mary Anne Hollmig, and I would get together and we often slept over at each other's homes because we were all alone in a fairly big house in a strange community. That's how we got through the times when the guys weren't there.

"The row houses had an alley behind them with the garages. Late in the season someone came into the house through the back door while I was sleeping upstairs and stole the wallet out of my purse, which was sitting in the dining room. I didn't hear or see anything. I just knew when I went out shopping that my whole wallet was gone. After that I made sure that I slept over at someone's house while the guys were gone.

"We often went over to New York City on weekends when we were playing the Giants or the Dodgers to see shows and go to the ballgames."

After a big win Andy and Dick Sisler would often lead the guys in singing in the clubhouse shower or on the bus. Our favorites were old standards such as "Blood on a Saddle," "Detour," or "In the Evening by the Moonlight," and Andy and Dick would often ad-lib their own lyrics. Sometimes I would sing the verse to "Shine on Harvest Moon" and everyone would join in on the chorus. We all enjoyed belting the tunes out together. In fact, our singing received some notoriety late in the 1950 season. Granny, Puddinhead, Andy, and Dick were scheduled to appear on the Ed Sullivan show and sing a couple of songs. Our ballgame at the Polo Grounds ran long that day and "the quartet" arrived at the studio too late to get on the air in those days of live television. It might have been a good break that they were not able to get on. Although we were loud, I am not sure how good we were.

PAUL STUFFEL: "After we won a ballgame Eddie Waitkus would sing in the shower 'My Heart Goes Where the Wild Goose Go.' Dick Sisler would join in, too. Or the guys would sing 'Sawyer don't want no card playing around here. We don't care what Sawyer don't allow, we're going to play cards anyhow.' They were really loose."

The Whiz Kids were a fun-loving bunch of guys, even in the heat of a pennant race. Sisler, McDonnell, Seminick, and others would often entertain themselves by doing skits in the hotel lobby or out on the sidewalk.

MILLER: "Maje kept everybody going with his sense of humor. He and Dick Sisler were a riot together. They did some of the craziest things to keep us loose. I don't think we could have won the pennant without Maje McDonnell. He never threw one pitch, never got one hit, never stole one base or made a defensive play, but his value in the clubhouse was something money couldn't buy."

McDONNELL: "We would get out in front of a building with some of the team around us and we would look up and say, 'They're they go. Look at them now! Oh no, they're going to jump!' and passersby would stop and try to see what we were looking at. In Florida one day we had 200 people gathered around us.

"In New York, we would take the subway to Ebbets Field and Dick would get on one end of the subway car and I would get on the other end. He'd yell, 'Maje, how are you?' I'd yell back, 'Hey, Dick how's everything? How's your family?' Dick would say, 'Well, my wife's still drinking. I don't know what the hell I'm going to do with the kids.' I'd say, 'No kidding, your wife is still drinking.' And Dick would say, 'Yeah, she was bombed today.' And we would go on and on for the benefit of the whole crowded subway car.

"Sometimes in the subway or in the hotel lobby we would all sit reading the paper pretending we didn't know one another. It might be Andy, Dick, Bubba, and me, and all of a sudden Dick would say, 'Do a half,' and we would cross our legs together. Then in a few minutes Dick would say, 'Give me a time and a half,' and we would cross our legs, uncross them, and cross them again, all in unison. Or he would say, 'Let's do two,' and we'd cross and uncross our legs twice. People thought we were really crazy."

SEMINICK: "Sometimes Dick Sisler and I would sit on opposite ends of a couch in a hotel lobby and we would get into a mock shouting match about something stupid, like the size of the room. I would say, 'It's 20 by 20,' and Dick would argue, 'No it's not, it's 30 by 25,' and we would go on and on. It was just something to keep us loose and relax the tension."

Del Ennis was very quiet and businesslike, but he loved to play practical jokes, particularly on Benny Bengough and Cy Perkins.

ENNIS: "Benny was husky and Cy Perkins was real slim, so I used to change their shorts all the time. Or I would put powder in their shoes so when they would start walking with their blue serge suit white powder would start coming out through their laces. Bengough's number was 11 so I used to put two strips of adhesive tape over his number. Then he would go out to coach third and his uniform would look like it didn't have a number. They always knew it was me whenever anything like that happened. Sometimes I would grab Benny and write my pass list on top of his bald head."

SAWYER: "Del was a practical joker but didn't have much to say. Del would plant exploding cigars in Benny Bengough's locker. Benny would take any cigar so he'd light them up and they would explode. Or he would give him cigars that gave off smoke that looked like dandelions. Everybody would be laughing at the strange smoke and Benny wouldn't know what they were laughing at because the smoke was up above his head."

RIDZIK: "Benny Bengough wore sneaker-type shoes and he would just set them in front of his locker. Delmer got a couple of long spikes, the kind that hold the bases down, and drove them right through Benny's shoes, through the wooden floor. Bengough would always dress, put his uniform on, sit down, slide into his shoes and tie them. After doing all this, he went to get up to walk and took a header, right into the locker."

We enjoyed each other on the Whiz Kids. We played hard and were united in our goal to win the pennant. Under Eddie Sawyer we were relaxed and confident and it showed off the field as well as on it.

Our strong bonds and camaraderie overcame even some occasional testiness caused by a tough loss. One time I had dropped a 3–2 heartbreaker to the Cubs in Wrigley Field on a late-inning home run by Hank Sauer. It took me a long time to unwind after a defeat like that and I would usually be the last to leave the clubhouse. Dick Sisler had had a bad game and we were both feeling kind of punk and keeping to ourselves.

In those days there was no team bus after a road game unless we were leaving town and had to get to the train station. We were all on our own getting to and from the ballpark. I really liked it that way because I could unwind after a game and leave whenever I was ready. As I mentioned, I would often walk back to the hotel. In any event, on this day Dick and I were the last two guys in the visiting clubhouse.

We ended up in the shower together, neither of us saying anything to the other. All of a sudden Dick said, "My old man says anytime you let a home run hitter beat you late in the game you are a bad pitcher."

I was not in the mood to hear that kind of talk so I said, "I tell you something. If you hit like your old man, I wouldn't be in so many close ballgames."

Now in the wake of that tough defeat neither one of us was joking. Dick kind of looked at me and left the shower. I was not sure what was going to happen next because we were both a little upset. Dick was a big guy and if we started to fight no one was there to stop us except the visiting clubhouse boy.

I got out of the shower and was toweling off when Dick came around holding two beers. He gave me one and said, "That wasn't called for. We've talked enough, haven't we?"

And I said, "Yes we have, Dick." So we sat there and drank a beer together.

We took losses hard, especially those who had made a bad play or somehow contributed to the defeat. But the Whiz Kids were a very resilient team, in part because we were so young. We never carried little tiffs over and we seemed to always be able to bounce back and play well after a difficult loss. And, of course, we were winning most of the time. Little annoyances do not multiply and are easily forgotten when you are in first place.

Eddie Sawyer's leadership had a lot to do with our team camaraderie. He simply did not put any pressure on us, nor did he exhibit any frustration or panic when we did not perform well. I never saw

Sawyer emotionally upset. He was the same in July 1948 as he was down the stretch in 1950, even through all the adversity we would face in September.

MILLER: "Gee, I got along good with the Skipper. I never saw so many guys that loved and respected a man as much as we did Eddie Sawyer. Everybody. I never heard anyone say a discouraging word about Eddie Sawyer. There was no second-guessing any of his moves. We had nothing but complete love and trust for him and we do to this day."

MEYER: "Eddie would let you go, but if he saw that things were getting out of hand a little bit with you, he wouldn't make a big deal out of it. He would just say, 'Hey, slow it down a little bit.' He wouldn't tell you to stop it, he'd just say, 'Slow it down. Use your head.' He was a great guy to play for."

SAWYER: "I didn't want to give them too much to think about. It's an easy game if you play it right. If they were doing something wrong, I'd change them. We tried to get them doing things right in the minor leagues and then you don't have to change anything when they get to the majors. That's why the Dodgers have been so successful over the years. They teach them how to play in the minor leagues and they should know how to play when they come up. We tried to do the same thing. The '50 Phillies were playing well and they didn't have to be changed. I told my coaches just leave them alone, not to bother too much with them until there was something wrong. They just needed a little confidence. They could already play. I think you can you confuse them more than you can help them sometimes.

"We tried to keep the pressure off them all we could. I didn't hang around the players but stayed off with the coaches and the press more than anything. A lot of that was to keep the press away from the players."

We began our western trip in high style, sweeping a two-game series from the Reds, 4–3 and 6–4, on August 22 and 23. For the year we had won 16 of 19 from Cincinnati. I won my seventh straight by a 4–3 score in the opener, thanks to Del Ennis's game-winning ninth-inning single, to run my record to 17–5. Bob Miller won his 11th (and it would turn out, final) game in 100-degree heat in the second contest 6–4, with ninth-inning relief help from Konstanty. Andy and Del continued their hot hitting with homers off of Willard Ramsdell and Harry Perkowski, respectively. For Andy it was his seventh circuit clout in 14 games.

Next we moved to Pittsburgh, following the Dodgers, who had kept pace with us by sweeping their two-game set with the Pirates. The night before, the Bums had taken 17 innings to win 7–5 and remain 5½ back; Boston had dropped 8 games back and St. Louis, plagued by pitching problems, was in fourth, 9 games behind. It was becoming more and more obvious that Brooklyn would be our main obstacle to the pennant.

Bubba Church pitched us to a 4–2 win in the series opener to run his season record to 6–2. The second game of the series proved to be a 15-inning marathon. Curt could not hold a 3–0 lead, uncharacteristically getting chased in a six-run Buc fifth. We rallied to tie the score at six in our seventh on two walks, a sacrifice fly, a ground out, and Richie Ashburn's clutch single. Jim Konstanty replaced Russ Meyer, who had relieved Curt, in the seventh and proceeded to pitch the next nine innings, allowing only five hits and a single run in his most impressive outing yet.

Andy put us ahead in our 10th on his 19th homer, but Ralph Kiner tied us again in the bottom half with a long poke of his own. Jim permitted no more damage and we finally manufactured two two-out runs in the top of the 15th to give him his 11th win of the season. Jim even drove in our second run in the 15th with a single off of Pirate loser Cliff Chambers.

Kiner's 10th-inning homer broke Jim's string of 25⅓ scoreless innings. In his last 31 innings, since July 23, he had allowed only 12 hits and that one run.

> **SAWYER:** "Jim was in great shape. He was probably the best-conditioned athlete that I had. He did his work every day and wanted to pitch every day. He really wanted the ball. He had great control; he could throw the ball over the plate where he wanted to. And we had these guys who could throw hard like Curt and Robbie. Then I would bring Konstanty in and he throws so soft it's like trying to hit a feather by comparison. But he could strike good hitters out. And he pitched better when he was tired. He seemed to have more break on his ball if he had pitched a lot.
>
> "If he wasn't pitching he would pitch batting practice, which the players hated. They didn't want to mess up their swings trying to hit Konstanty. Or he would throw in the bullpen if we didn't use him. The years he had with me in '49 and '50 were excellent."

CHURCH: "Jim felt that he should pitch every day. He had that kind of arm and that mentality."

ASHBURN: "I felt about hitting the way Konstanty felt about pitching. He never thought a hitter should get a hit off of him. If a hitter ever got a hit, he didn't credit the hitter, he blamed himself."

McDONNELL: "Jim was cocky. He thought nobody could beat him, thought nobody could hit him. Very, very cocky."

MEYER: "Konstanty didn't throw hard, but he could hit that black all day long. He could hit it in his sleep. And with his palm ball he kept the ball down. Puddinhead made a hell of a crack one night. He said to Jim, 'You know they put that speed gun on Feller. If they put that gun on you I don't think it would work.' But I never saw a guy put together two years like he did in '49 and '50. It just goes to show you that you don't have to throw hard to be successful."

I started the series finale looking for my 18th win and our sixth straight, but it was not my day. The Pirates chased me in the fifth of what became a 14–4 rout. Meanwhile Brooklyn won their fourth straight over Cincinnati, their tenth in a row overall, to close the gap to four games.

Immediately after our last-game shellacking at the hands of the Pirates we had to travel to Chicago to face the Cubs in a doubleheader the next day, August 27. Eddie had sent Bubba Church on ahead and, well rested, Bubba pitched another superb game in the opener, defeating the Cubs 6–1 on four hits before 39,000 in Wrigley Field. Mike Goliat's second-inning homer with Dick Sisler aboard got us off to a good start and Bubba did the rest, allowing only a disputed home run to Bill Serena.

Bob Miller fell behind 4–1 in the second game but we rallied in the fifth to tie the score 4–4 on key hits by Bugger himself, Eddie Waitkus, Del and Puddinhead. Rubber-armed Konstanty relieved Bob with two on and one out in the eighth. He not only got out of that jam, striking out Roy Smalley and Rube Walker, but pitched three more perfect innings before darkness halted play after 11 innings. Just two days earlier Jim had pitched the equivalent of a complete game in Pittsburgh.

Since the game was called, under National League rules we had to replay it in its entirety. That meant we had to play another doubleheader the following day. We lost a tough one in the opener, 7–5 as Hank Sauer hit three successive homers off of Curt. In the second game we regrouped to come out on top 9–5 behind another spectacular relief effort by Konstanty, his third in four days. Eddie brought Jim in to relieve Russ Meyer with one out in the sixth and the score tied 5–5. Konstanty held the Cubs at bay the rest of the way while we scored four runs off Johnny Klippstein to give Jim his 12th victory, all in relief.

SAWYER: "Jim had a difficult personality. I didn't have a lot of conversation with him because I didn't want to. He was doing all right and I avoided him. I didn't want to bother him. He wasn't very well liked on the ballclub either because he was pitching in place of some of the other pitchers. A fellow like that isn't very well liked if he isn't winning, but Jim wasn't very well liked when he was winning.

"Jim was a little older and had a family and he didn't join the other fellows in having a beer. He didn't drink or smoke and he kept himself in great shape."

ASHBURN: "Jim Konstanty was an interesting guy. We used to talk a lot. We never agreed on much but we talked a lot. Jim wasn't a drinker. I wasn't a drinker but I did hang around with guys who were. Jim wasn't really one of the boys. He stayed off on his own most of the time."

McDONNELL: "Konstanty was different than everybody else. He was his own man. He didn't drink and he didn't like the fact that a lot of the guys did. He would argue with them, 'Were you guys out last night?'

"'Yeah, but we'll be out there doing the job for you today. You get the ball over the plate and we'll do the job.' They would really get on each other in the clubhouse.

"Jim worked hard. He ran every day, every day. If he didn't pitch, the next day he would throw five minutes of batting practice. He threw every day and wanted to pitch every day."

CHURCH: "I used to run the fence with Jim. We ran. We had our own routine and Jim was a hard worker. You can bet that he was going to get his work in. He was extremely regimented and ordered. He could look in his black book and tell you who hit what pitch when and where it went. He believed in keeping records of his pitching. Jim was not aloof but he kept to himself, although he was a nice person and a good guy."

While Konstanty had established himself as the premier relief pitcher in the league, the Whiz Kids were hitting like they had in spring training. Waitkus had 8 hits in the first Chicago doubleheader and 10 hits for the series. Andy remained on fire with 6 hits, including a double, a triple, and his 20th homer in the second doubleheader, raising his season average to .308. Richie had 8 hits in the series and had his average up to .308 as well. Del, leading the league in RBIs, was at .301, while Dick was at .292, Puddinhead at .288, and Granny, with many clutch hits to his credit, at a solid .279.

At this point in the season, Eddie was going with a set lineup, day in and day out. In fact Andy, after getting a day off in Pittsburgh, had caught both doubleheaders in Chicago.

There was no rest for the weary, however. After the successive doubleheaders in Chicago, we took a train down to St. Louis for a two-game series with the Cardinals beginning the next night, August 28. I got back on track in the first game, beating Howie Pollet 5–3 before 27,000 on a hot and muggy evening. The game was not, however, without some anxious moments. I went into the ninth with a 5–1 lead but gave up two runs on a walk, an error, two hits, and a sacrifice fly. With two outs, Eddie brought in Konstanty for the fourth time in five days. This time Jim needed only one pitch to get the job done; Rocky Nelson grounded his first offering to Granny at short for the third out and the win.

The game the next day proved to be a real donnybrook. Ken Johnson started against his old team but could not repeat his earlier magic and quickly fell behind 3–0. The Cards were up 4–0 after five innings but we showed life in the sixth on successive singles by Waitkus, Ashburn, and Jones that loaded the bases. Del Ennis then sent a hot shot over second, driving in two runs and sending Cardinal starter Max Lanier to the showers. Dick Sisler greeted reliever Al Brazle with a base hit to reload the bases, and Granny drove in our third run with a fielder's choice ground out.

Unfortunately, the Redbirds came right back in their half with two runs off Ken Heintzelman, pitching in relief of Johnson, to make the score 6–3.

But the Whiz Kids were not through either. Caballero led off our seventh with a pinch single to center, and Waitkus worked Brazle for a base on balls. St. Louis manager Eddie Dyer brought in Harry Breechen to pitch to Ashburn, but Richie doubled to right, scoring Putsy. Puddinhead grounded to Tommy Glaviano at third, who made a low throw in an unsuccessful attempt to nail Waitkus at the plate. Del then singled to center to drive in Richie for the tying run before the Cardinals got out of the inning.

Once we tied the score, Sawyer brought in Konstanty to stem the tide, his sixth appearance in seven days. Jim pitched a scoreless seventh but ran into trouble in the eighth, surrendering two runs to send us to the ninth trailing 8–6.

Again showing the resilience that makes champions, we came back from a multiple-run deficit for the third time in the game. Del greeted Cardinal pitcher Gerry Staley with a line single to center. With one out, Granny shot a base hit over shortstop and Andy coaxed a walk to load the bases. Eddie sent Dick Whitman to bat for Konstanty, and Dick responded with a clutch double to right center to tie the score and push the go-ahead run to third. Jimmy Bloodworth, playing second after Mike Goliat had been lifted for a pinch hitter in the seventh, was next. Jimmy stroked a long fly to left that scored Bubba Church, running for Andy, to finally send us into the lead, 9–8.

Milo Candini opened the bottom of the ninth, but Eddie brought in Curt when Milo walked Glaviano, the first batter in the inning. Curt shut the door with a vengeance, retiring Marty Marion, Stan Musial, and Enos Slaughter to secure Konstanty's 13th victory and send us into September $6\frac{1}{2}$ games into the lead.

That ballgame typifies the kind of win that a team must have to win a pennant. It is one of the most memorable of that year because it was truly a team win. We managed to win a game it looked like we would lose because everybody chipped in and did their job. It demonstrates very vividly that we would not have won the pennant without the contributions of guys like Putsy Caballero, Dick Whitman, Jimmy Bloodworth, and Milo Candini.

We had won 8 of 10 (with one tie) on the western portion of our road trip and faced only a three-game set with the Braves in Boston before returning home to Shibe Park. And we finally had a day off, although we spent it flying from St. Louis to Boston.

By 1950 baseball teams were starting to fly sometimes on long hauls, and our TWA charter on a Lockheed Constellation on August 31 was the first team flight in club history. Our indoctrination was a rough one, particularly given that none of us had flown much, if at all. First, our 8 A.M. departure was delayed an hour and a half by mechanical difficulties. Then, once airborne, we flew into the middle of a severe thunderstorm.

It was very foggy in Boston, and when we finally touched down, we cheered the pilot, happy to be back on solid ground. That first flight was one of the worst I ever experienced in baseball.

> **SAWYER:** "It was about a 24-hour trip by train from St. Louis to Boston so Bob Carpenter said, 'Go ahead and fly.' There was a storm when we got to Boston and it was really raining. When we hit Logan Airport there was water all over and it looked like we were in the bay. But the newspapers made it sound worse than it really was. We were never in any danger.
>
> "The first person who called our room after we got to our hotel was Howard Hughes, who owned TWA. He was checking on us because had heard about our so-called mishap. Frank Powell answered the phone but we both talked with him. We told him there was nothing much to it except the newspapermen made more of it than there really was."

On our day off Brooklyn clobbered Boston 19–3, behind Gil Hodges's record-tying four home runs, to close to 6 games. The Braves remained in third place, 8½ games in arrears, while St. Louis had dropped into a fourth-place tie with the Giants, 11½ games back.

Bubba started our September in style with another strong outing, defeating the Braves 7–3 for his eighth victory. Andy legged out an inside-the-park homer in the sixth when his long drive off Max Surkont hit the center field wall and caromed off the Braves' Sam Jethroe. Richie had two hits to extend his hitting streak to 13 consecutive games (27 for 62) and raise his average to .313, while Dick Sisler, playing despite a sprained wrist, lifted his average to .299 with three hits of his own. Brooklyn lost to the Giants 4–1; our lead was seven and climbing.

Curt was even tougher the following night, outdueling Johnny Sain 2–0 for our 10th win in our last 12 games. The Dodgers beat the Giants by the same score to stay seven back.

Curt's win was his 17th and for the first time in his career he did not walk a single batter. While it looked then like we would coast to the pennant, neither Curt, Bubba, nor Bugger would record another victory in 1950. Tougher times were ahead for the Whiz Kids.

Chapter 13
SEPTEMBER ADVERSITY

R ain washed out the final game of our series in Boston. The rainout would necessitate a makeup game on our next trip to Beantown, which would unfortunately occur during the last week of the season.

But for the moment we were glad to be returning home after our last long road trip of the season. On the 17-day trip we had won 11 of 14 with one tie and extended our lead to 7 games over Brooklyn and $10^1/_2$ over Boston. The Cardinals had faded to fifth place, 14 games back, while the Giants had taken over fourth, $12^1/_2$ games behind us.

The team again took to the air, flying an American Airlines DC-6 charter home to Philadelphia. Little did we know that we would be treated to a heroes' welcome when we touched down at the Philadelphia airport. About 30,000 fans jammed the airport and the streets leading to it to greet us. String bands played and the people cheered until we got to our cars. The roads were so jammed that it took those living in Center City two and a half hours to get home; the flight from Boston had only taken an hour and a half.

This incredible reception had a significant impact on us. It was the first time that most of us realized how big a part of the city we were and how important our success was to the people of Philadelphia.

Our home stand began with a Labor Day doubleheader against Leo Durocher and his Giants, the team we loved to hate. I was to have pitched our last game in Boston and so Eddie Sawyer started me in the first game against New York, with Bob Miller to pitch the second game. I was going for my 19th win of the season.

I pitched well, allowing only two runs in eight innings before being lifted for pinch hitter Dick Whitman. Unfortunately, Jim Hearn pitched better, shutting us out on five hits to prevail 2–0. Sal Maglie completed the Giants' sweep in the nightcap, also shutting us out while his teammates chased Miller in the fourth on their way to a 9–0 victory. Twenty-year-old rookie Steve Ridzik made his only appearance of the year for us in the second game, pitching three innings of relief.

> **RIDZIK**: "I was shaking like a leaf and threw three balls to the first batter, Monte Irvin. I'd pitched against him in the International League many times. Lopata ran out and said, 'Come on Steve, get the ball over. You're going to be okay.'
>
> "I thought, 'I gotta start throwing strikes,' so I laid it in there and he hit it about 480 feet on the roof.
>
> "Lopata said, 'You're ready now. Let's go.' So I pitched three innings and got them out after that."

For the twin bill we had 14 hits, no runs, and two losses. Fortunately, Brooklyn also lost a doubleheader to the Braves and we were able to maintain our seven-game advantage.

After our disappointing homecoming we got a break from the schedule, a much-needed off day at home before facing the Dodgers in a key four-game series. While we were resting, the Giants beat the Dodgers 8–5 in Ebbets Field to extend our lead to 7½ games.

Our series with Brooklyn began with a September 6 twi-night doubleheader. Don Newcombe faced Bubba Church in the opener and the two quickly hooked up in a pitching duel. The Dodgers scratched out runs in the first and eighth innings while Newk extended our scoreless streak to 32 consecutive innings to win 2–0. He gave up only three singles, two to Richie Ashburn and one to Dick Whitman, who pinch hit for Bubba in the eighth, and did not allow a Phil past first base.

Newk's victory was his sixth in succession and his third shutout in four games. He was throwing so well that Dodger manager Burt Shotton, trying to gain ground on us in any way possible, started Don in the second game as well. Curt Simmons started for us in what we thought might be his last game before his activated National Guard unit was shipped out to Indiana, effectively ending his season.

We finally broke our scoring drought and touched Newcombe for a run in the first on Ashburn's single and Del Ennis's two-out double to right. We added another run in the third to go up 2–0 thanks to some long-awaited good fortune. Eddie Waitkus led off the inning with a line drive deep to right. Carl Furillo backed up to the light standard and looked like he would make the catch when he slipped on the concrete base of the standard. The ball then ricocheted off the fence for a triple. Richie then drove Eddie in with a sacrifice fly.

Meanwhile, Curt was invincible for eight innings, giving up only a fifth-inning infield single to Gil Hodges. He whiffed Eddie Miksis for his seventh strikeout to start the ninth, and it looked liked we had evened the score for the day. But Lefty walked Pee Wee Reese and Tommy Brown singled sharply to left to put men on first and second.

At this juncture, Eddie Sawyer waved in Jim Konstanty to secure the victory, as he had so many times before. When Curt left the mound, the 32,000 fans in attendance, believing it might be Curt's last appearance, rose and gave him a thunderous standing ovation. When the crowd finally quieted, Jim quickly got ahead of the first batter, Jackie Robinson, 0–2 before Jackie sent a hard grounder into the hole at shortstop. Granny Hamner made a nice play to get a glove on the ball but he had no play at any base, leaving the bases loaded with one out.

Jim bore down to fan the dangerous Furillo on four pitches and we were one out from victory. But he could not get Hodges, who already had two home runs off Jim for the year. Gil lined a single to left to drive in Reese and Brown with the tying runs. On the play, Granny cut off Dick Whitman's (playing because of Dick Sisler's sore wrist) throw to the plate, trapping Hodges who had headed for second on the throw. Granny threw to Goliat at second but Robinson had rounded third and was heading home with the go ahead run. Mike fired to Seminick at home, now trapping Jackie off third. It seemed like Robinson always got out of these jams, and he did this time as well, scoring the lead run when Andy's throw skipped by Puddinhead Jones at third.

Dan Bankhead, pitching in relief of Newcombe, who had finally been lifted for a pinch hitter in the eighth, got us out in our ninth and we had defeat snatched from the jaws of victory. Thanks to our second consecutive doubleheader loss our lead was 5½ games.

We topped the one million attendance mark the next afternoon as I started against Brooklyn on two days rest. Unfortunately, our losses stretched to five and our lead shrunk to 4½ as I lost another tough decision, 3–2. After two innings I was down 3–0 thanks to consecutive doubles in the first and home runs by Hodges and Bruce Edwards in the second. Del got us back to 3–2 with his 29th and 30th homers of the season off of Carl Erskine in the fourth and sixth innings, and I settled down meanwhile to withstand any further damage.

Richie led off our eighth with a triple over first, convincing Shotton that it was time to bring in Ralph Branca in relief. All Branca did was strike out Puddinhead and Del and induce Jack Mayo, just up from Toronto, to foul to third to escape the inning. He mowed us down one, two, three in the ninth and we had dropped another one-run game. Our lead was down to 4½ games.

We were hit with more bad news that afternoon when we learned that Bill Nicholson would be lost to us for the season. Nick had not looked well in recent weeks and seemed to be losing weight. He had uncharacteristically dropped a fly ball against the Giants on Labor Day in a scoreless tie in the game I eventually lost 2–0 and had shown little pop in his bat.

On Wednesday, Nick and I were standing together in the outfield during pregame practice and I said, "Bill, you don't look good."

He said, "I don't feel too good. I've lost about 15 pounds."

I said, "If I were you, I'd check with the trainer about that." So Nick went in to talk to Frank Wiechec and ended up in the hospital that day for tests. It did not take the doctors long to diagnose the problem as diabetes, which required immediate treatment and ended Nick's baseball for the year. Eddie Sawyer quickly called up Jack Mayo from Toronto, where he was hitting .304 with 11 round-trippers, and requested permission from the league office to add Jack to the World Series roster. Except in case of injury, those rosters had to be submitted by September 1.

Although Jack Mayo was a fine defensive outfielder, the loss of Nick for the season was a real setback. Nick was the consummate professional, and the way he conducted himself in the clubhouse and on the field was a positive influence on all of us. Once considered the best right fielder in the National League, injuries had curtailed his playing time the last two years. But he had produced several clutch hits for us, including two game-winning homers earlier in the year, and had contributed in many ways to our success.

Eddie Sawyer called a rare team meeting before the series finale with Brooklyn the next evening. It was only the third meeting Eddie had held since taking over as manager in July 1948. In his calm, quiet way he told us to keep hustling and fighting and that we would be all right once the breaks started evening out again. He wanted us to relax, not to be overanxious, and to remember that we had come out of five-game losing streaks earlier in the year with great success. He also reminded us that we had a 4½ game lead and were still very much in the driver's seat.

That meeting was typical of the way Eddie handled us, always trying to build us up and keep us loose and confident. Once again we responded, beating the Dodgers 4–3 behind the clutch pitching of Russ Meyer, who with the emergence of Bubba Church had not pitched much in recent weeks. Monk had every chance to blow in the second when, with a 2–0 lead and Furillo on first, Puddinhead booted Hodges's tailor-made double-play ball to put two runners on. Bruce Edwards followed with a run-scoring single that sent Hodges to third.

Faced with runners on first and third and no outs, Russ bore down, getting Billy Cox on a pop to short, fanning Dodger hurler Erv Palica, and inducing Reese to hit back to the box. We stretched our lead to 4–1 before Snider's eighth-inning homer closed it to 4–3. But Russ hung in for the complete-game victory and our lead was back to 5½ games. We led the season series with Brooklyn 10 games to 8 with 4 to play.

We continued to bounce back the next day, September 9, against Boston, in town for two games and still in third place only seven games back. Eddie decided to start Curt on only two days rest, knowing it would be his last pitching of the season. Curt, who had to depart for Camp Atterbury, Indiana, the following afternoon, did not have his good stuff but nonetheless pitched valiantly.

The Braves got two unearned runs in the second to jump to a 2–0 lead before we got on the board with a run in the fourth on Del's bunt single, Jack Mayo's ringing double off the right field fence (Jack was playing for Dick Sisler, who was still hampered by his sore right wrist), and a ground out.

Curt held the Braves until the seventh when they rallied for two more runs to extend their lead to 4–1, prompting Eddie Sawyer to bring in Bob Miller. As Curt left the mound for the last time, all 15,000 fans rose to give him a rousing and lengthy ovation. They realized, as did we, that the Whiz Kids would not be sitting in first place without Curt's 17 victories.

We quickly rebounded to tie the score in the bottom half of the inning on key hits by Whitman and Ashburn, in the process chasing Braves starter Max Surkont and ensuring that Curt would not go out a loser. In our eighth we forged ahead 6–4 on Del's sharp double along third, Jack Mayo's bunt single, Granny's run-scoring single, and Andy Seminick's sacrifice fly. But Konstanty, pitching after Whitman hit for Miller, for once could not hold the lead, giving up a two-run homer to Bob Elliot in the ninth.

Fortunately we had the last at bat in this seesaw game. Eddie Waitkus led off our ninth by singling to center off of Braves rookie David Cole. Southpaw Mickey Haefner came in to pitch to the left-handed batting Ashburn, who sacrificed Waitkus to second. Willie Jones, in the throes of a batting slump, belted the third pitch on a line to left to drive in the winning run. The Dodgers lost to the Giants 2–0 and, although we had lost Nick and Curt in quick succession, our lead was 6½ games.

MILLER: "I remember what a gutsy, thick-skinned guy Curt Simmons was. Curt, Bubba, and I were all single and we lived together at the Germantown Cricket Club that summer. We drove Curt down to his National Guard unit that Sunday morning and, boy, he heard a lot of gruff remarks and catcalls from the other guys in the National Guard, but he just smiled, grinned and bore it."

SIMMONS: "Frank Powell had been telling me all along that the club was going to get me an extension. We were activated September 5, but we spent a week at the armory at Broad and Diamond before shipping out. I had to be there 7 to 5 and then I'd go to the ballpark. And Frank Powell is saying, 'You're not going to go.' So on Sunday morning I'm getting on the train to go to Camp Atterbury and Frank says, 'We're going to get you back. Don't worry.'

"They did have lawyers working on it, but there was a lot of political pressure because of the Korean conflict, so I missed it."

BICKNELL: "After Curt and I got to Camp Atterbury we tried to throw a little to each other to keep in some kind of shape. We built a little mound out in a field to throw from. He used to catch me and I'd catch him. But I didn't even have a catcher's glove. I had to catch Curt with just a fielder's glove and that was tough. He beat my hand to death. It would swell way up. I tried to catch the ball in the web as much as I could but sometimes I couldn't. I put two fingers outside the damn glove and that helped quite a bit. He had a helluva sinker and that sucker was hard to catch. I sure as hell would not have wanted to hit against him."

SAWYER: "Curt hit his stride in '50 and he had almost as many wins as Robbie did [17 as opposed to 18] when he was called to active duty. He was pitching very well and many of the teams in the league, those with a lot of left-handed hitters, just couldn't beat him. The Giants really had a tough time with him. We would have would won much easier if we had had him the whole year. The other pitchers like Robbie would have had more rest."

Eddie would start Curt in the first game of a twi-night doubleheader in the Polo Grounds and we would be in the third or fourth inning before the Giants could even see the ball because of the shadows and Curt's fire-power. No one threw the ball any harder than Curt and his ball really moved. In one game, Henry Thompson, the Giant third baseman and a left-handed hitter, struck out three times against Curt. Henry used to be a switch hitter, and after his third kayo he supposedly told Leo Durocher, "Leo, I can't hit this guy left-handed."

Leo allegedly said, "Well, try him right-handed." So Thompson went up and struck out right-handed on three pitches. In many games that year Curt was as dominating a pitcher as ever took the mound.

The day Curt left—Sunday, September 10—was also Eddie Sawyer's 40th birthday, and we hoped to celebrate it with another victory over the Braves. Bubba started for us against John Sain and pitched well but still found himself down 3–1 after five innings. Two miscues had led to two of the three Boston runs. We had several chances to break through against Sain, finally tallying a run in the fifth on Richie's run-scoring two-base shot just inside the first base line.

In our sixth, Mayo laced a ball against the light tower in right for a home run and Hamner followed with a sharp single to left. Granny's hit was followed by a cloudburst that halted play. After a delay of an hour and 52 minutes the umpires called the game, which reverted back to the last completed inning, the second time rains had turned a possible win into defeat. Jack Mayo's home run was wiped out and we were 3–1 losers. It would be Jack's only homer of the year and it did not even count. On July 24 rain had nullified Waitkus's two-run homer in the top of the seventh against Pittsburgh, relegating us to a 2–1 defeat.

The loss dampened the postgame birthday celebration for Eddie Sawyer a little. We gave Eddie a huge cake inscribed "Happy Birthday to Our Skipper" and a box of his favorite cigars. Our "Happy Birthday" rendition was helped by the fact that the Dodgers had again lost to the Giants, keeping our lead at 6½ games.

After a welcome off day, the Cardinals came to town for a two-game series. St. Louis had faded to fifth place, 12½ games out, but were still a very dangerous club with Stan Musial (leading the league with a .359 average), Enos Slaughter, Red Schoendienst, and company.

I hooked up with Max Lanier in the first game in a classic pitching duel. Lanier, always tough against us, already had beaten us three times. Schoendienst led off the game with a double and I walked Marty Marion to immediately get into a tight spot with Musial coming to bat. But I got Stan to ground into a force out and with runners on first and third, struck out Bill Howerton on four pitches. We emerged from the inning unscathed when Andy threw out Musial attempting to steal.

Andy was in the throes of an 0-for-20 batting slump. His first time up he tried unsuccessfully to bunt before popping up softly to Marion at short. He then led off the fifth and with the count 1–1 teed off on the next pitch, driving the ball against the upper deck facade in left for his 22nd homer of the year. Fittingly, it was Grandpa Whiz's 30th birthday.

Andy's homer turned out to be the only run as I pitched a five-hit shutout for my 19th win in a game that was over in one hour and 41 minutes. Afterwards, Andy was all smiles in the clubhouse, lighting up a victory cigar. The Dodgers remained 6½ back, beating the Reds 3–1.

The following season Andy had another memorable encounter with Lanier. Early in the year Lanier, a left-hander, hit Andy on the head with an inside fastball. Some of us thought that Lanier was carrying a grudge way too far.

SEMINICK: "We got some helmet liners to try out the day that Max Lanier beaned me. I picked one up in the clubhouse before the game and tried it on. I remember thinking, 'This thing won't do much good' so I just tossed it down. Then Lanier really hit me hard and I wished I had tried one of those new helmet liners.

"I don't think Lanier was trying to hit me to even the score or anything. But I was in pretty bad shape. My heartbeat went down to 38 and I could barely raise my arm. I spent a day in the hospital and then tried to come back too soon, on the third day. I started feeling real bad again and they rushed me back to the hospital. I was okay but it seemed like it affected my hitting the whole year. I never could get back in a groove in 1951."

After our first-game win, the second game of our series with St. Louis was postponed a day by rain. Russ Meyer, who after a rough start had come on to win four of his last five outings, started for us against southpaw Harry Brecheen. With Curt gone, we needed the Monk to continue to step up, as he had against Brooklyn six days before.

Russ struggled mightily for $6^2/_3$ innings, giving up eight hits and eight walks. But he was tough in the clutch and kept us in the ballgame, leaving in the seventh for Konstanty with the score tied 2–2. The bases were loaded at the time, however, and Jim got Schoendienst to pop to Granny to escape the inning. Jim had to work out of his own jams in the eighth and ninth innings but managed to keep the Cards from scoring. The Cardinals had left a total of 18 runners on base in their nine innings at bat.

Mike Goliat started our ninth promisingly with a single to center off of St. Louis reliever Al Brazle. Caballero ran for Mike and was promptly forced at second by Konstanty's failed sacrifice attempt. Waitkus then sent a shot over third for two bases, sending Jim to third. Bubba came in to run for Konstanty but was thrown out at home on Richie's bouncer to third baseman Eddie Kazak, with Waitkus advancing to third on the play at the plate.

With two outs, Puddinhead was up. After the Cardinals huddled to discuss how to pitch to him, Willie, as he had so often, smashed the first pitch back through the box and into center field to drive in Eddie with the winning run.

Puddinhead's hit made Jim a winner for the 15th time, all in relief. It was a good thing we won, because the Dodgers swept a doubleheader from Cincinnati to close to six games.

The Reds came to town next for three games, including a September 15 twin bill to start the series. The two games would be as memorable as any we had played thus far.

Eddie tapped Bubba Church to start the first game and me to pitch the nightcap. In the opener we tallied a run in the second of Reds starter Willard Ramsdell on Goliat's RBI single. In the Reds' third Bubba walked Johnny Wyrostek on four pitches with two out, bringing up Cincinnati's brawny first baseman, Ted Kluszewski.

Bubba fired in a first pitch fastball and big Klu met it squarely, sending it back at Bubba like a rocket. It struck Bubba in the face, opening a gash under his left eye. Bubba clutched his face, spun completely around, and finally sank to his knees as teammates Sisler, Meyer, Bloodworth, and trainer Wiechec rushed to him.

CHURCH: "I missed with a fastball on Kluszewski by about a foot. I got the ball out too much over the plate and he got around on it and drove it right back up the middle. I saw the ball off his bat and got my glove up and thought I had it. The ball must have sailed because the next thing I know is something hit me and I turned and watched the ball go out to right field. Once I turned I couldn't stop, and I think I did a 360-degree turn because I wound up on my knees, facing home plate. My glove ended up about halfway to second base.

"Somebody had once told me about a fan in the first base stands getting hit in the eye with a foul ball in a game in Birmingham in the Southern Association. He said, 'Bubba, that man's eye just ran out of his hands.'

"Now, that's what I'm thinking, because I've got my hands up to my eye and blood is coming out of my hands. I'm on my knees and I'm thinking, 'Oh my God, I'm not going to be able to see.' But it was only blood."

MEYER: "I think I was the first guy out there, and I thought Bubba was dead. It was really scary. The ball went all the way over to where the stands in Shibe Park angled back toward the field down the right field line. That's a hell of a long way from the pitcher's mound off of a guy's face."

ENNIS: "I fielded the ball way down the right field line when Bubba got hit in the eye. I didn't know what to think; it looked like his eye was hanging out of his head and that he was really badly hurt."

SAWYER: "I was one of the first ones out on the mound. The ball hit right in the socket of his eye and sucked the eyeball right out of the socket. He was all bloody and his eyeball was hanging down the side of his face when I saw him. It looked like he had been stabbed. It was gruesome."

SEMINICK: "I was catching Bubba when Kluszewski hit him. That was an awful sight. It scared me. The ball bounced into right field and by the time I ran out and got to Bubba, he was staggering around. All I saw was blood all over his eye and I thought his eyeball was hanging out. The ball cut him right under the eye and the flesh was open and I thought that was his eyeball. It was an awful looking sight."

CABALLERO: "Fellows that were in the service said that Bubba reacted just like when a guy got shot. When we rushed out to the mound it seemed like Bubba had blood coming out of his mouth and his nose and his eyeball. We thought he was gone. It was the most tragic thing I'd ever seen, but thank God he came out of it okay."

Bubba never lost consciousness. He started to walk off the field but staggered as he reached the foul line. Bloodworth and Wiechec picked him up and carried him fireman-style into the clubhouse.

BLOODWORTH: "He kept asking me if we got that guy out. I told him, 'Sure we did Bub,' and he said, 'You're lying to me Bloodworth, I know we didn't.'"

ANNE ZEISER: "Andy Seminick lived with his family right around the corner from Shibe Park that year. His son, Andy, Jr., was in the clubhouse when they brought Bubba in. Little Andy, who was only four or five, ran home yelling, 'Mom, Mom, a man just got killed at the ballpark.' Bubba was hit in the first game of a twi-night doubleheader and the whole ballpark was under a veil the rest of the night."

CHURCH: "They carried me into the clubhouse and laid me on the training table. Blix Donnelly came in and said, 'We know you're all right, it hit you in the head. If it had hit you in the foot it would have really hurt you.'

"They took me to the hospital and it turned out I was fine. I had a large cut from my nose all the way under my left eye but nothing was broken and my eye was okay. They had to wait a couple of days for the swelling to go down and a plastic surgeon came in and sewed me up. My first visitor in the hospital was Bill Nicholson, who was in there with his diabetes and had been listening to the game on the radio."

Bubba was out of action about 10 days but could not get on track when he came back in late September. He would not record another victory in 1950.

Eddie Sawyer brought in Ken Heintzelman after Bubba's injury on September 15 and Goober was superb, escaping the third unscathed and allowing only one run over the last 6⅓ innings. Andy Seminick polled his 23rd homer in the fourth for what turned out to be the winning run in a 2–1 ballgame. Kenny, a 17-game-winner in 1949, won for only the second time in 1950.

I pitched the nightcap, looking for my 20th win, against the Reds' Howie Fox. After two scoreless innings, Virgil Stallcup, the Cincinnati shortstop, was the leadoff batter in the third. He hit my first pitch on a line right back at me. Luckily for me, unlike Bubba, I was able to catch the ball.

The Reds scored three runs on a couple of errors in the third and I gave up single runs in the fourth and fifth, so by the end of five innings I was trailing 5–0. But we battled back for two runs in the seventh and a run in eighth on a key pinch hit single by Bloodworth to close to 5–3.

In our ninth, Ennis beat out a one-out bunt against Reds reliever Ken Raffensberger. Stan Hollmig, batting for Jack Mayo, drilled a clutch two-bagger to put runners on second and third, causing Reds manager Luke Sewell to replace Raffensberger with Herm Wehmeier. Granny Hamner greeted the new pitcher with a ringing double to left, scoring Del and Putsy Caballero, running for Stan, to tie the score.

Wehmeier got out of the inning without further damage and hooked up in an incredible pitching duel with Konstanty. Jim had pitched the ninth in relief of rookie Jack Brittin, who had pitched a scoreless eighth after I had been removed for a pinch hitter during our seventh inning rally. For eight more innings Jim and Wehmeier pitched scoreless baseball, leaving us still tied 5–5 heading into the 18th inning. At that point it was after midnight and Jim, after pitching nine scoreless innings, finally tired, walking the bases loaded and eventually surrendering two runs.

Down 7–5 and again facing defeat, we rallied once more in the bottom of the 18th. Del led off with a short fly that center fielder Lloyd Merriman could not hold after a long run. Del, hustling all the way, ended up on second with a double. Dick Sisler singled to right to advance Del to third, and Granny brought him in with a timely sacrifice fly to center. Stan

Lopata, who had caught the last half of the game in relief of Andy, then followed with a resounding triple to right center to score Dick and bring us even again.

We looked like winners with Stan on third and only one out, but Wehmeier showed his mettle and retired Mike Goliat and Ken Silvestri, batting for Konstanty, to send the game to the 19th inning.

Eddie brought in Blix Donnelly to pitch the 19th, and he was greeted by Connie Ryan's two-bagger. But Blix bore down and retired the Reds without giving up a run. In our half, Eddie Waitkus led off against new Reds hurler Ed Erautt with a single to left. Richie followed with a beautifully placed bunt down the first base line that stayed fair, and we had runners on first and second. Then Puddinhead worked a walk to load the bases with no one out and Del ended it with a smash against the left field wall, our 23rd hit of the game, to plate Waitkus.

Our Friday twi-night doubleheader had lasted well into Saturday morning, and we had played almost seven hours of baseball. It was a night that was hard to believe, with all that had happened. But we had won both ballgames, and again everybody contributed to our success. After the second game Blix Donnelly, referring to the fact that Heinz and he had been the winning pitchers, observed, "Some Whiz Kids. They're taking us old men out of camphor to win."

Meanwhile Brooklyn had lost to the Cardinals 6–2, meaning that after the dust settled our lead had risen to $7\frac{1}{2}$ games over the Dodgers and 8 games over the Braves. We had only 15 games remaining while the Dodgers had 20 to play and the Braves 19.

Almost unbelievably, we lost our second starting pitcher in 24 hours the following afternoon. Bob Miller started against Ewell Blackwell and was touched for an unearned run in the first inning. Bugger then blanked the Reds until the sixth, when they scored another run to go ahead 2–0.

MILLER: "I first felt some pain in my shoulder in the fourth inning. By the sixth, it was starting to really bother me and I told Andy that I was having real trouble and didn't know how long I could last. Then I couldn't throw at all when I tried to warm up in the seventh. I'd had more stuff than I'd had in a long time, and then—just like that—I couldn't throw anymore."

Although rookie Paul Stuffel and Milo Candini blanked the Reds the rest of the way, we could do nothing against Blackwell, who blanked us on only three hits. On the positive side, both the Dodgers and the Braves also lost, so our 7½ game lead remained intact.

In the course of a week we had lost three starting pitchers: Curt, Bubba, and Bob. Curt was gone for the season and we knew Bubba and Bugger would need at least a couple of weeks to recover from their respective injuries. In addition, it had only been nine days since we had lost old pro Bill Nicholson for the duration of the year, and Dick Sisler had not been able to play for more than a week because of his sore right wrist.

To shore up our depleted team Eddie had called up pitchers Jack Brittin, Paul Stuffel, Steve Ridzik, and Jocko Thompson from Toronto and added outfielder Stan Hollmig. Brittin, from my hometown and considered one of the top Phillies prospects, had experienced an up-and-down year with the Maple Leafs, compiling a 7–11 record. He missed two months of the season there because of numbness in his legs. Although a doctor told him to quit baseball, Jack battled back and pitched well for Toronto late in the year, earning his call-up for the stretch drive.

Jack continued to experience frequent problems with his legs in subsequent years and was finally forced to quit baseball altogether in 1954 after achieving some success in the minor leagues. It was not until 1956, however, that doctors finally diagnosed Jack's ailment as multiple sclerosis. Its onset had caused Jack's leg numbness in 1950. Although Jack would have a productive life as a teacher and later as a state education administrator, he would battle MS for the rest of his life.

Pittsburgh came in for an unusual one-game series on Sunday, September 17. It was Granny Hamner Day, and after the fans honored Granny with gifts in a pregame ceremony hosted by broadcaster Gene Kelly, Granny stole the show. In the fifth inning, with two runs in, two on base, and two out, Granny smashed a Bill Werle offering into the upper deck in left for a three-run homer and a 5–0 lead. In the top of the sixth, with two Pirates on and no one out, Granny made a sensational stop of Ralph Kiner's hard shot in the hole and forced a runner at third to take the steam out of the Buc rally.

Russ Meyer again came through with a clutch performance, pitching into the ninth with a 5–1 lead before tiring. In the ninth Gus Bell beat out an infield hit and Russ came up lame covering first on the play. Although we initially thought that we would lose our third starting pitcher in three days and fourth in a week, Russ stayed in the game after hobbling around a bit. But after Wally Westlake, the next batter, blasted a two-run homer to close the deficit to 5–3, in came Konstanty, who on Friday night had pitched 10 innings in our 19-inning win. It took Jim just seven pitches to retire three Pirate hitters and secure the victory.

We were still 7½ games in front, but the Braves and Dodgers had switched positions. Boston picked up a half game and had overtaken Brooklyn by sweeping a twin bill from Cincinnati, thanks in part to Warren Spahn's 20th victory. Meanwhile the Dodges had dropped a 3–2 game to Chicago to fall 8½ back.

After a welcome off day on Monday the Cubs came to town for a two-game set. Eddie tabbed me to pitch the September 19 opener against Frank Hiller. Unfortunately for us, Frank pitched the game of his life, facing only 27 batters and allowing only two hits. We could not advance a runner beyond first base, as only Jack Mayo and Granny got hits and both were immediately erased. At least we did not leave anybody on base.

I pitched almost as well, scattering four hits. Unhappily, one was a fifth-inning home run by Hank Sauer for the only run of the game as I lost 1–0 to go to 19–9 on the year. The game was over in one hour and 35 minutes, the fastest of the year. On the positive side, we played without incurring any more injuries.

When I went out to warm up for the fifth inning in that ballgame I noticed that the ball was kind of dirty. After I made my warm up throws to Andy the umpire noticed the ball and asked Andy for it. Sauer said, "Aw, it doesn't matter," so Andy just threw it back to me. I used it and Sauer hit it into the upper deck. I wished I'd had a clean ball.

The Braves edged the Cardinals 8–7 to close to within 6½ games of the lead, while the Dodgers swept a doubleheader from Pittsburgh to climb back to 7½ games out.

Russ Meyer again took the mound the following afternoon, September 20, against Cubs rookie Warren Hacker. We jumped to a 4–1 lead after two innings, chasing Hacker in the process. But Chicago came back against the Monk, taking a 5–4 lead in the sixth.

Then Mike Goliat took over with one of his periodic offensive explosions. First, he quickly tied the game in our sixth with a solo home run against reliever Johnny Schmitz. We retook the lead in the seventh when Richie beat out an infield roller, advanced to second on a fielder's choice, and came home on Del's slashing double to left on a 3–2 pitch. Then in the eighth, Mike followed singles by Granny and Andy with another home run clout to left, this one off of Bob Rush for three runs and a 9–5 lead.

Meanwhile Jim Konstanty had relieved Russ in the sixth and allowed only a ninth-inning run in the last $3^2/_3$ innings to wrap up his 16th win of the season. It was his third rescue job in five games, during which he had pitched $14^2/_3$ innings.

The Dodgers kept pace by defeating the Pirates 7–2 while the Braves fell back into a second-place tie with Brooklyn, losing a tough one to St. Louis 1–0 as Vern Bickford failed for the third time to win number 20. Both clubs were $7^1/_2$ games behind. We had 11 games to play while Brooklyn and Boston both had 14 remaining.

We got a break from the schedule makers, getting both Thursday and Friday off before Brooklyn came to Shibe Park for our final two home games of the year. The break in the schedule meant that I could start the Saturday game on my normal three days rest, although it would be my third start in our last six games and my second in three games. In addition, Dick Sisler, out 10 days and hampered for almost a month with his sore wrist, would be ready for action again.

Brooklyn and Boston both won on Thursday to stay deadlocked in second place and close to within seven games. Both were idle on Friday, so the Dodgers came to town with some rest as well.

My mound opponent was again Brooklyn ace Don Newcombe, 18–10 on the year. As expected, we turned in another taut pitcher's duel. After a good start, I ran into trouble in the second, giving consecutive singles to Jackie Robinson and Carl Furillo. Gil Hodges, up next, twice failed to sacrifice, but then worked the count full.

In those days I was not too proud of my breaking ball, which was generally a big looping job, and I did not throw many unless I was ahead in the count. But Hodges was known as strictly a fastball hitter, so I figured if I got a curveball over I could get him. I was mistaken. Hodges hit my 3–2 breaking pitch on a line into the left field stands for a three-run homer.

Saddled with a 3–0 deficit, we tried to rebound in the third. Goliat, still hitting Newk like he owned him, reached second on a hit and an error. I followed with a clean single through the right side of the infield but Furillo threw a strike to nail Mike at the plate, effectively killing the rally.

We were unable to break through until the seventh when Del opened the inning with a bunt single. With two down, Andy laid into Newcombe's first pitch and drove it into the left field stands for his 24th homer of the year, closing the gap to 3–2.

Richie then led off the eighth with a drive to left center and tried for two bases, only to be nipped by Duke Snider's perfect throw to Pee Wee Reese. Del began the ninth with a single but we could not get him across, sealing our 3–2 loss and reducing our lead to six games. The Braves lost to the Giants 4–3 in 10 innings to drop to third, although remaining seven games back.

It was tough to lose a ballgame because someone who had been unable to lay down a sacrifice bunt had hit a home run instead. But although I had failed three times to get my 20th win, we still had a very healthy lead, and we had Bubba Church poised to start Sunday's game. Bubba had made a remarkable recovery; it was only nine days since his frightening injury against the Reds.

> **CHURCH:** "I was anxious to get back out there. I wanted to get back with that ballclub and I wanted to pitch. So when they let me out of the hospital after the plastic surgeon sewed me up I headed straight for the ballpark. I got Maje to go with me down the left field line and hit balls back at me. I wanted to find out for myself if I was going to flinch or shy. Once I satisfied myself that I wasn't going to be gun shy I started throwing to get ready to pitch again."

Bubba's return was not a successful one as we played our worst game of the year and got shellacked 11–0. Bubba pitched creditably until the fifth, when the roof fell in. Jackie Robinson clubbed a two-un homer to left, and a few batters later Dodger pitcher Erv Palica poked a grand slam home run to the stands in left center. We committed a season high five errors and could not get a hit off Palica until Seminick singled to right to lead off the eighth. Palica finished with a two-hit shutout and our lead was down to five games. Fortunately, the Braves failed to gain any ground, losing to the Giants 12–4.

It was a sobering end to our home season, but we had little time to dwell on our last game performance or on the fact that we had managed only 8 wins in our 18-game home stand. We left immediately after the game on a charter flight to Boston, where we had a Monday doubleheader with the Braves, who were still contenders. Our final nine games would all be on the road: three in Boston; four in the Polo Grounds against the tough fourth-place Giants, who were nine games back; and a season-ending two-game set in Ebbets Field with the powerful Dodgers.

Eddie Sawyer called a rare team meeting before the September 25 twin bill. He let us know that he was unhappy with our shoddy play but told us to put it behind us and to go out and play the way we knew how to. As usual, the skipper never raised his voice, speaking very calmly and quietly. But we got the message loudly and clearly.

SAWYER: "We weren't hitting very much. The other teams were pitching their best pitchers against us, too. And they had pretty good pitchers, one and two and sometimes three. We were getting all of them because everyone was trying to knock us off.

"We had a few breaks going against us, too. Hitting balls right at somebody, not finding the holes. We were getting good pitching but we couldn't score any runs.

"So we wanted to go over things and let everybody know we hadn't given up on them and try to keep them from pressing. We were still in first place, and we just wanted to give them a vote of confidence more than anything else."

Eddie started Ken Heintzelman, who had pitched so well in relief when Bubba had gotten hit by the line drive, against Warren Spahn, already a 21-game winner. Goober, who had pitched in tough luck all year after his brilliant 1949 campaign, had only two 1950 victories.

SAWYER: "Heinz had usually pitched pretty well against the Braves, particularly up there. I always allowed for that. Some pitchers pitched better in certain parks and that was one of his better parks.

"In '51 we were playing the Cardinals in St. Louis and the Dodgers were battling them for the pennant. I used Jocko Thompson against Harry Brecheen, one of their best pitchers. Oh, Brooklyn was upset that I was using Jocko Thompson. But Jocko always pitched well in St. Louis and he beat them 3–2."

Games are won and lost on the playing field, not by comparing statistics. We proved that beyond a doubt by driving Spahn from the mound with a four-run first-inning attack. After three innings we had extended our lead to 8–1, allowing Heinz to coast to a 12–4 win. Dick Sisler, still wearing a wrap on his wrist, celebrated his return to the lineup with four sharp singles in five at bats, and Mike Goliat continued his hot streak with a single, a double, and a triple. Eddie Waitkus also chimed in with three hits.

Monk Meyer toed the rubber against Max Surkont in the second game. With single runs in the second and the fifth, we led 2–0 going into the Boston fifth. A great play by Gene Mauch on Seminick's shot behind second had kept us from adding another run. Mauch knocked the ball down and caught Puddinhead in a rundown between third and home for the final out in our fifth.

With Russ pitching well, we still seemed to be in good shape. But the Braves loaded the bases in the fifth on three consecutive one-out hits. Russ then got ahead of Sam Jethroe two strikes, but Sam managed a weak bat-handle grounder to short for a scratch hit, scoring a run. After Russ walked Earl Torgeson on a 3–2 pitch, tying the score, Eddie Sawyer, with the bases still loaded, brought in Konstanty for 70th time, tying the league record set by Ace Adams of the 1943 New York Giants.

Jim got the dangerous Bob Elliot to pop to Puddinhead at third for the second out. He then walked Sid Gordon, perhaps remembering Gordon's grand slam homer at Shibe Park earlier in the season, to give the Braves a 3–2 lead, before retiring Tommy Holmes to end the inning.

Sisler continued to make his presence felt, tying the score in the seventh on a mammoth 420-foot homer deep over the center field fence. But Boston struck for two runs off Konstanty in the bottom of the eighth, with pitcher Surkont's third hit of the game the big blow. We came up short in the ninth and had to settle for a split for the long, bone chilling day. The twin bill had begun at 1:30 and ended at 7:00 with the lights on. Jim's record fell to a still impressive 16–6 for the year.

Boston had staved off elimination from the pennant race by its second-game victory, while Brooklyn had split its own doubleheader with the Giants, winning 3–2 and losing 4–3, to remain five games in arrears. The Dodgers had nine games remaining, while we had seven.

Our final game in Boston was the following afternoon, Tuesday, September 26, another cold, overcast day. Eddie started Bob Miller, pitching for the first time since his September 16 shoulder injury. Vern Bickford was on the mound for the Braves, trying for the fifth time to gain his 20th win and attempting to keep his team's pennant chances alive.

We struck first in the seesaw game, scoring a run in the third on singles by Waitkus, Ashburn, and Ennis. The Braves came back in their fourth to take a 2–1 lead on a homer by Torgeson with a man on, the only hit Bob allowed for the first six innings.

We rallied and surged ahead 5–2 in the top of the seventh to chase Bickford. Waitkus again started the rally with a single, and Ashburn followed by beating out a bunt in front of third. Sisler then crossed up the Braves, who were expecting a sacrifice bunt, by lashing a game-tying single. Ennis clubbed Bickford's next pitch over the wall in left for three runs and a 5–2 advantage. It was Del's 31st circuit blast, and his RBI count reached a league-leading 123.

With Bugger pitching so well, our three-run lead seemed quite safe. But Bob ran out of gas in the bottom of the seventh, allowing a walk, a double to Elliot for one run, and, after a fly out, a single to center by Tommy Holmes for another. At this juncture Sawyer brought in Konstanty for a record 71st time. Unfortunately, Jim faltered again, giving up three more hits good for three more runs before getting out of the inning. After the dust settled, Boston had retaken the lead 7–5.

The Braves' lead was short-lived, however, as we rallied from behind for the second time in two innings in the top of the eighth. This time we got some help from Boston. Dick Whitman, batting for Konstanty, drew a walk off of Braves reliever Bob Hall to open the inning. Then Hall retired our next two hitters on a pop out and a ground out and looked to be avoiding difficulty. But Dick Sisler singled to left to keep the inning alive and give Del a chance.

Ennis lifted a pop foul in back of first but Torgeson, with a late break, could not quite reach it. Given a second chance, Del singled to center to score Whitman and send Caballero, running for Sisler, to third. Puddinhead followed by knocking a high bounder to Sibby Sisti at short for what looked like the third out. But Sibby booted the ball, allowing Putsy to score the tying run. Granny then followed with a solid single to center to score Del and we were back in front, 8–7.

Eddie had me warming up in the bullpen with Blix Donnelly.

> **SAWYER:** "I had Robbie down warming up but I brought in Blix Donnelly. Somebody said, 'Oh wow, you really confused them there.' But Blix always said the one team he could beat was Boston."

Blix responded by holding Boston hitless and scoreless in the last two innings to secure our victory. The official scorer awarded Blix the win, even though Konstanty was the pitcher of record when we took the lead in the eighth. It was our 90th win and 30th one-run victory of the year and officially eliminated Boston from the pennant.

Brooklyn kept pace, defeating New York 8–4 to remain five games back with eight to play. We had six games to go, including consecutive doubleheaders with the Giants in the Polo Grounds over the next two days, the result of rainouts during our last trip to New York. We knew all too well how tough the Giants were, particularly given their hot September, which had lifted them into fourth place. We then finished with two games against the Dodgers in Ebbets Field over the weekend.

Our magic number was three, meaning that any combination of three Phillies wins or Dodgers losses would give us the pennant. If we could sweep the Giants the next day, September 27, and Brooklyn split their doubleheader with Boston the same day, the pennant would be ours. Likewise, if we split with the Giants and Brooklyn was swept by Boston, we would clinch.

Bob Carpenter, seeking to give us every advantage, had arranged for us to fly to New York rather than take the train. We were in the air within an hour after the end of our last game in Boston.

I started the first contest in New York, my fourth try to get my 20th win. I was not really aware of that, however; I just wanted to help us win the pennant that was so far eluding us. But it was not to be a good day for me or the team. Monte Irvin ripped a line drive homer off of me in the second, followed by Bobby Thomson's triple and Alvin Dark's run-scoring single, and I was down 2–0. It got worse before it got better. In the fourth Hank Thompson lofted a home run into the right field stands and the Giants scored two more runs before I could get the side out. After four innings the score was 5–0.

Eddie Sawyer decided to rest me after that and sent Putsy Caballero up to hit for me in the fifth. Putsy grounded out, but with two out Richie legged out a hit behind second off of Giant starter Monte Kennedy. Puddinhead followed with a ringing double to center, sending Whitey to third. Del then singled to drive in both, closing the gap to 5–2.

Unhappily, New York extended its lead to 7–2 in the sixth, scoring two runs on two walks and a Don Mueller triple off of Jack Brittin. Mueller tried for an inside-the-park homer but was cut down by Goliat's relay to Seminick at the plate.

We finally got to Kennedy in the top of the eighth, mounting one of our finest comebacks of the season. Three consecutive singles to start the inning scored a run and led Giant manager Durocher to bring in Sal Maglie in relief. Maglie promptly plunked Andy in the ribs with a fastball to load the bases. Mike Goliat then lashed a single to left, driving in our second run of the inning and keeping the bases full.

Dick Whitman came up next, batting for Milo Candini, who had succeeded Brittin on the mound. Dick, who led the National League in pinch hits in 1950 with 12, stroked a grounder between first and second for a two-run single, to bring us to 7–6. Durocher had seen enough of Maglie and brought in Dave Koslo to pitch to Eddie Waitkus. But Waitkus slashed Koslo's first pitch to center to drive in Goliat with the tying run. Koslo shut the door after that, thanks to Thomson's running shoestring catch of Ashburn's liner. Whitman, thinking the ball was going to fall, was doubled off at second.

Nonetheless our five-run rally had turned a certain defeat into a possible victory, and we had Konstanty taking the mound to hold the Giants. Jim blanked New York in the eighth and ninth innings with comparative ease while we could do nothing against Koslo, who held us in check in the ninth and tenth innings.

In the bottom of the tenth, Jim walked Monte Irvin to start the inning. Bobby Thomson sacrificed Monte to second, bringing up Alvin Dark, the Giants' shortstop. After a ball and two strikes, Dark poked a single between first and second. Irvin, running all the way, beat Del's throw to the plate and slammed into Andy Seminick's left ankle, scoring the winning run.

Andy was knocked into the air by Irvin's slide and came down on his face. For a scary moment he lay there motionless, and when we reached him and turned him over he was still clutching the ball. It looked like we had not only lost a ballgame but our catcher who was having his career year.

> **SEMINICK:** "Monte Irvin slides into me just as I get the ball and come around to tag him. The umpire says, 'Safe!' and of course that's the winning run. The game is over. And I'm laying there. My leg is killing me. I'm in agony. I thought, 'Oh my gosh, I really did it this time.'
>
> "He slid in fairly high on me but I just didn't get turned around in time. I should have prepared myself a little better, like Cy Perkins had taught me. Instead of having my toe pointed at third base, I had it more turned toward second base. And he hit me and turned my ankle over and broke a bone in it.
>
> "They wanted to carry me off the field but I said, 'No, I'm going to walk off.' The clubhouse in the Polo Grounds was a long way back there, behind center field, about 500 feet away. And my ankle was killing me every step of the way. But I wasn't going to

let them know that they had hurt me. It was silly, I guess, in a way, but I wouldn't let them know that they had hurt me.

"They took me to the hospital and X-rayed it and it showed a bone separation."

In the nightcap, we had to try to bounce back from both a tough 10-inning loss after we had come from five runs down to tie in the eighth, as well as the loss of our catcher on the last play of the game. Bubba Church, making his second start since his eye injury September 15, went against Jim Hearn, pitching on only two days rest.

Bubba started well, retiring the first two batters. But Mueller and Hank Thompson singled and Irvin drew a walk and all of a sudden the bases were loaded. Bobby Thomson then hit a long drive to deep left center field, clearing the bases and scoring himself without a play at the plate for an inside-the-park grand slam home run. That, it turned out, was the ballgame, as we again could not dent the plate against Hearn, who scattered 7 hits. Although Milo Candini, Jocko Thompson, and Paul Stuffel pitched well in relief of Bubba, the final score was 5–0.

The day was not a complete washout since the Dodgers, after winning the first game of their doubleheader with Braves 9–6, had lost the second game 4–2 as Johnny Sain posted his 20th win of the season. Although our lead was now four games, our magic number was down to two. If we could sweep the Giants the following day, September 28, we would clinch. Likewise, if we split with New York and Brooklyn split its doubleheader with Boston, we would win the pennant.

Russ Meyer's arm was bothering him again, so Eddie selected Ken Heintzelman to start Thursday's opening game. Amazingly, Andy Seminick was behind the plate.

> **SEMINICK:** "They shot my ankle full of Novocain to deaden it, and Wiechec strapped it up with tape to make it stiff, like a boot. I couldn't run much at all. The Novocain would wear off and they would have to take the tape off in the middle of the game and give me another shot."

> **SAWYER:** "Andy was tough. If Andy could stand the pain and wanted to play, there was no reason to not let him play. It didn't hurt his speed any because he couldn't run anyway. Lopata was healthy and could have played, but Andy was used to catching all the pitchers. Stan hadn't been in too much in the latter part of the season. But Andy wanted to play, that was the main thing.

Of course, we didn't know it was as bad as it really was. We thought it was just a bad sprain. But at that point in his career he was a fine catcher and he really played well on that bad ankle."

Durocher sent Maglie to the mound to redeem himself for his poor relief performance in game one the day before. Maglie, whose season record was an outstanding 16–4, again started slowly, giving up game-opening singles to Waitkus and Ashburn. Sisler advanced both runners with a slow roller to first and Durocher elected to pass Del Ennis intentionally, loading the bases with one out. But Maglie fanned Willie Jones and Granny Hamner lined to Thomson in center to turn us away without a run.

Goober was pitching well but gave up a solo homer to our nemesis Thomson in the second to fall behind 1–0. We drew even in the third when Richie led off with a single and then scored on a walk, a sacrifice fly, and a ground out. But the Giants immediately retook the lead in their half on a walk and Monte Irvin's two-out, run-scoring double.

We had a good chance to knot the score in the fifth when, with one out, Whitey lined his third single of the game and flew around to third on a wild pitch. But neither Dick Sisler nor Del Ennis could get Richie home and Maglie again escaped without damage. After that Sal really got tough, retiring the last 14 Whiz Kids in a row. Bobby Thomson connected for yet another homer in the sixth to make the final score 3–1 Giants.

With three losses in a row to the Giants, we really wanted to salvage the last game of the series. Eddie gave me the ball for the second game and I was happy to take it, even though I had pitched four innings the day before. Andy, as banged up as he was, was behind the plate again. Sheldon Jones, a Giants stalwart, was on the mound for New York.

Eddie Waitkus got us off to a great start with a lead-off home run into the right field stands, only his second round-tripper of the year. Ahead 1–0, I ran into trouble in the third when Dark singled and I walked Wes Westrum, the Giants' catcher. But Andy, bad wheel and all, came to the rescue. With Sheldon Jones at bat, we expected a sacrifice. As Waitkus broke for the plate to field the anticipated bunt, Westrum took a long lead off first. But Goliat snuck in behind Westrum from second and Andy picked off the runner with a bullet throw to first for the initial out of the inning.

Dark then stole third and I ended up walking Jones to put runners on first and third. With Eddie Stanky up, one of my pitches got away from Andy, dribbling about 10 feet behind him. Jones took off for second and Andy nailed him by three feet for his second assist of the inning. Dark had to stay at third on the play. I walked Stanky as well but finally got out of the inning by inducing Whitey Lockman to ground into a force out at second.

I held the slim lead until the sixth when Stanky knocked a ball into the left field stands to tie the score 1–1. Lockman followed with a double to left and Don Mueller sacrificed him to third for out number one. With Henry Thompson at bat, Andy made his third great play of the game. With the count 3–2, Thompson took a big swing and foul-tipped the ball. Andy quickly reached down and actually caught the ball barehanded for the second out. Although Durocher and the Giants argued vehemently, umpire Augie Donatelli stood by the call.

With two outs and the lead runner on third, I would need still more help to escape the inning. Monte Irvin, the next hitter, smashed a deep drive towards the Giants' bullpen in far right center field. Del Ennis, off at the crack of the bat, made a wonderful running stab of the ball with his back to the infield for the third out of that hair-raising inning.

Mired in a team batting slump, we still could do nothing against the offerings of Jones. Still struggling, I got back into trouble immediately in the seventh. Bobby Thomson, who seemed to own us in this series, led off with a double to right. But brilliant defense again came to the rescue when Dark followed with ground ball to Waitkus. Eddie made a fine stop of the ball and then threw across the diamond to Puddinhead at third to nip Thomson trying to advance.

I then fanned Westrum for the second out and it looked like we had dodged another bullet. But pitcher Jones dunked a hit in front of Del in right and, my control still off, I walked Stanky to load the bases. Then fate seemed to intervene. I got one strike on the next batter, Lockman, and then threw him a fastball on the inside part of the plate. Whitey tried to hold up on his swing but made contact and plunked the ball beyond Granny's reach behind third for what can only be described as an accidental base hit. Two runs scored and we were all of a sudden down 3–1. I was beginning to think that the gods really were against us.

We finally got something going against Jones in the top of the ninth when Del led off with a sharp single to center. Willie Jones, who had been battling an upset stomach all day, followed with his first hit of the doubleheader, a single to right, sending Del to second. Granny was next and attempted to bunt the runners over but failed on the first two pitches. He missed the second pitch completely, but so did Giant catcher Westrum, allowing Del to take third on the passed ball.

Now with runners on first and third, Granny hammered the 0–2 pitch on a line toward right. For an instant it looked like a sure double and a tie game, but first sacker Irvin, playing near the bag to hold Puddinhead close, made a sensational across-the-shoulder stab for the first out. He then trotted to first to double off Willie, who was off with the crack of the bat, for an unassisted double play and the second out of the inning. Andy popped to Dark at shortstop and we had lost our second consecutive doubleheader to the Giants, our fifth straight, and our seventh defeat in the last nine games.

SAWYER: "We played pretty well but we couldn't score. We had a hitting slump after Labor Day and we didn't hit much. The Giants had come on strong, the pressure was off and they were a good ballclub. Of course, they won it the next year.

"The pressure was on us and we just couldn't buy a base hit when we needed it, although our pitching was all right. They got a few lucky hits, too, with balls going over the bag. It all added up to two doubleheader defeats."

STUFFEL: "The last couple weeks of the season the singing in the clubhouse stopped. Everyone tightened up. It was kind of like everyone woke up and realized, 'My God, if we're not careful, we're going to win the pennant.' We were a young team and most of us had never been in a pennant race before."

Brooklyn again split a twin bill with Boston, winning 6–5 and losing 8–4. Our lead was down to three games, but, more importantly, because the Dodgers had lost another game, our magic number was now one game. If Brooklyn lost just one of their four remaining games the pennant was ours. So even though we had lost consecutive doubleheaders, we were in fact closer than ever to the pennant.

We were in one of those stretches where we could not believe how difficult it was to win a ballgame. It seemed like we would never clinch the pennant. But, as tough as our schedule was that last week, it was even tougher for the Dodgers, although they did not have the injury problems that we did. While we got Friday off before our season-ending two-game series in Ebbets Field, the Dodgers had to play their third consecutive doubleheader with the Braves. If the Bums lost either game, we would back into the pennant. By then we would have gladly have taken it. In fact, we were all praying for a Braves win.

SIMMONS: "I was following the guys from where I was in Indiana. I'd get the paper or hear the radio. I was checking on them and they kept losing. And all my new buddies, all dressed alike, were getting on me because the Phils couldn't win and clinch the pennant."

MEYER: "That last week was a nightmare. Those games were pressure packed and we just couldn't win. The Dodgers just kept on winning."

CANDINI: "Jimmy Bloodworth was my roommate and we were really concerned. Jimmy said, 'Oh boy, it looks like we're not going to make it.' It was terrible."

Since we were already in New York, several of the Whiz Kids took the subway to Ebbets Field the next day to watch the doubleheader.

MEYER: "I went to the Braves games with Eddie [Waitkus], Maje, and a couple of other guys. There was a photographer there who saw us and kept taking our picture. We asked him a half a dozen times, 'Hey, leave us alone. We're just here to watch the ballgame.' So this SOB stuck his camera right in front of me and I popped him. I said, 'Now will you get the hell out of here?'

"So that night I'm in my pajamas in my room at the Commodore watching TV and there's a knock on the door. It's the damn photographer with a police officer. So he has me arrested for popping him.

"So I called Eddie [Sawyer] and we finally got the damn thing straightened out. The guy admitted that he was wrong and I admitted that I was wrong and that I shouldn't have hit him. I didn't hurt him. I didn't really pop him. I hit the camera more than I hit him."

The rest of the team watched the doubleheader on television in our hotel. I stayed in my room and watched both games by myself. It turned out to be an agonizing day not only for Russ but for all of us.

In the first game, 19-game winner Preacher Roe started for the Dodgers against the Braves' Max Surkont, a late season call-up who had pitched extremely well down the stretch. Brooklyn jumped to a 2–0 first-inning lead before Boston fought back to take a 3–2 lead in the fourth. Two more runs in the top of the eighth extended the Braves' lead to 5–2 and gave me considerable optimism that we would win the pennant while I sat in my hotel room. But the Dodgers came right back in their half of the inning to score five runs with the help of two Boston errors to go ahead 7–5. Dan Bankhead retired the Braves in the ninth and our wait continued.

Vern Bickford, trying for the sixth time to win his 20th (a frustration I could identify with), pitched the second game against Brooklyn rookie Chris Van Cuyk. A first-inning Duke Snider triple again propelled the Dodgers to an early 1–0 lead. Boston again came back, taking a 2–1 lead in the second on Bickford's two-run single. The Braves extended their lead to a healthy 4–1 in the next inning on Bob Elliot's two-run double, which chased Van Cuyk. The Dodgers closed to 4–3 in the fourth behind Hodges's double and Roy Campanella's 30th home run of the season.

Boston got two men on in the fifth when Elliot and Torgeson both singled. Sid Gordon grounded to the usually reliable Billy Cox at third, but Billy threw so wildly past first that both runners scored, making the score 6–3 Braves.

Before I could get too excited, Brooklyn fought back once again in the sixth. Hodges singled and Campy again drove him home, this time with a double. Cox drew a walk and Eddie Miksis, batting for reliever Jim Romano, sacrificed both runners over. Cal Abrams bounced out to score Campanella, and Cox scored a moment later on a wild pitch to tie the score 6–6.

The Braves could not score in their seventh against Carl Erskine. Jackie Robinson led off the bottom half of the inning by smashing Bickford's first offering far into the left center field seats to put Brooklyn ahead 8–7. Erskine then held the Braves at bay the rest of the day and our long wait for the pennant continued.

We would have to win the National League championship on the playing field by taking one of the last two games at Ebbets Field. With two games remaining, our lead had shrunk to two.

Chapter 14
THE FINAL WEEKEND

Saturday, September 30, was my 24th birthday and I had high hopes that it would be the day we clinched the pennant. We knew we had the flag in our grasp, but we just had not been able to win a ballgame to bring it home. While we had struggled, losing 7 of 9, Brooklyn had surged, winning 12 of their last 15. It all came down to a fall weekend in Brooklyn.

EDDIE SAWYER: "The club was tired. We had had a long year, beginning in spring training. After the games in Florida we made that long haul by train through Louisiana and Texas because our scouts had some prospects there and they wanted them to see who the Phillies were. By the time we started the season we'd had a pretty good season already. In September everybody was tired because we were a young team and weren't used to playing that many games.

"We weren't fielding as well as we had earlier in the year and we couldn't buy a base hit when we needed it, except for that game in Boston. We were averaging only two runs a game and we needed to get at least three to win any. It had been a long year and we had a young team which had never played under that kind of pressure."

Eddie chose Bob Miller to start from our depleted pitching corps. Burt Shotton sent out right-hander Erv Palica, who six days before had thrown a two-hit shutout at us in that 11–0 shellacking that ended our home season.

SAWYER: "We didn't have too many healthy guys at that time. I didn't have a whole lot of options. Brooklyn was a right-hand hitting club and Bob had pitched pretty well against them at different times. I talked to Russ Meyer about pitching but he wasn't quite right. He was all right to relieve but he couldn't start. At that point I thought we had a better chance with Bob Miller. I was saving Roberts, of course. If we lost, Robin could still pitch Sunday with two days rest."

We played well from the start, full of hustle and confident that we could beat the Dodgers as we had many times before that season. Bob seemed sharp early, scattering three hits over the first four innings and holding Brooklyn scoreless. We could still not solve Palica, however, and the game remained a scoreless tie going into the bottom of the fifth inning.

Bugger struck out Campanella to start the inning but then gave up a single to Cox. Palica hit back to the box and was out at first as Cox took second. With two out we had little cause for concern. But Abrams singled to center to score Cox and Pee Wee Reese laced a drive to deep right center for a triple, driving in Abrams with the second run.

At this point the Skipper decided that Bob had gone as far as he could. In came Konstanty, making a record 74th appearance, to face the dangerous Duke Snider. But Jim could not stem the tide as he had done so often. Duke drove one of his first offerings over the fence in right for a two-run homer. Although Jim got out of the inning without further damage, Brooklyn had rocked us for four two-out runs and now led 4–0. It seemed like a large hill to climb, given our team hitting slump and particular ineptitude against Palica.

But as we had done so many times, we mounted a rally in our next at bat. Eddie Waitkus began with a sharp single to left and Richie Ashburn followed with another base hit to the same field. Dick Sisler was next and struck a sizzling liner that caromed off Snider's glove as he attempted to short-hop it. Two runs scored while Dick tried to reach third as Snider retrieved the ball and fired home. Palica cut the ball off and threw to Cox at third as Dick slid to the bag. But the peg was wild and bounced to the stands, where a fan reached over the rail and picked up the ball. Umpire Larry Goetz immediately ruled fan interference and waived Dick home with our third run of the inning, closing the gap to 4–3.

Even though no one was out, Palica quickly regained command and retired the side. Konstanty held the Dodgers in the bottom of the sixth and Andy Seminick, playing despite his damaged ankle, walked to lead off the top of the seventh. Since Andy was basically immobile, Putsy went in to run for him. But Mike Goliat failed to get down a sacrifice and then grounded into a double play. Konstanty blooped a hit over third, but Waitkus grounded to Gil Hodges to end the inning.

There were no more scoring threats until the Dodger eighth when Jackie Robinson opened with a walk. He advanced to second when Carl Furillo looped a base hit over Goliat's head at second. Konstanty made a nice play on an attempted sacrifice by Hodges, forcing Robinson at third. But Roy Campanella drove Jim's second pitch deep into the center field bleachers for the knockout blow, a three-run homer. Palica shut us down in the ninth to win 7–3. Our lead was one game with one game left on the schedule.

SAWYER: "I had to pitch Konstanty an awful lot, and they were getting used to him and he was wearing down a little. But he always wanted that ball. He literally wanted to pitch every day."

ANNE ZEISER: "Frank Powell had gotten us box seats for the games. Unbeknown to us, on Saturday Bill Campbell, one of our announcers, had told the TV cameramen to focus on us behind home plate to capture some real Phillie fans in action. It turned out that there was a priest sitting in front of us. I wound up hitting him over the head with my scorecard because he was rooting for the Dodgers and the Dodgers won. I swore that he prayed them into that win. That night when we got back to the hotel, Bill met us and told us that I was on television beating up a priest. And I said, 'Well, that's all right, Bill. The priest turned around and said 'With fans like you, the Phillies deserve to win it. I'll say a prayer for them tomorrow.'"

Nonetheless we were now faced with it: the prospect of the most colossal collapse by a league leader in National League history. Just 11 days earlier, on September 19, we had held a 7½ game lead over the Boston Braves and a seemingly insurmountable 9 game lead over the Dodgers, including 7 in the loss column.

For the third time that year we had suffered through a five-game losing streak. Both other times we had come up with key wins to stop the streak, but the importance of those games paled by comparison to our last game of the season.

If we lost again on Sunday we faced an immediate three-game playoff, with the first game in Ebbets Field and games two and, if necessary, three in Shibe Park. A playoff, given the weariness of our pitching staff and Andy's injury, was something we hoped to avoid. We knew our best chance was simply to win on Sunday.

That evening I ate in the hotel and turned in early. It was, to say the least, a very tense atmosphere.

BETTY ZEISER: "We were in New York for that last weekend. All the Phillies were saying, 'We're going to be all right,' but you could see a lot of sorrow in their eyes. You could tell that they were really afraid that they were going to blow it. You could have cut the atmosphere in the lobby of the Commodore with a knife.

"That Saturday night my sister and I went to the little church that was around the corner from the hotel. We wanted to say a few prayers, thinking God would hear our prayers and the Phillies would win. And there in the first pew we saw Putsy Caballero, praying and crying like a baby.

"Later we were in the lobby of the hotel and Willie Jones and Johnny Nee, the scout who had signed Willie, came into the hotel feeling no pain. Johnny Nee was crying and hanging onto Willie and hollering, 'You're leavin' me down, Willie, you're leavin' me down.' It was really sad to see the two of them together like that."

I have already recounted how we won the pennant by beating the Dodgers on Sunday, October 1, in the most important and most thrilling game I ever pitched. The game, with the pennant on the line, was certainly one of the most exciting ever played. It was a game no one on the Whiz Kids would ever forget.

SAWYER: "I think Robin knew he was pitching but I told him anyway in the clubhouse before the game. I felt pretty good about our chances anytime I gave him the ball."

ASHBURN: "We lost three-fifths of our starting rotation in September, so it was Robin there toward the end, carrying the load for us. But I figured we were going to win that last game. But, of course, I don't think I ever went into a game thinking, 'Hey, we're going to lose this game. Even with the '62 Mets I thought we were going to win every game we played.

"I'd rather have Robin out there than any pitcher I've ever seen—especially a game like that one that we had to win. I knew that no matter how the game came out we would get the best out of Robin Roberts. He wasn't going to give the game away. If you were going to beat him you were going to have to hit him. I know he never walked away from a game thinking that he could have tried any harder. That's the most you can ask out of a ballplayer. He was as perfect to play behind as you can get. He threw strikes. He didn't fool around out there. And always had that ability, if he got in trouble, to reach back somewhere and get something extra."

BUBBA CHURCH: "The last week was a nightmare. It seemed like everyone was hurt. We were really depleted. I had proven by then that I wasn't reliable after getting hit, even though I was getting stronger every day. Robbie had pitched a lot but I was certainly glad he got that last ballgame."

SEMINICK: "I had a feeling we were going to win. How, I don't know. But with Robbie pitching we knew we had a good shot. And we had to win. But I was a little leery about myself. I couldn't move. I was hurting pretty bad. I asked Sawyer and Carpenter both, 'Don't you think Lopata should start this game?' But Sawyer said, 'No, we want you to start. Go as long as you can.' So I said, 'All right.' Then I didn't ask them anymore.

"My ankle hurt awful bad. I'd sit up at night on the commode with my foot in a tub of hot water. That would ease the pain a little and that's the way I would get my rest."

CABALLERO: "We went into Brooklyn with a two-game lead but we were in a slump. Granny was my roommate and we were listening to the radio in the room when Jackie Robinson was quoted as saying, 'The Phillies better straighten out. If they do get in the World Series, they're not going to be a very good representative of the National League.' Hamner said, 'Listen to that guy, knocking us already.' But the Dodgers beat us anyway on Saturday and we had to win on Sunday."

DEL ENNIS: "We couldn't win one in New York and then lost in Brooklyn on Saturday. When it got down to that last game and Sawyer started Robbie, we knew we were going to win."

BETTY ZEISER: "On Sunday we had box seats up front with Lou Louderback from Louderback Movers. Through the whole game, I cried. From the first pitch to the last pitch, I cried. I was so nervous and upset I couldn't do anything else. Anne sat through the game with her rosary beads. Lou said, 'I don't know if we are going to get prayed out or flooded out of the box that we're in.'"

ENNIS: "We were ahead 1–0 when Pee Wee Reese hit a ball off the screen in right. It had backspin on it and balanced itself on the ledge. I kept waiting for the ball to come down but it spun and spun until it came to a dead stop on the ledge for a home run. I should have thrown my glove at it because then it would have been a triple instead of a home run."

SEMINICK: "That was terrible when Reese hit that crazy home run. I was hollering at Ennis, 'Throw your glove at the ball,' because at least then it would be only a triple."

ASHBURN: "Reese's ball stuck up on that ledge wasn't covered by the rules because it had never happened. If it had happened the next year, it would have been a ground rule double. Meanwhile, Pee Wee ran around the bases, laughing at his good fortune."

MEYER: "Talk about a million-to-one shot, the damn ball sitting on that ledge. We couldn't buy a hit, so I thought there was the whole damn game, sitting out on that ledge."

MAJE McDONNELL: "If Reese's ball doesn't stay on that ledge, it's a single. This was crushing to us, sitting in that dugout. I mean Newcombe's throwing BBs. He was throwing hard."

DICK WHITMAN: "Reese's home run on that ledge was brutal. I thought, 'Ah man, if we lose on that, that's really awful. After the game I told Pee Wee, 'I thought you had us after you hit that Chinese home run out there.' Pee Wee said, 'What do you mean a Chinese home run? That ball was a smash.'"

SAWYER: "Reese's homer was just a lazy fly ball. It wasn't really hit good. He just slopped it to right field. It looked like one of the Giants' hits from earlier in the week. But it was covered by the ground rules and there wasn't any doubt that it was a home run even though it stayed in the ballpark."

The score remained tied into the bottom of the ninth when, to open the inning, I walked Cal Abrams on a 3–2 pitch that I still think was a strike. Reese, after fouling off two sacrifice bunt attempts, lined a single to left to put runners on first and second with no one out. All at once I was pitching in sudden death. A base hit would likely spell defeat and force the playoff that we wanted to avoid.

Duke Snider was the next batter and, as I mentioned earlier, I thought that with no outs he would be bunting.

ASHBURN: "With the winning run on second in the bottom of the ninth you would normally shorten some. You have to gamble a little in that situation. But against Duke Snider you couldn't shorten much because of his power, so I came in only a couple of steps.

"I've heard some people say that we thought he was going to bunt. Well, I didn't think there was any possible way that he was going to bunt, for a couple of reasons. Not only was he such a good hitter but he hit Robin pretty well.

"So Snider nailed a single to center field, a line drive, one-hop single. He smoked it; it was a perfect ball for an outfielder to handle, right at you, you could charge the ball, it was hit sharply. I have been criticized for my throwing arm, sometimes I think unfairly because although I did not have a great arm, I did not have a bad arm. I worked very hard at charging the ball and getting rid of it quickly and throwing it accurately. If you can do that you're going to get a lot of base runners, and I led the league in assists two or three years.

"Snider's hit was a one-hopper, bang, bang, and I did just what I had practiced a thousand times. Charged the ball, threw the ball, threw it accurately, and Abrams was out by thirty feet. Here was a guy who should not have been sent, with nobody out in the bottom of the ninth.

"The third-base coach, Milt Stock, got fired because of that play. Oddly enough, he went from the Dodgers to St. Louis with his son-in-law, Eddie Stanky, who was managing the Cardinals. In one game when Milt Stock was coaching third base for the Cardinals, if memory serves me right, I threw out three guys from center field. He never thought I could throw, I guess.

"Anyway, Abrams was out by a mile. I've heard people say, 'Well, Ashburn was backing up second in case Snider bunted.' That wasn't even in the picture. First of all, if there had been a bunt play, the play wouldn't have been at second, it would have been either at third or first. I mean that was preposterous. I have heard that I was running in toward second to back up a pick-off play by Robin. Robin didn't have a pick-off play to second; he didn't even have one to first. So that was preposterous.

"But what happened was that I had come in a couple of steps with the winning run on second. Cal Abrams was a pretty good runner. It was not a good situation to be in, so sometimes you have to gamble a little bit. I wasn't really worried about Snider hitting a ball over my head because I could run like hell. To hit it over my head, he probably would have had to hit the ball into the stands. I played a shallow center field anyway."

LOPATA: "Andy Seminick was really hurting with his ankle but he had started the game. He walked in the eighth inning and Mr. Sawyer put in a pinch runner and then brought me in to catch.

"It never even crossed my mind that Snider might bunt. Whitey was playing short on Snider's hit and picked the ball on one bounce and threw it to me on one hop and I had Abrams by maybe 20 feet, if not more. I just ran after him because I didn't want the other runners to advance any farther.

"I had made up my mind that I was going to block home plate and I don't think Abrams ever touched the plate. I was no slouch at blocking home plate. That was one of the greatest plays in baseball, and I figured as big as I was, and with the shin guards and the chest protector, if they wanted to run into me and try to knock me over, go ahead, they were welcome to it. I really loved blocking that home plate.

"I think Abrams was just rounding third base when I had the ball. We should have sent Milt Stock a World Series share, I'll tell you that. Milt probably didn't look back at where the outfielders were playing like he was supposed to. But I think you can blame Abrams, too. They both should have looked around after every pitch to see where Whitey and the other outfielders were playing. I always did when I was on second base so that if a ball was hit to the outfield I would have a general idea of how far I could go. I mean knowing where Whitey was playing, and with the ball hit so sharply, I don't think I would have ever tried to score in that situation, even if the coach tried to send me.

"We practiced pick-off plays all the time in spring training, but I don't think we ever even tried a pick-off play at second during the season. Andy and I used to get on Robbie to try to get him to hold the runners on first closer, to give us a chance to throw a guy out. Robbie didn't have a very good move and didn't even like to throw over much. Robbie said, 'Hey, don't worry about it. If a guy gets on first base and steals second and third, he still has to go another 90 feet to score.' And he knew what he was doing. Many times he would have a runner on third with nobody out and they wouldn't score. In the seventh, eighth, and ninth innings, he could rare back and get that extra from someplace. He was the best pitcher I ever saw at getting that something extra when he needed it. I don't know where he got it."

BLOODWORTH: "Abrams bounced about halfway back to third base after hitting Lopata. He didn't even jar Stan. Stan Lopata was much of a man."

SAWYER: "Richie always played short in parks where center field wasn't too deep like Ebbets Field. He could go back on a ball very well. I liked to have my outfielders work out in the infield during batting practice so they would get used to handling ground balls and charging them. And that is what Richie did. It wasn't a real long throw but it was fairly long. But he was very accurate with his arm, although he didn't have a great arm. He led the league in assists a couple of times in his career.

"We didn't think that Stock was going to send Abrams in. Abrams could run pretty good. He wasn't a great runner. We were very much surprised when he tried to score. He was out by a good 10 feet and Lopata went up the line to keep him away from the plate. Sometimes in Brooklyn runners would be called safe when they never reached the plate. But that didn't happen with Larry Goetz behind the plate. He was never influenced by the crowd and he was a fine umpire."

MEYER: "Ashburn made the throw of his life to throw Abrams out. We could see from the bullpen that Richie had moved in because we were afraid that he was coming in too close. But he still made the throw of his life."

Now with runners on second and third and one out, Eddie Sawyer came out and told me to put Robinson on to set up a force at home. That brought the dangerous Furillo to the plate. Eddie had reminded me to keep the ball down on Carl, who was an excellent high-ball hitter. My first pitch was about eye high but with something on it. Carl swung and popped to Waitkus in foul ground.

I was still not out of the woods with Hodges, a powerful right-handed batter, coming up. With the count 1–1, Gil sent a fairly deep fly ball to right field.

> **ENNIS:** "Hodges's ball hit me right in the chest. I lost it in the sun; the line drive hit me in the chest and dropped right in my glove. After the game I had the seams from the ball in my chest. Gene Kelly, our broadcaster, was saying, 'Easy fly ball to right field.' Easy all right. I lost the ball in front of me. I knew it was coming right at me, so I just stood there and it hit me right in the chest and dropped in my glove."

Looking back at those at bats by Furillo and Hodges, I sometimes wonder if my wife Mary, who later concluded that baseball all came down to luck, did not have something. But I still like to think that skill plays some part in who wins and who loses.

After our miracle escape in the ninth inning, Eddie let me bat in the top of the tenth and on the second pitch I bounced a single up the middle.

> **SAWYER:** "Robbie was a good hitter left-handed, although he wasn't too good right-handed. He could hit Newcombe. Also, we didn't have a lot of guys to use. If Nick [Bill Nicholson] had been with us, I might have changed. But Robin was still the best pitcher we had, even though it was late in the game. Our best shot at winning was with Robbie on the mound. In fact, if it had been a left-handed pitcher, I probably would have let him hit anyway."

Waitkus followed by looping a single to center, and we were in business against Newcombe with runners on first and second and no one out. Richie then forced me at third trying to bunt us over, as Newk made a great play to get to the ball and just nip me sliding headlong into the bag.

ASHBURN: "I really got a pretty good bunt down but Newcombe bounced off the mound and made a good play to force Robin at third. He would have had no play on me at all. It would have been a great bunt if I had been bunting for a base hit. But it was my fault because Newcombe broke for the third base line as soon as he threw the pitch. In that situation I have to bunt it hard enough to make the third baseman field the ball."

Now with runners on first and second with one out, Dick Sisler stepped to the plate for the biggest at bat in Phillies history. Dick already had three hits off of Newk for the day, but Don went after him with fastballs and got ahead two strikes. Dick laid off a high outside fastball for ball one and then fought off the next pitch, fouling it back into the press box behind home plate.

SISLER: "Newcombe was a fastball pitcher. Overpowering. He was the kind of guy whom I liked to bat against. I was a good fastball hitter. He tried to pitch me inside but he got one out over the plate a little too far. I hit the ball to left, the opposite field, but I didn't know it was a home run at first. I knew I had hit the ball good and I was hopeful that it was out, but I was past first base when I saw that it was a home run. Boy, that was the greatest feeling in the world. That was the greatest thrill I ever had in baseball."

BETTY ZEISER: "Anne didn't see Dick Sisler's home run. She was sitting there but she didn't see it. She didn't know what everyone was hollering about."

ANNE ZEISER: "I didn't see it. I was praying so hard, I had my eyes closed and I didn't see it."

BLOODWORTH: "We were expecting Sisler to hit the ball hard because he already had three hits. Newk got the ball just a little bit outside and Dick jumped on it like a hound on a rabbit. Just as soon as he hit it we knew it was gone."

MILLER: "In the bullpen, everybody thought the Big Cat's [Sisler's] home run was a routine fly ball when it left the bat. But the guy's so doggone strong that it got out of there."

MEYER: "When Dick hit the ball, I didn't think it was hit that good, watching from out in the bullpen. But the ball kept drifting and drifting and I'm looking at the left fielder Abrams go back to the wall and looking at the ball and I said, 'It's got a chance, it's got a chance.' Then I thought, 'Well, it's going to hit the top of the wall anyway,' because I didn't think Abrams could get to it. He was playing in left center and the ball was hit to straightaway left. It was really something when that ball got over the fence, it was really something."

WHITMAN: "I fell right off the bench when Dick hit that home run."

CANDINI: "The dugout in Ebbets Field was ground level and the top of the dugout was not very high. When Dick hit the home run I jumped up and cracked my head against the roof. Ow, it hurt like hell."

ASHBURN: "I was kind of glad to see Sisler up there. He hit Newcombe well and he had been swinging the bat well all game. I didn't know Sisler's ball was out right away. I knew it was a hit. I knew it wasn't going to be caught and I would score from first if it had gone off the wall, I was sure of that.

"I felt quite a sense of relief to see that ball go into the bleachers out in left field. In my mind the game was over with Robin pitching. No question, the season was over and we had won the pennant."

SEMINICK: "When Dick's ball went out it was like a big load had been lifted off our shoulders. We had had a pretty tough 10 days."

CHURCH: "After Dick hit the home run, that ballgame belonged to Robbie. I don't care who the Dodgers would have had coming up to home plate. With so much on the line in those last two innings, Robbie never pitched better in his life."

BLOODWORTH: "I figured Robin would handle the Dodgers in the 10th because he had a great arm but he had a greater head. And he had an even bigger heart. He knew nothing but to rise to the occasion."

MEYER: "Out in the bullpen I said, 'I'll tell you right now, I like our chances with that horse out there and a three-run lead.'"

MILLER: "Robbie came out in the 10th like a man possessed. I never saw a guy throw better than he did that last inning."

SAWYER: "This is why I kept Robin in there. If we had only gotten one run we would have been fine. He is in Cooperstown."

In the bottom of the 10th I retired Campanella on a line drive to Jack Mayo in left to open the inning.

MAYO: "I went into left field for Sisler after he hit the home run. I wasn't much of a hitter but I was a good defensive outfielder. I made a pretty good running catch on the ball that Campanella hit."

I struck out pinch hitter Jim Russell on four pitches for the second out. Then Tommy Brown, another pinch hitter, skied a pop-up to Waitkus in foul territory. As Eddie squeezed it for the third out, my teammates rushed to the mound to celebrate the pennant we had finally won. They carried me off the field as we felt exhilaration and a great sense of relief all at once.

McDONNELL: "When Robbie got the last three outs we all ran to the mound. I saw Jones and Waitkus, two hard guys, with tears in their eyes, and I started crying with tears of joy. I'll never forget that. As long as I live I'll never forget that moment."

ANNE ZEISER: "When Robbie shut them out in the 10th we just all went crazy. We got out in the middle of the field and paraded around it, we were so happy."

McDONNELL: "As we ran to the dugout, down through the runway to the clubhouse, I stopped for a minute and knelt down and said a prayer. I said, 'If You never give me anything the rest of my life, if You never give me nothing, I just want to thank You for this. This is the greatest thrill of my life and it will be the greatest thrill of my life, because this is something that people live for and never get, and I want to thank You.' And I got up and ran into the clubhouse.

"That morning I was in a cab with Dick Sisler going to the ballpark for the game. There were four or five of us sharing the cab. Another cab pulled up along side of us at a red light with an Italian family from South Philly in it. There was a father and his three sons and they were going to the game. The father said to our cab driver, 'Hold it,' and he got out with a red rose in a glass and he gave it to Sisler.

The Whiz Kids before our first plane trip. We always traveled in coats and ties. The flight, from St. Louis to Boston, turned out to be a rough one because of foul weather. *(Courtesy of Maje McDonnell)*

Curt and I before he left for National Guard duty. Camp Atterbury got a great pitcher. *(Courtesy of Ted Silary)*

Bubba Church being carried off the field after being hit by a line drive off the bat of Ted Kluszewski. I was in the locker room and missed that terrible scene.
(Courtesy of Rich Westcott)

Jack Brittin. His promising career was cut short by multiple scelorosis.
(Courtesy of Ted Silary)

Jim Konstanty in the clubhouse listening intently to the game on the radio during our last home stand. We needed him in the bullpen. *(Courtesy of Ted Silary)*

Jim Konstanty after his record-tying 70th appearance of the season against Boston on September 25. *(Courtesy of Ted Silary)*

Andy Seminick on the ground, his ankle dislocated after Monte Irvin slid into him to win the first game of the September 27 doubleheader with the Giants, 8–7. *(Courtesy of Andy Seminick)*

Andy is helped to the clubhouse by Willie Jones and another teammate after dislocating his ankle. *(Courtesy of Andy Seminick)*

Trainer Frank Wiechec cools off Jim Konstanty during our September 30 loss to Brooklyn. Bubba Church is wearing the jacket and Benny Bengough looks at the camera. *(Courtesy of Ted Silary)*

Stan Lopata tagging out Cal Abrams trying to score the winning run. Ashburn's throw was right on the mark. No big deal — right! *(Courtesy of Ted Silary)*

Dick Sisler's welcome after his 10th-inning home run. This was a big deal! *(Courtesy of Associated Press)*

Dick Sisler *(right)* and I celebrate the pennant in the clubhouse. The fans thought we looked alike. *(Courtesy of Ted Silary)*

The clubhouse scene was a wild one. *(Courtesy of Bettmann Archive)*

Left to right: Eddie Sawyer, me, and Dick Sisler celebrating on the train ride back to Philadelphia. Even our singing sounded good then. *(Courtesy of Rich Westcott)*

Fans mobbing us at 30th Street Station in Philadelphia. They knew we could do it! *(Courtesy of Rich Westcott)*

Eddie Sawyer taps Jim Konstanty to open the World Series. Who is Howard Ehmke, anyway? *(Courtesy of Rich Westcott)*

Cover of the official program for the 1950 World Series. The photo shows *(left to right)* me, Mike Goliat, Bob Miller, Maje McDonnell, Willie Jones, and Stan Lopata reacting to Richie Ashburn's two-out, ninth-inning single against Chicago on June 25, which gave me my ninth victory by a 2–1 score.

Jim Konstanty *(right)* with Phillies pitchers Russ Meyer, me, Ken Heintzelman, and Bubba Church before Series opener. *(Courtesy of Ted Silary)*

Allie Reynolds and I pose for photographers before Game Two of the Series. We didn't do much talking. *(Courtesy of Ted Silary)*

Andy trying to console me after DiMaggio's 10th-inning home run. Adam, I should have walked him. (Adam was a friend of Curt's who always told Curt I should have walked DiMaggio.) *(Courtesy of Temple University Archives and Ted Silary)*

Glum Whiz Kids trudge back to our dressing room after our final defeat to the Yankees in the 1950 World Series. Stan Hollmig is in the foreground, followed by Jimmy Bloodworth and Granny Hamner.

Richie Ashburn and Andy Seminick at the train station in Philly after our loss to the Yankees in the World Series. *(Courtesy of Ted Silary)*

"The father said in broken English, 'I went to church this morning and I took this flower off the altar. I want you to have it. Put it on top of your locker.' And Dick told the man, 'Thank you.'

"After the game was over and I ran into the clubhouse, I saw that flower above Dick Sisler's locker. And he is the one who hit the home run. Isn't that amazing?"

WHITMAN: "When Robbie got that last out I was the happiest man in the world. When you play against your old team, you're not mad at them but naturally you want to beat them. In Brooklyn they put the flag of whoever was leading the league up behind center field. So it was nice to see that Phillie flag up there in Ebbets Field at the end of the year.

"While we were celebrating in our clubhouse I took a bunch of beer over to the Dodger clubhouse and told them, 'If you can't win at least you can have some beer on the winners. Then Pee Wee came into our clubhouse and congratulated us and told me, 'You did it again. Second year, I don't understand it, but you won again.'"

MAYO: "It was an indescribable feeling when you win like that. You hear people on TV try to describe it, but it is indescribable."

SEMINICK: "There was a lot of jubilation in that clubhouse with everyone hugging one another and showering everyone with champagne. Of course, I was laying on the training table, getting treatment from Frank Wiechec on my ankle."

SISLER: "In the clubhouse we were throwing beer all over the room. We were the happiest bunch who ever lived. It's hard to imagine the feeling we had from finally winning the pennant.

"My dad [Hall-of-Famer George Sisler] was scouting for the Dodgers at that time and had real mixed emotions. But he was really proud of me, even though he got ribbed quite a bit by Branch Rickey and others with the Dodgers."

Amid all the celebration I was sitting by my locker. I was overwhelmed that we had pulled it off but really beat physically. While I was sitting there Eddie Sawyer came over and kissed me on the cheek. That is the only time he ever did that.

McDONNELL: "Frank Yeutter, sportswriter with the *Philadelphia Bulletin*, had a big walrus mustache. He had said that he would shave off his mustache if we won the pennant, so a bunch of the guys grabbed him and shaved it off. Everybody was pouring beer and champagne all over the place. We were so relieved and happy."

SAWYER: "The first guy who called to congratulate me in the clubhouse was Durocher. He wanted us to beat the Dodgers, because they had fired him in 1948. I said, 'Why didn't you think about that earlier in the week,' when the Giants were beating us."

SIMMONS: "I was playing touch football that Sunday afternoon at Camp Atterbury because I couldn't stand to listen to the game. Finally a guy hollers out, 'Hey, Sisler hit a home run! The Phillies won!' What a relief it was to hear that."

CHURCH: "We were all so glad that Robbie had won his 20th. He had pitched so well and so often and we really wanted him to get that 20th win, as well as win the pennant. In the clubhouse we were an excited bunch. We were all on such a high. I expect that you get that high maybe once in your life. I know I've only experienced it once in my life."

MILLER: "The Dodgers showed a lot of class, particularly Jackie Robinson, who came into our clubhouse and shook hands with everybody and wished us well in the Series."

MEYER: "Jackie Robinson was a class act. He came in to congratulate us after we won the pennant, even though Dusty Cooke was still one of our coaches."

Robinson's sportsmanship was remarkable considering how tough the Phillies were on him when he broke in in 1947. I am not sure I would have thought to do the same at that time if the roles had been reversed and the Dodgers had won the pennant on the last day of the season.

SAWYER: "Several of the Dodgers came in to congratulate us, including Newcombe. The Dodgers and we respected each other. We played them a lot and they were all tough games. They appreciated our rivalry and so did we. They appreciated us and we appreciated them. They were good, hard competitors."

CABALLERO: "Bob Carpenter came into the clubhouse and asked everybody, 'You want to have a victory party here or back in Philadelphia?' And we all wanted to go back to Philadelphia because that's where our wives and families were."

McDONNELL: "We took the bus to the train station to go back to Philly, and when we came out of the clubhouse people were yelling and jeering and even spitting at us."

One woman kept calling to Richie as we were boarding the bus outside Ebbets Field. When he finally turned around to look at her, she spat right in his face. I had to restrain Whitey from going after her and push him onto the bus. I guess some of those Brooklyn fans really took that loss a little hard.

BETTY ZEISER: "Lou Louderback offered us a ride back to the train station in his limousine. So our group plus others we picked up formed a congo line in the middle of the street outside Ebbets Field to get to the limousine. We had to crowd into the limo and Anne had to sit on my lap. Traffic was very bad, so by the time we got to the train station my leg was asleep. When I tried to get out of the car, I fell. But I was all right in a few minutes."

ANNE ZEISER: "They held the train for the team to get there. Lou had rented a compartment and had set up some drinks, and we were inviting the players back one by one to have a drink and celebrate. Andy hobbled back and he was all smiles.

"At one point there was a lot of commotion up in the dining car, so we went up to see what was going on. Dick Sisler was sitting there trying to eat. Every time he would put the fork up to his mouth some drunk standing in the aisle would hit him in the back and send the fork anywhere but Dick's mouth. Putsy Caballero was sitting there signing his autograph 'Ralph Joseph "Putsy" Caballero' to anybody who wanted it."

McDONNELL: "We had three private cars on the train and it was just bedlam all the way home. There were about 30,000 people at the train station in Philly and we couldn't find our wives. They had been told to go to the Warwick Hotel, where the celebration was going to be. We all finally got down there in cabs, but it took a long time to get there because the streets were so packed."

ANNE ZEISER: "We were supposed to go to the victory celebration at the Warwick and meet Andy and his wife there. When we pulled into the North Philly Station there were hundreds and hundreds of people. Amazingly, we looked out the window and there stood our mother, our aunt, our cousin, and our baby sister. So we got off to give them our luggage to take home for us and then the conductor wouldn't let us back on the train, which was going down to 30th Street Station. Traffic was so bad that we never did make it down to the celebration at the Warwick."

MARY ROBERTS: "Carolyn Jones, Mary Anne Hollmig, and I went to meet the train, but we couldn't get anywhere near the train station. We didn't know what to do, but we finally found out that the party for the team was going to be at the Warwick Hotel. We never got close enough to the station to even get out of the car, so we met the boys at the hotel."

CABALLERO: "When we got back to Philadelphia that night the crowds were trying to push the train off the track, that's how excited Philadelphia was. They went nuts. It gives me goose bumps to think about it, 40-some-odd years later. Then we had our big party at the Warwick. Everyone was there and we were so elated because it was the first pennant for the Phillies in 35 years."

SAWYER: "The train station was mobbed. There must have been 50,000 people at the station. We could hardly get off the train. It was almost impossible to get a cab to get to the Warwick. I don't know how my wife got to the station to meet me in that mob. You know, I don't think I ever asked her how she made it down there. We ended up staying at the Warwick until about 3 A.M."

SIMMONS: "That night the guys called me from the Warwick and I went over to the company office to take the call. I talked to Rob and Willie Jones and a bunch of the guys. They were all pretty excited and having a real good time."

Mary and I did not stay at the Warwick very long, although it was a great party with a band and all the food and drink one could want. It was great to see everyone associated with the Whiz Kids celebrating and so happy, but I was really drained by that time. Mary was eight months pregnant with Robby, Jr., who was born on October 20, and I knew she was in no shape to be out late and I was anxious to get home as well.

MARY ROBERTS: "This was my first year of marriage and I suppose I was as dumb as a doornail because this winning the pennant I thought was going to happen real often. I was eight months pregnant, so the party wasn't as much fun for me as for everyone else, but I thought we would have these parties lots of times. I didn't realize what a difficult accomplishment it is to win the pennant."

Although we left early, the party went on until the wee hours. Granny Hamner apparently joined the band at one point and led the singing.

Winning the pennant that day in Brooklyn gave me a feeling that I never had experienced in sports and, although I would pitch in the big leagues for another 16 years, I never really got that same feeling again. It was complete exhilaration, elation, and great relief all rolled together.

Although we had played extremely well that entire year, the season and the pennant had come down to that final day in Brooklyn. Without Richie's throw, Dick's home run, and my getting the Dodgers out in the ninth and tenth innings, we might well have been just another Cinderella team that fell short. If that had occurred, I am afraid no one would remember the 1950 Phillies. But because of the 1950 season and that last ballgame in Ebbets Field, the Whiz Kids are one of baseball's most memorable teams. And I am proud to have been a part of that special group.

Epilogue: The World Series and Beyond

We had two days to get ready to play the Yankees in the World Series, which opened on Wednesday in Shibe Park. The Yankees had survived a tight pennant race of their own with the Detroit Tigers and Boston Red Sox to win the pennant by three games, clinching on the day before the season ended. They were led by Joe DiMaggio, Yogi Berra, Johnny Mize, American League MVP Phil Rizzuto, and the formidable starting pitching of 21-game-winner Vic Raschi, along with Allie Reynolds, Eddie Lopat, and a rookie named Ed "Whitey" Ford, who had gone 9–1 after a late season call-up from Kansas City.

Eddie Sawyer gave us Monday off, so we had our only pre-Series workout on Tuesday. Curt Simmons had gotten a pass from his National Guard unit to join us for the Series but could not be activated, since the Series rosters were set; besides, he had not really pitched in several weeks. He did throw batting practice for us, and several of the guys complained that it was tougher hitting against Curt's half-speed throws than it was against most pitchers in games.

The Skipper had delayed naming the opening game starter, but on Tuesday he surprised everyone by tapping Jim Konstanty to pitch the first game. Jim had made 74 appearances, all in relief, on the way to his 16–7 record. He had thrown 155 innings and had a number of appearances in which he had pitched five, six, or even more innings effectively.

SAWYER: "I was looking for somebody different. Back in 1929 Connie Mack had started Howard Ehmke in the World Series opener against the Cubs. He couldn't throw hard and struck out like 13. So this was what I was thinking of. Konstanty would be something different for the Yankees to look at. We had to stop the Yankees' left-handed bats, Berra, Bobby Brown, and Mize. Those guys were pretty good hitters. Konstanty had pitched seven innings for me a lot of times in Toronto, pitching the short games in doubleheaders. So I figured he can start it and go as far as he can and then I would bring in somebody else."

By starting Jim, I could pitch the second game with my normal three days rest and could still start two games in the Series. Also, the Yankees were known as a free-swinging bunch with the likes of Berra, Mize, Hank Bauer, and Gene Woodling, and Jim's off-speed deliveries would likely give them trouble.

Eddie's analysis turned out to be correct: Jim scattered four hits over eight innings before Dick Whitman pinch hit for him in the eighth. But our hitting slump continued, thanks in no small measure to the bullets thrown by the Yankees' Vic Raschi, who lived up to his nickname, the Springfield Rifle. All afternoon we were only able to touch Raschi for two fifth-inning singles.

The game was decided in the fourth inning when Yankee third base-man Bobby Brown doubled to left, advanced to third on Bauer's long fly to Richie Ashburn in center, and scored the game's only run on Jerry Coleman's long sacrifice fly to Dick Sisler in left.

Following our 1–0 opening game defeat, I started the second game, played Thursday, October 5. Yankee manager Casey Stengel named Allie Reynolds, who had posted a 16–12 record, including several low-scoring one-run losses, to throw for New York.

I struggled at the start, allowing two hits in the first before escaping with no damage. Then with two out in the second I walked Coleman. Reynolds, a .185 hitter, followed by poking a single to right to send Coleman to third. Leadoff hitter Gene Woodling then topped a high bounder to Puddinhead Jones's left. Willie could not get to the ball, but Granny Hamner fielded it deep in the hole. With no play at the plate, he fired to Mike Goliat at second to try to force Reynolds, but Allie just beat the throw. Coleman scored on the play and we were down 1–0.

I was not in a good groove and did not have good rhythm for the first five innings. I managed to scatter the Yankee hits, but I really was struggling. In fact, with the exception of that last inning in Brooklyn, I had not thrown well for the last two or three weeks of the season. But about the fifth inning I began to get the feel of it, which meant I was pitching within myself and not trying to overthrow. When I did that I threw relaxed and had good movement on my fastball.

After blowing a couple of scoring opportunities early, we finally scored our first run of the Series in the fifth. Goliat started with an infield hit that Coleman made a great play to simply glove. I popped to Reynolds for the first out trying to sacrifice Mike along. Eddie Waitkus then hit a routine-looking grounder to second that suddenly bounced crazily over Coleman's head and into right field, allowing Mike to go all the way to third. Richie got the run home by stroking a long fly to left to bring us even at 1–1.

Although we had runners in scoring position in the seventh, eighth, and ninth innings, we could not break through against Reynolds again. Meanwhile, I survived a one-out jam with runners on second and third in the eighth. I set the Yankees down in order in the ninth, and Granny gave us hope with a one-out double in our half. Dick Whitman pinch hit for Ken Silvestri, who had gone in to catch after Putsy Caballero had run for Andy Seminick in the seventh, and Stengel ordered an intentional walk to bring up Goliat.

With runners at first and second and one out, Mike worked the count to 3–1 against Reynolds. Mike was a free-swinger, and on the next pitch he swung at a chin-high fastball, grounding a two-hopper to Rizzuto for an inning-ending double play.

The little things in baseball will drive you buggy if you dwell on them, but if Mike had taken that pitch we would have had the bases loaded with one out. I was on deck, and Eddie would probably have hit for me, and who knows if we would have scored. But in a short series small things can have a big impact, especially when you lose close games like we did.

The first batter to face me in the top of the 10th was none other than Joe DiMaggio. Although I was not overconfident, I had handled Joe well all day, popping him up to the infield in his four previous tries, once with two runners on base. This time I got behind him two balls and no strikes. I then threw him a low fastball out over the plate a little too much and Joe walloped it into the first row of the upper deck in left for a home run. I got the next three hitters, but we went to the bottom of the 10th trailing 2–1.

Eddie put Jack Mayo in to pinch hit for me to start our half of the inning, and Jack worked Reynolds for a five-pitch walk. Waitkus sacrificed Jack to second and we had a runner in scoring position with only one out. But Allie bore down to get the two final outs and close out the victory. We had lost 2–1 in another very tough game and were suddenly down 2–0 in the Series.

After the game, DiMaggio told the press that he had hit a slider for the home run. I know, of course, that Stan Lopata had called for a fastball because I did not throw a slider. But my fastball did tend to slide away from a right-handed hitter when I got it down and away, and it was effective in that location. If I got it up or too much over the plate it tended to flatten out and was not that great of a pitch.

The Series quickly moved to Yankee Stadium without interruption for a travel day. Eddie named Kenny Heintzelman to start the third game against the Yanks' Ed Lopat, who had compiled an 18–8 record. Although Kenny had had a disappointing year, he had pitched well in a couple of key games in September and seemed to be regaining his 1949 form.

The contest promptly became another pitchers' duel, as Goober and Lopat were on top of their games. The Yankees scored in the bottom of the third when Phil Rizzuto drew a seemingly harmless two-out walk. Rizzuto took off for second on the next pitch and Andy's throw bounced into center field, enabling Phil to go to third. Coleman then singled to left to drive in the first run of the game, although Dick Sisler threw Jerry out trying to stretch for two bases.

Although we had early scoring opportunities, most notably in the second when we had runners on first and third with only one out, our hitting slump continued. Heading into the sixth inning we had still scored only one run in the entire Series. But with two outs Del Ennis got his first hit with a slashing double over Mize at first. Dick followed with his first hit of the Series too, a line single over Rizzuto at short to drive in Del and tie the score at 1–1.

Granny, who was our leading hitter in the Series, singled to begin the seventh inning. Andy successfully sacrificed him to second and Mike Goliat laced a single to center. Granny, running hard, beat DiMaggio's throw to the plate and we had our first lead of the Series at 2–1.

When Heinz retired the Yankees in order in the bottom half of the seventh and got the first two batters in the eighth, it looked like we were on the way to victory. But Ken walked Coleman on a 3–2 count and then walked Berra and DiMaggio to load the bases.

Kenny was out of gas and Eddie brought in Konstanty to get the third out. Stengel sent Bobby Brown, who already had three hits in the Series, up to bat for Bauer. Jim got ahead two strikes when Bobby knocked a ground ball to Granny at short. Granny, appearing a little overanxious to get the force at second, bobbled the ball and all hands were safe. Coleman scored on the play and we were knotted again, 2–2. Konstanty bore down and forced Mize to pop to Puddinhead in foul ground for the third out.

In the top of the ninth Granny immediately redeemed himself with a smash to deep left center off of reliever Tom Ferrick. DiMaggio made a great barehand stop of the ball to hold Granny to a double; if Joe had not cut it off, Granny would have had at least a triple. Andy then popped a sacrifice bunt attempt toward third baseman Billy Johnson, who, though the ball was catchable, let it drop. Granny, after hesitating, sneaked into third while Johnson, after starting for Granny, easily threw out Andy, running on his broken ankle, at first.

Stengel ordered Goliat intentionally walked to put runners at the corners with one out. Eddie countered by inserting Dick Whitman to hit for Konstanty. Dick topped a slow bouncer that first baseman Joe Collins charged. Hamner was off on contact, and Collins threw to Berra to nip him at the plate and effectively kill the rally. With Goliat on second and two out, Waitkus flew out to Cliff Mapes in right to end the inning.

Russ Meyer came on to pitch the bottom of the ninth. He retired the first two hitters, and it looked like we were again headed for extra innings. But Gene Woodling hit a tricky grounder that Jimmy Bloodworth, in for Goliat, bobbled behind second for an infield hit. Rizzuto followed with a liner over second. Jimmy dove and knocked the ball down, but he could not come up with it in time to make a play, and there were suddenly runners on first and second.

Coleman was next and hit a fly ball between Ashburn and Mayo in left center field. Richie and Jack appeared to hesitate slightly and the ball fell in for a single, driving in Woodling with the winning run. The 3–2 defeat was our third consecutive one-run loss of the Series and put us down three games to zero.

After losing three tough ballgames, we were discouraged. The Yankees were playing well and had made some great defensive plays that had tipped the scales. But because we had played them so well thus far, we still believed that we could give the Yankees a run for their money. We just needed to get that first victory, but time was running out.

Eddie selected Bob Miller to start game four but let the pitching staff know that he might use all of us if need be. The Yankees started 21-year-old rookie southpaw Ed "Whitey" Ford. Eddie Waitkus began by drawing a walk, and after Richie flew out to Woodling in left, Puddinhead laced a drive to right that bounced into the stands for a ground-rule double. With only one out we had runners on second and third in a most promising beginning.

Del followed and worked the count to 3–0 before taking a strike. On the next pitch Del grounded to Bobby Brown at third, who came up firing to nail Waitkus at the plate. Dick Sisler took a called third strike and our chance to get an early jump was gone.

Unhappily, the Yankees did just that to us in the bottom of the first, scoring two runs on some shaky fielding, a wild pitch, a single by Berra, and a double by DiMaggio. The Skipper, pulling out all the stops, brought in Konstanty with one out to get us out of the inning.

We had another good chance in the fourth when Del topped a slow roller that hugged the third base line for a single. With one out Granny again came through with a hit-and-run single to right to send Del to third. But once again disaster struck. Andy hit a slow bouncer to Mize near the bag at first. John stepped on first and then threw home to Berra, who tagged out Del attempting to score. The double play knocked us out of another scoring opportunity and kept the score at 2–0.

Konstanty pitched well until the sixth when Berra opened the inning by clubbing a 3–2 offering into the right field stands for a home run. DiMaggio was hit by a pitch, and with one out Brown drove him home with a triple to deep center. Bauer singled Brown home to make it 5–0 before Jim could get out of the inning.

Meanwhile, we could not break through against Ford. Eddie brought me in to pitch the eighth after removing Konstanty for a pinch hitter. I held New York scoreless, but we were down to our last at bat, still trailing 5–0.

Puddinhead opened with a whistling single to left center and Del was hit by a pitch to put runners on first and second. Ford settled down to get the next two batters, bringing up Andy Seminick as our last chance. Andy poled a long drive near the 402-foot sign in left center that Woodling, after a long run, lost in the sun and dropped. Running with two outs, Jones and pinch runner Ken Johnson scored to bring us to within 5–2.

Andy could get only to first on his bad ankle, and Eddie brought Jack Mayo in to run for him. Mike Goliat kept our hopes alive with a sharp single to left to bring the tying run to the plate.

At this point Casey Stengel decided to bring in Allie Reynolds, to the displeasure of Yankee fans who wanted to see Ford finish the game. I was the scheduled hitter, but Eddie brought in Stan Lopata to pinch hit. Stan got behind 0–2, took a ball low, and struck out on a high fastball. The Series was over and we had never gotten that first victory, although we had been in every game to the end.

The World Series was a big disappointment to us. In some ways the Series might have been anticlimactic because we had had such a tough time winning the pennant and had felt such a sense of relief when we finally beat the Dodgers in Ebbets Field on the last day of the season. But we were all thrilled to have the chance to play the Yankees in the Series.

If we had played the Series in early September, before all of our injuries and before we lost Curt Simmons to active duty, it might have been a different story. That, after all, was the Whiz Kid club that had built the sizable lead that gave us the cushion we needed to win the pennant. But they play the World Series in October, not September, and we gave it the best we had.

We had exceptional games against the Yankees, but we just did not hit, continuing our team hitting slump from the last 10 days of the regular season. Of course, the outstanding Yankee pitching certainly had something to do with our .203 Series average as a team.

We fully expected to win several more pennants in the coming years and return to the World Series. We thought we would have other shots at the Yankees. But it did not happen. We fell to fifth place in 1951, 23½ games out, with Curt on active duty the entire year.

> **SAWYER:** "Not having Curt Simmons all year really hurt us in 1951. Some of the other guys tailed off a bit. And the farm system stopped paying off like it had before. A couple of guys like Paul Stuffel and Jack Brittin never made it and they should have. But we weren't signing the top prospects like we had in the late 40s. Other scouts for other teams weren't letting us sign some of the top guys out of high school and college. They were a little envious of our success. So we had to make trades to try to get players we needed, and you really can't do it that way, you've got to develop your own kids."

In 1952 we were mired in sixth place in late June when Bob Carpenter fired Eddie Sawyer and replaced him with Steve O'Neil. Under Steve we got hot and won 59 and lost only 32 the last three months of the season. I had the best season of my career, going 28–7, but we still finished only fourth, 9½ games out. We tied for third in 1953, but 22 games off the pace.

In mid-July 1954 we were in third place, three games over .500, when new general manager Roy Hamey fired O'Neil and brought in Terry Moore. We ended up fourth, again 22 games behind and 4 games under .500. Mayo Smith took over in 1955, and we again finished fourth with a 77–77 record.

We slipped to fifth in 1956 and 1957 before finishing the decade as National League cellar dwellers. The 1950s ended with Eddie Sawyer again at the helm, trying once more to turn the franchise around. Eddie resigned after the first game of the 1960 season, uttering the famous quote, "I'm 49 years old and I want to live to be 50."

When I was elected to the Hall of Fame in 1976 I was very grateful, but I was unhappy with the plaque that the Hall of Fame prepared for my induction. It said something about my having pitched mostly for second division clubs and failed to mention the Whiz Kids at all. Although the Phillies fielded poor teams in the late 1950s, the plaque really bothered me because the Phillies had solid first division teams when I was winning 20 games every year. It made it seem like I had won 286 games without any help at all. And in omitting the Whiz Kids, it ignored the team I am most identified with. So I eventually got my plaque changed, and my association with the Whiz Kids is prominently stated.

I have often wondered whether the Whiz Kids won too soon. Brooklyn, of course, suffered heartbreaking defeats in 1950 and 1951 before winning four of the next five pennants. Would that kind of adversity have improved us in the long run? If we had blown that October 1 game in Brooklyn, would our organization have made moves to shake up our team? Because we won, did we stand too pat?

ASHBURN: "We had a good team in the early and middle 50s. But while we were pretty much staying the same, the Dodgers, Pirates, Braves, and Giants were all bringing up black ballplayers. Roy Campanella told me many times that he had wanted to play with the Phillies. He was born and raised in Philadelphia. He once went to Shibe Park for a tryout and they wouldn't even let him in the ballpark. Can you imagine our club with Roy Campanella on it? But that is the way it was then. The Phillies were just slow to change.

"I think if we had been able to get our share of black ballplayers in the early 50s we would have contended for the pennant every year."

Of course, the fact that we did not win again should not overshadow our success of 1950. If we had not won that October 1 ballgame, no one would remember the Whiz Kids. Under the leadership of Eddie Sawyer we were an exceptional team with great camaraderie, considerable talent, and a real will to win.

Bob Carpenter, Herb Pennock, and Eddie Sawyer had taken the franchise out of the doldrums and built a pennant winner in fairly short order. Eddie was the perfect manager for the Whiz Kids, always remaining calm, letting us play, and instilling confidence in us that we could win the pennant. He believed we could do it, and that alone meant a lot to us. I have always been grateful that we did not let him down.

In writing this book with Paul, I went back through the 1950 season game by game. In doing so, I was reminded how everyone on that Whiz Kids ballclub contributed to our winning. So-called reserves like Jimmy Bloodworth, Bill Nicholson, Dick Whitman, and Stan Lopata had key game-winning hits, while Ken Johnson, Blix Donnelly, and Milo Candini won crucial games during the year. Of our regulars, Andy Seminick, Dick Sisler, and Mike Goliat had career years and almost everyone else had very good years. Rookie pitchers Bubba Church and Bob Miller were simply outstanding until injured.

But perhaps what stood out most in reviewing the year were the tremendous seasons that Jim Konstanty, Del Ennis, and Curt Simmons delivered for us. Curt had won four games in 1949, but before he went into the service he had pitched just about as well as anyone ever had in the big leagues. Jim simply had one of the finest seasons ever for a relief pitcher, while Del drove in 126 runs to lead the league. For certain stretches of the year, he carried us almost single-handedly with his bat.

The Whiz Kids were the only pennant winner that I and most of my teammates ever played on. For us 1950 was truly a season to remember. It was a special time and a special team and holds great memories for me.

I am convinced that baseball fans will never forget the Whiz Kids. Even now, 45 years later, wherever I go I am asked more about the Whiz Kids than anything else. Surprisingly, until now, fans have not had much of an opportunity to read about us. But now, if anybody wants to know about the Whiz Kids, as Casey Stengel used to say, "It's in the book. You can look it up."

Appendix A
WHAT HAPPENED TO THE WHIZ KIDS

RICHIE ASHBURN was the starting center fielder for the Phillies through 1959. He won batting titles in 1955 and 1958, and also finished second twice. Richie was traded to the Cubs in 1960 and finished his career by hitting .306 for the 1962 New York Mets. He has broadcast Phillies games for over 30 years and for many years wrote a weekly column for the *Philadelphia Evening Bulletin.* He lives in suburban Philadelphia. Richie was (finally) elected to the Baseball Hall of Fame in 1995.

BENNY BENGOUGH coached for the Phillies until retiring in 1959. He then worked in the Phillies' public relations office, where he was a very popular after-dinner speaker. He died on December 22, 1968, at the age of 70, after coming out of church after mass.

CHARLIE BICKNELL was sold to Boston Braves in spring training 1950, where he pitched for Braves' minor league teams in Milwaukee, Atlanta, and Hartford before his National Guard unit was activated in September. He was in same unit as Curt Simmons and served with Curt in Germany until early 1952. He pitched in 1952 for the Hartford Chiefs in the Eastern League, where on August 29 he was involved in an automobile accident with three teammates. The car rolled twice and caught on fire. Bicknell escaped and returned to pull two teammates, one who was dazed and one who was unconscious, out of the car just before it was engulfed in flames. He pitched for Toledo in the American Association in 1953, 1954, and 1955, leading them to their first pennant in over 50 years in 1953 with a 16–9 record. He also pitched winter ball in Venezuela with Paul Stuffel. Charlie pitched for the Atlanta Crackers and the Memphis Chicks in 1956 and 1957 before retiring from baseball. He then worked as a factory rep for Champion Spark Plugs in Memphis for 20 years. He is now retired and lives in Germantown, Tennessee.

JOHNNY BLATNICK never made it back to the big leagues after the Cardinals sent him down to Houston early in 1950. He played in the International League with Rochester, Syracuse, and Buffalo until retiring from baseball in 1956. John worked for many years for the Worker's Compensation Bureau of the State of Ohio and also refereed college and high school basketball and football for 25 years. He is now retired and lives in Lorraine, Ohio.

JIMMY BLOODWORTH played for the Phillies in 1951, then managed in minor leagues for two seasons. He served for a time as a deputy sheriff and worked for many years with a paper company in his hometown, Apalachicola, Florida, until retiring in 1976. He still lives in Apalachicola.

JACK BRITTIN appeared in three games for the Phillies in 1951 before being optioned to Baltimore in the International League. Released by the Phillies in the spring of 1952, he was signed by the Atlanta Crackers of the Southern Association, where, after a slow start, he became one of the top pitchers in the league. He pitched for the Crackers in 1953 but was plagued with undiagnosed arm and leg problems. He then pitched for Huron, South Dakota, in the Basin League before retiring from baseball because of health problems. He was finally diagnosed as suffering from multiple sclerosis in 1956. Jack taught physical education and coached at elementary schools in Springfield, Illinois, until he was forced to quit in 1958 because of his deteriorating health. He became reacquainted with Wilma Oschwald, a childhood classmate, in 1961, after a gap of 23 years. He learned to dance and married Wilma in 1963. He returned to work that year with the Office of Public Instruction of the Illinois State Board of Education. Jack later worked for the Teachers' Retirement System and the State Board of Education in special education before retiring in 1989. He died on January 5, 1994, of a heart attack brought on by his MS. He was 69.

RALPH "PUTSY" CABALLERO continued as a utility infielder for the Phillies through 1952. He then played for Baltimore and Syracuse in the International League until retiring from baseball after the 1955 season. Putsy worked as a salesman for the Miller the Killer Exterminating Company in New Orleans along with future jazz stars Al Hirt and Pete Fountain. He eventually started his own exterminating firm, D A (Deadly Action) Exterminating in Metairie, Louisiana, where he still lives and works.

MILO CANDINI appeared in 15 games for the Phillies in 1951, his last season in the big leagues. He pitched for Oakland in 1952 and for Sacramento from 1953 through 1957, both in the Pacific Coast League, before retiring from baseball at age 40, wrapping up a 20-year career in professional baseball. Milo owned and operated a liquor store in his hometown of Manteca, California, for many years. He retired in 1978 and still resides in Manteca.

BOB CARPENTER had assumed that the 1950 pennant was the first of many. He purchased Connie Mack Stadium (formerly Shibe Park) in 1954, when the Athletics left for Kansas City. He sold the ballpark to a developer in 1961, although the Phillies continued to play there. For many years he led the fight for a new stadium, which culminated with the opening of Veterans Stadium in 1971. He served as president of the Phillies until November 1972, when he became chairman of the board while his son Ruly took over as president. He died at his home near Wilmington on July 8, 1990, at the age of 74.

BEN CHAPMAN coached and managed for several years in the minor leagues. He served as a coach for the Cincinnati Reds in 1952, his last year with a big league team. After leaving professional baseball, he sold insurance and coached Babe Ruth and American Legion teams in Birmingham, Alabama. He died on July 7, 1993, at his home in Hoover, Alabama, at the age of 84.

EMORY "BUBBA" CHURCH won 15 games for the 1951 Phillies. He was traded to Cincinnati early in 1952, and then to the Cubs in 1953. He made his last big league appearance in 1955, retiring to enter the real estate business. He returned to baseball as a player-coach for the Miami Marlins in the International League in 1957 and 1958. Bubba then entered the life insurance business before returning to his hometown of Birmingham, Alabama, as a manufacturer's rep for medical surgical supplies. He later founded and operated a linen service for medical clinics and doctors until retiring in 1988. He lives in Birmingham, where he recently scored his first hole-in-one.

ALLEN "DUSTY" COOKE continued as a Phillies coach until 1952, when new manager Steve O'Neil brought in his own coaches. He then returned to his native North Carolina, where he and his wife Daphne operated a small variety store in Raleigh. He suffered a series of strokes and died in Fuquay-Varina, North Carolina, on November 25, 1987, at the age of 80.

SYLVESTER "BLIX" DONNELLY pitched briefly for the Boston Braves in 1951 before bowing out of the major leagues. He became a barber and then owned and operated an anhydrous ammonia business for many years in his hometown of Olivia, Minnesota. He died on June 20, 1976, at the age of 62.

DEL ENNIS started for the Phillies through 1956, when he was traded to the Cardinals and proceeded to drive in 105 runs, his seventh season with over 100 RBIs. He finished his career with the Reds and the White Sox before retiring at age 34 after the 1959 season. For many years he owned a bowling alley in Philadelphia and later raced greyhounds, many of which he named after his Whiz Kid teammates. Del died on February 8, 1996, at his home in suburban Philadelphia of complications from diabetes. He was 70 years old.

MIKE GOLIAT was sent to the Phillies' farm club in Baltimore at the start of 1951 but was later recalled and sold to the St. Louis Browns in September. He played in three games for the Browns in 1952 before being released. Mike never returned to the majors but played in the International League at Toronto for eight years and at Montreal for one year, winning the MVP award in 1956. In 1957 he hit .294 with 28 home runs and 102 RBIs. He was a player-coach for Spokane in the Pacific Coast League in 1961 before retiring from baseball. He operated a small trucking business in Cleveland and then worked for Ford Motor Company for five years. He also became an excellent bowler. Mike is now retired and lives in suburban Cleveland.

GRANVILLE "GRANNY" HAMNER was the Phillies' starting shortstop for most of the 1950s before being traded to Cleveland early in the 1959 season. He managed in the minor leagues for the Kansas City Athletics while working on his knuckleball (he had pitched in four games for the Phillies in 1956 and 1957). Granny pitched in three games in 1962 for the Kansas City Athletics before retiring as a player. He served as a minor league instructor and coach for the Phillies for many years. Granny died of a heart attack in Philadelphia on September 12, 1993, at the age of 66, waiting to be interviewed for this book.

KEN HEINTZELMAN pitched for the Phillies through 1952, when he retired from baseball. He worked many years for the McDonnell-Douglas Company in St. Louis, Missouri, as an expediter. Ken retired in 1980 and now lives in St. Peters, Missouri.

STAN HOLLMIG made his last big league appearances as a pinch hitter in two games for the 1951 Phillies. He played in the minor leagues for Baltimore, Atlanta, Schenectady, Louisville, Richmond, Nashville, and San Antonio before retiring from baseball in 1958. He then scouted for the Cincinnati Reds and Houston Astros for 23 years while living in New Braunfels, Texas. Stan died of cancer on December 4, 1981, at the age of 55.

KEN JOHNSON pitched for the Phillies in 1951. He was sold to the Detroit Tigers before the 1952 season, and was later optioned to Buffalo. He pitched for Buffalo and Toronto in the International League before retiring from baseball after the 1955 season. He recently retired from a successful career as an insurance executive in Wichita, Kansas, where he still lives.

WILLIE "PUDDINHEAD" JONES started at third base for the Phillies until midway through the 1959 season, when he was traded to the Cleveland Indians. Less than a month later he was traded by the Indians to Cincinnati, where he finished his 15-year career, retiring early in 1961. He worked as a car salesman in Cincinnati for many years before dying of cancer at the age of 58 on October 19, 1983, just a few minutes after talking to his old Whiz Kid roommate Del Ennis.

JIM KONSTANTY compiled only a 4–11 record for the 1951 Phillies. He pitched for the Phillies through 1954, when he was sold to the Yankees. He amassed a 7–2 record for the 1955 Yankees but was released in 1956 and picked up by the Cardinals. He pitched for San Francisco in the Pacific Coast League in 1957 before retiring from baseball. Jim owned and operated the Jim Konstanty Sporting Goods Store in Oneonta, New York, for many years, and served as a minor league pitching coach for the Cardinals in 1963 and the Yankees in 1965. He became athletic director at Hartwick College in Oneonta in 1968 and led the development of a nationally prominent college soccer program there before retiring in 1972. Jim died of cancer on June 11, 1976, at the age of 59. The undertaker at his funeral was Andy Skinner.

STAN LOPATA spent most of 1951 with Baltimore in the International League. He returned to the Phillies in 1952 and remained until he was traded to the Milwaukee Braves during spring training in 1959. His best year was 1956, when he hit 32 home runs and drove in 95 runs. He retired from baseball early in 1960 and worked as a salesman and later vice president of sales for a concrete materials company in the Philadelphia area before retiring several years ago. He now lives in Mesa, Arizona.

JACK MAYO was up and down with Phillies through 1953, spending a lot of time with Baltimore in the International League. He retired after the 1954 season, at the age of 29, and became a very successful land developer and real estater broker in his hometown of Youngstown, Ohio, where he still lives and works.

ROBERT "MAJE" McDONNELL remained a coach with the Phillies through 1957, then scouted for the team for 3½ years before coaching baseball and teaching for 9 years at a Philadelphia area prep school. He returned to the Phillies in 1973 in their community relations department, where he still works. Maje organizes tryout camps, leads tours, and gives 75 to 100 speeches a year for the Phillies. Recently elected to the Pennsylvania Sports Hall of Fame, he lives in Philadelphia.

RUSS MEYER pitched for the Phillies through 1952 before being traded to Brooklyn, where he appeared in the 1953 and 1955 World Series. He later pitched briefly for the Cubs, Reds, Red Sox, and Athletics before retiring as an active player in 1959. He was manager and part owner of a bowling alley in Gary, Indiana, for several years before coaching baseball at Illinois Valley Community College in LaSalle-Peru, Illinois. More recently, he served for 12 years as a pitching coach in the Yankee organization before retiring in 1993. Russ lives in Ogelsby, Illinois, very near his hometown of LaSalle-Peru.

BOB MILLER pitched for the Phillies through the 1958 season, though he was plagued by a bad back. He was picked up by the Cardinals in 1959 but was released before the season. Bob lives in Detroit, where he is retired from a successful career in the life insurance business. He has coached baseball at the University of Detroit for 33 years.

SAM NAHEM retired from baseball after his release from the Phillies in 1948. He worked for many years for a major oil company in California, where he became a very active trade unionist, eventually heading his local Oil, Chemical and Atomic Workers chapter. He retired in 1980. A widower for 20 years, Sam lives in Berkeley, California.

BILL NICHOLSON came back from his illness and played for Phillies as a reserve outfielder and pinch hitter through 1953. He retired to his 120-acre farm near his hometown of Chestertown, Maryland, until his death on March 8, 1996.

CY PERKINS served as a Phillies coach until 1953 and later coached the baseball team at Valley Forge Military Academy in Wayne, Pennsylvania, for several years. He died in Philadelphia on October 2, 1963, at the age of 68.

LOU POSSEHL spent 1950 with Toronto. He pitched in two games for the Phillies in 1951 and four games in 1952 while pitching mostly for Baltimore in the International League. He hurt his arm in 1953 and retired from baseball early in 1954. Lou worked for many years as a salesman for Yellow Freight Systems in Chicago before retiring in 1987. He now lives in Bradenton, Florida, and plays a lot of golf with Steve Ridzik.

STEVE RIDZIK, still plagued by an injured knee, spent 1951 with Baltimore in the International League before sticking with the Phillies in 1952. He pitched for Phillies until early in 1955, when he was traded to Cincinnati in a multiple-player transaction (Andy Seminick was traded back to the Phillies in the deal). He then pitched for the Giants and Indians before injuring a disc in his neck in 1958. He pitched in the minors for Fort Worth and Toronto until 1963, when he was purchased by the expansion Washington Senators. After pitching with the Senators through 1965, Steve finished his career back with the Phillies, appearing in two games in 1966. Altogether, he pitched 21 years in professional baseball. After baseball, he worked as regional manager in the food brokerage business in Washington, D.C., selling to U.S. military commissaries world-wide. He is retired and lives in Bradenton, Florida. Steve is one of the cofounders of the Major League Baseball Players Alumni Association (MLBPAA).

ROBIN ROBERTS pitched for the Phillies through 1961, winning more than 20 games six straight years, through 1955. His best year was 1952, when he went 28–7 and was the only 20-game winner in the National League. He pitched for the Baltimore Orioles from 1962 until midway through 1965. Subsequently, he pitched for the Houston Astros and Chicago Cubs before ending his big league career in 1966 with a total of 286 wins. He was instrumental in hiring Marvin Miller to head the players' union in 1965. After baseball, he worked as a stockbroker and Phillies broadcaster and was part owner of the Philadelphia Firebirds, a minor league hockey team, before becoming baseball coach at the University of South Florida for eight years. Elected to the Baseball Hall of Fame in 1976, he is now retired and living in a suburb of Tampa, Florida. Robin serves on the Board of Directors of the Baseball Hall of Fame and of B.A.T. (Baseball Assistance Team).

LYNWOOD "SCHOOLBOY" ROWE pitched in 1950 for San Diego in the Pacific Coast League before retiring as a player. He managed Williamsport in the Eastern League in 1951 and served as pitching coach with the Detroit Tigers in 1954 and 1955. He subsequently scouted for the Tigers until his death on January 8, 1961, at the age of 48.

EDDIE SANICKI made the Phillies coming out of spring training in 1951 but in May was sent to Schenectady in Class A when the team had to trim its roster from 28 to 25. He retired from baseball in 1952 and returned to college at Seton Hall, completing his degree. Eddie taught physical education to mentally handicapped children in Clifton, New Jersey, until retiring in 1986. He lives in Old Bridge, New Jersey.

EDDIE SAWYER managed the Phillies until he was fired by Bob Carpenter in June 1952. He worked for a golf ball manufacturer, rising to become vice president in charge of sales, until he was rehired to manage the Phillies in July 1958. Eddie quit after the first game of 1960, saying, "I'm 49 years old and I want to live to be 50." He returned to work for the golf ball manufacturer but scouted for the Phillies in the 1960s. The expansion Kansas City Royals hired him in 1968 to help draft players from other American League teams, and he was instrumental in drafting a team that became the most successful expansion franchise in its first year. He worked as a special assignment scout with the Royals until retiring in 1973. Eddie lives in Valley Forge, Pennsylvania, and is a member of sports hall of fames in Pennsylvania, Maryland, Virginia, Rhode Island, and, most recently, Binghamton, New York.

ANDY SEMINICK was traded to Cincinnati after the 1951 season, and then traded back to the Phillies early in the 1955 season. He became a Phillies coach in 1957 and coached, managed, and scouted in the Phillies system until retiring in 1986. A widower, he lives in Melbourne, Florida, and is very involved in the athletic program at Florida Tech, which has named its baseball field after him.

KEN SILVESTRI was on the active player roster until early in 1953, when he officially became a Phillies coach. He then managed in the Yankees system until 1959, when Eddie Sawyer brought him back as a Phillies coach. Replaced after the 1960 season, he began a 16-year association with the Braves organization, including three games as interim manager of Atlanta in 1967. He went on to work as a minor league coach and instructor for the Twins, Indians, and White Sox until his death on March 31, 1992, in his hometown of Tallahassee, Florida, at the age of 74. Altogether, Ken spent 55 years in organized baseball.

CURT SIMMONS served with the National Guard in Germany until early 1952 and then pitched for the Phillies into the 1960 season. He was released and picked up by the Cardinals, where he pitched successfully, peaking with 18 wins in 1964 and starting two games in the World Series. He was sold to the Cubs in 1966 and went to the California Angels in 1967 before retiring after 20 big league seasons. He is part owner (with Robin Roberts) and operator of Limekiln Golf Club in suburban Philadelphia, where Robin Roberts, Jr., serves as assistant manager.

DICK SISLER was traded after the 1951 season to Cincinnati, who shortly thereafter dealt him to the Cardinals. He was St. Louis's regular first baseman in 1952 but played little in 1953, his last year in the majors. He played and managed in the minors until 1961, when he became a coach for the Reds. He succeeded an ill Fred Hutchison as the Reds' manager in late 1964 and piloted the 1965 Reds to an 89–73 record but was still fired after the season. He went on to coach for the Cardinals, Padres, Mets, and Yankees. Dick is now retired and lives in Nashville.

PAUL STUFFEL pitched for Baltimore and Schnectady in 1951 and briefly for the Phillies in 1952 and 1953, spending most of those two years with Baltimore in the International League. He was sold to the White Sox and pitched for Memphis, Atlanta, Mobile, and Austin before retiring from baseball in 1957. After baseball, he operated his own insurance agency in his hometown of Alliance, Ohio. Paul retired in 1992 and still lives in Alliance.

JOHN "JOCKO" THOMPSON appeared in 29 games for the 1951 Phillies, his last year in the majors. After retiring from baseball he worked as a sales manager in Maryland. Jocko died on February 3, 1988, at the age of 68.

EDDIE WAITKUS married one of the nurses who cared for him after he was shot. He played for Phillies through 1953 before being sold to Baltimore. He was sold back to the Phillies during the 1955 season, after which he retired. Eddie worked as a floor manager in a Waltham, Massachusetts, department store before passing away on September 15, 1972, at the age of 53.

HARRY WALKER spent part of 1950 and most of 1951 with Rochester in the International League. He became a very successful player-manager with Rochester and managed the St. Louis Cardinals in 1955, also going 5 for 14 at bat. He later managed the Pittsburgh Pirates (1965 through mid-1967) and Houston Astros (1968 through late 1972) and coached baseball at the University of Alabama–Birmingham. He is known as one of the leading batting coaches in baseball. Now retired, he lives in a house in Leeds, Alabama, he has owned since 1948.

DICK WHITMAN was traded in June 1951, back to the Dodgers, who sent him to St. Paul in the American Association. He never returned to the big leagues but played in the International League and Pacific Coast League through 1955 before becoming a player-manager with San Jose in the California League for two years. He then worked as a manager for the San Jose Water Company for 29 years. Dick is now retired and living in Peoria, Arizona.

Appendix B
BOX SCORE OF PENNANT-WINNING GAME, OCTOBER 1, 1950

Phillies	AB	R	H	PO	A	E
Waitkus, 1b	5	1	1	18	0	0
Ashburn, cf	5	1	0	2	1	0
Sisler, lf	5	2	4	0	0	0
Mayo, lf	0	0	0	1	0	0
Ennis, rf	5	0	2	2	0	0
Jones, 3b	5	0	1	0	3	0
Hammer, ss	4	0	0	1	2	0
Seminick, c	3	0	1	2	1	0
a-Caballero	0	0	0	0	0	0
Lopata, c	0	0	0	2	0	0
Gollat, 2b	4	0	1	1	3	0
Roberts, p	2	0	1	1	6	0
Totals	38	4	11	30	16	0

Brooklyn	AB	R	H	PO	A	E
Abrams, lf	2	0	0	2	0	0
Reese, ss	4	1	3	3	3	0
Snider, cf	4	0	1	3	0	0
Robinson, 2b	3	0	0	4	3	0
Furillo, rf	4	0	0	3	0	0
Hodges, 1b	4	0	0	9	3	0
Campanella, c	4	0	1	2	4	0
Cox, 3b	3	0	0	1	2	0
b-Russell	1	0	0	0	0	0
Newcombe, p	3	0	0	3	2	0
c-Brown	1	0	0	0	0	0
Totals	33	1	5	30	17	0

PHILLIES	0	0	0	0	0	1	0	0	0	3	—	4
BROOKLYN	0	0	0	0	0	1	0	0	0	0	—	1

a-Ran for Seminick in ninth b-Struck out for Cox in tenth c-Fouled out for Newcombe in tenth.

Runs batted in—Jones, Reese, Sisler 3. *Two-base hits*—Reese. *Home runs*—Reese, Sisler. *Bases on balls*—off Roberts 3. Newcombe 2. *Struckout*—by Roberts 2. Newcombe 3. *Double plays*—Reese, Robinson and Hodges. Roberts and Waitkus. *Left on bases*—Phillies 7. Brooklyn 5. Time of game—2:35—Attendance 35,073. Umpires—Goetz, Dascoli, Gorda, Donatelli.

Appendix C
INDIVIDUAL STATISTICS FOR THE 1950 PHILLIES

PITCHERS	Age	Bats	Throws	G	IP	H	BB	SO	W	L	PCT	ERA
Borowy, Hank	34	Right	Right	3	6	5	4	3	0	0	.000	6.00
Brittin, Jack	26	Right	Right	3	4	2	3	3	0	0	.000	4.50
Candini, Milo	32	Right	Right	18	30	32	15	9	1	0	1.000	2.70
Church, Bubba	24	Right	Right	31	142	113	56	51	8	6	.571	2.73
Donnelly, Blix	35	Right	Right	14	21	30	10	11	2	4	.333	4.29
Heintzelman, Ken	34	Right	Left	23	126	122	54	39	3	9	.250	4.10
Johnson, Ken	27	Left	Left	16	63	61	46	32	4	1	.800	3.98
Konstanty, Jim	33	Right	Right	74	151	109	51	54	16	7	.696	2.68
Meyer, Russ	26	Both	Right	33	161	193	66	74	9	11	.450	5.29
Miller, Bob	23	Right	Right	35	174	190	57	46	11	6	.647	3.57
Ridzik, Steve	21	Right	Right	1	3	3	1	2	0	0	.000	6.00
Roberts, Robin	23	Left	Right	40	304	283	76	146	20	11	.645	3.02
Simmons, Curt	20	Left	Left	31	215	178	87	146	17	8	.680	3.39
Stuffel, Paul	23	Right	Right	3	5	4	1	3	0	0	.000	1.80
Thompson, Jocko	30	Left	Left	2	4	1	4	2	0	0	.000	0.00

CATCHERS	Age	Bats	Throws	G	AB	R	H	HR	RBI	PCT
Lopata, Stan	24	Right	Right	58	130	10	26	1	11	.200
Seminick, Andy	29	Right	Right	130	393	55	113	24	68	.288
Silvestri, Ken	33	Both	Right	11	20	2	5	0	4	.250

INFIELDERS	Age	Bats	Throws	G	AB	R	H	HR	RBI	PCT
Bloodworth, Jimmy	32	Right	Right	58	110	7	25	0	13	.227
Caballero, Ralph	22	Right	Right	46	24	12	4	0	0	.167
Goliat, Mike	24	Right	Right	145	483	49	113	13	65	.234
Hamner, Granny	22	Right	Right	157	638	78	172	11	80	.270
Jones, Willie	24	Right	Right	157	610	100	162	25	88	.266
Waitkus, Eddie	29	Left	Left	154	641	102	182	2	43	.284

OUTFIELDERS	Age	Bats	Throws	G	AB	R	H	HR	RBI	PCT
Ashburn, Richie	23	Left	Right	151	594	84	180	2	39	.303
Blatnick, John	29	Right	Right	4	4	0	1	0	0	.250
Ennis, Del	24	Right	Right	153	595	91	186	31	125	.313
Hollmig, Stan	24	Right	Right	11	12	1	3	0	1	.250
Nicholson, Bill	34	Left	Right	40	58	3	13	3	10	.224
Sisler, Dick	29	Left	Right	141	523	79	156	13	83	.298
Whitman, Dick	29	Left	Right	75	132	21	33	0	12	.250
Mayo, Jack	23	Left	Right	18	36	1	8	0	3	.222

Appendix D
THE 1950 NATIONAL LEAGUE RACE MONTH BY MONTH

May 1	W	L	PCT	GB
Brooklyn	7	3	.700	—
Chicago	3	2	.600	1½
Pittsburgh	6	5	.545	1½
St. Louis	6	5	.545	1½
Boston	6	6	.500	2
PHILLIES	6	6	.500	2
Cincinnati	4	6	.400	3
New York	1	6	.143	4½

June 1	W	L	PCT	GB
Brooklyn	23	14	.622	—
St. Louis	23	14	.622	—
PHILLIES	23	15	.605	½
Boston	20	16	.556	2½
Chicago	18	17	.514	4
Pittsburgh	16	24	.400	8½
New York	13	21	.382	8½
Cincinnati	11	26	.297	12

July 1	W	L	PCT	GB
PHILLIES	37	26	.587	—
St. Louis	38	27	.585	—
Brooklyn	35	27	.565	1½
Boston	35	29	.547	2½
New York	32	31	.508	5
Chicago	31	31	.500	5½
Pittsburgh	23	41	.359	14½
Cincinnati	22	41	.349	15

August 1	W	L	PCT	GB
PHILLIES	59	40	.586	—
St. Louis	54	41	.568	3
Brooklyn	52	40	.565	3½
Boston	53	41	.564	3½
New York	45	47	.489	10½
Chicago	41	51	.446	14½
Cincinnati	39	56	.411	18
Pittsburgh	34	61	.358	23

September 1	W	L	PCT	GB
PHILLIES	79	47	.627	—
Brooklyn	69	51	.575	7
Boston	68	55	.553	9½
New York	66	57	.537	11½
St. Louis	65	58	.528	12½
Chicago	54	70	.435	24
Cincinnati	49	73	.402	28
Pittsburgh	43	82	.344	35½

October 1 (Final)	W	L	PCT	GB
PHILLIES	91	63	.591	—
Brooklyn	89	65	.578	2
New York	86	68	.558	5
Boston	83	71	.539	8
St. Louis	78	75	.510	12½
Cincinnati	66	87	.431	24½
Chicago	64	89	.418	26½
Pittsburgh	57	96	.373	33½

Appendix E
Game-by-Game Summary of the 1950 Phillies' Season

Date	Opponent	W-L	Score	WP	LP	Record	Standing
4-18	Brooklyn	W	9-1	Roberts	Newcombe	1-0	1(T)
4-19	Brooklyn	L	7-5	Podbielan	Meyer	1-1	3(T)
4-21	at Boston	T	2-2*			1-1	5
4-22	at Boston	L	3-2	Spahn	Simmons	1-2	5
4-23	at Boston	L	4-3	Sain	Donnelly	1-3	
"	at Boston	W	6-5	Konstanty	Hogue	2-3	5
4-25	at New York	L	8-4	Jansen	Meyer	2-4	5(T)
4-26	at Brooklyn	L	5-4(10)	Ramsdell	Donnelly	2-5	6
4-27	at Brooklyn	W	9-2	Roberts	Roe	3-5	6
4-28	Boston	W	6-1	Simmons	Sain	4-5	5(T)
4-29	Boston	W	2-1	Miller	Bickford	5-5	4(T)
4-30	Boston	L	4-1	Roy	Meyer	5-6	
"	Boston	W	9-3	Roberts	Donovan	6-6	4(T)
5-2	at Chicago	L	10-8	Rush	Heintzelman	6-7	5(T)
5-3	at Chicago	W	5-2	Johnson	Klippstein	7-7	5(T)
5-4	at St. Louis	W	9-6	Simmons	Staley	8-7	3(T)
5-5	at St. Louis	L	3-2	Brecheen	Roberts	8-8	6
5-6	at St. Louis	W	11-7	Miller	Lanier	9-8	5
5-7	at Cincinnati	W	6-0	Heintzelman	Fox	10-8	
"	at Cincinnati	W	6-4	Simmons	Blackwell	11-8	2
5-8	at Cincinnati	W	6-5	Johnson	Wehmeier	12-8	2
5-11	at Pittsburgh	W	3-2	Roberts	Dickson	13-8	1
5-13	New York	W	7-1	Simmons	Koslo	14-8	1
5-14	New York	L	4-3	Jansen	Heintzelman	14-9	1
"	New York	S†					
5-16	Cincinnati	W	1-0	Roberts	Blackwell	15-9	1
5-17	Cincinnati	W	5-4	Johnson	Wehmeier	16-9	1
5-20	Chicago	L	7-2	Rush	Simmons	16-10	2
5-21	St. Louis	L	6-5	Staley	Roberts	16-11	
"	St. Louis	W	4-2	Simmons	Boyer	17-11	2
5-23	Pittsburgh	L	6-0	Macdonald	Meyer	17-12	2
5-24	Pittsburgh	W	6-3	Konstanty	Werle	18-12	2
5-25	Pittsburgh	W	3-0	Miller	Chambers	19-12	2
5-26	at New York	W	3-2	Roberts	Kramer	20-12	2
5-27	at New York	W	8-5	Simmons	Jones	21-12	1(T)
5-28	at New York	W	5-2(11)	Konstanty	Hansen	22-12	
"	at New York	L	3-1	Koslo	Heintzelman	22-13	1
5-30	at Brooklyn	L	7-6(10)	Roe	Konstanty	22-14	
"	at Brooklyn	L	6-4	Banta	Meyer	22-15	3
6-1	at Chicago	W	8-4	Simmons	Hiller	23-15	3
6-3	at Chicago	W	6-2	Church	Rush	24-15	2
6-4	at St. Louis	L	6-2	Lanier	Heintzelman	24-16	3
6-5	at St. Louis	W	6-5	Roberts	Munger	25-16	2
6-6	at St. Louis	L	5-4	Pollet	Simmons	25-17	3
6-7	at Cincinnati	W	4-0	Miller	Ramsdell	26-17	2
6-8	at Cincinnati	L	8-4	Raffensberger	Meyer	26-18	3

*Game called because of rain and snow in the bottom of the 8th.

†Game suspended because of Sunday curfew with Phillies leading 9-7 after 8 innings. Completed July 5.

Appendix E: Game-by-Game Summary of the 1950 Phillies

Date	Opponent	W-L	Score	WP	LP	Record	Standing
6-10	at Pittsburgh	W	7-6	Konstanty	Law	27-18	
"	at Pittsburgh	L	5-4(12)	Werle	Donnelly	27-19	3
6-13	St. Louis	L	6-3	Brecheen	Simmons	27-20	3
6-14	St. Louis	L	4-2	Lanier	Heintzelman	27-21	3
6-17	Cincinnati	W	5-2	Roberts	Blackwell	28-21	3
6-18	Cincinnati	W	4-3	Simmons	Wehmeier	29-21	
"	Cincinnati	W	4-2	Miller	Fox	30-21	3
6-20	Pittsburgh	W	7-3	Meyer	Law	31-21	3
6-21	Pittsburgh	L	5-3	Macdonald	Roberts	31-22	3
6-22	Pittsburgh	W	7-4	Miller	Borowy	32-22	2(T)
6-23	Chicago	L	7-4	Lade	Simmons	32-23	2(T)
6-24	Chicago	W	5-4	Meyer	Hiller	33-23	2(T)
6-25	Chicago	L	11-8	Schmitz	Konstanty	33-24	
"	Chicago	W	2-1	Roberts	Rush	34-24	2
6-27	at Boston	W	3-2	Simmons	Spahn	35-24	1
6-28	at Boston	L	3-1	Sain	Meyer	35-25	2
6-29	at Boston	L	3-2	Bickford	Heintzelman	35-26	2
7-1	Brooklyn	W	6-4	Miller	Podbielan	37-26	1
7-2	Brooklyn	W	6-4	Meyer	Branca	38-26	
"	Brooklyn	T	8-8(10)*			38-26	1
7-3	Boston	L	3-1	Bickford	Heintzelman	38-27	2
7-4	Boston	W	14-5	Roberts	Roy	39-27	
"	Boston	L	12-9	Hogue	Konstanty	39-28	2
7-5	New York	W	9-7†	Konstanty	Jones	40-28	
"	New York	W	10-3	Meyer	Hartung	41-28	2
7-6	New York	W	9-6	Miller	Jones	42-28	2
7-7	at Brooklyn	W	7-2	Simmons	Branca	43-28	1(T)
7-8	at Brooklyn	W	4-1	Konstanty	Newcombe	44-28	1
7-9	at Brooklyn	L	7-3	Palica	Meyer	44-29	1
7-13	at St. Louis	W	3-2	Simmons	Pollet	45-29	1
7-14	at St. Louis	L	4-2	Staley	Roberts	45-30	1
7-15	at St. Louis	L	8-6	Martin	Konstanty	45-31	1(T)
7-16	at Chicago	L	8-0	Dubiel	Meyer	45-32	
"	at Chicago	L	10-3	Lade	Miller	45-33	2
7-18	at Chicago	L	5-2	Minner	Roberts	45-34	
"	at Chicago	W	8-3	Church	Rush	46-34	1(T)
7-19	at Pittsburgh	W	3-2(11)	Simmons	Werle	47-34	
"	at Pittsburgh	L	4-2	Macdonald	Meyer	47-35	2
7-20	at Pittsburgh	L	10-8	Dickson	Donnelly	47-36	2(T)
7-21	at Pittsburgh	W	4-1	Church	Queen	48-36	1(T)
7-22	at Cincinnati	W	2-0	Roberts	Ramsdell	49-36	
"	at Cincinnati	L	6-1	Fox	Heintzelman	49-37	1(T)
7-23	at Cincinnati	W	12-4	Simmons	Raffensberger	50-37	
"	at Cincinnati	W	7-4	Meyer	Blackwell	51-37	1
7-24	at Pittsburgh	L	2-1‡	Macdonald	Miller	51-38	2
7-25	Chicago	W	7-0	Church	Klippstein	52-38	
"	Chicago	W	1-0	Roberts	Rush	53-38	1
7-26	Chicago	W	6-4	Candini	Dubiel	54-38	1
7-27	Chicago	W	13-3	Simmons	Lade	55-38	1
7-28	Pittsburgh	W	4-1	Miller	Macdonald	56-38	1
7-29	Pittsburgh	L	7-4	Werle	Church	57-39	1
7-30	Pittsburgh	W	10-0	Roberts	Queen	57-39	
"	Pittsburgh	W	4-2	Konstanty	Dickson	58-39	1
8-1	Cincinnati	W	6-4	Miller	Smith	59-39	
"	Cincinnati	L	4-1	Blackwell	Simmons	59-40	1
8-2	Cincinnati	W	2-0	Church	Ramsdell	60-40	1
8-4	St. Louis	W	4-2	Roberts	Pollet	61-40	1

*Game called after 10 innings because of Sunday curfew. Game to be replayed in its entirety, although individual records count.

†Completion of suspended game of May 14.

‡Game called because of rain after six innings.

Date	Opponent	W-L	Score	WP	LP	Record	Standing
8-5	St. Louis	W	2-1	Meyer	Staley	62-40	1
8-6	St. Louis	L	7-1	Boyer	Miller	62-41	
"	St. Louis	L	2-0	Lanier	Church	62-42	1
8-7	St. Louis	W	9-0	Johnson	Brecheen	63-42	1
8-8	at Brooklyn	W	6-5	Roberts	Newcombe	64-42	1
8-9	at Brooklyn	W	5-4	Meyer	Palica	65-42	1
8-10	New York	W	6-5(10)	Konstanty	Koslo	66-42	1
8-11	New York	L	3-1	Maglie	Simmons	66-43	1
8-12	New York	W	5-4(11)	Konstanty	Koslo	67-43	1
8-13	New York	L	2-0	Hearn	Johnson	67-44	1
8-15	Boston	W	9-1	Simmons	Sain	68-44	1
8-16	Boston	W	5-1	Roberts	Bickford	69-44	1
8-18	at New York	L	7-4	Hearn	Meyer	69-45	1
8-21	at New York	W	4-0	Simmons	Jansen	70-45	1
8-22	at Cincinnati	W	4-3	Roberts	Raffensberger	71-45	1
8-23	at Cincinnati	W	6-4	Miller	Ramsdell	72-45	1
8-24	at Pittsburgh	W	4-2	Church	Law	73-45	1
8-25	at Pittsburgh	W	9-7(15)	Konstanty	Chambers	74-45	1
8-26	at Pittsburgh	L	14-4	Dickson	Roberts	74-46	1
8-27	at Chicago	W	6-1	Church	Minner	75-46	
"	at Chicago	T	4-4*			75-46	1
8-28	at Chicago	L	7-5	Leonard	Simmons	75-47	
"	at Chicago	W	9-5	Konstanty	Klippstein	76-47	1
8-29	at St. Louis	W	5-3	Roberts	Pollet	77-47	1
8-30	at St. Louis	W	9-8	Konstanty	Staley	78-47	1
9-1	at Boston	W	7-3	Church	Surkont	79-47	1
9-2	at Boston	W	2-0	Simmons	Sain	80-47	1
9-4	New York	L	2-0	Hearn	Roberts	80-48	
"	New York	L	9-0	Maglie	Miller	80-49	1
9-6	Brooklyn	L	2-0	Newcombe	Church	80-50	
"	Brooklyn	L	3-2	Bankhead	Konstanty	80-51	1
9-7	Brooklyn	L	3-2	Erskine	Roberts	80-52	1
9-8	Brooklyn	W	4-3	Meyer	Palica	81-52	1
9-9	Boston	W	7-6	Konstanty	Cole	82-52	1
9-10	Boston	L	3-1†	Sain	Church	82-53	1
9-12	St. Louis	W	1-0	Roberts	Lanier	83-53	1
9-14	St. Louis	W	3-2	Konstanty	Brazle	84-53	1
9-15	Cincinnati	W	2-1	Heintzelman	Ramsdell	85-53	
"	Cincinnati	W	8-7(19)	Donnelly	Erautt	86-53	1
9-16	Cincinnati	L	2-0	Blackwell	Miller	86-54	1
9-17	Pittsburgh	W	5-3	Meyer	Werle	87-54	1
9-19	Chicago	L	1-0	Hiller	Roberts	87-55	1
9-20	Chicago	W	9-6	Konstanty	Schmitz	88-55	1
9-23	Brooklyn	L	3-2	Newcombe	Roberts	88-56	1
9-24	Brooklyn	L	11-0	Palica	Church	88-57	1
9-25	at Boston	W	12-4	Heintzelman	Spahn	89-57	
"	at Boston	L	5-3	Surkont	Konstanty	89-58	1
9-26	at Boston	W	8-7	Donnelly	Hall	90-58	1
9-27	at New York	L	8-7	Koslo	Konstanty	90-59	
"	at New York	L	5-0	Hearn	Church	90-60	1
9-28	at New York	L	3-1	Maglie	Heintzelman	90-61	
"	at New York	L	3-1	Jones	Roberts	90-62	1
9-30	at Brooklyn	L	7-3	Palica	Miller	90-63	1
10-1	at Brooklyn	W	4-1(10)	Roberts	Newcombe	91-63	1

*Game called after 11 innings because of darkness.

†Game called because of rain after 5 innings.

AFTERWORD

Although few would argue that the Philadelphia Phillies of 1950 were one of baseball's all-time great teams, they are certainly one of the most famous and memorable. Even casual fans have likely heard of the Whiz Kids, and anyone at all knowledgeable about baseball history knows of their last-minute clinching of the pennant against the mighty Brooklyn Dodgers.

Given that, it is most surprising that their story has not previously been told in depth, for there is much to tell. They were the youngest team ever to win a pennant and they were an engaging bunch from all sections of the country. Even their nicknames were extraordinary by baseball standards, where colorful monikers are the rule. But no other team can compete with the likes of Puddinhead, Putsy, Swish, Bubba, Goober, the Mad Monk, Bugger, Maje, Stash, Yimca, Lop, Hawk, Wasil, Hooks, Granny, Blix, Whitey, Putt Putt, and Lefty.

My own fascination with the Whiz Kids came after the fact, during the late 1950s when the Phillies were National League cellar dwellers. Growing up in Wyoming, I had nonetheless become an avid Phillies fan through my grandfather, who lived in Jenkintown, Pennsylvania, and was a lifelong Phillies supporter. Robin Roberts was my favorite, and I struggled along with him and the rest of the Phillies during those years.

When I was 12 and at the height of my little league career (and, it would turn out, my baseball career) the mailman one day brought an envelope postmarked Phillies Spring Training, Clearwater, Florida. In it was a letter from none other than the great Robin Roberts, exhorting me to do my best in the coming season. My grandfather had prevailed upon Joe Scott, a mutual friend of his and Robin's, who had seen to it. I remain convinced that never has the mail brought such a treasure to a 12-year-old.

That was my only contact with Robin until June 1992, a span of 32 years. Talmage Boston, a good friend who is a true baseball nut, called me up one day to invite me to an Equitable Old Timers' luncheon that the Texas Rangers were putting on in conjunction with their Old Timers' weekend. I am not crazy about large, impersonal luncheons, but Talmage told me that Bob Gibson was speaking and, since I was free, I agreed to go.

We were seated at the lunch and well into our salads when in walked Robin Roberts. I had no idea he would be there. All of a sudden I felt like I was 12 years old again; my heart raced, my hands became sweaty and my voice shaky.

Talmage, with much more assertiveness than I ever could have mustered, decided that I had to meet Robin. But of course Talmage did not know him either. So after lunch he caught Robin by the elevator while I slinked behind, finally presenting myself. Robin, who had a tee time, suggested breakfast the next morning with his wife Mary. So Talmage and his wife Claire, my wife Lynn, and I met Robin and Mary for a delightful two-hour breakfast the following day.

Robin mentioned at breakfast that he had no interest in writing an autobiography, so when I approached him some months later with the idea of doing a book on the Whiz Kids, I did so with some trepidation. But Robin readily agreed, for the reasons set forth in his introduction, and the project was hatched.

Although I immediately discovered that Robin's baseball memory is superb, we agreed that I should talk to as many former Whiz Kids as possible, as their recollections and anecdotes could serve only to enrich the book. Robin suggested we start with Eddie Sawyer, who proved to be most cooperative and an incomparable resource.

Unfortunately, I missed interviewing Ben Chapman by only 10 days or so. Bubba Church had arranged for me to see Ben on my visit to Birmingham in the summer of 1993 but he passed away shortly before I arrived.

Even more bizarre was my near interview with Granny Hamner. I traveled to Philadelphia in September 1993 for a Whiz Kids Reunion centered around a baseball card and memorabilia show. Bubba Church and Robin introduced me to Granny at a Saturday evening dinner, and Granny agreed to an interview the next morning at 11:00, giving me the room number in his hotel.

I turned up for the interview a few minutes late and rang the room, with no answer. After scouting around the hotel and calling the room number several more times, I ventured up to the room and knocked on the door. Still no answer, although I could hear what sounded like a radio or television playing on low volume.

I finally gave up and went to the card show, where Granny was scheduled to appear at 2:00. I thought maybe I could catch him for a few minutes there. Again he failed to appear, for the saddest of reasons. I learned the next day that Granny had been found dead, slumped in a chair in his hotel room, shortly after I had left. Housekeeping, whom I had noticed was cleaning the room next to Granny's, had called hotel security when they could not get into the room.

With that sobering reminder of the mortality of even the Whiz Kids, I forged on, ever more convinced that theirs is a story worth telling. I hope that you now agree.

Writing this book with my boyhood hero Robin Roberts has been more fun than the law allows. When I hatched this project and Robin immediately came on board, I felt a little like the dog who catches the car he is chasing and thinks, "What do I do with it now?" But Robin's enthusiasm and the wonderful cooperation of his teammates and Eddie Sawyer made my initial anxieties disappear. Meeting and interviewing the Whiz Kids, all now senior citizens, has been a true delight. They are a terrific bunch of guys and in my mind deserve that 1950 pennant on that basis alone. But, of course, I am not particularly objective on that issue.

All of those quoted in the pages that precede graciously allowed me to interview them without compensation. Maje McDonnell was especially helpful in putting me in touch with his former teammates. Robin, Maje, Eddie Sawyer, Andy Seminick, Curt Simmons, Charlie Bicknell, Lou Possehl, Bubba Church, Stan Lopata, Dick Whitman, Andy Skinner, Dot Sisler, Wilma Brittin, Mary Anne Hollmig, Mary Konstanty, and Anne and Betty Zeiser all readily provided photos for inclusion and were all most cooperative and kind. Bubba and the late Peggy Church went far beyond the call of duty taking care of me and my daughter Jillian on our visit to Birmingham. Eddie Sawyer was incredibly accommodating in allowing me to pester him frequently.

Talmage Boston's enthusiastic support was instrumental in helping me figure out what to do with this "car" I had chased and caught. Pat Williams lent his creativity and infectious enthusiasm late in the project, encouraging me to go the last mile. He, Talmage, Sam Dann, John Esch, Dr. Bobby Brown, Mary Roberts, Jimmy Roberts, Richie Ashburn, Bo Carter, and Mike Best read all or parts of the manuscript, all to its betterment. My wife Lynn's painstaking review of the manuscript for the non-baseball afficionado helped tremendously. The late Dwight Sharpe, Mike Amedeo, Bill Werber, Rich Westcott, Ernie Montella, Ruly Carpenter, Jim Konstanty Jr., Liz Ennis, Tom Chandler, Ray Leicht, John Thorn, Michael Gershman, Peter Salmon, Carroll Beringer, Howard Green, Rich Westcott, Ted Silary, Rob Neyer, Jim Bradley, Stan Kotzen, and Jon Jackson were helpful and supportive in many other ways. Greg Ivy provided wonderfully able and cheerful research and archival assistance throughout the project, and Elyse Feller, Sherrie Devlin, Lisa Montez, Sharon Magill, and Debbie Seiter at SMU were unwavering in their help and support.

Lastly but mostly I wish to acknowledge the debts I owe my family. For my love of baseball I owe my uncle, Carl Galloway. For my devotion to the Phillies and early appreciation of the Whiz Kids I am indebted to my late grandfather, Bart Pfingst. I am grateful for the immediate enthusiasm, understanding, and lasting support of my mother, Leigh Galloway Rogers, and the encouragement of my father, C. Paul Rogers, Jr. But my greatest debt is to my immediate family, my wife Lynn and daughters Heather, Jillian, and Ruthie. It is they who never complained when I was off somewhere conducting another interview or glued evening after evening and weekend after weekend to the word processor upstairs. Thanks, special ones, for allowing me this labor of love.

Paul Rogers

SELECT BIBLIOGRAPHY

Books

Archibald, Joseph. *The Richie Ashburn Story*. New York: Julian Messner, 1962.

Barber, Red. *1947, When All Hell Broke Loose in Baseball*. Garden City, N.Y.: Doubleday, 1982.

Bartell, Dick, with Norman L. Macht. *Rowdy Richard: A Firsthand Account of the National League Baseball Wars of the 1930s and the Men Who Fought Them*. Berkeley: North Atlantic Books, 1987.

The Baseball Encyclopedia. New York: Macmillan, 1969.

Bilovsky, Frank, and Rich Westcott. *The Phillies Encyclopedia*. New York: Leisure Press, 1984.

Blake, Mike. *Baseball Chronicles: An Oral History of Baseball through the Decades*. Cincinnati: Betterway Books, 1994.

Bragan, Bobby. *You Can't Hit the Ball with the Bat on Your Shoulder*. Fort Worth, Tex.: Summit, 1992.

Fedo, Michael. *One Shining Season*. New York: Pharos Books, 1991.

Golenbock, Peter. *Bums: An Oral History of the Brooklyn Dodgers*. New York: G. P. Putnam's Sons, 1984.

Honig, Donald. *The Philadelphia Phillies: An Illustrated History*. New York: Simon & Schuster, 1992.

———. *The Man in the Dugout*. Chicago: Follett, 1977.

———. *Baseball between the Lines*. New York: Coward, McCann & Geoghegan, 1976.

Kaufman, Alan S., and James C. Kaufman. *The Worst Baseball Pitchers of All Time*. New York: Citadel Press, 1995.

Kuklick, Bruce. *To Every Thing a Season: Shibe Park and Urban Philadelphia 1909–1976*. Princeton: Princeton University Press, 1991.

Lewis, Allen. *The Philadelphia Phillies—A Pictorial History*. Virginia Beach: JCP Corporation of Virginia, 1983.

Lieb, Frederick G., and Stan Baumgartner. *The Philadelphia Phillies*. New York: G. P. Putnam's Sons, 1953.

Paxton, Harry T. *The Whiz Kids*. New York: David McKay, 1950.

Peary, Danny, ed. *We Played the Game: 65 Players Remember Baseball's Greatest Era, 1947–1964*. New York: Hyperion, 1994.

Reidenbaugh, Lowell. *The Sporting News Selects Baseball's 25 Greatest Pennant Races*. St. Louis: Sporting News, 1987.

Robinson, George, and Charles Salzberg. *On a Clear Day They Could See Seventh Place: Baseball's Worst Teams*. New York: Dell, 1991.

Shatzkin, Mike, ed. *The Ballplayers: Baseball's Ultimate Biographical Reference*. New York: William Morrow, 1990.

Sugar, Bert Randolph. *Baseball's 50 Greatest Games*. North Dighton, Mass.: JG Press, 1994.

Trachtenberg, Leo. *The Wonder Team: The True Story of the Incomparable 1927 New York Yankees.* Bowling Green, Ohio: Bowling Green State University Popular Press, 1995.

Tygiel, Jules. *Baseball's Great Experiment: Jackie Robinson and His Legacy.* New York: Oxford University Press, 1983.

Van Blair, Rick. *Dugout to Foxhole: Interviews with Baseball Players Whose Careers Were Affected by World War II.* Jefferson, N.C.: McFarland, 1994.

Westcott, Rich. *Diamond Greats: Profiles and Interviews with 65 of Baseball's History Makers.* Westport, Conn.: Meckler Books, 1988.

Westcott, Rich, and Frank Bilovsky. *The New Phillies Encyclopedia.* Philadelphia: Temple University Press, 1993.

Wilber, Cynthia J. *For the Love of the Game: Baseball Memories from the Men Who Were There.* New York: William Morrow, 1992.

Yeutter, Frank. *Jim Konstanty.* New York: A.S. Barnes, 1951.

Articles

Ashburn, Rich. "Jim Konstanty: He Gave Relief Pitchers Dignity." *Baseball Digest,* September 1976.

———. "When Dick Sisler Had His Moment in the Spotlight." *Baseball Digest,* September 1975.

———. "The Day Seminick Wiped Out the Giants' Infield." *Baseball Digest,* August 1974.

———. "Will the Phillies Sweat Their Way Back?" *Sport Magazine,* April 1952.

———. "The Philadelphia Phillies." *Sport Magazine,* August 1951.

———. "The Brains behind the Phillies." *Sport Magazine,* January 1951.

———. "Like Sisler, Like Son." *Sport Magazine,* August 1950.

———. "The Phillies Gamble on Youth." *Sport Magazine,* June 1950.

———. "Harry Walker: The Hard Luck Kid." *Sport Magazine,* July 1948.

Baumgartner, Stan, and Harry T. Paxton. "He Pitched the Phillies to the Pennant." *Saturday Evening Post,* January, 13, 1951.

"The Big Leagues' Youngest Team." *Life Magazine,* March 27, 1950.

Bjarkman, Peter C. "Those Fabulous Whiz Kids." *The Diamond,* January/February 1994.

Bloodgood, Clifford. "Eddie Sawyer, a Baseball Educator." *Baseball Magazine,* October 1948.

Brown, Hugh. "Mr. Roberts: Story of a Winner." *Sport Magazine,* August 1956.

———. "Did They Overwork Roberts?" *Sport Magazine,* February 1954.

———. "Roberts Pitches to Win." *Baseball Yearbook,* 1953.

———. "The Terrible-Tempered Russ Meyer." *Sport Magazine,* December 1952.

———. "The Bonus Baby Who Made Good." *Sport Magazine,* October 1952.

———. "Hamner of the Whiz Kids." *Sport Magazine,* September 1952.

Brundige, Bill. "Richie Ashburn: The .100 Hitter with the .300 Average." *Baseball Life Stories,* 1952.

"Bubba Church: After Popsicles, Pitching Was Easy!" *Baseball Life Stories,* 1952.

Burick, Si. "Page-ing Jim Konstanty." *Baseball Digest,* August 1950.

Burnes, Robert L. "Why the Waitkus Deal?" *Baseball Digest,* March 1949.

"The Call for Casimer," *Newsweek,* July 17, 1950.

Connell, George. "How the Pirates Suddenly Solved Johnson." *Baseball Digest,* June 1951.

Daley, Arthur. "Miracle in Philadelphia." *New York Times Magazine,* September 17, 1950.

Davis, Russ. "Ennis Hits Vicious Liners." *Baseball Digest,* March 1948.

———. "The King of Swing." *Collier's,* May 17, 1947.

Dexter, Charles. "Seminick—Key Man of the Phils." *Baseball Digest,* November 1950.

Donaghey, Don. "Phils a Far Cry from Old Days." *Baseball Digest,* November 1950.

Drebinger, John. "The MVP Winners for 1950." *Baseball Magazine,* January 1950.

Duncan, Andy. "Jim Konstanty: The All-Time Fireman." *Sport Magazine,* May 1951.

"The Fanatic Fan." *Newsweek,* April 24, 1950.

Fay, Bill. "Sawyer of the Phillies." *Collier's,* July 2, 1949.

———. "They Woke the Busher Up!" *Baseball Digest,* May 1947.

Graham, Frank, Jr. "How Del Ennis Won His War with the Wolves." *Sport Magazine,* May 1956.

"Harry the Hat." *Time,* August 18, 1947.

Hillman, Serrell. "The Whole Story of Pitching." *Time,* May 28, 1956.

Hochman, Stan. "Robin Roberts Remembers the 'Whiz Kids.'" *Baseball Digest,* July 1972.

"How Roberts Does It." *Sport Magazine,* September 1953.

Hurwitz, Hy. "Brotherly Love." *Baseball Digest,* November 1947.

Kelly, Gene. "Robin Roberts: The Pitcher Who Couldn't Pitch!" *Baseball Life Stories,* 1952.

Kelly, Wilbur (Bill). "The Robin Roberts You Didn't Know!" *Baseball Magazine,* Spring 1953.

"The Kid from Nebraska." *Time,* June 14, 1948.

Lewis, Allen. "When Ennis Climbed the Wall." *Baseball Digest,* September 1949.

Lieb, Frederick G. "Best Since Matty: Robin Roberts." *Baseball Magazine,* September 1953.

Lundquist, Carl. "Meet the Watch Dogs of the Whiz Kids." *Baseball Magazine,* July 1951.

Miller, Hub. "Dick Sisler, Son of George." *Baseball Magazine,* January 1951.

———. "Harry the Hat." *Baseball Magazine,* January 1948.

Morrow, Art. "Robin Roberts—Baseball's Greatest Pitcher." *Inside Baseball,* March 1953.

Motley, William. "What's Wrong with Philadelphia?" *Baseball Magazine,* June 1952.

"A Neurotic Fan with a Rifle." *Newsweek,* June 27, 1949.

Newcombe, Jack. "Roberts Is the Phillies' Stopper." *Sport Magazine,* June 1952.

———. "The Making of Richie Ashburn." *Sport Magazine,* September 1951.

———. "The Old Man of the Phillies." *Sport Magazine,* April 1951.

Paxton, Harry T. "Sport's Greatest Teams: The Whiz Kids." *Sport Magazine,* January 1964.

———. "Baseball's Biggest Winner." *Saturday Evening Post,* January 10, 1953.

———. "The Ballplayer Nobody Wanted." *Saturday Evening Post,* June 30, 1951.

———. "What"s Got into the Phillies?" *Saturday Evening Post,* July 8, 1950.

———. "The House Where the Ballplayers Live." *Saturday Evening Post,* September 10, 1949.

"The Phillies Come to Life." *Time,* July 8, 1946.

"The Phillies Pitching Pals." *Sport Magazine,* October 1953.

Pollock, Ed. "Undertaker Gives Him New Life." *Baseball Digest,* November 1950.

"The Professor Leads the Phillies." *Complete Baseball Magazine,* Summer 1950.

"Richie Ashburn's Speed Helps Him Bat over .300." *Look,* July 27, 1954.

Robert, Harry. "The Strange Discovery of Del Ennis." *Baseball Magazine,* July 1947.

Roberts, Robin, as told to George Vass. "The Game I'll Never Forget." *Baseball Digest,* February 1976.

"Robin Roberts: So Good—You Can't Believe He's Real!" *Baseball Stars 1953.*

Rummil, Ed. "A Reporter Calls on Jim Konstanty." *Baseball Magazine,* November 1950.

———. "'Puddinhead' of the Phillies." *Baseball Magazine,* April 1950.

———. "Gran Hamner, a 154 Game Player." *Baseball Magazine,* January 1950.

———. "The Only Cub Regular Who Hit .300 in 1946." *Baseball Magazine,* March 1947.

Ryan, Jack. "From Redneck to Blueblood by Way of Poise and Avoirdupois—That"s the 'Inside' on Cub's Russ Meyer." *Baseball Digest,* September 1948.

Silverman, Al. "The Del Ennis Puzzle." *Sport Magazine,* August 1952.

Small, Collie. "The Terrible Tempered Mr. Chapman." *Saturday Evening Post,* April 5, 1947.

Stockton, J. Roy. "Goliat's Comeback Chance." *Baseball Digest,* November 1951.

———. "Them Phillies or, How to Make Failure Pay." *Saturday Evening Post,* October 4, 1941.

Taylor, Sec. "Being Sisler, Jr., Helps, Hurts." *Baseball Digest,* July 1946.

Thom, John. "The 1930 Phillies." *The National Pastime,* 1993.

Williams, Edgar. "How Robin Roberts Wrestled His Way to a Comeback." *Baseball Digest,* December/January 1959.

———. "Has Roberts Lost His Fast Ball or Did He Merely Suffer an Off-Year?" *Baseball Digest,* January/February 1957.

———. "His Control's Built-In! Phillies' Amazing Roberts Always Could Put Ball Where He Wanted It." *Baseball Digest,* August 1953.

———. "First Robin of Fling." *Baseball Digest,* January 1953.

Yeutter, Frank. "They Can't Bump Off Waitkus." *Baseball Digest,* September 1953.

———. "Ennis—Mild Bull of the Phils." *Baseball Digest,* April 1952.

———. "Hamner Bristles: I'm Better Than McMillan!" *Baseball Digest,* March 1952.

———. "They Call Him Mister Putt-Putt!' *Baseball Digest,* October 1951.

———. "The Kid Who Looks Like Diz." *Sport Life,* September 1951.

———. "No Peace for a Quaker." *Complete Baseball,* Summer 1951.

———. "Goliat—Phil's New Goliath?" *Baseball Digest,* June 1951.

———. "Wild Wildcat Oilman." *Baseball Digest,* May 1951.

———. "Konstanty and the Kids." *Complete Baseball,* Fall 1950.

———. "Second Sizzling Sisler." *Baseball Digest,* August 1950.

———. "At Bat, in the Field, Del Ennis Is a Quaker City Cutie." *Complete Baseball,* Summer 1950.

————. "Sawyer Has a Way with Him." *Baseball Digest,* January 1950.

————. "Slide, Richie, Slide!" *Sports World Magazine,* September 1949.

————. "First Robin of Fling." *Baseball Digest,* June 1949.

————. "Poppa Seminick's Son, Andy." *Baseball Magazine,* June 1947.

Newspapers

Philadelphia Inquirer, 1948, 1949, 1950.

The Sporting News, 1948, 1949, 1950.

Miscellaneous Sources

The Baseball Register, 1947–1954.

Who's Who in Baseball, 1947–1951.

The Phillies Yearbook, 1949–1955.

INDEX